IN THE TRENCHES

RECENT SOCIOLOGY TITLES FROM W.W. NORTON

Code of the Streets by Elijah Anderson

The Cosmopolitan Canopy by Elijah Anderson

Social Problems, 2nd Edition by Joel Best

A History of Future Cities by Daniel Brook

The Glass Cage: Automation and Us by Nicholas Carr

The Family: Diversity, Inequality, and Social Change by Philip N. Cohen

You May Ask Yourself: An Introduction to Thinking Like a Sociologist, 4th Edition by Dalton Conley

The Vanishing Neighbor: The Transformation of American Community by Marc J. Dunkelman

Citizen Coke: The Making of Coca-Cola Capitalism by Bartow J. Elmore

The Real World: An Introduction to Sociology, 4th Edition by Kerry Ferris and Jill Stein

Introduction to Sociology, 9th Edition by Anthony Giddens, Mitchell Duneier, Richard P. Appelbaum, and Deborah Carr

Essentials of Sociology, 5th Edition by Anthony Giddens, Mitchell Duneier, Richard P. Appelbaum, and Deborah Carr

Mix It Up: Popular Culture, Mass Media, and Society by David Grazian

The Contexts Reader, 2nd Edition edited by Douglas Hartmann and Christopher Uggen

The Society Pages: Crime and the Punished edited by Douglas Hartmann and Christopher Uggen

The Society Pages: The Social Side of Politics edited by Douglas Hartmann and Christopher Uggen

The Society Pages: Color Line and Racial Angles edited by Douglas Hartmann and Christopher Uggen

Thinking Through Theory by John Levi Martin

Doing Race edited by Hazel Rose Markus and Paula M.L. Moya

Readings for Sociology, 8th Edition edited by Garth Massey

Families As They Really Are, 2nd Edition edited by Barbara J. Risman and Virginia Rutter

Social Construction of Sexuality, 3rd Edition by Stephen Seidman

The Sociology of News, 2nd Edition by Michael Schudson

Sex Matters: The Sexuality and Society Reader, 4th Edition edited by Mindy Stombler, Dawn M. Baunach, Wendy O. Simonds, Elroi J. Windsor, and Elisabeth O. Burgess

Gender: Ideas, Interactions, Institutions by Lisa Wade and Myra Marx Ferree

Naked Statistics: Undressing the Dismal Science by Charles Wheelan

Cultural Sociology: An Introductory Reader by Matt Wray

American Society: How It Really Works, 2nd edition by Erik Olin Wright and Joel Rogers

To learn more about Norton Sociology, please visit: wwnorton.com/soc

W. W. Norton & Company has been independent since its founding in 1923, when William Warder Norton and Mary D. Herter Norton first published lectures delivered at the People's Institute, the adult education division of New York City's Cooper Union. The firm soon expanded its program beyond the Institute, publishing books by celebrated academics from America and abroad. By midcentury, the two major pillars of Norton's publishing program—trade books and college texts—were firmly established. In the 1950s, the Norton family transferred control of the company to its employees, and today—with a staff of four hundred and a comparable number of trade, college, and professional titles published each year—W. W. Norton & Company stands as the largest and oldest publishing house owned wholly by its employees.

Editor: Karl Bakeman
Associate Editor: Nicole Sawa
Project Editor: Rachel Mayer
Assistant Editor: Lindsey Thomas
Editorial Assistant: Mary Williams
Manuscript Editor: Lynne Cannon Menges
Managing Editor, College: Marian Johnson
Managing Editor, College Digital Media: Kim Yi
Production Manager: Andrew Ensor
Media Editor: Eileen Connell
Media Editorial Assistant: Ava Bramson
Marketing Manager, Sociology: Julia Hall
Art Director: Jillian Burr
Design Director: Rubina Yeh
Designer: Anna Reich
Assistant Photo Editor: Kathryn Bryant
Permissions Manager: Megan Jackson
Permissions Clearer: Elizabeth Trammell
Composition: Achorn International, Inc.
Manufacturing: Sheridan Books, Inc.

Permission to use copyrighted material is included on p. 333.

ISBN: 978-0-393-91877-9

W. W. Norton & Company, Inc., 500 Fifth Avenue, New York, NY 10110-0017
wwnorton.com

W. W. Norton & Company Ltd., Castle House, 75/76 Wells Street, London W1T 3QT

1 2 3 4 5 6 7 8 9 0

IN THE TRENCHES

TEACHING AND LEARNING SOCIOLOGY

MAXINE P. ATKINSON
NORTH CAROLINA STATE UNIVERSITY

KATHLEEN S. LOWNEY
VALDOSTA STATE UNIVERSITY

W.W. NORTON & COMPANY, INC.
NEW YORK • LONDON

ABOUT THE AUTHORS

MAXINE P. ATKINSON grew up in Georgia where she went to Reinhardt, a small two-year school, graduated from the University of Georgia, got her master's from Georgia State, and taught at Oxford College of Emory University. She moved across the country to the Pacific Northwest to get her PhD from Washington State.

Maxine moved back east to take her first post-PhD job at NC State, and she has been on the faculty there since with only a two-year break for a post-doctoral fellowship at Duke University in aging and statistics. Maxine has taught graduate-level statistics, graduate family courses, graduate courses in the sociology of aging, and her favorite graduate course, "Teaching Sociology." At the undergraduate level, Maxine has taught gender, upper-level division and introductory family courses, along with Introduction to Sociology. She has taught large sections of introductory courses along with small seminars for first-year students only, service learning courses, and courses in NC State's London study abroad program.

Maxine originally focused on family, aging, and gender publishing in journals such as the *Journal of Marriage and the Family*, *Journal of Gerontology*, *Criminology*, and the *Journal of Adolescent Research*. More recently Maxine has focused on the scholarship of teaching and learning (SoTL) with publications in edited books and journals such as *Teaching Sociology*. She is most proud of her SoTL research with NC State graduate students.

She has won a number of teaching awards in sociology including the American Sociological Association Distinguished Contributions to Teaching

Award, the Carla B. Howery Award for Developing Teacher-Scholars, the Hans O. Mauksch Award for Distinguished Contributions to Undergraduate Sociology, and the Distinguished Teaching Award from the Southern Sociological Society. Maxine was the first woman at NC State to win the North Carolina university system teaching award, the Board of Governors' Award for Excellence in Teaching, along with being inducted into NC State's Academy of Outstanding Professors, and winning the Outstanding Teacher award, the Richard Felder Award for Outstanding Service in Support of Teaching and Learning, the First-Year Student Advocate Award, the Lonnie and Carol Poole Award for Excellence in Teaching. In her home department she also won the Gary D. Hill Students' Choice Teaching Excellence Award and the Outstanding Advisor award.

Maxine spent almost two decades as an administrator, serving as her department's Associate Head, the Director of NC State's First-Year Inquiry Program, and most recently as Department Head. She most enjoys her time as teaching mentor. As Director of the First-Year Inquiry Program she led teaching workshops focused on inquiry-guided teaching techniques, critical thinking, and first-year student development. She conducts teaching workshops at NC State, at professional meetings, and on campuses around the country. She also conducts departmental curriculum reviews as a member of the American Sociological Associations Departmental Resource Group, sociologists trained to evaluate curriculum and conduct teaching workshops. Currently, Maxine serves as an NC State TH!NK Faculty Fellow, a faculty mentoring position associated with NC State's Quality Enhancement Plan, which focuses on critical and creative thinking. Maxine mentors individual faculty in a variety of disciplines and conducts teaching workshops for faculty from across the campus.

KATHLEEN S. LOWNEY graduated from the University of Washington with double majors in sociology and comparative religions. Three months later she moved across the country to begin her PhD at Drew University, majoring in religion and society. While at Drew, she not only found her life's work, but the love of her life, Frank Flaherty. During their engagement, Frank moved to South Georgia for a tenure track job, and Kath followed. For almost 30 years they have taught at Valdosta State University.

While at Valdosta State, Kath has taught Social Problems, Mass Media and Popular Culture, Sociology of Religion, Domestic Violence, Sociology of Disability, Religion and Culture, Introduction to Applied Sociology, and for the past five years, she has specialized in large sections of Introduction to Sociology courses.

Her research agenda is eclectic, but she nearly always uses the constructionist perspective. She has written about gender roles in the Unification Church, kudzu as a social problem, adolescent Satanism, stalking as a new crime problem, mass media constructions of social problems, and recently, how the media constructs nurses who are serial killers.

She has been active in the teaching movement in the discipline of sociology since 1992. She has published nearly thirty manuscripts on the scholarship of teaching and learning and in 2009 became the editor of *Teaching Sociology*. She was asked by her university administration, in 2013, to become the Fellow-in-Residence of the IDEA Center (Innovative Designs for Enhancing the Academy)—the new teaching and learning center at Valdosta. Working with other faculty fellows, she creates programming, organizes media campaigns for all IDEA Center activities, and coaches/mentors many faculty. In 2014, she was the recipient of the American Sociological Association's award for Distinguished Contributions to Teaching. Helping students to engage their sociological imagination is Kath's passion.

To our students—past, present, and future—and to yours too.

KATH
To William M. Lowney—I miss you, Dad.

MAXINE
To Jerome David Slatta, my son, who taught me that good teachers can change lives. I hope that I can be for my students what your inspiring teachers have been for you. And, to my mother, Marrine Moore Davis, who taught me how to laugh when I need to most.

CONTENTS

INTRODUCTION

This book is intended for sociologists who want a basic guide to teaching well. While we see the primary audience as sociology instructors new to teaching, anyone who is interested in improving her or his undergraduate teaching will find something in the book that appeals. While the emphasis is on basic teaching techniques, we also introduce teaching strategies used by more advanced instructors. The model for the book is Svinicki and McKeachie's (2011) *Teaching Tips,* but this book is aimed at sociologists rather than a more general audience. The text is research based but also relies on the wisdom of practice developed by the authors over a career of teaching. The authors are both winners of the American Sociological Association's Distinguished Contributions to Teaching Award as well as the highest teaching awards in their respective university systems.

We write in a conversational tone that reflects our approach to teaching our undergraduates and to mentoring others, including each other. While we agree on most teaching issues, there are some about which we are not in agreement. For example, Kath assigns traditional research papers in some of her classes (primarily in theory and the institutions courses she teaches, because those are programmatic requirements negotiated by all faculty). She believes that learning to think and write using the scholarly language of our discipline can shape how students perceive our discipline, their role in it, and helps them to learn to see themselves as having insights worth listening to, because they are apprentice sociologists. In many other classes, however, Kath creates assignments which model the work that applied sociologists do, and for which her program is preparing students to take. Maxine argues that professional articles are written for professionals to talk to professionals and that to require students to read and synthesize this material is counterproductive. Too few of our undergraduates are going to graduate school in sociology to make this worthwhile. She asserts that there are many other kinds of written assignments that are more appropriate and more likely to help students use sociology as an analytical tool. It does not surprise us that we disagree about some things nor does it concern us. Ultimately any teaching strategy is only as effective as its implementation.

Most of us begin our teaching portfolios with our philosophy of teaching. This book begins the same way for the same reason. Teaching philosophies make explicit our beliefs about teaching, our goals, and some ideas about how we will go about accomplishing those goals. We believe that teaching, and teaching well, is absolutely necessary for the survival of higher education and the advancement of an educated populace. We cannot survive the challenges of the twenty-first century in ignorance. While higher education certainly has its weaknesses, and we will draw attention to many of those, some form of higher education must exist if knowledge and skills are to be created and maintained. To state the obvious, as sociologists, we are convinced that the social sciences make fundamental contributions to the general knowledge base required of educated people and those who major in sociology have unique perspectives to offer.

While we hope that this broad introduction does not serve as simply a painful elaboration of the obvious, we begin this book in this manner because we believe that far too much is taken for granted too often when it comes to teaching. Far too many myths about teaching are unchallenged, unfounded, sacred truths. Let's start with some common myths and taken-for-granted notions about teaching.

Myth #1. Teaching is not important because real scholars do research and that is how scholars are and should be judged.

Myth #2. Teaching is all about personality. I am who I am and there is not much I can do about it.

Myth #3. What I want my students to learn is perfectly obvious from my syllabus.

Myth #4. When I was a student, I learned from lectures and my students will learn the same way.

Myth #5. You learn to teach as you practice teaching. It just evolves that way.

Real scholars do traditional research and publish it in referred journals and books. There is no argument about that. However, most of us also teach—even those of us who have positions in some of the most highly ranked programs in the country. Some of us teach more than others but very few of us work in research institutes with no teaching obligations. The extent to which teaching is valued may also vary across institutional types, but it is highly doubtful that any university takes pride in bad teaching. Few of us as individuals take pride or pleasure in doing a job poorly. This book will make contributions toward helping readers be more effective and efficient teachers who can take pride in a job well done.

Certainly our personalities manifest themselves in our classrooms! Our personalities also manifest themselves in our professional writing but that does not mean that we do not have to work at writing well. Teaching is at least partially a skill and skills can be honed. All of us can improve our teaching by learning more about teaching well. One of the goals of this book is to help instructors choose and develop those techniques that are most consistent with our individual strengths.

We too often take for granted that our syllabi and courses are constructed such that our goals are as obvious to others as they are to us. While we are careful to define our research questions and explicate how we answer them, the same is not true of our teaching. Indeed, too often, we cannot articulate what we want our students to know or to be able to do beyond "understand"! Good teaching is explicit teaching with thoughtfully constructed goals. One of our primary emphases will be helping instructors learn to be more intentional teachers who achieve instructional goals by carefully explicating goals and objections and by organizing our teaching around them.

Perhaps one of our biggest challenges as instructors is that we are, by definition, very successful students of sociology. Most of us were taught by faculty who lectured most of the time and yet we thrived in the academy. Lecturing is what we know best. We teach as we were taught. To assume that our own students will thrive as we did is a very risky assumption. We are not like our students. Very few of them will get PhDs and even fewer will get PhDs in sociology. Moreover, the larger social world and the academic environment have changed considerably since most of us were undergraduates. New media have been created which—like it or not—are changing not just *how* our students learn but how they *expect* to learn. Not recognizing these changes—even if we choose not to use all these new ways of communicating with our students—is a choice which is fraught with peril. Additionally, since the recession of 2008, many academic institutions have faced difficult economic choices, some of which have impacted student learning (e.g., larger class enrollments, online delivery of content). Many of us are struggling to use the best teaching practices in these bigger and different teaching and learning environments. If we are to realize even a small bit of the potential of the power of sociology, we must teach using the most effective strategies available. Our research-based methods are far more likely to be effective than relying on simply what we remember worked for us. This book will focus on teaching techniques backed up by evidence.

Our goals for this book are to provide sociologists with a basic foundation for teaching undergraduate sociology well, suggest means of successful course planning and provide examples, offer instructions for effective teaching strategies, address a variety of forms of grading and assessment, discuss the most significant challenges in twenty-first-century pedagogy, and help sociologists envision the twenty-first-century teacher-scholar.

We divide the book into five sections: course development, day-to-day challenges, assessment and grading, emerging issues, and building your career as a teacher-scholar.

SECTION 1: COURSE DEVELOPMENT
- Chapter 1, "Learning Goals, Objectives, and Outcomes," concentrates on planning a course with a focus on objectives and learning outcomes. Course goals, objectives, and student learning outcomes take you from fuzzy thinking to knowing exactly what you want to accomplish. Explicit statements of what you want your students to know and be able to do at the end of the course is the first step toward a successful course for you and your students.
- In Chapter 2, "Syllabus Construction," we outline the essential parts of a syllabus. This is one of the most basic chapters and you will find no big surprises here, but the chapter will help you understand what the various parts of the syllabus help you accomplish. We walk you through each part of an effective syllabus.
- Chapter 3, "How Much Content to Cover," deals with one of the biggest challenges we all face in our teaching: the coverage issue. We are all in love with our content and our passion for our discipline can serve as an obstacle to good teaching. The chapter reiterates the need for planning, taking into account the requirements of your specific institution and curriculum. We discuss depth and breadth in detail, outlining the importance of focus in introductory and advanced-level courses.

SECTION 2: DAY-TO-DAY LIFE IN THE CLASSROOM

The second section of the text is the longest and reflects the text's emphasis on a variety of teaching techniques.

- Chapter 4, "Choosing Teaching Techniques," discusses the process of choosing specific teaching strategies to help students meet the learning outcomes of the course. This chapter is more philosophical than some of the other parts of the text but is consistent with our emphasis on the importance of course planning. We provide criteria for choosing specific techniques while balancing your student learning outcomes, the difficulty of the material to be taught, student backgrounds, class size, and instructor comfort and confidence with the techniques.

- Chapter 5, "Constructing a Lecture," explores the most common teaching technique in most all of our teaching tool kits, the lecture. While lecturing is often presented as the technique that no one should use, we assert that lectures can be powerful. We probably all lecture. The point is to lecture well and turn monologues into meaningful interaction with our students.

- Chapter 6, "Active Learning," is the chapter that most of us expect to be included in a text on effective teaching. It focuses on the importance of having our students actively involved in our classes rather than simply filling a seat.

- Chapter 7, "Inquiry-Guided Learning," discusses the array of active learning/teaching techniques that highlight the importance of dynamic questioning. Inquiry-guided learning refers to a category of teaching methods that focuses on questioning and helps students move toward knowledge construction. Inquiry-guided learning is a more advanced active learning technique that most of us will practice as we become more experienced teachers, but we can all move toward emphasizing the process of inquiry.

- In Chapter 8, "The Importance of Writing for Learning," we argue that writing is fundamental to good teaching and that writing and thinking are inextricably linked. We emphasize informal, low-stakes writing but also provide examples of more formal writing assignments. We argue that writing is such a powerful tool that it should be used during every class period.

- Chapter 9, "Guiding Discussion," presents a review of using guiding discussion in our classes. Discussions can be used for a variety of purposes, ranging from encouraging students to focus their attention to creating a setting that inspires students to think deeply.

- In Chapter 10, "Critical Thinking," we review one of the most important goals for specific courses—and indeed, a college education in general: critical thinking. We address the variety of definitions of critical thinking but focus on two major typologies.
- Chapter 11, "First-Day Activities," discusses the most important day of any course: the first day! While a successful first day of class does not guarantee a fully successful semester, it certainly sets the scene. The literature on first-day activities is also a good source of engaging strategies that can be used throughout the semester.
- The title for Chapter 12 sounds gloomy: "Teaching Failures." However, we stress that while failure is likely for all of us at some point in our teaching careers, valuable lessons are there to be learned, and failure can lead to greater success.

SECTION 3: ASSESSMENTS, GRADING, AND EVALUATIONS

- Chapter 13, "Measuring Student Learning," focuses on the importance of knowing if and what our students are learning. We provide examples of a variety of assessment techniques.
- In Chapter 14, "Grading," we turn our attention to grading. In contrast to chapter 13, here we focus on the microlevel everyday experience of grading for our classes. We will discuss the idea that not all learning by students must be graded—or graded at a very detailed level—and how that realization can be very freeing for faculty. We'll also think about our feelings as we grade—how to pay attention to those feelings and use them to shape our behaviors. We'll talk about some best practices in grading and how to own the "little things" that are idiosyncratic to each of us and then help students to know about them so that they can avoid them.
- In Chapter 15, "Class Evaluations," we discuss student evaluations. Getting such student feedback is not always an easy process, so we'll talk about how and when to read your evaluations. Then we'll talk about interpreting them: what messages are outliers and best to let go of and which are important and need to be internalized. We will end the chapter by talking about how student evaluations play crucial roles in the careers of those who are not the typical faculty member (i.e., nontenure track, faculty of color, and women faculty) and how to use your student evaluation statistics in ways that can benefit your career.
- Chapter 16, "Assessing Your Program," discusses program assessment, including rationales and tools for this level of assessment. The chapter discusses a way for sociologists to come together to talk about their pro-

gram, threats to it from without and within; and from those conversations, develop concepts, theories, and sociological skills which majors should take away from the program when they graduate. Working backward, faculty should figure out where all those concepts and skills should be introduced to students and then reinforced in other courses. The chapter concludes with a discussion of potential problems that might occur during the assessment process.

SECTION 4: TWENTY-FIRST-CENTURY PEDAGOGY

- Chapter 17, "Teaching and Technology," focuses on two compelling questions: Is the technology being used in and out of class advancing student learning? How do you know that it is? We will talk about best practices in using some common technologies, all the while keeping in mind that what matters is how much sociology students are learning.
- Chapter 18, "Making Your Course Accessible to All Students," is a rare discussion on making classes accessible to all students. While most texts of this type do not consider accessibility, we feel strongly about our moral responsibility to make sure that we are not making learning harder for some of our students. The chapter talks about the shift from the medical model of disabilities to the social justice model, and how that transition parallels the shift to the universal design of classes. We offer a variety of tips for using PowerPoint, Word, and other software in an accessible manner.
- Chapter 19, "Teaching Large Classes," focuses on the pedagogy needed for teaching large classes. While many of our pedagogical techniques are scalable, there are some unique challenges which large classes pose. We suggest ways to increase active engagement while keeping grading time within reasonable limits.

SECTION 5: BUILDING YOUR CAREER AS A TEACHER-SCHOLAR

- In Chapter 20, "The Scholarship of Teaching and Learning," we argue that a more inclusive definition of SoTL is most likely to be to the benefit of students and provide suggestions for building a career as a SoTL scholar.
- Chapter 21, "Creating Your Teaching Philosophy and Teaching Portfolio," provides three examples of teaching portfolios created by recent PhDs as models for creating your own portfolio.
- In Chapter 22, "What the Best Sociology Professors Do," the text concludes with advice from winners of the ASA Distinguished Contributions to Teaching Award. We hope this book makes a contribution toward producing the next decade of the best sociology teachers.

ACKNOWLEDGMENTS

We both want to thank Karl Bakeman, Nicole Sawa, and Kate Feighery from W. W. Norton. They have made our ideas better and clearer.

We gratefully acknowledge the winners of the American Sociological Association Outstanding Contributions to Teaching award who shared their vision of what the best sociology teachers do. They are Caroline Persell (2005), Kathleen McKinney (2006), Ed Kain (2007), Liz Grauerholz (2008), Carol Jenkins (2008), Keith Roberts (2010), Katherine Rowell (2012), Diane Pike (2012), and Rose Brewer (2013). These teacher-scholars serve as an inspiration to us as they do to many others.

We also acknowledge and thank Andrea Hunt, Sarah Epplen (Rusche), and Kris Macomber who so generously allowed us to use their teaching portfolios as exemplary teaching portfolios. All three received their PhDs at NC State University and served as Maxine's graduate student colleagues and coauthors.

Kath wants to thank her husband, Dr. Frank Flaherty, for his support, his uncanny ability to make her laugh just when she needs it, his ability to solve nearly all the technology problems that arose during these years, and for his unending love. Kath also wants to thank Sara Tehrani, who worked as a researcher in 2012 on this project. Sara was always able to find just the right source. And to Maxine—thank you for sharing your teaching journey with me as we wrote this manuscript. I have learned so much from you and appreciate the amazing teacher that you are. Thank you for inviting me on this intellectual journey.

Maxine thanks her husband, Dr. Richard W. Slatta, for his belief in her ability and expertise, the pride he has shown in her work, and his own professional teaching accomplishments. He has been her teaching partner as well as her life partner. Maxine also wants to thank Andrea Hunt who worked as her research assistant and without whom Maxine's chapters could not have been written. And to Kath, my partner and my friend. I will forever be grateful for your expertise, your patience, and your unceasing support. I am proud to have my name linked with yours.

SECTION 1

COURSE DEVELOPMENT

►►► CHAPTER 1
LEARNING GOALS, OBJECTIVES, AND OUTCOMES

In this chapter we focus on the realization of more specific goals for a course and detailed planning. With a successfully planned course, you will never again wake in the middle of the night wondering, "Now what was I supposed to do tomorrow in class?" You will be more relaxed, more secure, and ready to enjoy teaching. You will never again have your students complete a creative activity only to find that it did little more than entertain.

The biggest mistake we have made and the single biggest mistake we see others make is a failure to plan. For many of us, the most difficult part of teaching is the prerequisite for success, both for us and for our students; that is, course planning, specifically creating goals and student learning outcomes. There is very little chance that either you or your students will find your class successful if you have not planned it well. While that is certainly a truism, all too often we charge right in without the planning necessary to be successful.

We confess. We are both hoarders. We collect all the cool activities and films and good ideas for things to do in class that we can find. We are especially excited about interactive projects, class activities, and assignments. Our imaginations go a little wild thinking about our students comparing music of various types from different eras, analyzing toys and commercials about toys, viewing thought-provoking films, and analyzing interview and quantitative data. There are always new materials to consider, and it is great fun to review new textbooks and readers as they are published. We love pondering the assortment of articles that have worked so well for each of us in the past and the great new ones we could incorporate. The new activities we have carefully collected are enticing. We feel that finding an interesting activity is a little like falling in love.

Then we realize, we have done it again. Time after time, we have focused on materials, activities, and assignments while merrily skipping the core work we need to do for any course, whether it is the first time we teach it or the twentieth. Simply having assembled a collection of activities and assignments without careful consideration of what skills or knowledge they contribute may be entertaining for professors but that is not effective teaching. Engaging students with enticing activities is better than boring them with yet another fact-filled lecture, but it does not meet the standard of effective teaching.

Maxine is often reminded of two examples of "great" classes she taught that were completely ineffective. Brouillette and Turner (1992) published a fascinating article in *Teaching Sociology* about social construction using spit and saliva as examples. Maxine laughed aloud the first time she read it and knew that she just had to use it in her class. She practiced that presentation repeatedly, until she had her timing and delivery perfect. Her students were enthralled, and she left that class beaming. Then, we had the first exam. She asked students to use the spit and saliva lecture in an answer. No one had a clue what the interactive lecture meant. She had done the "debriefing the day of the class," so she did not think that could be the problem. Maxine discussed the exam and the exercise with her class. The students remembered the class and thought it was great fun, but not a single student could integrate it with the rest of the class materials or activities.

A similar thing happened the first time her class played Classopoly (Coghlan and Huggins 2004; Fisher 2008; Jessup 2001). Students had a wonderful time playing the game and, again, although she did a careful job of helping them make sense of the game during the class period they played, their learning was still problematic. They simply did not see how the game fit into the larger picture. In both instances, students loved the class and seemed to understand the point of that specific activity on that day, but they did not know how the activity fit into the larger context of the course. Maxine had what she calls "the entertainment problem"; that is, she entertained but did not teach.

The activities failed for several reasons, but the first is that she had not carefully considered what she wanted students to know or be able to do because of that presentation. Second, she had only vaguely thought about how the activity helped the class meet course goals. Students did not know how the activities fit into a larger context because she was only vaguely aware of the contributions the activities would make. In both instances Maxine had written course goals, but once she wrote them she never thought of them again, and she had no related student learning outcomes. Somehow, she believed the students would magically make connections, synthesize all the activities, readings, and other materials she assigned, and finish the course as excited about sociology as she was. It did not happen. It is not likely to happen for any of us. It is not realistic to expect students to make connections that we ourselves have not made.

However, sometimes students can surprise us and see these connections more quickly than we can. In 2010, Kath and her 270 Introduction to Sociology students created a flash mob. They danced to Lady Gaga's "Bad Romance" music video. The entire semester had built to this day—there had been exercises where students had to count traffic patterns on the main campus; the students had created over 100 hypotheses about how people would react to 200 people starting to dance, etc. They had a plan that the flash dance would be videotaped from the top of three buildings (Campus Media Services volunteered to do this), so that we would have visual data to use to test our hypotheses. But five minutes before the flash dance, Media Services told Kath they decided to put the cameras at ground level. When they sent the film to her later in the day, she quickly realized that it would not allow for hypothesis testing. Over one hundred hours of dance practice outside of class, four class assignments which gathered data—all were for naught. But Kath's students were the ones who rescued the assignment. They convinced her to let them write on the topic of the social construction of reality instead. The campus was congratulating the class for a successful flash mob, while the class all considered it a failure. They said this was when they really understood what the social construction of reality meant, and they wanted to write about it. So they took a "pedagogical lemon" and made lemonade.

We would be willing to bet that you have ideas about what should be in your course and what you want your students to get out of the course. Your ideas may be vague or overly ambitious, but it is difficult to imagine that you have no ideas about the desired outcomes for your students. Knowing you will teach a course but not having yet planned for it is much like knowing you want to write on a particular topic for your dissertation or an article. You have something in mind, but you really need to narrow it down so that you can get to work. This is where course goals, objectives, and student learning outcomes take you from fuzzy thinking to knowing exactly what you want to accomplish. If you do not know where you want to go, there is no telling where you will end up. If you only know which continent you are aiming for, it is very difficult to buy an airline ticket! Explicit statements of where you want to go will take you a long way on the journey toward excellent and rewarding teaching for you and your students.

GOALS, OBJECTIVES, AND OUTCOMES

learn how these terms are used @ univ.

First, let us deal with the language of goals, objectives, and outcomes. Unfortunately, the terms are not used consistently in either the general teaching literature or in the sociological literature. The terms are certainly not consistent across campuses. We all have to make sure who our audience is and communicate clearly. You need to find out how the terms are used on your campus and adapt your language. More of us teach more introductory courses than any other, so in this chapter we will focus on writing goals and objectives for these courses, specifically an Introduction to Sociology class.

Usually goals and objectives refer to what you want your students to accomplish in the most general sense. Outcomes are the specific behaviors, attitudes, or knowledge that you want students to acquire. For example, being better critical thinkers is a goal or objective many of us have for our students. In this book, we will use the words "goal" and "objective" for the more abstract accomplishments we want for our students and "outcomes" for the more specific. That is, in this book, we use the term "goal" or "objective" for some generalized aspiration for the students in our course. By "outcome," we mean something we want our students to know or be able to do that helps them reach the more general goals of the course. In sociological terms, the goals or objectives are comparable to theories we are testing, and outcomes are comparable to hypotheses. Like hypotheses, outcomes are measurable; and like theories, goals and objectives are not.

If we have planned our courses competently, we will have general goals and specific outcomes, not just for our course but for sections of the course and even for each specific time the course meets. If you are teaching online, your goals and outcomes should be planned for concrete time periods in the course, such as a specific week. While there are any number of different types of goals and outcomes—such as affective, cognitive, behavioral, and attitudinal—the most common goals and outcomes are cognitive. Let us start there.

outcomes = measurable
most common goals = cognative

questions about what we want stdnts to know / do

How do we construct goals and objectives? (Remember that goals and objectives are more abstract.) Ask yourself these questions: In general, what do we want our students to know or be able to do after completing their first course in sociology? Do we want them to "understand" the sociological imagination? Do we want students to "appreciate" a sociological perspective? Do we want students to "value" diversity? Do we want students to "think critically"? These are common and laudable goals for sociology courses.

Choosing goals is perhaps the easiest part of planning. Your course may fit into general education requirements; if so, some goals may be defined for you. "Develop critical thinking skills" may be the most common college goal, but critical thinking is taught in the context of a discipline or field of study. You have to decide what it means to think critically in sociology. What does it mean to "understand" the sociological imagination? How do you operationalize and measure "understanding"? That is, what would your students be able to do or what knowledge would they have that would convince you that they "understand the sociological imagination"? Strong student learning outcomes are clear, concise, and measurable.

If you are confused about the more abstract goals and more specific outcomes, a visual representation may help illustrate the relationship. Consistent with the literature on what sociologists consider some of our discipline's important goals (Grauerholz and Gibson 2006; Persell 2010; Wagenaar 2004), Figure 1.1, "Goals and Student Learning Outcomes" illustrates three goals

FIGURE 1.1 GOALS AND STUDENT LEARNING OUTCOMES

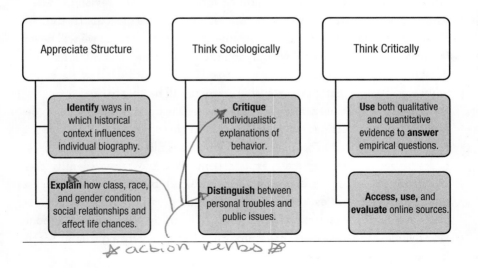

appreciate the soc. imagin.

★ action verbs ★

and two student learning outcomes for each goal. Following Grauerholz and Gibson's (2006) lead, we chose two goals that focus on the discipline: "appreciate structure" and "think sociologically." We also chose a third goal that is more generally shared across many disciplines: "think critically." Two student learning outcomes that will help students achieve the goal to "appreciate structure" are "identify ways in which historical context influences individual biography" and "explain how class, race, and gender condition social relationships and affect life chances." If we use "think sociologically" as our goal, two student learning outcomes might be "Critique individualistic explanations of behavior" and "Distinguish between personal troubles and public issues." When critical thinking is our goal, we might measure it by asking students to "Use both qualitative and quantitative evidence to answer empirical questions." We might also choose "Assess, use, and evaluate online sources."

Student learning outcomes orient the course to the students' perspective. Outcomes clearly tell students what they are supposed to know or be able to do at the end of the course. Remembering this one fact leads us to strategies for developing solid outcomes. Start with conceptualizing what students should be able to do at the end of the course, given the goals you have specified. We argue that outcomes have three major characteristics. Outcomes are measureable, achievable, and reasonable given the context of the curriculum, level of the course, and what is known about the students.

For example, it makes no sense to expect first-year students to have the same skills as graduate students writing their dissertations. Sociology majors should be able to complete more complex tasks than nonmajors should. Nilson (2010:30) provides a useful rubric for evaluating and revising student learning outcomes. Her category of "missed the point" is most instructive. We have missed the point when our outcomes only list the topics we will cover. We have missed the point if we only refer to internal states of mind like "understand" and "appreciate." We have missed the point if we fail to use action verbs and do not clearly indicate what learners will be able to do.

One of the most useful ways to state student learning outcomes is to deploy a verb that describes an observable action. (In Figure 1.1, the action verbs are presented in bold.) Fortunately, the literature is filled with good examples of action verbs, including: state, explain, compare and contrast, identify, construct, provide examples, apply, and illustrate. Even better, as we will discuss in the chapter on critical thinking, the literature provides examples of verbs that have been linked with varying levels of cognitive outcomes (Diamond 1998; Nilson 2010). Once you have a list of active verbs, writing student learning outcomes is a much simpler task.

For most of us, it is much easier to write a goal than it is to construct a student learning outcome. With these three goals, you could choose a variety of different student learning outcomes just as we might choose a large range of measures of any abstract concept. How do you decide which student learning outcome to use with which goal? The obvious answer is "it depends." It depends on your vision of sociology and your judgment about what is most important for your students to be able to do. For example, appreciating structure and thinking sociologically are obvious goals for courses in our discipline. How we might measure them is less obvious and will vary from one instructor to another. Though constructing student learning outcomes may seem intimidating and perhaps even bureaucratic, they can be one of the most creative parts of teaching. While constructing student learning outcomes is a challenge, it gets easier with practice.

USING GOALS AND OUTCOMES TO STRUCTURE YOUR COURSE

Once you have created your goals and student learning outcomes, you are at the stage we consider one of the most exciting parts of teaching. Your learning outcomes serve as a set of criteria, guiding your choice of teaching materials, activities, and teaching techniques. Many think of outcomes as a road map for your course. Materials, activities, and teaching techniques are chosen if and only if they contribute to your students' ability to meet the student learning outcomes. Your students will accomplish your goals and student learning outcomes by these means.

We can use the three goals proposed in Figure 1.1 (appreciate structure, think sociologically, and think critically) and the proposed accompanying student learning outcomes to illustrate how goals and outcomes help structure a successful class. As we consider these goals and outcomes, we note three important characteristics. First, our goals overlap significantly. At least from our perspective, it would be very difficult for students to "appreciate structure" and not be able to "think sociologically" and vice versa. We also see being able to "appreciate structure" and "thinking sociologically" as good examples of "thinking critically." That is reassuring because it means that the outcomes for one goal may also be used as outcomes for another goal.

Although it is not necessary to explicitly rank order these outcomes and goals, especially given the considerable overlap between them, we find it helpful to decide ahead of time exactly where each of us will place the most emphasis. Others might prefer to focus more on breadth and less on depth. If that is your choice, you would place more equal emphasis on each outcome. Either way, goals and outcomes should guide course construction.

As we write, rewrite, and reflect on how we will measure these goals, we realize that some are more important to us than others. Two student learning outcomes are most central to our understanding of sociology. First, like many sociologists, we see race, class, and gender as constituting the core of sociology (McKinney et al. 2004). Second, we also place a lot of emphasis on using evidence to answer empirical questions. While we take care to measure each of the student learning outcomes, we knowingly stress these two. Given the outcomes, each of our course materials needs to focus on race, class, and gender. We need classroom activities that are consistent with helping students deal with controversial topics. Our teaching methods will take into account the sensitivities surrounding these social justice issues.

Where do you start? First, ask if your department has adopted a text for your course. If so, you may still be able to supplement with favorite readings. ASA's TRAILS (American Sociological Association 2010) has a vast collection of syllabi and scads of materials and suggestions for activities for introductory-level courses. *Teaching Sociology* publishes reviews to consider. Your colleagues may also have suggestions, and usually departments have sample copies of texts from all the major publishers. If you are a novice instructor, we recommend using a text. Many experienced instructors see texts as unduly restrictive, but texts have advantages. They already have an organizational structure that will add coherence to your course, and many come with an amazing array of support materials. As you gain experience, creating your own course structure will give you more choices.

This book will hopefully be of help in choosing activities and teaching methods. In addition to ASA TRAILS and *Teaching Sociology,* other good sources include McKinney and Heyl's (2009) activities, the TeachSoc list serv (TeachSoc 2005), and the Facebook group Teaching with a Sociological Lens. You probably already have some idea of the types of activities that you prefer. Maxine tends to focus on writing to think exercises (see chapter 8) and inquiry-guided activities (Atkinson and Hunt 2008, see chapter 7), while Kath uses a significant amount of clicker questions in her introductory-level courses to engage students and assess learning. The ideal is to have all of your activities chosen before the beginning of the class, but most of us do not meet that standard when we begin to teach. Having some already planned, however, will go far toward not only helping your students meet the course goals, but it will also help you feel more confident and excited about teaching.

EVALUATION METHODS

[handwritten: ⟶ used to measure outcomes]

Ideally, evaluation methods are chosen after materials, activities, and teaching methods. Exams, assignments, and ungraded exercises should be designed to measure student learning outcomes. What is most appropriate given the other choices made for the class . . . exams, papers, group projects, graded or ungraded assignments, etc.? Again, the right answer is, "it depends." Student learning outcomes and the means by which students have been taught to meet those outcomes are the primary considerations. If lectures are the only teaching method used and students have been asked only to memorize materials (not recommended!), perhaps multiple-choice recall questions are all that are needed. However, if the goals and outcomes for a course look like the ones we have presented, it is unlikely that measures of simple recall will assess the extent to which students have met these outcomes. For example, if we think about the outcomes in Figure 1.1, *identify, explain, critique, distinguish, use, answer, access,* and *evaluate*, it is clear that learning to perform these tasks will require more than memorization. If your student learning outcomes are similar to the ones we have posed here and you have planned only to lecture, it is time to revisit your goals and outcomes.

The evaluation method we use most often is a variation on what is usually referred to as a "minute paper." At the end of the class period, we ask students, "In a sentence or two, tell me one thing you learned today." On the other hand, we may ask, "What is the clearest point today's exercise illustrated for you?" Another alternative to consider is, "What is it that you are still unsure about?" It is often a good idea to ask students to respond at the beginning of a class about an assignment. Caution is in order; if you overuse any evaluation method students are likely to see it as pro forma, and the method is likely to lose its effectiveness. There are several good sources of types of useful evaluations, but the classic reference is Angelo and Cross's (1993) *Classroom Assessment Techniques.*

Maxine usually proceeds inductively; that is, as with these exercises, student learning outcomes are first addressed by having students complete active learning exercises and then the exercise is examined in context. For assessments and grading, Maxine uses a series of low-stake methods, including group quizzes, individual quizzes, and free writes. A free write is simply having students "freely write" or informal exploratory writing (Bean 2001) in response to a prompt. For a graded assignment, students write a short take-home essay explaining how gender is socially constructed and how these

[handwritten: low-stake methods ⟶ grp. quzs., quzs., free writes]

FIGURE 1.2 CONNECTING TEACHING METHODS, READINGS, AND ASSESSMENTS TO OUTCOMES

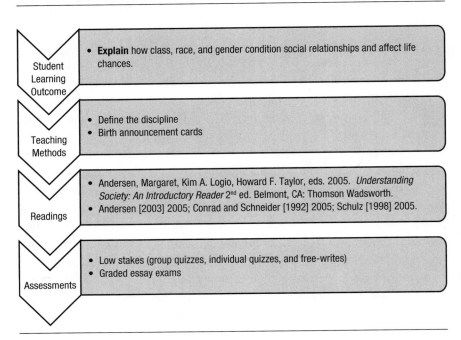

constructions affect men and women's life chances. (See chapters 14 and 15 for a thorough discussion of grading and evaluation.) Note that these integrated teaching methods and readings and assessments all target a specific student learning outcome.

To illustrate how student learning outcomes are used, we offer an example from one of Maxine's classes. She concentrates here on the student learning outcome "Explain how class, race, and gender condition social relationships and affect life chances." Figure 1.2 visually represents a partial layout of the teaching methods, readings, and assessments Maxine used to help students achieve this outcome.

The first day of class, students complete an activity that asks them to make identity statements, share the identity statements with a partner, and introduce their partner to the class (Atkinson 2010). The data that students generated is then analyzed in a most basic way. When a student is introducing a woman, the identity statement is written on the board under a column labeled "women"; conversely, when a student is introducing a man, the identity statement goes under a column labeled "men."

Students work with the same partner they introduced and look for patterns in the data generated by the entire class. Typically, women identify themselves in relation to others, for example, "daughter," "sister," or "friend." Male students often initially greet this exercise with blank stares but proceed with encouragement and mention identities such as "soccer player" or "from Hometown, North Carolina," or "engineering major," a high status group on our campus. The class ends with a discussion of these patterns.

Students are fascinated with themselves and each other so this is a fun exercise for them. We are working on several outcomes simultaneously, but we are also laying the groundwork for the two outcomes that are the focus represented by this outcome, that is, explaining how class, race, and gender condition social relationships and affect life chances.

The next day in class, students write a short paragraph describing what the first class told them about sociology as a discipline and what they could expect of the class. Their attention is drawn to the student learning outcomes. Students are typically pleased that they are already "doing sociology" and that they can see what the class will be like and what will be expected of them. A foundation for later classes is created. Students' written responses provide faculty with an initial impression of student skills. As the class proceeds, students are reminded of this exercise. The next time gender is the focus of the class, students complete another exercise. This time students analyze birth announcement cards for what they tell us about gender expectations (Clark and Atkinson 2008). If the class is small, an assortment of cards can be shared among students, but it is easy to adapt this exercise to a larger class by scanning the cards and having them available online. Students examine the cards, then answer a series of descriptive questions and a synthesis question. Examples of the descriptive questions include, "What colors are used in the card?" and "What words are used to describe the child?" The synthesis question is, "What are the cards saying about how girls and boys should be?"

The assigned readings add depth and provide a richer sociological context to the activities. If activities are to go beyond the "entertainment problem" described in the beginning of this chapter, teaching methods and readings must be woven together to address student learning outcomes. These two gender activities are framed with the lens of social constructionism. A reader is assigned for this class, *Understanding Society* (Andersen, Logio, and Taylor 2005) and three readings addressing this perspective (Andersen [2003] 2005; Conrad and Schneider [1992] 2005; Schulz [1998] 2005).

PROGRAM ASSESSMENT AND THE SCHOLARSHIP OF TEACHING AND LEARNING

Goals and outcomes are not only essential for your individual course planning, but also for program assessment. In chapter 16, we explore the relationship between course planning and program assessment, but program assessment warrants a brief mention here. Whether the course or courses you teach are a fundamental component of your department's assessment efforts probably depends on the role your course plays in the curriculum. Spalter-Roth and Seelza (2009) find that departments across institutional types tend to focus on capstone courses, senior theses or projects, and student surveys to assess their programs. Even if the course you teach this semester may not be directly involved in your department's assessment efforts, the ability to do course planning matters for program assessment purposes.

The logic of course planning and the logic of program assessment is the same. In both, you must set goals and then decide how you will determine if you met those goals. Both course planning and program assessment require that you determine what destination you need to reach and what path you need to travel. Abstract goals are set and concrete measurements are constructed. Once you have some practice creating goals and outcomes for your course and evaluating them, you will become a valuable partner in your department's assessment efforts.

The scholarship of teaching and learning (SoTL) and constructing goals and outcomes are also strongly related. For example, if you wanted to publish a teaching "note" in *Teaching Sociology*, you would need to provide what the journal calls "outcome data." When you assess or evaluate your student learning outcomes that is exactly what you will be doing. You are collecting "data" to measure the outcomes you posed. Earlier, we argued that a goal is much like a theory and an outcome is a type of hypothesis to be tested. This is the dominant model used in SoTL. See chapter 20 for a more detailed discussion of the scholarship of teaching and learning.

SUMMARY

Goals and student learning outcomes also provide you with the basis for evaluating your own courses. In this chapter, Maxine used explicit examples of activities, readings from a course she recently taught, and their corresponding assessments. At the end of the semester when Maxine was evaluating the course, she realized that she had placed more emphasis on gender and social class than she had on race. She also placed too little emphasis on historical context for it to be a major student learning outcome. The next time she teaches the course, she will include more emphasis on race and will drop or replace the student learning outcome, "Illustrate how historical context influences individual biography." Explicitly stating her goals and outcomes allows her to evaluate the structure of the course more clearly.

Goals and student learning outcomes comprise the skeleton of any successful course. Without them, the course may meander along pleasantly enough, your students may love you, and they will probably learn bits and pieces of the discipline; but you cannot construct a coherent learning experience retroactively. Trying to teach a course without goals and outcomes is like trying to do research with no planned relationship between methods, theory, and literature. Teaching and research require careful planning. You can only teach a course as well as you have planned it.

goals → be confedent in what(ever) you
knw. abt. soc.

  ◦ use campus resources

  ◦ interact w/ class

outcoms → start to see wrld./ major
w/in a soc. imagin.

▶▶▶ CHAPTER 2
SYLLABUS CONSTRUCTION

It happens to all of us. That moment when we have to face it—the blank computer screen, staring back at us. It's time to draft a syllabus.

We have all had that experience—of being ready to construct (or reconstruct) a course. For Kath and Maxine, there's a mixture of exhilaration, dread, and anxiety that is hard to express. But more than anything, we feel hopeful that students will strive enough to get what they need to from the course; hopeful that we can find that "sweet spot" which balances readings and assignments just right; hopeful that our planning is enough but not too much, which can get in the way of spontaneous learning experiences.

We bet you have been there (or soon will be). Whether you use a computer or paper—there is that moment, pregnant with hope for you and your students. Hold on to that feeling—it can sustain a professor through a lot of the "down moments" in a term. The document that you are about to create—the course syllabus—should be the map of where the journey is to take you and your students. It should provide the key facts about the trip, what supplies are needed for the journey; and it should show the students the pace of the journey ahead. ◀—

Like trip planning, syllabus construction is highly individualistic. Some of us are super-organized, planning out every second of the trip, and others of us live for the spontaneity of the journey. Kath is more the former than the latter, so her syllabi have been as long as 30 pages. However, since she began using the university's learning management system (LMS) for every class, her syllabi have shrunk. Now she no longer includes some things in the syllabus, but only posts them online.

Maxine dislikes overly wordy documents of any kind, so she is more likely to make the error of not being explicit enough. She works hard to flesh out her syllabi without overwhelming her students or hiding information in a sea of verbiage. So please see these as guidelines, following those which make sense to you, bending others, and ignoring those which do not fit with your teaching style or which violate your institution's best practices.

PACKING THE NECESSITIES FOR YOUR SOCIOLOGICAL TRIP TOGETHER
Basic Information about the Class

- Name of course/course number and term (date)
- Name of professor
- Location of classroom
- Days/times when the class meets (including if there is a secondary class-room used regularly for certain classes, i.e., a laboratory versus lecture room)
- Ways to contact you (phone number[s], e-mail, etc.)
- Website address or link to LMS if one or both is being used
- Course description as it appears in the course catalog. Be sure to include any prerequisites or corequisites which are necessary for success in the course
- How grades will be calculated and the grade distribution

These pieces of information seem so fundamental that we sometimes forget that they need to be in every syllabus. But most institutions see these as the barest minimum amount of information needed in a syllabus. We want to encourage you to see these as the warm-up for your course. There is so much more information that students need to know about the class—about your expectations for them and for yourself, and the final destination for your sociological journey—that you don't want to end here. Some faculty put these basics in a shaded text box on the first page, so that they are easy for students to locate. What else should be included?

LEARNING GOALS AND OUTCOMES

Students have a right to know what kinds of learning goals you set for them, why those goals were chosen and not others, and how you will be measuring their learning. Some of us might include them simply because accrediting bodies require their presence in the syllabus, but we believe that with the proper explanation and coaching learning goals and outcomes really can become useful to students. Think of the goals and outcomes as how the travelers on the sociological journey (your students and you) will measure whether the trip was a success. These are the most important things to pack for your trip, for they should shape the rest of the journey that you and your students will take. (See chapter 1 for how to develop these for your course.)

REQUIRED READINGS

Students care about what they will be expected to read. Often they care most about the number of pages per week than anything else, but they need to know if you are requiring that they purchase one or more books or if there are additional readings, and how they can access them. Are you requiring the ASA's *Style Guide*? Have you created a customized reader which will be sold in the bookstore? Have you placed PDFs of required readings in the LMS or have you put hard links of journal articles online? If you do the latter, you might want to consider giving them directions for how to access the articles, including whether a password is necessary. Many libraries require use of a password when accessing library resources from off-campus and not all students know that, or how to find the password (which may change every term). If you have optional readings, the syllabus needs to delineate clearly which are required and which are optional.

Students also care about the cost of the required readings. We urge you to consider that as well. For many faculty, the cost of required books (textbooks or monographs) is one of many factors they consider as they create a syllabus. It's not easy to weigh the cost compared to the benefits of any particular reading. And for some faculty, the balance shifts depending on the course level. They tend to use more textbook-like readings in lower-division courses and more monographs and scholarly articles in upper-division ones. For the latter, we try to link articles via the hard link in our library databases, so that students do not necessarily have to copy what we want them to read. For other courses, we might scan readings and post them to the LMS. As a caution, in chapter 18 we will address problems with scanned readings if they are posted as PDFs. In addition, you must recognize that there are copyright issues which might arise as well.

DESCRIPTIONS OF REQUIRED ASSIGNMENTS

Whether we like it or not, many students attend the first day of class in what we like to call "tasting" mode. They will size up the amount of work required for the course, their impressions of the professor and class (size, room [e.g., distance from previous and next class]), and so on. One of the things that they will be examining closely is the required workload, and so they quickly will gravitate to this section of the syllabus. Most of us will create this section of the syllabus alone, in our office, but for an alternative strategy—cocreating the assignments with your students during the first few days of class—see Hudd's (2003) article.

One of the decisions to make is where you include the full description of assignments. If you include only brief descriptions in the syllabus, we strongly suggest you insert a note at the end of the brief description which tells students where the full assignment is located (in LMS? separate assignment directions, etc.?). Descriptions need to describe accurately what students will be asked to do. "Write a paper" is too vague. Is it a 3-page paper? A 20-page paper? Are there a minimum number of scholarly references to be used? Does the paper require students to create a logical argument using a particular theoretical perspective or a concept? Is the paper a review of sociological literature on a topic of the student's choice or will you have topic approval? The more your description can clarify your requirements for students, the more informed they will feel.

For many faculty, this section of their syllabi undergoes frequent revision from term to term, just because some details, like dates and assigned classroom, need updating. Here is a bit about how Kath has seen her syllabi's class calendar evolve. She used to have a relatively short class calendar: breaking the course into however many parts she had planned, the dates for that entire section, required readings, and any assignments that were due. She did not give a day-by-day list of topics, etc. Trust us, she now looks back and cringes! She has come to believe that students need to know the plan for every day of class and finds that having this plan helps her to focus too. So the calendar now lists each day, the topic for the day, all required readings, any assignments that are due that day, and any additional resources that she wants students to

FIGURE 2.1 IT'S IN THE SYLLABUS

IT'S IN THE SYLLABUS

This message brought to you by every instructor that ever lived.
WWW.PHDCOMICS.COM

Source: "Piled Higher and Deeper" by Jorge Cham. www.phdcomics.com.

bring to class (i.e., a theoretical perspectives handout which she posts in the LMS in a folder called "Class Resources" that she wants students to read outside of class and then bring to class on the days when the class is discussing the perspectives). She reminds them where the handout can be found as well. She also includes key institutional dates on the class calendar, such as the last day to withdraw from the class. For each assignment, we suggest you list its due date and how students are expected to turn it in (i.e., "Assignment #1 is due on [insert date] by 8:00 a.m., submitted as a Word document, via the learning management system only").

CLASS POLICIES

Many faculty find this section to be the one part of syllabi that they change the most from term to term. We rarely feel that we have gotten our policies "just right." And we often add new policies based on what went wrong in the last term. So please let us talk a bit about policies in general and then address some specific ones you might want to consider.

Classrooms are sites for social interaction which are centered around learning (Macomber, Rusche, and Atkinson 2009). As sociologists, we know that, but we sometimes do not apply that knowledge to our own classrooms. We like to think about policies using that interactional lens. What behaviors do you want to encourage in order to foster learning? What behaviors do you want to control, in order to enhance learning? For both of us, those are questions without easy answers. In fact, neither of us are sure there are "perfect" answers to those questions—not for us. We think that engaging in the introspection and struggle that constructing policies entails is what is important, perhaps even more important than what the rules will be. In part, we believe that your policies will likely vary depending on the level of the course, the size of the class, the way the classroom is designed, and in what kinds of active learning you want your students to be involved. Even the time and the length of the class play a part in constructing policies. So what are some policies to consider?

Accessibility statement. It is very likely that your institution has an official policy statement which should be included in your syllabus. Check with your school's office (it might be called the "Access Office" or the "Disabilities Office") which works with students who have disabilities, to acquire the recommended nomenclature in your syllabus. Remember, though, that what the office requires is the minimum standard. As we will discuss in chapter 18, many of these offices are undergoing a paradigm shift—away from the medical model and toward the social model of disabilities. If your school has made this shift, then the policies and procedures will likely look very different—less required documentation and more focus on creating a hospitable, accessible atmosphere for all students. Try not to think just about meeting the minimum legal requirements of accessibility—you want to ensure that all your students succeed; students with disabilities are simply a subset of your students who might need alternative ways to access course content.

As you are choosing texts and videos, don't forget that both need to be accessible. Are all the videos you use (in or out of class) captioned? They need to be. If not, you will need to provide a transcript for students who request one.

Attendance. It is difficult to learn if students are not present to engage with the material and be active learners. So of course we want them physically present in a face-to-face class—it increases the chance of learning! How can you create a learning atmosphere that will make students want to come to class? Will taking attendance every day accomplish that? How will you take attendance, if you decide you will require it? Will you call roll every day? Or will you assign seats and quickly scan the room for empty seats? Will you have a student assistant who could do it for you? Is there any technology available to you which could assist monitoring attendance (see, for example Cordell [2011] and Jones [2010])? What will be the consequences for not attending class? Most schools have an attendance policy to which you are expected to adhere (for example, one of our universities states in the *Undergraduate Catalog* that missing 20 percent of the class constitutes a failing grade). There are often official permutations to the rule, for example, that students who are off on "official university business" (e.g., sanctioned field trips, or more commonly, athletic events) are given official excuses and cannot be counted as absent. And what constitutes "attendance" in an online class? If there are mandatory synchronous events, then attendance is easier to assess, but what if there are not? Are there certain tasks which must be completed every week to count as being "present"? If so, your syllabus has to alert students to that requirement.

Attendance rules also mean that you will become the designated listener of the myriad of stories that students will tell you to account for their absences—especially if you state that you will allow some absences for reasons above and beyond the university's policy. What additional excuses will be valid? What kind of documentation will the student have to provide to you? Are you prepared for the emotional labor required to listen to their accounts? Kath finds it exhausting—and she often feels icky if she has to ask a student to provide some sort of documentation when the student tells her there was a death in the family or some other tragedy.

Your policy should take into account the time it would take to call the roll or to gather the information in some other way, the class size, how you will handle non-normative behavior, and the emotional toll it can take on the student to ask for "special treatment." Please remember, too, that not every student will be brave enough to come forward and offer an excuse, even if he or she knows it would be considered an excused absence. Don't forget about that student as you create your policy.

Late work. Will you accept late work or not? If you say "yes, you will," does the late work receive the same grade as work that was turned in on time? If it loses points, how many points? Is there a time beyond which you will not accept late work? Do students have to provide you with a reason for the late work, and then you will decide if you accept it or not? These are just some of the possible permutations of late work policies. As you think through the answers to these questions, remember the pedagogical purposes of the work which you assign: to help students learn. For both of us, what matters most is that we still give students who turned work in late the feedback that other students received who turned the work in on time.

Here's Kath's policy about late work: it will be read and she will offer the same amount and quality of comments to the student, but it earns no points. And she defines late as "not turned in to her by the start of class" or if it is to be turned in via the LMS, within one minute of the time that she has designated. However, she mitigates that policy just a bit. She has found that she doesn't like to deal with excuses for late work, so she has created what she calls the "Lowney Loan" plan. Each student can use the Lowney Loan once a semester. It gives the student a set amount of additional time (usually 12 hours, although it can change somewhat if the class meets once a week, etc.) without point loss. Kath created a form that each student who uses it must sign and attach to the late assignment (see Figure 2.2), which states that the student understands that the assignment was late and should have received a zero grade. The student turns it in to her, the departmental secretary, or another faculty member—not student workers in the departmental office.

Extra credit. There is tremendous disagreement on whether extra credit assignments are a good pedagogical idea (Moore 2005; Norcross, Dooley, and Sevenson 1993; Slay 2005; Streich 2008). Again, we think the question to ask yourself is, "Why are you offering it?" Is it because you feel the distribution of grades, after all the preplanning work you did, is too unbalanced? Or that you think students have not buckled down for most of the term and now they are ready to do so, but most of the points are "gone," so if you do not offer the extra credit, most will fail the course? Or is it that you are unhappy with the amount of learning that they seem to be doing and want them to have one more opportunity to succeed? If you choose extra assignments, they should help students learn sociology and it is a good idea to include your policies in the syllabus.

Plagiarism. These policies need to be on the syllabus! We both believe in having students write in every class we teach, no matter its enrollment. But that also means that we often confront plagiarism.

Part of creating our policies about plagiarism involves crafting carefully the kinds of assignments that we assign students. In many classes, we create assignments which require students to apply material to a particular applied scenario. These kinds of assignments, while requiring grounding the paper in scholarly literature, make it harder to plagiarize than the standard "Write a 10-page paper about X"—where X is a pretty common topic with lots of available resources from which students might lift information. While the assignment might stay the same whenever we teach the course, we change the details

FIGURE 2.2 THE "LOWNEY LOAN" PROGRAM FOR ADDITIONAL TIME

Papers in my class are due on time or else you will lose **all** the points. Just as in any job, there are deadlines and those deadlines have consequences. However, I recognize that **in rare circumstances** something can happen and you may not have your paper done on time. So I will give you a "break"— **once and only once this semester!!!!!** Here's how it will work.

You have the option to turn a paper in late once during the term—and it will not be penalized as late. However, you have to obey the following rules:

1. You have until **12:00 noon** the next school day to turn it in. You must turn it in to me (if I am in the building) or to the departmental secretary or to another departmental faculty member. The faculty member/departmental secretary must initial the front of the assignment and write down the correct time that you turned the paper into him/her. It is your job to ask politely for the person to do this, it is NOT her/his job to remember it.

2. **You cannot turn your paper in to a student worker in the departmental office**. I do not accept their initials/time markings—I will assume that the paper came in late. **BUT** if you turn it in to someone other than myself, you must get the faculty member or the departmental secretary to put the time you are turning it in, the date you are turning it in, and his or her initials on the first page of the assignment. If you do not, it will be considered late, and will receive a zero. It is **your** responsibility to remember to have them do this, not theirs.

3. If you try to use the "loan program" more than one time during the semester, the second assignment will receive a zero **and** you will lose general class participation points. **This is a one-time offer, folks**, don't make it a habit to be late!! For a group project assignment, have a group member who has not used the Lowney Loan turn in the assignment.

4. You must complete the following (or print a copy from the learning management system) and turn this page in with the late paper:

****
Lowney "Loan" Application

Print Your Name _____

I understand that I am requesting that this paper not be considered late and should be graded. I can use this loan of "time" just once this semester. I have had a departmental staff member (faculty or secretary) sign this, and initial the day and time.

This is a "gift"—**I understand that the paper was late and should have received a zero.**

_____/_____
Sign your name above please   Date

enough to make it difficult for students to plagiarize from previous students in the course.

While few of us are perfectly happy with our policies about plagiarism, here are the processes that we use to arrive at them. First, examine your school's policies—what do they say? What constitutes plagiarism? What constitutes convincing evidence of plagiarism—for you? for administrators who would oversee a report of plagiarism which you would make? The institution's policy should form the basis of your policies, so that you know you will have support if you report a student for academic dishonesty.

Then we believe you need to be clear what your policies are—in the syllabus, of course, but we have found that it helps to repeat those policies, briefly, in the directions of every assignment. Talk about them in class—not just what the punishment is for plagiarism, but about why correct citing is important, how every discipline has its own citing style and how scholars always use the ideas of others but that we have to show the chain of ideas and how we found them—that is what citations give to the reader. (We both require ASA style for all classes for majors but are more flexible in classes primarily for nonmajors.) Again, the concept to have front and center when constructing policies about plagiarism is that they are, overall, more aimed at helping students to learn how to cite correctly rather than simply punishing them.

Technology policies. Perhaps the most basic question we all need to address is how much student technological use will we allow in class? Can students fire up their laptops or tablets and take notes on a regular basis during class? Will you allow cell phones to be turned on during class? Can they be on vibrate? There are many factors that influence the answers to these questions: The number of students, the physical boundaries of the classroom, the kind of material which the course covers, the course level (i.e., for first-year students or seniors), etc., might all impact your decisions.

A policy that we have had to create, because we each use a LMS for nearly every class, concerns what happens if the LMS stops working around the time that an assignment is due. It is important that our students understand that we are aware of the fickleness of technology and we create a policy that codifies this awareness. You might want to provide an automatic extension to your deadlines if the system goes down, for example.

Of course, students often will use technological excuses for late work. Having a policy such as the "Lowney Loan" (explained above) takes away some of students' worries about technological glitches. In chapter 17 we will offer some advice for how to deal with this issue.

If you use student response systems (i.e., "clickers"), then you should consider establishing policies about them. In particular, do you want to create a norm that says that any student can only have his or her clicker on the desk? Is it an instance of academic misconduct to input data on someone else's clicker, if that student is not present in class that day? If you see two or more clickers being used by one student, what will you do?

A FEW LAST HELPFUL HINTS—OR PLEASE, LEARN FROM OUR MISTAKES!

Double-check your addition, to be sure that you have not made any math errors in the grade calculation section of the syllabus! We often go back and forth about how much assignments should be worth as we are creating the syllabus, so force yourself to double-check this section before either posting the syllabus to the LMS or starting to Xerox it for students. Take the few minutes to do the same.

Proofread for spelling and grammar errors. This is *especially* important if, like each of us, you grade students on their grammar and spelling! Use the built-in tools in software like Word or Open Office or do it the "old-fashioned" way—going line by line. But do it!

Make sure that the class schedule doesn't skip days or weeks accidentally and that deadlines are correct. If you have each assignment as a separate file, open it up and double-check that the day and time it is due is the same on the assignment directions as on the calendar schedule in the syllabus and as in the calendar in the LMS (if used).

Accept that you might not catch every mistake. Use that as a learning opportunity. Kath has a unique way to get students to see proofing as a useful step in the writing process. In her-upper-division sociological theory course, where writing and ASA style are emphasized, she deliberately makes several grammatical and style errors. She posts the list of errors to the LMS, but locks it, so that students cannot open it right away. Then, after she and the class have talked about the ASA style, the syllabus becomes a test of their learning—they have 24 hours to find the ASA errors she made. This is a win-win scenario: they actively read the syllabus applying their new knowledge of style requirements while also reading the syllabus several times!

LAST THOUGHT: YOU AS TRAVEL GUIDE

The remaining piece of advice about constructing a course syllabus we want to offer is never to forget that it is an introduction to who you are for students. Yes, it is a document that has many other functions and many audiences, but don't ignore this one. If you have a particular "style" or "tone" in class, we think it should be present in your syllabus too. Kath likes to use creative titles for the parts of the course—similar to how she talks in class. Consider using a graphic or a cartoon or an epigram if that is in keeping with who you are as a person and as a professor (with appropriate permissions and a citation, of course!). Don't make the syllabus so legalistic and bureaucratic that students lose the fact that you—unique, intriguing, with talents and flaws—made the syllabus. We firmly believe that they will be more likely to want to take the sociological journey with you if they get a sense of who you are in the syllabus.

►►► CHAPTER 3
HOW MUCH CONTENT TO COVER

Perhaps one of the most difficult decisions faculty face as we design our courses is the quandary of how much content should be covered in a term. There is no clear answer to this dilemma; rather what we want to do in this chapter is help you to consider some questions to ask as you contemplate this decision.

Course design should not happen in a vacuum; ideally it should have a significant collective component to it. While much of the actual design process might happen while we are alone, working at a desk in our campus office or at home, there should be significant input from others involved as we build our courses. Colleagues who have (hopefully) constructed a cohesive program of carefully planned learning for their students, one's institution curricular policies, accrediting bodies' standards, and even our students—their prior learning, their expectations about coverage, amount of work which is "normal" in this type of course at your institution, etc.—all should play a role in our decision making. Figure 3.1 illustrates the social context of the course design process.

We believe that asking some questions about your class, the overall curriculum of your sociology program, and your institution's curriculum, can serve as a guide for beginning to answer the depth versus breadth issue.

FIGURE 3.1 THE SOCIAL CONTEXT OF THE COURSE DESIGN PROCESS

POSSIBLE INPUTS

Core Curriculum/Gen Ed learning goals and required assessment activities

Major or Program learning goals and outcomes and required assessment activities (including writing and style requirements)

Your Students, some who come with prior knowledge (accurate or not) and others who do not have prior knowledge. Can be "book" knowledge or learning via life lessons.

Prerequisite Courses (if there are any) and the knowledge students should have acquired there.

You (your own teaching and research interest, your workload, your private life, etc.)

YOUR COURSE

Do you have copies of the inputs which are written down to help you in your design process?

Where and how does your course incorporate these inputs?

How do the readings you select mesh with these inputs? Are the connections clear to students? If not, how will you help them to see those connections?

How do your assessments attempt to measure accurately your learning goals and objectives?

Have you created a grading scale flexible enough for students to have some troubles and yet still overall achieve academic success?

Does your grading scale give multiple opportunities to show learning?

Do you have enough points by the midterm grading period for students to make an accurate assessment of the likelihood of their academic success?

Is your course accessible for students?

Can you balance this course with your other courses and still stay engaged, energetic, and caring?

POSSIBLE OUTCOMES & RESPONSIBILITIES

To Your Students: They will have been introduced to concepts needed for future success in their major or program. Your assessments created meaningful opportunities for appropriate feedback to them. Within reason, all can access your content in order to have equal opportunity for success.

To Your Colleagues: You have followed requirements for the course/program and provided meaningful assessments and feedback to your students. Your students are prepared to be successful in their next course.

To Your Discipline: Your course is sharing up-to-date information—including unsettled debates—at the appropriate content level for the course.

To Your Institution and Accrediting Agencies: Your course will be evidence of completing institution's and program/major's learning goals and objectives.

To Yourself and the ones you love: You will stay balanced, not just in your work life, but in all parts of your life.

Source: Created by K. Lowney and S. Gravett. July 2012.

QUESTION 1: HOW SHOULD STUDENTS' SOCIOLOGICAL KNOWLEDGE GROW BECAUSE THEY WERE IN YOUR CLASS?

This is a crucial question to consider as you think about designing a course. Another way to determine this is to begin at the end—what is often called "backward design." Once you know what you want students to take away from the course, you can select readings and active learning experiences, and create assessments which collectively build these skills with your students. Using the principles of backward course design, Wiggins and McTighe (1999) provide a way to move from "covering the curriculum" to "creating curriculum" and understanding with technology. They offer a three-stage diagram of the backward design process that includes: identify desired results, determine acceptable evidence, and plan learning experiences and instruction.

We encourage you to begin by asking questions about outputs. What should your students know by the end of your class? What concepts will they have had "first contact with" in your class and which others should their prior learning in other classes have deepened by completing your course? The more specificity you can bring to creating this list, the better. You are on your way to creating learning goals. "They should learn sociology" is not as helpful as "Students should be able to identify correctly the theoretical perspectives involved in a written scenario" and "Students should be able to propose solutions to the problems in the scenario based on those theoretical perspectives," for instance. But again, we hope that this is not a solitary project; the sociology faculty, including you, should do this work collectively.

Now think about the concepts/theories/theorists/skills, etc., on that list. How will you design assessments—be they tests, papers, in-class activities, writing assignments, active learning exercises in class, etc.—which can measure how well your students learned the sociology you want them to learn? Which ones are more likely to need repeated assessment in order to give students time to move from mere memorization to deep learning and the ability to apply the concept or skill (Brown, Roediger, and McDaniel 2014; Chew 2010; Lang 2012)? (For more information on designing assessments see Stiggins et al. [2004].)

In particular, consider if your class is a prerequisite for any other courses in the curriculum. What are the expectations about the amount of sociological knowledge that faculty teaching those courses will have for your students? Even if your class does not directly flow into another, as prerequisites do, there should be curricular expectations for what students should have learned in it, which get at the depth versus breadth debate. (If there are no curricular expectations, why are students taking the class? Even elective courses should have a list of concepts/skills/theories which will be attained.) For example, at Kath's school, there are two parts to the degree. There are the concentration courses in Applied and Clinical Sociology, and the foundations courses. The latter are: (1) theory; (2) research methods; (3) self, society, and culture; (4) social inequalities; and (5) social institutions. There are several classes from which students choose one course in each of the latter three areas, which they must pass with a C grade or better. Years ago, we created shared expectations of what, for example, a "social institutions" class should cover, because we wanted to be sure that students learned about all the institutions and their roles in shaping social structure and social life as well as the sociological knowledge about *the* particular institution which was the focus of the class they chose. We also decided that students would be asked to write a review of literature in whichever institutions course they took, as well as in their sociological theory course, so that we knew students would have at least two opportunities in their time-in-major where they would obtain and use that specific writing skill. Now to be truthful, we have not always done a good job of remembering what these shared expectations were and are working on re-creating—and more importantly—renegotiating them in order to hold ourselves and our students accountable.

If your program does not have such expectations, then we suggest that you read *Liberal Learning and the Sociology Major* (Eberts et al. 1990) and *Liberal Learning and the Sociology Major Updated: Meeting the Challenge of Teaching Sociology in the Twenty-First Century* (McKinney et al. 2004). Both documents can give you some guidance about how to envision fitting together a curriculum, which can help you to situate the kinds of academic content which best fits the course you are teaching, to the kinds of students you have, etc.

For other types of classes (i.e., general education courses which might double as required for the major, such as Introduction to Sociology or Social Problems), there likely will be required general education assessments or assessments from accrediting bodies which will need to be completed at some point in the term. These might involve pre- and post-test assessments or a portfolio of student work, for example. You will need to understand how these can be used in your class so that you are not violating procedures. (For instance, can the assessment be included as part of a regularly scheduled test or must it be freestanding? Can students earn points—or extra credit—for it or not? And so on.) Be sure you understand when these requirements must be completed during the semester, so that you are sure students have covered the material thoroughly enough to show their learning by the time of the assessment.

You will need to know all these "outputs" as you sit down to construct your course. Ideally, they will be easily accessible to you, written in clear and understandable language, and you will not only agree with them all (or even better, you were a part of creating them!), but can easily see how you will accomplish them. But many of us don't work in departments and institutions which function this way. You might find that colleagues are reluctant to share their syllabi, even though they teach the class which follows yours in a sequence, or you are a new hire or an adjunct and have no say on existing agreements. Some of you might be lucky to get anyone to talk with you, let alone share if there are any such curricular agreements. What to do then?

We suggest you spend some time reading all you can about your program and your institution. Look in the course catalog (sometimes called the course bulletin), which frequently has a listing of all courses offered at the school. Take notes on, for example, the sociology courses, and list all courses you are scheduled to teach. Then, in another column, list all other courses for which a course you are teaching is a prerequisite or a corequisite. That will give you some clues about how the faculty may see the connections between classes. Are there any courses you are teaching which fit into a category in the curriculum, such as Kath's example of social institutions courses above? If so, think about what are the overarching sociological theories/methods/concepts/theorists/skills for the entire category and assume that your course should address them as well as the specific content based on the particular title, and so on. This isn't the best of situations, but see it as another time to hone your content analysis skills.

QUESTION 2: WHAT DO THESE EDUCATIONAL OUTPUTS REQUIRE?: DEPTH VERSUS BREADTH

Any discussion of breadth versus depth for each individual course has to consider where the course fits into the larger curriculum (Hirsch 2001). Given the current context of higher education's focus on assessment, it is likely that most courses have preexisting goals and outcomes. If not, then those tasks need to come first, before deciding on the amount of sociological coverage that is best for the course which you are teaching (see chapter 1 for advice on creating them). Learning goals and outcomes—whether created by you or by a group of faculty—provide the road map for the intellectual journey that you and your students will take. Clear understanding of goals and outcomes is crucial. So for instance, Schweingruber (2005) argues that the choice of textbooks needs to be guided by course goals and more research needs to focus on this. What kind of language do the books you choose utilize to discuss the key concepts you will be covering? Does the language match how you intend to teach about the concept? Does the language imply depth or breadth or something in between?

The standard way that learning goals are written almost inevitably involves breadth. For instance, in chapter 1, the learning goals we used as examples were that "students can appreciate structure," that they can "think sociologically," and that students can "think critically." Consider the "think sociologically" learning goal; can you imagine any concept which we teach in a sociology course which would not fit with that goal? That's both good and bad. Luckily, the learning outcomes help to narrow the coverage options. Again, from chapter 1, one of the learning outcomes linked to that goal was that students should be able to "distinguish between personal troubles and public issues." Having that as a learning outcome means that the concept of the sociological imagination will need to be covered in the course, so that students have the chance to succeed at that learning outcome.

However, the fact that it needs to be addressed in class is not yet a complete answer to the coverage question. Faculty will still need to consider how much we want students to focus on that topic. And "in depth" can mean different amounts to different instructors. For example, imagine the concept of "the sociological imagination" is addressed in a variety of ways: one full day of in-class discussion; coupled with two days reading about the concept in course texts; as well as a required discussion board conversation where students must show not just a definitional knowledge but the ability to apply the concept to a situation of their choosing and to respond to others' posts; a short written assignment where students had to "see" the concept at work in a video and correctly applying it; and finally, to answering successfully several different types of test questions about the concept. Is that "in depth" coverage of the sociological imagination? Or is it "about average" coverage of the concept? Or is it too little coverage?

We think the answer is, "it depends." If this is an introductory-level course for nonmajors—and part of your program's learning goals is to get students to begin to think and to analyze the world around them using the sociological imagination—then these assignments and test questions may be a good series of assessments which build on each other to help students learn the concept. But if you are teaching a research methods course and you want to mention the concept briefly in the first week of class during an overview of the sociological perspective, then such a focus on the sociological imagination is probably too much. We don't mean that it is "wrong," but rather that the amount of time (in and out of class) spent on this concept—given the topic of the class—seems out of balance. Requiring this much work for a concept that should be more in the "remember this from earlier classes?" category of student learning in addition to the new methodological content may exhaust the students. They may possibly give up or disengage (see Brown et al. [2014] for recent scholarship on the amount of time and energy needed for students to create learning versus recalling information).

With upper-division major courses, it could make pedagogical sense for faculty to construct courses which encourage deep learning by students. These courses are often smaller, which can allow for more in-depth discussions and active learning opportunities. But again, many such courses are scaffolded, and thus a certain amount of sociological knowledge must be covered in order to allow students to succeed in the next course in the major.

For each class you will have to situate it in your program's and institution's curricular goals and objectives and analyze which concepts ought to be in the class and then how much about it. There are no easy or obvious answers. Instead, there are lots of inputs which can help you to reflect on the pedagogical choices which you are making.

QUESTION 3: WHO ARE YOU AS A TEACHER IN THIS CLASS?

Thinking about the content in this chapter has made each of us pause to consider what kind of professors we are. Before we share our profiles, let's talk a bit about the two ends of the teaching coverage continuum—breadth to depth: are you a "speed sociology" kind of professor (one who focuses on breadth of coverage) or are you a "teaching minimalist" who focuses more on depth of coverage? Or something in between? Kath thinks of a "speed sociology" professor this way: he or she primarily teaches one of the introductory courses (e.g., introduction to sociology, social problems, or marriage and family) and uses one of the more popular "big standardized texts" which has 40 to 50 chapters. And this faculty member goes through them all in one term. This pedagogical choice emphasizes breadth—giving the students numerous tastes of what sociology is. As in speed dating, though, students barely catch a glimpse of the richness of what sociological insights can offer about any particular topic or concept before the attention shifts to another topic, another chapter. By the end of the term, students may have touched on most of what the discipline does, but what will they take away from this exceedingly brief exposure to an "everything and the kitchen sink" pedagogical approach? The answer to that last question often remains unclear.

The other end of the continuum focuses on depth of coverage, not breadth. These faculty members are more minimalistic, focusing on a limited number of concepts. While students can gain significant sociological knowledge with this kind of a pedagogical approach, the range of knowledge is often much more circumscribed. Of course, if this is the student's sole course in sociology, one wonders if he or she got enough of an introduction to the discipline. Will the limited coverage allow students to move on to other sociology classes with enough background to succeed? The answers to those questions depend on what the faculty member decided to cover.

Both of us are much more minimalists than "speed sociologists." Kath chooses more depth than breadth, especially in lower-level courses such as Introduction to Sociology (see Pershell, Pfeiffer, and Syed [2007] to uncover what students should understand after taking Introduction to Sociology). She covers—at most—six or seven chapters of a traditional Introduction to Sociology textbook. She wants to stress that sociology is a way of thinking about the world more than anything else, so she begins with culture. On the first day of class, by about 15 minutes into the class, she has asked her students if—only by her accent—they can guess where she was born. (She was born in Montana, moved to Seattle when she was barely 2, lived there until she was 21 when she moved to Northern New Jersey for 5 years of grad school, and now has lived in South Georgia for 27 years.) Most guess that she is not "from here" but struggle with exactly where she has lived, based on her accent. That conversation morphs into how different regions of the country use different words for the same material object (often Kath uses the "Pop vs. Soda" website [McConchie 2014] to illustrate this point) and the class has become intrigued with how culture has shaped us—exactly the first-day experience she wants! She and her students spend about two-and-a-half weeks on culture, covering concepts such as the sociological imagination, norms and values, the role of language and nonverbal symbols in creating social solidarity, and how sociologists study cultures—our own and others. These topics bring up the nature of the relationship between the individual and larger social groups/ social forces, so they next discuss socialization—how culture shapes our personality. Conversations about socialization raise questions about the role of groups in our lives, and that is where the class turns next. Included in this section are days where the class discusses the types of groups, social structure, statuses and roles and their problems, how groups work, including bureaucracies. This section ends by studying the largest group: society. That topic allows for the transition to the next section of the course, on how key sociologists have examined society. Here students learn how the discipline came to be, some of its foundational thinkers (e.g., Comte, Durkheim, Marx, Weber, DuBois, Addams), the theoretical perspectives and exemplars of each, and finally, the logic of science, and how sociologists use the scientific method, including an extensive conversation about the role of ethics in sociology. Throughout the course, Kath uses examples of how societies construct stratification systems about race, class, gender, ableism vs. disability, and age, so students are exposed to these concepts, but the actual chapters about them are not always assigned. This "works" because her sociology colleagues and she have constructed general education assessments which focus primarily on the sociological imagination, understanding how social structure shapes and constrains choices and behaviors at the individual and collective levels. Had the faculty constructed learning goals and objectives which emphasized, for example, more focus on stratification, then this approach to teaching the course would be less successful and she would have to revise it in order to help her students to succeed on the general education assessments and have the knowledge base required for future sociology courses.

Maxine, too, is a minimalist. In fact, she just might even be more philosophically committed to this way of teaching than Kath is and the issue of coverage is perhaps the most frustrating of all teaching challenges. For example, Maxine mentors a lot of graduate students in their teaching. Most of them use textbooks and she agrees that for a new instructor, that is probably a good choice. On the other hand, the use of textbooks often encourages the "It is the third week of class so we must be teaching family (or some other content area)" approach. Once you have assigned a text for a class to use, the temptation is to cover the entire book so that students do not feel that they have wasted their money. The result of this choice is a breeze-through of a lot of content with little depth. The big questions, the fundamental ideas, are often addressed in the first chapter of a text and never referred to again. Students can all too easily finish a course with little more than a vocabulary exercise and no in-depth understanding of the discipline. From Maxine's perspective, this approach is a waste of everyone's time.

QUESTION 4: BUT WHAT ABOUT WHEN THE COURSE IS MY SPECIALTY?

Ah, that wonderful moment when you are assigned a course in your specialty! Many of us know that rush of excitement, that "finally I can show all that I have learned" moment. We encourage you to enjoy the elation of such a moment, but we think teaching one's specialty can often be more difficult than might be believed.

Exactly because something is our specialty, and we know so much detailed content, it can be very difficult to figure out the "sweet spot" in the breadth versus depth debate—how much sociological content about the specialty area is appropriate to the level of the course, its place in the program, etc. It can be tempting to share *every* single thing we know with our students—and to expect them to want to learn it too! If it helps you to begin with a detailed syllabus for your course—go for it—but then let it sit for a while. When you come back to it, try to let some of the excitement go and examine ruthlessly the proposed content and your learning goals and objectives, your readings, and your assessments. Are they truly appropriate for the level of the course? Or have you gotten caught up in the "desire to share all you know" phenomenon?

This is where those inputs—a curriculum which has shared learning expectations and which is scaffolded to let students gain and practice with their sociological toolkit before they move on to more advanced coursework, with a clear assessment plan—can provide the checks and balances we need to temper our pedagogical enthusiasm.

QUESTION 5: EGAD, I WAS JUST ASSIGNED AN IN-DEPTH CLASS IN AN AREA OF SOCIOLOGY I KNOW NOTHING ABOUT: WHAT NOW?

Our first suggestion is to breathe. The moment when this happens almost feels like falling into a bottomless sinkhole. But don't despair. If you feel that you can do this safely, career-wise, you might consider asking for a one-term reprieve in order to take more time for your preparation.

If that is not an option, then we suggest you be a sociologist (imagine that!) and start gathering data. Get copies of the common agreements which impact your course from the department head or Sociology Coordinator. Those are the bare bones of what you must do in the course—keep them front and center as you prepare. Then ask for copies of syllabi from your colleagues who have taught the course (or at least those you think would be willing to share, but who don't feel you must teach it "their" way). Contact the publishing representatives who visit your institution and get copies rushed to you of books on the subject they might have. This doesn't mean you have to use their books; they are one of many resources for you. If you don't have a subscription to TRAILS (American Sociological Association 2010) this might be the time to join. TRAILS is the online database of peer-reviewed teaching ideas sponsored by the American Sociological Association. The "old" bound syllabi collections have been digitized and are in the TRAILS database. We would first suggest searching the database for syllabi, and then for ideas about concepts the course will be covering. Then look in *Teaching Sociology*, one of the American Sociological Association's journals, as well. It is indexed in many databases, such as JSTOR.

Some other places to seek advice are Facebook groups such as Teaching with a Sociological Lens and Shared Teaching Resources for Sociology. Send a request to join and the group administrators will quickly give you permission. Go ahead and post a "help me please" message and then wait for some good ideas to come your way. The Society Pages (2014) has a wealth of great ideas for teaching, not only at the Teaching TSP link, but in many of their community pages, such as Sociological Images and Graphic Sociology. There are a growing number of other websites aimed at helping sociological faculty to teach. Try, for example, Sociology in Focus (2014) or SociologySource .org (2014). And many publishers now have websites—either around specific books they publish or more general pedagogical-oriented sites. Now is the time to make use of this accumulated knowledge.

Once you feel you have a sense of how some others have taught the course, spend some time alone, writing down your thoughts. What are the most important concepts you feel students need to know from this class as they move on to other parts of the curriculum? Who are important theorists they need to know about and why? What kinds of meaningful, well-structured assessments can you give students which will allow them opportunities to show depth of learning?

If we had only one suggestion to offer, it would be to not do too much the first time you teach a new in-depth course. When we don't know a subject well—and want to build confidence and not show weakness/ignorance to our students—we often overprepare. So create a draft syllabus and then go through and see what content might be realistically cut. Assume that in-depth learning can take more time and build that into the class. Give yourself time too; often we teach these classes the first time and feel that we're just one day ahead of students in learning the material. So feel free to slow down a bit and be sure you are giving yourself and your students the time to process the sociological content at this level of learning. Be sure you are meeting the required content, but don't feel you have to do "everything" to show colleagues that you can "do" this class.

QUESTION 6: BUT DON'T I HAVE ACADEMIC FREEDOM TO TEACH MY CLASS HOWEVER I WANT TO TEACH IT? WHY DO I HAVE TO PAY ATTENTION TO ALL THESE LEARNING GOALS, OBJECTIVES, AND ASSESSMENT REQUIREMENTS?

Ah, academic freedom! This concept can sometimes be used as a trump card in conversations about aligning courses with learning goals and objectives. Let's be honest—the term has a long, complex legal history and neither of us are lawyers. But we do believe that any conversation about academic freedom is unbalanced without a similar conversation about academic responsibilities. Academic freedom, in part, gives a faculty member some protections against capricious decisions by administrators concerning legitimate academic choices. But those freedoms come with a parallel set of responsibilities to our students, our institutions, our discipline, and so on (see Figure 3.1, right column). (For more information on academic freedom and academic responsibility see AAC&U Board of Directors Statement [2006].) Students deserve a coherent curriculum which maximizes their learning potential. Our colleagues need to be able to count on us—and we, them—to cover sociological material designated for any particular course. Too often these responsibilities are overlooked. Few of us are "academic islands," alone, with no obligations to others. These obligations temper our complete freedom in the classroom.

BALANCING OUT DEPTH VERSUS BREADTH IN YOUR WORKLOAD

While many of us do not get much, if any, choice about what classes we are teaching during any given semester, some of us do get input into this decision. But if you do have choice, think about who you are as a teacher. Do you want a few classes that are more about breadth—and likely where you feel confident with the conceptual content—and then are you up for the challenge of a course-in-depth or two? Do you want to balance a heavy teaching load that way?

For Kath, what matters most is that if she has several "breadth" sections of the same course, such as Intro to Sociology—even with her minimalist approach—she needs them on the same days, and preferably back-to-back in the same room (less prep time needed before class begins). She struggles when, in one term, she has a section on a 75-minute/twice-a-week schedule and another section of the same class on a 50-minute/three-times-a-week schedule. So for Kath, the mix of classes is not as important as the scheduling of them. Even when she writes notes in her teaching journal, right after a class, about where she left off, she will sometimes forget which section was told a particular example, etc. If the classes are right after each other, in the same room, all her written notes and memory cues are still there, visible, for her to use.

Kath prefers to have her "depth" classes in the afternoons, twice a week. Some of that is her own preference; she likes that she and students have a longer time together every class, but also likes the spacing of this schedule. It allows students more time to read the material she has assigned, digest it, and come ready to talk and ask questions. Moreover, this "twice a week in the afternoons" schedule is the common pattern for upper-division classes, so majors in her department have come to expect classes at these times. Majors can get grumpy with a content-heavy course, for example, at 8:00 a.m.

Maxine prefers to have her undergraduate courses back to back for many of the same reasons, especially forgetting what she focused on in which section! The twice-a-week courses meet for a longer period of time, which gives Maxine more time for active learning activities. She teaches her "breadth" courses in such a minimalist way that the contrast between breadth and depth courses is not much of an issue for her. However, she certainly sees the challenge with her graduate students. Lately, Maxine's biggest breadth-versus-depth concern has been teaching Study Abroad classes. In these classes, the requirements for teaching intercultural skills and reflection are sometimes difficult to merge with the curricular requirements of the course content. Creating a balance and maintaining an emphasis on depth so as not to simply skim important questions is daunting.

CONCLUSION

There is no one correct answer to the question, "How much sociological content should I cover in this class?" The answer, however, can emerge if you begin to consider what role the course plays in your institution and degree program's curricula. Use that knowledge to build a sense of what you should be able to expect from your students at the beginning of the course and it will help you to shape your expectations for their learning by the end of the course.

SECTION 2

DAY-TO-DAY LIFE IN
THE CLASSROOM

►►► CHAPTER 4
CHOOSING TEACHING TECHNIQUES

What is the first thing most of us do when we are planning our courses? In our experience, most teachers first think of choosing a textbook. Or, their book orders are due long before they have had time to plan their course and they must choose a text first. We understand that this frequently happens. When it does, we urge you to resist the urge to let the text construct your course for you. Put the text aside. After you have done your course planning, you can come back to the text and fit the text into your plan rather than vice versa. If the text does not adequately present the material you need, you can always supplement it.

All too often after we choose our text, the second thing we do is think of "stuff we like to have students do." This is exactly what we did when we first started teaching and continued doing for many years. Maxine admits that she was especially guilty of hearing about a cool activity and trying it out in class with far too little thought of what the activity might actually help her students learn to do or understand and too little reflection about how the activity fit into the course overall. Before we can adequately discuss choosing teaching techniques, we need to review briefly how you choose the content of what you will teach.

KNOW WHAT YOU WILL TEACH

This story shows how important it is to question constantly what we are teaching. Recently Maxine observed a graduate student instructor teaching a class. This was a dedicated young teacher in whom Maxine has a lot of confidence. The assigned unit in the textbook was on family. While overall the class went very well, Maxine wondered why the graduate instructor was asking students to know terms like *exogamy* and *endogamy* and to differentiate between *polygamy* and *polygyny*. They are cool concepts, at least for a family sociologist, and Maxine has taught them many times just as this instructor did. As she watched the students in the class dutifully copy the words down, it occurred to her that she did not understand the point. What was the big idea? When would students ever need to know those terms other than to identify them on a multiple-choice test? If that was their only use, was it worth the time and energy required to deal with the concepts? She asked the instructor if s/he thought the terms were important. The instructor replied that they were not, but they were in the textbook and so s/he taught them. The big idea here is that marriage rules are not universal but rather differ across cultures. Does memorizing these terms teach that lesson? Of course, that is an empirical question, but we doubt that this is the most effective way for students to learn about cultural variation in marriage patterns.

Wiggins and McTighe (1998:10) provide some useful guidelines for deciding what we will teach. They assert that we must distinguish between "enduring understanding," "important to know and do," and "worth being familiar with." When a topic or a concept has enduring value beyond the classroom and is applicable to new situations that are not limited to the specific, discrete term, Wiggins and McTighe (1998) assert that this is enduring understanding. They offer as an example the Magna Carta because it lays out the principle that the rule of law specifies the limits of a government's power and the rights of individuals. They offer us three other guidelines: We should teach that which lies at the heart of our disciplines. We should teach those ideas that require "uncoverage," i.e., the big ideas that require help from others, the not so obvious. Finally, they argue that the idea, concept, or process needs to have the potential to engage students. What are the big ideas in sociology? What is worth teaching that will be useful to our students in their personal and professional lives after college and/or graduate school? What has the potential to engage our students? Many of us would name the sociological imagination and many of us would argue that critical thinking skills rise to this level of significance.

Maxine applies Wiggins and McTighe's (1998) guidelines to her own teaching methods. She teaches the same fundamental concepts regardless of the name of the class or the level: sociological perspective, method and epistemology, structure, culture, and inequalities. For her these are the linchpin ideas, the fundamental concepts, in sociology, and they have valuable application throughout an individual's life cycle in both public and private spheres. They lie at the heart of the discipline, require deep thought and guidance to "uncover," and have the potential to engage students' imaginations. There is no need to clutter up your class with anything other than the vital lessons sociology has to teach!

What does this have to do with choosing teaching strategies? We argue that before you choose how you will teach anything, you must know what you will teach. We made the same argument in chapter 1 when we reviewed student learning outcomes and goals. We reiterate it here because it is fundamental. (Recall Figure 1.2 in chapter 1.) There are four steps to course design: (1) creating outcomes, (2) choosing teaching methods, (3) choosing materials such as readings, films, etc., and (4) deciding on assessment techniques. Choosing what you will teach is a part of creating student learning outcomes.

In addition to Figure 1.2 in chapter 1, some refer to the process of course planning as "backward design" (Wiggins and McTighe 1998). (Also see chapter 3.) That is, you begin with identifying the results you want, determine how you would know if you got the desired results, and then plan teaching strategies and choose materials. Simply put, we need to spend more time, return to the concept more often, use a wider variety of methods—and use more involved teaching methods—for those ideas and concepts that offer enduring understanding. We can spend less time and use less intense methods for those ideas that are important to know and even less time and less sophisticated methods on those ideas that are simply "worth being familiar with." Again, we cannot choose teaching strategies until we know what we will teach and what we want to accomplish in our courses. That is, we must specify our student learning outcomes and then decide how to teach them most effectively.

Techniques for Teaching a Fundamental Concept: The Sociological Imagination

We begin with some hypotheticals and assumptions. Let's assume that you want to teach the sociological imagination because it meets all the criteria for being important enough to teach. Let's assume that you have written a student learning outcome. The outcome we have chosen for illustration is:

Students will explain the sociological imagination in their own words and apply it to a variety of situations.

There are literally dozens of options or choices of strategies, but first let's start with some of the most commonly used techniques.

We first think of the two most common behaviors students can do to be actively involved in the classroom: they talk to each other and they write, and the two can be combined. If you know no other teaching methods start with these two: discussion (see chapter 9) and writing (chapter 8). There are a large variety of discussion and writing formats. Probably the most common discussion format is Think-Pair-Share. That is, ask students to think about a question, issue, or idea, then find a partner and talk about it. If we wanted to work on having students explain the sociological imagination in their own words we might first want students to write at least a few phrases describing the sociological imagination and then have them talk to a partner about what they wrote. Or, if you wanted to put more emphasis on writing, you might start with asking students to do a free write or a minute paper (see chapter 8). If you were asking students to apply the sociological imagination to a variety of situations, you could use the same two strategies. Notice that you are asking them to think at two different levels. If you ask students to put something in their own words, you are asking a comprehension question. If you ask them to use a concept in a variety of situations you are asking an application question. (See Bloom's Taxonomy [1956], chapter 10.)

The Sharp (2008) data we explain in chapter 7 is a good example of an exercise you can use in student discussion and/or writing and is also a good inquiry-guided technique. Sharp's data (2008) retrieved from the Social Security website presents the most popular baby names in 1907 and those in 2007. This data clearly illustrates the intersection of historical time and individual biography, a primary attribute of the sociological imagination. Students could be shown the data, asked to describe it, identify patterns, and explain how the sociological imagination helps us understand the patterns they identify.

If you wanted still more practice with mastering the conceptualization of the sociological imagination, or any other fundamental concept, you might try peer review. For example, students could be given the following prompt: "In your own words explain the two primary components of the sociological imagination as presented by C. Wright Mills. To illustrate the clarity and accuracy of your understanding, use an example from your own life to illustrate one of the components of the sociological imagination" (see Atkinson 2014).

Students are asked to bring their work to class, identified only with the last four digits of their student IDs. The examples are handed in and then redistributed to other students for their evaluation. After the students have evaluated their example, the papers and an evaluation rubric are returned to the original authors for revision or class discussion. We suggest providing students with a rubric like the following:

Evaluate the example you are given for clarity. Use the scale below. Circle your answer.
    5   Yes, the response is quite clear.
    4   The response is mostly clear but could use some improvement.
    3   The response is somewhat clear but needs quite a bit of work.
    2   The response has at least one point of clarity overall but needs to be completely rewritten.
    1   The response is not at all clear. The author needs to begin again.

Evaluate the example you are given for accuracy. Use the scale below. Circle your answer.
    5   Yes, the response is accurate.
    4   The response is mostly accurate but could use some improvement.
    3   The response is somewhat accurate but needs quite a bit of work.
    2   The response has at least one point that is accurate but needs to be almost completely rewritten.
    1   The response is not at all accurate. The author needs to begin again.
        (Atkinson 2014)

This example of peer review could be used with any fundamental concept. Note that clarity and accuracy are two of Elder and Paul's (2011) "universal intellectual standards" as discussed in chapter 10.

BALANCING CRITERIA FOR DECIDING ON STRATEGIES

Now let's assume that you have clearly decided what you will teach. You have chosen your fundamental concepts and the skills you want students to acquire or strengthen. If you have chosen critical thinking skills, as many of us do, Linda Nilson's (2010) work is most helpful. Nilson (2010) created a table organizing a number of teaching strategies by level of critical thinking as defined by Bloom's Taxonomy (1956; see chapter 10). That is, Nilson (2010) indicates which teaching strategies are most useful for teaching each level of critical thinking on Bloom's Taxonomy (1956; see Figure 4.1.) If your goal is to teach the application level in Bloom's Taxonomy (1956), for example, she suggests a number of different strategies including writing and speaking, the case method, and inquiry-guided teaching strategies.

In the section above, when we illustrated choosing techniques for teaching a fundamental concept like the sociological imagination, we suggested using a combination of strategies including discussion, writing, and inquiry-guided technique and peer review. For each concept you want to teach, thinking through which teaching method is most appropriate is a worthwhile exercise. What else do you need to consider? We suggest that there are at least four other criteria to take into account: (1) the difficulty of the concept or outcome and its relationship to other parts of the course, (2) the students' backgrounds, (3) the size of the class, and (4) the instructor's comfort and confidence with the technique.

FIGURE 4.1 BLOOM'S TAXONOMY

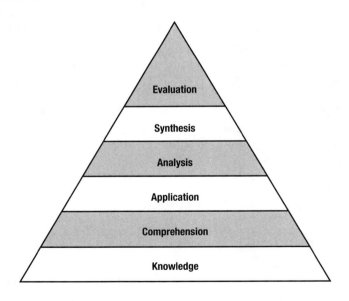

Source: Overbaugh, Richard C. and Lynn Schultz. *Bloom's Taxonomy*. Retrieved October 31, 2011 (http://www.odu.edu /educ/roverbau/Bloom/blooms_taxonomy.htm).

Difficulty of the Concept or Outcome and Its Relationship to Other Parts of the Course

Continuing with our example of teaching the sociological imagination, we might move up Bloom's Taxonomy (1956) to analysis, synthesis, and evaluation. If so, Nilson (2010) has a number of teaching methods to consider for each level. For example, if we wanted our students to analyze a situation, document, film, etc., Nilson (2010) suggests choosing one or more of the following strategies: writing and speaking exercises, classroom assessment techniques (Angelo and Cross 1993), student-peer feedback, the case method, inquiry-guided learning, problem-based learning, project-based learning, role-plays and simulations, service learning, and/or fieldwork /clinical. Note that Nilson (2010) recommends inquiry-guided learning for every level on Bloom's Taxonomy (1956). (See chapter 7 for examples of inquiry-guided learning exercises. This is the case because inquiry-guided teaching techniques are a variety of techniques, not just one strategy.) You get the picture.

Students' Backgrounds

We include student participation in this category. If you are teaching an introductory-level course to students from weak academic backgrounds you probably would not want to ask them to do sophisticated original research. You would, however, want to challenge them to think more critically. We suggest that you include some activities that require writing and speaking in every class. We also urge you to try at least to move even your least intellectually mature and skilled students to think at the application level. Note that Nilson (2010) suggests classroom assessment techniques to meet application goals. She is defining classroom assessment techniques here to mean informal in-class activities to allow you to see how your students are doing and to give them practice with the discipline. These activities are scattered throughout this book but you might check out chapter 6 on active learning especially. It is remarkably easy to find teaching activities. For example, we just searched for "teaching about social class" and found this website: http://cwcs.ysu.edu /teaching/teaching-class (2014).

On the other hand, what if you are teaching a class to majors? How would you choose teaching strategies for them? First, consider their preparation. Have they had a theory class? Have they had a methods class? We find it common to have students in our majors' classes who have a large range of experiences. At NC State, where Maxine teaches, all upper-level majors courses have as a prerequisite at least one introductory-level course and a methods class. Some students come to a major's class with that minimum; some are taking their last class. At Valdosta State students must have either Introduction to Sociology or Introduction to Social Problems before they can enroll in any upper-division class for majors. In addition, before taking Research Methods, students must take and pass the Statistics course with at least a C grade. At NC State, upper-level courses are also fairly small, with enrollment limits of 30 to 35. If your majors have at least an introductory-level class and a methods class, or an introductory-level class and a theory class, it is probably time to move them along in terms of cognitive development and critical thinking. Having them start with comprehension strategies is fine but they need to get beyond that level. We suggest that you develop at least one teaching strategy that challenges your students. Have them practice doing some of their own research; use a case, perhaps assign a project; role-plays and simulations are great strategies; service learning with a reflective component is very time-consuming but equally powerful. Whatever strategy you use, we argue that the strategy needs to include a writing component.

Should you assign a traditional term paper? We are split on the idea. Maxine is not a fan of the traditional research paper that requires students to read and synthesize professional literature. Why? Consider the audience for journal articles. They are written by professionals for professionals. In Maxine's experience, students find journal articles difficult to understand, boring, and tedious. Synthesizing professional literature is often beyond the skill level of even the most advanced students. The literature suggests that traditional term papers are not a very common assignment. In their analysis of over four hundred undergraduate syllabi in a large range of sociology courses, Grauerholz, Eisele, and Stark (2013) find that only 14 percent of writing assignments are traditional library research assignments. There are a variety of more commonly used writing assignments that are more likely to be effective, including student journals, field notes, reflections papers, essays, and research proposals. However, Kath disagrees, at least for some classes. She does assign these types of projects in her theory course as she outlines in chapter 14. Maxine notes that Kath's project is carefully scaffolded and broken down into several manageable assignments.

The Size of the Class

What about large classes? What are you going to do in the dreaded large lecture classes? In chapter 19 we suggest a number of different strategies based on the literature and on Kath's experience teaching large sections. We will be the first to admit that creating active learning activities in a large class is more difficult than in a small one. Kath "flips" her class, requiring students to post online, applying concepts. She then often starts a class with an anonymous post from an individual student and uses clickers to have the entire class evaluate the response.

Even in large classes we stress that choosing content is crucial to choosing teaching strategies. Risking redundancy we reiterate that we should focus on the content that is likely to be important outside the classroom and that is at the heart of our discipline. We should also consider the content that is most likely to be engaging for students. That gives us a large menu! Sociology is inherently interesting and is seen in our everyday lives if we give students the tools to "uncover" it. What does this tell us about teaching strategies for large classes? Use a larger number of activities on whatever you think is most important. Create more challenging assignments for the important content. Remember that you do not have to grade everything you assign and you can grade at the group level. If you have 100 students and create groups of four, you can grade 25 assignments rather than 100! The less important the content, the fewer number of activities you need to create. Do not forget that all lectures are not bad. We should not demonize lectures. They serve their purposes and can be done well if you create interactive lectures (see chapter 5). Writing should not be ignored even in very large classes. Informal "writing to think" exercises are very effective tools regardless of class size. You do not have to grade everything students write.

The Instructor's Comfort and Confidence with a Teaching Technique

This is as important a criterion as any of the others. We have recommended the most basic of techniques: writing to think and Think-Pair-Share. Using these two techniques to create an interactive lecture can take you a long way. However, we believe that most of us can intersperse a few more activities throughout the semester. Begin to create a teaching library for yourself, including your favorite strategies and a few "how to" books. We have cited many throughout this text. Maxine's favorite "how to" is Linda Nilson's (2010) *Teaching at Its Best*. Nilson's book (2010) is written for a multidisciplinary audience but she is a sociologist. Since Kath uses clickers so much in her classes, her favorite "how to" book right now is *Teaching with Classroom Response Systems: Creating Active Learning Environments* (Bruff 2009). There are also a large number of very good websites. Many are mentioned throughout this text. One of Maxine's favorites is The Center for Teaching at Vanderbilt

University (The Center for Teaching 2014). One of Kath's favorites is Faculty Focus (2014). Most every teaching and learning center has online resources; take a few hours and go Internet surfing. Even if you don't find something you need for that next class, you will get many ideas for future classes. And Kath can't let this opportunity pass without also mentioning the journal *Teaching Sociology* and the ASA online database TRAILS as additional pedagogical sources as well.

CONCLUSION

We close this chapter with two seemingly contradictory pieces of advice. First, do not rely solely on one type of activity. Students have different learning styles and if we only use one type of activity we disadvantage some and advantage others. Using only one activity also wears thin over a semester. Students need a bit of variety. A good balance between variety and having some notion of what to expect is a worthy goal to strive for.

Second, do not use too many types of activities, especially if you are inexperienced. Think-Pair-Share, writing to think, and interactive lectures can be used in any class, and you can develop more activities as you gain experience. You will discover your teaching voice over time. As you develop your toolkit, you can begin to innovate. In chapter 22, for example, Keith Roberts discusses how he gradually modified his courses.

To use a very old cliché, "Rome was not built in a day." Your skill with choosing and using teaching strategies will not be as strong in your first class as it will be as you gain experience. Be patient with yourself. Being approachable and kind can go a long way toward teaching success. Develop your toolkit over time by taking small risks every semester. If one of your exercises and activities fails, revise and resubmit!

►►► CHAPTER 5
CONSTRUCTING A LECTURE

Lecturing is probably the teaching technique more likely to be used than any other. Most of us were primarily taught through lecture and it is the method with which we are most familiar. If we cannot think of anything else to do, we lecture! In this chapter we explore the situations where lectures are most appropriate and suggest how to construct lectures that meet class goals.

Two of our favorite comedic quotes about lectures are, "College is a place where a professor's lecture notes go straight to the students' lecture notes, without passing through the brains of either" (attributed to Mark Twain, cited in Adsit [2014]) and "Some people talk in their sleep. Lecturers talk while other people sleep" (attributed to Albert Camus, cited by Adsit [2014]). These classic quotes should suggest what we are referring to as a "lecture." We will call a *lecture* the classroom experience where an instructor presents material and then is willing to answer any questions that arise. Often lectures end with "any questions?" Unless we clearly state differently, this is what we mean by a "lecture." We will also talk about interactive lectures but will let you know when we are moving on to this form of lecturing. We will refer to an *interactive lecture* as when an instructor presents material with breaks for students to be actively involved.

If everyone loves active learning, almost no one loves lectures, except perhaps the person delivering them, and for good reasons. We all like the sound of our own voices and most of us think we are more entertaining than we actually are. We like to talk more than we like to listen. We convince ourselves that lectures are just fine. Our professors lectured and we did well, right? (Yes; supposedly as sociologists we understand about generalizing from outliers, but that is an argument that you will hear all too often.) However, we suspect that the primary reason we lecture is that we simply do not know what else to do. And lecturing may seem like the only alternative in a large class. We suspect that most of us have heard by now that lecturing is not the most creative thing to do but we continue on.

What is the problem with lecturing? Lectures focus attention on the instructor rather than on the student. Lecturing is the very opposite of "student centered." Lecturing does require the lecturer to do a lot of intellectual work, but it requires very little of students; as a result, lectures are often truly "in one ear and out the other without engaging the brain"—at least the students' brains. (Our experience is that faculty work very hard on their lectures.) Since the 1920s research has demonstrated that lectures are not effective. Menges (1988) is the classic source on just how forgettable lectures are. According to Menges, the average student remembers 62 percent of material just presented. Three to four days later, there is a 45 percent recall rate, and only a 24 percent recall rate after eight weeks. Before the semester is half over, 75 percent of the material from a lecture is already forgotten. Imagine what the recall rate is a year after graduation from college. Do we really want students to spend four to six years doing something they will simply forget? Especially in times when the cost of higher education is considered especially high, the usefulness of the lecture is being strongly questioned.

For many of us, teaching *is* lecturing! But, as Barr and Tagg (2004) forcefully argued more than 10 years ago, we simply must move from a "teaching paradigm" to a "learning paradigm." Our courses should not be about our teaching but about our students' learning. Lecturing is about our teaching. Fortunately, it is very easy to move from lecturing to interactive lecturing and this is where we will focus our attention. Lecturing is a technique that will probably be with us for a long time for a variety of reasons, but we need to move from standard lecturing to interactive lecturing. That is the first step away from straight lecture, and it doesn't require much effort and will pay off in big ways. You may actually find yourself enjoying your teaching much more, and your students certainly will. Better yet, students are more likely to learn. In chapter 6, "Active Learning," we say that you can improve your teaching and your students' learning by using very simple techniques, including learning some student names, wait time, and Think-Pair-Share. Start there, although there are other ways to make your lectures as effective as possible.

TECHNIQUES FOR EFFECTIVE INTERACTIVE LECTURES

Chapter 6 discusses active learning and suggests some techniques to be used to move your teaching from lecturing to interactive lecturing, although some of the techniques we discuss in that chapter will be easier to use in a small class rather than a large one. Let's briefly review the ones we discuss that are most appropriate here.

The use of "wait time" is probably the most effective of the simple things you can do. When you throw out a question to your students, give them time to respond! Waiting at least 10 seconds can do wonders for students' participation. You might be surprised at how hard it is to wait 10 seconds, but it is well worth it.

In large classes, you may not be able to learn all student names but try to learn some. Knowing someone's name gives you power and increases her or his responsibility. Here are some tips we have for memorizing names. Most of us have rosters with pictures on them and those help. You can also practice using names in a variety of ways. When Maxine asks questions in class, she often begins with calling three names. She says something like, "Anyone can feel free to answer this question but I am going to ask Jennifer Jones or Jonathan Brown or Chris Tchipstky (fictional names) to take primary responsibility." Then, she follows with a question. (Both of us try to avoid calling on individuals to answer a question unless they have had time to think and preferably to write, and even then we are reluctant.)

Come to class early and leave late. Nothing tells students how unimportant they are than a faculty member who runs into the class at the last minute and leaves before they do. Coming in early gives you time to set up, to say hello, and to be available for questions. Leaving late also makes you available. Students who will not take the time to come to your office will stay late five minutes to ask you a question. Kath actually gets to her large supersection classes about 90 minutes early. She practices her slides for the day several times, edits any clicker questions which she thinks sound "clunky," and then is available for when the hundreds of students start to come in for class. She'll roam around the room, talking with different students each day, and is able to take the emotional temperature of her students. This helps her to learn names, by the way!

Here are our other top suggestions for effective interactive lectures.

Before class:

1. Make sure that your lecture helps you move toward meeting a student learning outcome or at least one of the goals you set for yourself. Before

constructing a lecture, ask yourself, "What will students know or be able to do as a result of this lecture?" If you can't answer that question, do not create that lecture.

2. Plan your interactive lectures and come prepared with notes but do not prepare a script. A script will tempt you to read to your students rather than making eye contact and using a conversational tone. Few strategies are less effective. Writing out a script is a waste of your time. It could easily require 25 to 30 pages and one lecture could take you hours to complete. Again, everyone loses.

3. Structure your lecture so that it has a beginning, a middle, and a conclusion. Your beginning should attract attention. The middle should carry the heft of the lecture and your conclusion should reflect the introduction and drive the point home. It is a good idea to end with a question that prompts students to think more deeply about the content.

4. Limit your lectures no longer than 10 to 15 minutes, punctuated by some student activity. Even the most riveting lecturer loses audience attention after about 15 minutes (Bligh 2000).

5. Limit the material you present in one lecture and make sure that you speak slowly. A lecture that goes on too long, with too much material presented too quickly is a surefire way to put students to sleep and these lectures will take you a long time to create. Everyone loses.

During class:

6. Make sure to begin your lecture with something that will attract attention. Start with a statement that is counterintuitive or provocative. For example, you might begin by saying something like, "Children born in the United States are more likely to survive than those born in any other country, or are they?" Follow up by showing the class infant mortality rates and asking them to evaluate your statement. Try to avoid critiquing the United States yourself; instead, show students data and let them come to conclusions. Or, start with a provocative story that your lecture will address. Maxine often tells the story of her son, at age six, demanding information about Santa. Sometimes she uses the story to illustrate the power of myth; sometimes she uses it to illustrate how hard it is to resist culture even if you do not entirely buy into it. You only need a few good stories in your toolkit and you can find a variety of uses for each. Ask your students for stories; you might be surprised at the stories they contribute.

7. Make eye contact. Eye contact helps students believe that you are talking to them personally. Make sure you are making contact with students in all parts of the room including the sides and those in the back row.

8. Use visuals! Scan comics, use YouTube, and show a photo—on every occasion try to find a visual way to depict material. Your students can be a great help with creating your collection. Ask them to bring in examples of advertisements, find relevant YouTube videos or other visuals that help illustrate a sociological story. Even after one class you will have a good collection of visuals.

9. Use contemporary culture as examples of the concepts and ideas you are illustrating in your lecture. Movies, television, music, sports, and advertisements help connect sociological knowledge to the worlds in which our students live. If you struggle to find contemporary examples, let the students help you out. Assign them to find music and lyrics that address the issues in your class. Ask them to find YouTube videos that make a point. Maxine is not a TV person so every semester, she asks students to vote on the three best current TV shows and she watches at least one episode of each one. (This is often not a fun task so think about whether you really want to do this. Maxine is just a glutton for punishment.) The older you are, the less likely you are to be knowledgeable about the youth culture your students are a part of, but that is okay. Students will enjoy teaching you. Your lack of knowledge gives them a valuable opportunity to be a part of the learning community you are creating. Let them bring you examples you can use in the class you are teaching and in other classes.

10. If you have the opportunity to use clickers, take advantage of them. They will help assure student participation. (See chapter 17 for more discussion.) Or, you can simply have your students raise their hands in response to a question. If students are responding by raising their hands, divide the class into zones and have a student count hands in that zone. A lot of different strategies will be effective. Just be sure that you have a way for students to respond to you and to each other.

11. Minute papers (see chapter 8) are excellent ways to get your students actively involved. You need not grade them all, but looking through what students write will give you a good idea of how much they understand. If you do not want to use enough time to have students write for a long period of time, ask them to do "jottings" or simple notes that will help them think through their response.

12. Think-Pair-Share exercises are perfect for any size class (see chapter 6). Pose a question that goes beyond a "yes-or-no" response. Ask students to first think of their own answer, then talk to the person next to them and share their ideas.

13. Fishbowl is a great exercise to use in a large lecture class. Announce ahead of time that a small group of students will be asked to be a part of a discussion during the next class period. After a short lecture pointing out critical issues, choose the group and have them come down front or sit in the middle of the room to discuss the topic. You can run the discussion or if your students are more sophisticated, ask one of them to do so. Make sure that the observers have an opportunity to respond to the discussion either in writing or by responding in class. You might require that students create a question they want the class to respond to during the next class period. Or, you could always start the class with a fishbowl and use your lecture time to make sure that the points you think are most important are addressed.

14. Create a real-world problem for students to solve based on your lecture and the readings you assigned that accompany your lecture. For example, you might ask students to critique a relevant university policy, or a state or federal law. Ask them to work in pairs and allow pairs to present their reply to the entire class. Be sure to include students who are sitting on the periphery of the class.

At the end of class:

15. After a short lecture, present one to three multiple-choice questions that capture the most important points of the lecture or that require students to go beyond the scope of your lecture. Ask students to record their answers and then compare them to a partner's answers. The key here is to ask strong questions that help students think critically. Consider using Bloom's Taxonomy (1956; see chapter 10) to guide your question construction.

Figure 5.1 shows what happens to students' heart rates as lectures progress. Notice the precipitous downturn as the lecture goes on and how much the heart rates increase when a student asks a question or intervenes in some other way. This graph is based on data from medical students! It is rather sobering, isn't it? See how impressive a simple visual can be?

FIGURE 5.1   STUDENTS' HEART RATES IN CLASS

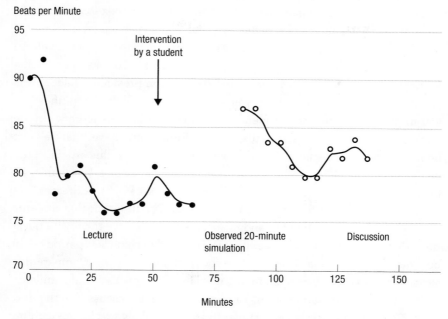

Source: Bligh, Donald A. 2000. "What's the Use of Lectures?" San Francisco: Jossey-Bass.

CONDITIONS UNDER WHICH INTERACTIVE LECTURES ARE MOST APPROPRIATE

There are circumstances under which interactive lectures are appropriate. If, for example, there are some basic facts you want students to know that would require them to read more than you want to require, you might synthesize it for them. For example, you might want students to know Durkheim's contributions to sociological theory as compared to Weber as compared to Marx. You could provide 12 to 15 minutes of lecture to teach your students the basics of these theoretical paradigms. Then, think of how you will structure the interactive part of the lecture. A good way to start this lecture might be to joke about sociologists referring to Durkheim, Marx, and Weber as dead white men. Show a picture of them, pretend to use their voices, and don't be afraid of sounding silly. Get their attention. Get students involved by at least asking them to raise their hands in response to relevant questions. You might ask them how many of them are Protestants and emphasize the place of religion to Durkheim as compared to Weber as compared to Marx.

There might also be material that is simply too complex for students to comprehend without your help. Suppose you want your students to read a refereed journal article that you know is beyond their experience level. An introductory interactive lecture could get them started. For example, Cecilia Ridgeway's 2013 American Sociological Association presidential address is about the importance of status. If you were teaching a class on stratification, you might reasonably want students to be able to differentiate between the ideas of resources, power, and status, and why Ridgeway believes that we must be more attentive to status. An effective way to introduce this article would be to review those ideas and provide some concrete examples. We could then turn to Ridgeway's article (2013) and review the issues she addresses. We would need to define a few of the concepts she uses in the article that students are likely to be unfamiliar with and make sure that we leave them with questions that they can answer by reading the article. The next class period could be a discussion of the article based on the questions we pose. Compare this strategy to what usually occurs in lecture classes: simply assigning students to read the Ridgeway article (2013) and asking them to discuss it in the next class. That might work, but our students are more likely to be successful in reading difficult texts if we provide some scaffolding for them. An interactive lecture can do just that.

If there are some basic skills students must know in order to do assigned work, you might use an interactive lecture to gauge student skill levels and get students up to speed. Maxine tries to teach quantitative literacy in all her classes. She uses interactive lectures to ascertain how much work students need to do on reading and constructing simple tables. She begins by showing a table percentaged on the columns, moves to tables percentaged on rows, and then to tables percentaged on the entire sample. After each table she asks students to answer multiple-choice questions based on the table. Finally, she asks students to write a brief comparison of the different tables. If the students can answer the questions correctly, she moves on. If not, she offers more practice. Reading tables is a skill her students need to be able to master in order to do work in the course, so it is important that she knows where her class is with this ability and that she can teach the skills she wants them to have if they need review.

One of the classic examples of lectures that can either be a waste or very effective are lectures in our statistics classes. Many of us have had the math teacher who wrote the equations on the board with his (and we do mean "his") right hand and erased them with the left! Or more commonly, we had a teacher who presented an hour-long lecture on a technique and then sent us home to do more complicated problems on our own. The easy work was done in class and the hard work was supposed to be done alone. Chances are that many of us were frustrated if not totally lost. Compare this to what might be the case if students were assigned to read about the basic technique and given a simple problem with which to practice. The follow-up in class could be an extension of the problem, with the instructor there to help and other students to practice with. This example illustrates the weakness of traditional lectures and suggests ways that interactive lectures might be more effective.

Lectures are not likely to go away and they shouldn't. They provide us with a way to provide more examples, to work through problems with our students, to synthesize literatures, and to help our students conquer more complex materials. The point is not to throw lectures out of your teaching toolkit but to transform them into the effective technique they can be. You will be glad you did and so will your students!

▶▶▶ **CHAPTER 6**

ACTIVE LEARNING

While members of the academy disagree about any number of issues, there is strong agreement about the importance of active learning. If you want to improve your teaching, a good beginning is to think about how to actively engage your students. Almost any teaching strategy other than continuous lecture could be considered "active learning." In this chapter, we focus on the basics of active learning and why we should all be striving to have our students engaged with the ideas and materials in our courses.

Second only to the belief in the importance of critical thinking, active learning has become a mantra for many. Lecturing is considered the antithesis of active learning: derisive terms include "the banking method," the "empty vessel" perspective, and the "sage on the stage" instructor.

If the class is centered on the faculty rather than on the students, chances are that students are not actively involved. Ask yourself two simple questions: "Who is active in this class? Who is doing the intellectual work in this class?" If the answers are that you are the only active participant and you are the one doing the intellectual work, it is time for a change. Scholars like John Dewey and Maria Montessori are famous for advocating more active learning strategies, and since the 1980s teaching experts from every discipline and at every level of education were beginning to agree that active learning is a requirement for effective teaching (Meyers and Jones 1993).

In reality, however, our guess is that many instructors still do not meet the goal of having students truly and actively involved in learning. If active learning is so powerful, why don't more instructors use it? Think about your experiences as a student: you were probably taught by well-meaning faculty who simply lectured. Most PhDs have never had a class or any type of formal training on how to teach, including ourselves. We have little if any training. Most of us teach the way we were taught because we do not know what the alternatives are.

One of Maxine's defining moments as a teacher was when a student asked, "How do I study for this class, how do I learn this material?" As is her wont, Maxine blurted out the truth: "I don't know how to tell you how to learn anything in this class. PhDs have no training to teach; we are substantive experts." The student was shocked to hear that someone whose job it was to teach her knew nothing about how to teach. Maxine was shocked that she had so impulsively, and perhaps unadvisedly, revealed this weakness in both her own skills and the academy. On the other hand, truth is sometimes difficult to ignore. This moment was humiliating and painful, and it prompted a time of self-doubt and reassessment. Maxine began to see higher education from the point of view of the students and their parents. These students and/or their parents paid tuition money and state taxes for her salary. There was no other institution that was responsible for teaching these students. Why was she getting paid to do a job that she obviously could not do? Then, she thought about her own teachers. A few were inspiring. Most were not. She wondered about the meaning of doing a job year after year and facing student after student with no idea how to teach them. That day was the beginning of a promise that she made to herself and her students. She promised that she would either find a better way to teach or find another job. She could not live with herself otherwise. Maxine already had tenure so she was not a new teacher, but she had focused on publishing that next article and then the next and then the next. The job was losing its meaning for her.

Maxine's teaching career has had three stages: "fill-up," "Oprah," and "revise and resubmit." The "fill-up stage," where she planned to teach by thinking of how she would "fill up" the time in every semester, she saw as a sort of a fill-in-the-blanks exercise. If she could get all the blanks or every class session filled in with something, she'd won! But then the "fateful day of truth," as she now sees it, happened, and she had to change. She began the "Oprah stage." She entertained. She figured out that students feared boredom as much as anything else and she learned to put on a show. Maxine most often teaches family sociology so it isn't all that hard to find interesting and often controversial materials. She and her students spent lots of time talking about the history of love and why men and women truly aren't from different planets, and what constitutes a family after all. At this stage, class was fun and Maxine loved her students and they liked her. Her teaching evaluations soared. But, as you may have guessed, there was still a problem. Students wanted to do well on tests and Maxine had no idea how to construct a test, much less how to teach her students how to do well on them. The "Oprah" routine was not working. It was better than the "fill-up stage" but not nearly good enough.

The third stage is the one we are in now: the "revise and resubmit" or "try and try again" stage. It is the stage all effective teachers stay in. There is no such thing as a course that is finished. The minute anyone thinks her/his courses need no further revision is the day the teacher fails the class. Maxine has been teaching in college for 34 years; Kath has been teaching for 28 years and we are still trying new things in our classes! We go to teaching workshops, we talk with other teachers, and we assess our classes both informally and formally. (Daily activities are usually assessed informally and the course is assessed formally. See the chapters in Section 3 for more detail.) We read every issue of *Teaching Sociology* from cover to cover, we read teaching blogs, and we "revise and resubmit," over and over again. We have both been teaching for more years than we care to remember, and we still try new things in our classes and seek out new teaching opportunities. Kath recently did a "flash mob" and Maxine is trying very hard to create more visual materials. Kath is the outgoing editor of *Teaching Sociology* and loves this job because it allows her to read about others' innovative ideas and even to help shape them. Maxine recently began teaching a study abroad course and is working hard on the balance between the experiential and the academic.

We encourage you to seek help from other instructors. We were fortunate enough to find a group of teacher-scholars who care about teaching. Colleagues who are truly invested in their teaching are much easier to find these days, both on our own campuses and at professional conventions. While we depend on colleagues on our own campuses more than others, the Listserv TeachSoc is a very quick way to get feedback from scholars across the country. There are also Facebook groups you can join, including Teaching with a Sociological Lens. Having other teachers to talk with is an essential resource. If you do not have someone to discuss teaching with, find someone. You will be glad you did!

How do you begin to do better? The good news is that you already have. If you are reading this book, it is a good indicator that teaching is important to you and you want to do a good job. (Or, maybe you are simply overwhelmed and need help.) Fortunately, there are some very easy ways to quickly make a big difference for you and your students. The first three require very little effort but pay huge dividends: learning your students' names, coming early and leaving late, and practicing wait time.

If you know students' names, they are much more likely to be actively involved in your class. It is easy to ignore a professor who asks a question anonymously, who obviously does not know who you are, or who does not seem interested in you. Even if you have large classes, there are methods to use that are helpful. We just Googled "learn students' names" and ten pages of URLs appeared. (Isn't the web wonderful?) We won't take up your time here listing them. Try it for yourself! We all have our favorites. Maxine uses seating charts. She uses seating charts to take roll call and to learn names. Every day, she practices by saying "hello" to students as they are getting seated or by acknowledging them in class by name. Using seating charts is also useful for registering attendance. If a seat is empty, obviously the person who is assigned to that seat is not there. Students do need to be gently reminded that if their seat is empty, they are counted as absent. In small classes, Kath calls students' names every day as she hands back some assignment or writing exercise. In large classes, Kath requires students to hang a name tag off their desk or lose points! You might also try downloading student pictures from your class roll, labeling them, and memorizing.

Come to class early and leave late. This simple behavior tells your students that they are important to you. By being there when they arrive, you provide students an opportunity to ask a question and you have given yourself an opportunity to practice using their names as they walk in the door. If you are usually early and available at the end of class, the few times when you are rushing into class because of other commitments will barely be noticeable.

Practice "wait time." That is, when you address a question to your class, wait for their answer. All too often we rush to fill any gaps in silence. It is as if we cannot tolerate any time in our classes that is not filled with sound, usually the sound of our own voice. One of the easiest ways to make sure you give your students enough time to respond to your questions is by counting on your fingers. Maxine puts both hands behind her back and slowly and sequentially touches her thumb on her right hand to each finger, one at a time. Then, she does the same thing with her left thumb and fingers. That gives students five to ten seconds to respond. You will be surprised at how long this can seem. You may also be surprised at how effective it can be. It is certain that students will be more likely to respond and be actively involved in your class if they have an opportunity to respond than if they don't have an opportunity. When we ask a question and just as quickly answer it, students have no opportunity to respond and they are likely to stop listening to your questions.

After you've mastered the first three active learning techniques, the sky's the limit! There are far too many active learning activities to catalog them all but we will share a few of our favorites with you here. If you want even more active learning activities, there are a large number of online and print sources for class exercises, YouTube videos, and more. The American Sociological Association's TRAILS is a treasure chest for those who would like to improve their teaching. *Teaching Sociology* is already the source of a large variety of active learning approaches.

Our favorite and perhaps the most often used active learning technique is "Think-Pair-Share." The name of the activity tells you exactly what to do. Students need to think, then find a partner, and share what they thought. It is as easy as that. Of course, you have to come up with something for students to think, pair, and share about! Coming up with Think-Pair-Share content doesn't have to be a struggle. You can try Think-Pair-Share with something as basic as the sociological imagination. Imagine teaching this concept in two different ways: the traditional lecture versus Think-Pair-Share. In the lecture scenario, the professor rushes into class, struggles to get the notes organized, looks up at the class and says, "You were assigned to read about the sociological imagination. So, what is the sociological imagination?" Two seconds pass. The professor begins to lecture: "Well, as C. Wright Mills tells us . . ." What do you think the quality of this class is likely to be? Can you see the students in your mind's eye? We see blank stares, heads on desks, and texting under the desktop. Is this what your class might look like to an outsider? Is this how you were taught?

Imagine an alternative. The professor is in class chatting with students, looks up and sees that it is time for class to begin. The professor says, "Today we will practice using the sociological imagination to understand situations in our own lives. First, we need to make sure we agree about what we mean by the term 'sociological imagination.' We will practice our Think-Pair-Share technique. Take a minute to think about what you read and how you understand what Mills meant by the sociological imagination. Perhaps you will want to check the notes you took when you were reading the text. Then, turn to the person next to you to share your ideas. In a couple of minutes we will all talk together. Again, think about what the sociological imagination is, talk to a person next to you, and then we will all talk together." After about 90 seconds, say to the class, "If your partner has not had a chance to talk, make sure you give them a turn now." Walk around the class and listen to the conversations. When students begin their social chatter, it is time to bring the class back together. Now you can ask students to volunteer to explain the sociological imagination and begin your discussion. Most likely, you will follow up by asking students for examples—be sure to provide them with enough wait time to have a chance to think about their answers! Maxine's favorite follow-up is to ask students to jot down in their notebooks an example of the sociological imagination which she refers to as "jottings," meaning a simple phrase or even a word or two that helps students to think more about a topic or issue before speaking out loud. After students have had a bit of time to think, a general classroom discussion is likely to be more productive. Kath has a fun variation on Think-Pair-Share. She claps a pattern and students repeat it. Then she asks them to pair up to address a particular question. Then, she claps the pattern again to get the class back together.

Another of Maxine's favorite techniques is the jigsaw method (Aronson 2014). Jigsaw is a structured cooperative learning activity she uses for helping students acquire knowledge and information as well as developing higher-level thinking skills. Material or skill is divided into parts and students are assigned to be experts on each part. The group of experts must teach the other students their parts and the entire class is responsible for knowing the material or being able to use the skill. The experts first meet with each other in small groups to make sure they understand their part. Let's call them "Xs," "Ys," and "Zs." The Xs meet together, the Ys meet together, and the Zs meet together. They are each experts on some part of an assignment. Then, the expert groups are split up so there is one expert in each of the new groups. Let's call them "group 1," "group 2," and "group 3." Group 1 would be made up of one X, one Y, and one Z. Group 2 is also made up of one X, one Y, and one Z. The same for group 3. Each of the final groups has an expert on one part of an assignment. Using jigsaw helps students learn to depend on each other. It is a classic social psychological approach motivating students to do their best because their peers are depending on them.

Maxine has used this technique when teaching students to read important professional journal articles that might be difficult for undergraduates to understand. Maxine often assigns an article on the processes by which inequality is reproduced (see Schwalbe et al. 2000). The authors argue that there are four interactional processes that produce inequalities: othering, subordinate adaptation, boundary maintenance, and emotion management. Assigning a group of students to be experts on each process and then to teach it to the other students in the class makes this important theoretical work accessible, even to first-year students. Jigsaw is also put to good use when

[Handwritten margin notes: "jottings", "jigsaw → experts"]

[handwritten margin note at top: usefull when they don't need to know material in detail]

you want to get students to understand the basic ideas in several articles but you do not necessarily need them to master the material in detail. Or, you might want students to be introduced to ideas that you will refer to again and again throughout the semester but for the moment, you might want them to understand the big idea and develop mastery through repeated use. For example, Massey's (2012) *Readings for Sociology* begins with an excerpt from Berger's *Invitation to Sociology*, Mills's *The Sociological Imagination*, and Durkheim's *Rule of Sociological Method*. You might use jigsaw to make sure students were introduced to each big idea. You would create expert groups for each excerpt and assign them the responsibility of teaching the rest of the class.

Another of Maxine and Kath's very favorite active learning techniques are simulation games and puzzles. Stratification, especially, is often taught through the use of games and simulations, many of which can be done very quickly and with only a little preparation. Wetcher-Hendricks and Luquet (2003) teach students inequality by distributing an uneven number of crayons to students and then asking them to draw a picture of a generic experience or common object. Objects that are easier to draw—cars or apples, for example—quickly come to mind. You could also challenge students' creativity by asking them to draw experiences like waiting on a sidewalk for a traffic light to change or buying groceries. The students are asked to reflect on how they felt as the crayons are being distributed and as they are drawing their pictures. Those who have the most crayons will have the best experiences and those with the fewest are likely to feel deprived. Wills, Brewster, and Fulkerson (2005) also illustrate how the allocation of resources affects life chances in their simulation of stratification using puzzles. They ask students to work together in groups to put together puzzles for extra credit. The groups that finish first get the most credit. But, some of the puzzles are already preassembled and of course, those students finish first.

[handwritten margin note: using crayons]

Maxine recommends making use of Classopoly or Sociopoly (Coghlan and Huggins 2004; Fisher 2008; Jessup 2001), the game of Monopoly played with a different set of rules. That is, you play with the traditional Monopoly game but the rules are changed to reflect our stratification system. Using the sociology rules, some students start the game with more resources and get more money when they "pass go," for example. Classopoly does require a lot of class time and as with all games and simulations, careful follow-up is needed, but it is a fun yet powerful tool.

Let's think about how we might use Classopoly or Sociopoly to partially address goals and outcomes for an introductory course. One goal might be,

"Students will learn to appreciate social structure." An example of a student learning outcome to measure that goal is, "Students will explain how social class is an opportunity for some and an opportunity constraint for others." The assigned reading for the day is a selection from Ehrenreich's (2001) *Nickel and Dimed* (many readers include this selection including Massey [2012]). For the class period after the game, students are asked to write answers to the following questions: (1) Which group won the Classopoly game? (2) Why did this group win the game? (3) Did the winners work harder than the losers? (4) Were the winners more skilled than the losers? (5) How was the game similar and different from the lives depicted in Ehrenreich's *Nickel and Dimed* (2001)? (6) How was the game similar and different from life experiences you have observed? It is a good bet that your students have played Monopoly before, but after Classopoly they will never think of Monopoly in the same way again!

We strongly believe that trying to create an active learning classroom reminds us to take the spotlight off our performance and put it on our students and their learning. We hope that after you've read this chapter, you're excited to try some new techniques with your students! However, before you begin, we would like to add a caveat. Games and simulations are a lot of fun and students will enjoy them, but if not used with care, fun is all that will happen. Activity alone is not enough to ensure learning. To make games and simulations work, students must have readings assigned that address the concepts and issues at a deeper level, and those readings must be related to the games. Instructors must guide the students through a period of reflection and discussion of what happened in the game. If left on their own, students will likely remember the games but never understand why they played them. Games and simulations can produce "aha" moments or simply entertain. There are literally hundreds of cool things to do in class that will actively engage your students but the cool games and simulations are only as effective as the teacher who uses them.

Active involvement is crucial for mastery of material and the development of skills. If you are just beginning to work on your teaching, this is where to start. Simple strategies such as learning names, giving students time to think about responses to your questions (wait time), and asking students to work together (Think-Pair-Share) have big payoffs. Developing your toolbox of more sophisticated techniques and tools will take time but that is to be expected. All skills require starting with the basics and gradually becoming more sophisticated. The important thing is to start and you will soon find that you won't simply be filling up your semester or entertaining; you will be truly teaching. Teaching well can be exhilarating and it all starts with making sure your classes are focused on your students' active involvement rather than being focused on you and your performance. Once you have begun to turn your class into an area of active learning, you will find that it is too much fun to turn back. Your teaching will improve, your students will learn, and you will be making a difference. You are likely to fall in love with sociology all over again. The next chapters will help you develop more tools for your toolbox.

▶▶▶ **CHAPTER 7**

INQUIRY-GUIDED LEARNING

The classic example of inquiry-guided learning (IGL) is original research. That is, learning is guided by a question or a problem. It is as simple as that. IGL in sociology is a category of active learning techniques that are fundamentally organized around practicing the discipline. Students are actively involved in dynamic questioning and the construction of sociological knowledge. As Roberts (2002) argues, learning to ask questions and find answers should be a core requirement of our curriculum as well as our classes. In this chapter, we guide readers through the most basic practice of inquiry with students to examples of more complex teaching techniques.

Have you made statements like these in your class?

▶ The main concepts are highlighted in the text.
▶ Follow the directions step by step.
▶ If you do exactly as I tell you, you will do fine in this class.
▶ Our midterm exam will cover chapters 1 to 10 in the text.
▶ Look up any terms you do not understand in the glossary at the end of the book.
▶ Make sure you review all of your class notes as well as all of the chapters in the text for your exam (Roberson and Reimers 2008).

These statements are examples of what IGL is *not*, and they probably sound familiar to you. Both Kath and Maxine have said one or more of these during their teaching career. Maxine admits to having said them all at one time, and in the earlier years of her teaching she regularly made these statements in every class! These instructions emphasize students as passive recipients of knowledge. They emphasize the "banking method" and define the instructor as the person who does most of the intellectual work.

When we begin moving toward more effective teaching, using active learning techniques (see chapter 6) is the first step. If we think of effective teaching methods as a set of concentric circles we could conceive of active learning as the largest circle within which many others reside. IGL techniques are subsets of active learning. They are an advanced form of active learning. We can actively engage our students without using inquiry-guided techniques. If you ask students to read material and then summarize it, you have used an active learning technique. Certainly in that case students are doing much more intellectual work than if they simply listened to us lecture and repeated what we said, but inquiry-guided techniques go further. Or, if we think of a continuum from most basic to most sophisticated, IGL is further along the continuum toward sophistication.

IGL is not a specific type of teaching method but rather an umbrella concept. IGL refers to a category of teaching methods that focuses on questioning and helps students move toward knowledge construction. IGL techniques reflect the art of teaching and engaging students by asking questions that encourage critical thinking. IGL can be a very sophisticated and complex approach to teaching. We do not recommend that any novice instructor set as her or his goal a course completely based on IGL techniques. We *do* recommend that we all move toward emphasizing the process of inquiry in our classes as opposed to an emphasis on mastery of content.

IGL has at least two defining characteristics. First, IGL methods are inductive rather than deductive. Second, IGL techniques focus on constructing knowledge and promoting student learning through questioning and problem solving. Most of us are fairly familiar with the axiom that students who are actively engaged with material are more likely to retain more information over longer periods of time. Retaining information is a positive goal. Knowing something is certainly better than knowing nothing but being well educated requires much more than knowledge acquisition and retention.

Many of us use inquiry-guided learning techniques but are simply unfamiliar with the term. We are sometimes dismayed with the proliferation of technical terms to describe and categorize similar teaching practices and try our best to avoid this practice. "Inquiry-guided learning" may be one of those terms that appears to fall into this category. However, we argue that explicitly using the term "inquiry-guided learning" as an organizational category reminds us to focus on the process of inquiry and higher-level thinking skills. Practice defining and differentiating inquiry-guided processes from other teaching approaches creates a distinction that helps us choose effective teaching techniques.

While independent research and problem-based learning are probably the purest forms of IGL, less elaborate teaching methods also help students move beyond active involvement toward investigation of sociological phenomena. Although many would limit inquiry-guided techniques to problem-based learning and original research, we argue that a more inclusive definition is a more productive approach for the majority of us. In this book, we categorize teaching techniques under one label or another to help instructors become more effective teachers rather than in an attempt to add to the scholarly literature. Developing a familiarity with IGL gives us a sensitizing concept that moves us beyond the memorization of content toward deep learning. In this chapter we begin with an exploration of the principles of IGL and direct the reader from basic IGL practices through more sophisticated IGL teaching techniques.

It is important to begin your course with an attitude of inquiry. In chapter 11, we focus on first-day activities that will help you get off to a good start.

FIGURE 7.1 MEMORIZING CONTENT IS NOT THE MOST USEFUL SKILL TO MASTER IN COLLEGE

Source: "My Only Skill Is Taking Tests" by Harley Schwadron. www.cartoonstock.com.

There are some very simple ways to get in the habit of questioning rather than telling, beginning with helping your students to understand your syllabus and what is required for your course. For example, while we could read our syllabus to the students or emphasize the most important sections, another way to begin the course is to focus on allowing the students the opportunity to explore the syllabus and ask questions about our stated requirements. It can be as simple as asking students such questions as, "how many exams are scheduled in this course?" Or, "what is one thing on the syllabus that is unclear to you?" Of course, students should be allowed to ask their own questions.

There are other examples of ways that the syllabus itself can be constructed to emphasize inquiry-guided teaching. Instead of labeling a section of your course, "Social Class and Stratification," or something similar, you might label sections of the course with questions like "How do individuals get rich and stay rich?" Or, "Is everybody middle class?" Or, "How likely is it that those born poor will stay poor?" To help students address these types of questions, you could provide data to interpret, films to watch, and/or articles to read. None of these sources of information must directly address the question posed. It would be better if the material did not answer the question for the students, but rather provided evidence students could use to create an argument for their own response to the question. The way we construct our syllabus sets the tone of the course for both our students and ourselves.

Another basic approach for moving toward IGL is by helping students develop strong questions that go beyond recall of fact. Rusche and Jason (2011:343) provide a good set of guidelines for teaching students to focus on inquiry; that is, to ask questions rather than "learn" material. With a variety of activities, they require their students to ask questions throughout the semester and give their students the following suggestions for asking good questions: "Stay focused on the material. Ask more than one question when necessary. Give your readers something to work with and respond to by encouraging them to use the course material to respond. Refer to specific arguments, authors, and page numbers when appropriate. Ask questions that foster deep thinking."

These suggestions are good reminders for us too! Rusche and Jason (2011) describe several ways they put to good use the questions their students construct, including providing individual responses to the student-generated questions as a means to guide classroom discussion and a focal point for student pairings to carefully examine course material.

As a way of understanding IGL, let's practice with an inductive activity of our own. Spend some time with the data in Table 7.1 and address the questions posed. Do not skip to the end of the exercise where we explain the source of

TABLE 7.1 NAMING PATTERNS

DOB	Name of Newborn	Names of Parents	Relation of Newborn to Person with Same Name
1830	Adnor	Rose – Adnor	Father
1832	Hannah	Molly – Johnson	Mother's mother
1836	Betty	Nancy – Burge	Father's mother
1838	Stephney	Phoebe – Jack	Mother's father
1840	Gadsey	Duck – Wilson	Mother's mother
1846	Violet	Beck – John	Mother's father's mother
1847	Jenny	India – Primus	Mother's mother
1850	Gabriel	Fanny – Lewis	Father's father
1855	Linda	Little Sarah – Dave	Father's sister (dead)

Source: Gutman, Herbert G. *The Black Family in Slavery and Freedom 1750–1925*, p. 94.

the data and the interpretation the author assigned to the data. The point of reading this book is to learn; it is not to "get the right answer!" (Can you hear yourself saying this to your students?) Carefully examine the data and address the questions listed below. *love ths.!*

▶ What question generated this data?
▶ What is the possible significance of this data?
▶ What patterns do you see in this data?
▶ How would you classify these patterns? Are they strong? Weak?
▶ What else would you need to know to be convinced that this data is telling a story of significance?

Was this an easy task? Was it messy or straightforward? Were skills involved? Could you have learned the same thing if you had simply memorized material from a text? Could you identify with your students' struggles as you faced unfamiliar data?

The table was taken from Gutman's (1976) book *The Black Family in Slavery and Freedom 1750–1925*, page 94. Gutman (1976) uses this data to bolster his argument that slavery did not destroy the African family and that one of the ways we see this is through the naming patterns of children. Notice that children were often given the names of their grandparents.

We do not suggest that you use this particular exercise with your under-graduate students. It may be a bit sophisticated for undergraduates, and may be more frustrating than it is worth. Instead, we suggest that you present other forms of data for students to interpret. We chose this example to try to get you to remember what it feels like to struggle with the unfamiliar. Our students are novices and we need to remember what it is like to not be an expert. Because our tasks are easy enough for us, we have to be vigilant to remember students' perspectives. Maxine created this exercise for one of the multi-disciplinary teaching workshops she does on campus. The faculty from the science, technology, engineering, and mathematics (STEM) disciplines were stymied and none mentioned this exercise in their assessments as something they found useful. The social scientists did a bit better but they were also challenged. They did, however, see the exercise as useful. The historians and the English professors thought the exercise was easy and fun and wanted to do more like it! This is a good example of the point we are trying to make. We often forget that what is easy for us can be a huge challenge for our students.

While we do not suggest that you use the "Naming Patterns" exercise we present here, you can use the basic idea of table reading and interpretation in a format that is less challenging. Sharp (2008) creatively uses data from the Social Security Administration on baby names in 1907 and 2007 to illustrate that social influences shape some of our most personal and individualistic decisions—that is, what to name our children. This is a great set of data to use for this purpose. While we do not know how Dr. Sharp conducted her class, we could make use of her idea and the same data in the following three approaches: lecture, active learning, and IGL. We could do a straight lecture, making the point that while names might be assumed to reflect very personal and/or famil-ial decisions, those decisions are decidedly social. In this instance, we would use this data as evidence to back up our assertion. This is a common tactic but not an inquiry-guided technique. (There are circumstances when this would be an excellent approach. See chapter 5 on lectures where we return to this point.)

We might take an active learning (but not IGL) approach by presenting the data and asking students very concrete questions. For example, "What was the most popular name for males in 1907? What was the most popular name for females in 1907? How about 2007? Are the most popular names the same in 1907 as in 2007? Is there more or less concentration of the same names in 1907 and 2007?" Once students' attention was focused on the data, we could follow up with a more complex question like, "What do you think might account for the patterns you observe?"

Alternatively, we could present the data to the class and ask questions that made the concrete questions implicit and focus on more interpretive questions. We might ask students, as did Andrea Hunt (July 2012, personal communication), to look for differences and similarities across time and contrast patterns by gender. Further, we might ask students to speculate on why there are differences or similarities in naming patterns, and to consider what other information would be beneficial when examining naming patterns. We could consider these questions in a class discussion or in small groups. Or, we could go a step further and simply give students the URL for the Social Security Administration (2014), ask them to generate these tables, and address the same questions in writing.

As these examples illustrate, what makes an approach inquiry guided is the extent to which students are asked to investigate and interpret data. Concrete questions are used to focus attention as an alternative to simply lecturing and presenting facts. Even when questions are very simple, having students respond rather than talking at them is more likely to be engaging. The more they hear their own voice, and that of other students, the better. Questions that call for interpretation are used to help students justify, explain, and evaluate evidence or pose solutions to problems. The professor's job is to guide and to encourage engagement rather than providing all the answers. The approach you use would depend on your student learning outcomes and the students' developmental stage and skills. IGL techniques foster increasing intellectual independence as the course develops and as students mature.

There are numerous examples of inquiry-guided exercises and approaches documented in *Teaching Sociology*. Scarboro (2004) provides an excellent example of moving from active learning to IGL techniques. It was his practice to have students actively involved with the material in his theory class by including exercises that required students to apply theories and to discuss the readings. Still, students found the material to be somewhat irrelevant; just being actively involved did not bring the lessons home. The class became more successful when Scarboro (2004) moved to a more inquiry-guided approach by asking students to pose questions that related theories to their own lives and to describe the process by which they addressed their questions.

Kwan and Trautner (2011) describe an inquiry-guided activity that sensitized students to their own biases about physical attractiveness. Students were shown photographs of women who exhibited varying levels of physical attractiveness. They were then asked to evaluate the women on characteristics such as friendliness, rudeness or politeness, and intelligence. The results would not surprise most sociologists. Students rated attractive women as more likely to be a leader, more likely to be polite but also more likely to be untrustworthy. The follow-up is what distinguishes this activity as inquiry guided. Students were shown the data and then asked to explain why

good example

attractive people were perceived as more successful, more likely to be a leader, and more emotionally stable but also more selfish. A pretest/post-test evaluation, and students' own response to the exercise indicates that the module was successful in helping students see both general bias and their own personal bias based on physical attractiveness. The same exercise could be less inquiry guided in a variety of ways. If the students were simply presented with similar data and told to apply understanding gained from reading an article about the issue, the exercise would have been an example of active learning but not inquiry guided. If students were presented with similar data and told what the data implied, it would not be an example of an active learning technique nor an inquiry-guided exercise. The more students are asked and the less they are told, they more likely they are to learn at a deeper level. An activity is much more effective than passivity and original inquiry is more effective still.

We both believe that it is more difficult to implement IGL techniques in large classes than in small ones, but even in large classes, you can use inquiry-guided techniques. Chapter 19 presents several ideas for student engagement and questioning. Kath's most often-used technique in large classes is "Think-Pair-Share." To use this approach in an inquiry-guided approach, ask students to think about questions and share them with their partners. Rusche and Jason's (2011) requirement that students construct questions is adaptable for large classes. Students can be assigned to write questions and share them with a partner. Using clickers (see chapter 17), a table of data can be examined and interpreted. Students can be asked to generate questions that explore the meaning of data even if you choose not to use the clickers to display those questions. Mollborn and Hoekstra (2010) have their students address such complex questions as "How useful are human capital explanations of who does housework?" with the help of clickers.

IGL techniques challenge us to think critically and creatively about our teaching as we encourage our students to move beyond basic thinking skills toward more complex views and interpretations of our social worlds. In chapter 10, we explore critical thinking and suggest means by which we can help our students become more nuanced and sophisticated thinkers. We can help students move from memorization to the evaluation and creation of knowledge. IGL techniques help us meet some of the most common and highly valued goals in all the disciplines and fields in higher education and certainly in sociology. It is through our own inquiry-guided skills that we create knowledge. Think about it: What do you do when you practice sociology?

►►► # CHAPTER 8

THE IMPORTANCE OF WRITING
FOR LEARNING

There are "three learning objectives for which writing is critical (that is, goals that cannot be achieved without some type of writing): critical thinking, sociological thinking, and theoretical sophistication" (Grauerholz, Eisele, and Stark 2013:49). Shouldn't all our classes focus on sociological thinking and critical thinking? We would be surprised if sociological thinking were not paramount in all our sociology courses! We argue, in agreement with Grauerholz, Eisele, and Stark (2013), that the single most important task we can require of our students is that they write. When we write, we clarify what we think. Often we develop our ideas as we write. The same is true of our students.

We are strong proponents of writing, especially informal writing or writing to think activities. If your students are writing, they are more likely to be actively thinking about sociology, developing their critical thinking skills, and yes, practicing their writing skills. Using writing exercises, activities, and assignments will allow you to teach more effectively and grading can be more efficient than you might think. The good news is that even if you are not using writing in your classes now, writing is one of the easiest activities to incorporate in your teaching and has a big payoff.

We will focus on informal writing activities or those that are exploratory and do not require a finished product, as compared to formal activities that do require a finished product (Bean 2011). While we argue that both informal and formal writing are necessary for successful courses, we emphasize informal/ low-stakes writing activities because they are easily constructed, serve a large range of goals, and do not necessarily require any grading. Other than forcing us to take ourselves outside the center of all activities and putting students in the center, low-stakes, informal writing activities only require a bit of creativity on our part. We also consider formal writing assignments and discuss the necessary requirements for formal writing assignments to be effective. We provide you with examples of each from our own experiences and from the literature and discuss the choice of choosing writing skills as an outcome in and of itself. We conclude by suggesting how you might make the decisions about which type of writing assignments you will use.

The purpose of informal, low-stakes writing is student engagement with the ideas and materials in your course. It can be graded or not, but by definition it is not a polished, finished piece of writing that counts for a large proportion of the course grade. Informal writing is most likely to be low stakes and associated with writing to learn. Formal writing is more likely to be high stakes but it does not necessarily have to be a significant proportion of the course grade. Often, high-stakes writing assignments consist of more formal papers like research papers or essays that require multiple drafts and result in a polished form. Simply put, formal writing results in a finished product. Why is writing, especially informal/low-stakes writing, so important?

Let's consider a practical, everyday example of why writing is important. Not long ago Maxine was considering knitting something after not having practiced that craft for a while. She had no doubt that she could do it. The project was an easy one and she took it for granted that she would simply buy the yarn, sit down, and knit. It did not happen that way. When she got to the yarn store she realized that she did not know how much yarn to buy. When she started to knit she did not know where to start. All she knew was that she needed yarn and needles but she had no idea how much yarn, what kind of yarn, what size needles, or what type of needles. Anticipating the task, she believed she knew exactly what she was doing and how she was going to proceed. Much to her chagrin, she got no further than a store that had yarn—and there she was, stopped dead in her tracks.

All too often we assume we know more than we do! We have not thought through our understandings of our tasks. Our thoughts are fuzzy and our arguments are not well constructed. Without writing our "thinking" is most often not precise enough to accomplish any sophisticated intellectual task. It is too easy to gloss over even the most important construct. We take far too much for granted, as Maxine did with her knitting. That is why we often write out a lecture, or at least, an outline. Few of us would consider giving a paper at a conference without at least preparing notes and many of us write out the entire paper. Just assuming that we know what we are thinking is not enough. We write to decide clearly what it is we think, whether it is an intellectual task or even a task that is a part of daily living.

Our writing helps us construct our thoughts. For example, without a shopping list, few of us could even buy our groceries. It is not just a matter of remembering what we want to buy. We have to decide—that is, think about—what we need, using one form of organization or another. Before we can begin to make a list we have to think about the supplies we have and what we might need. Then, we have to organize a list, and the more formal the meals we are having, the more careful and structured our lists usually are.

Writing helps our accuracy and our recall. Writing helps us remember. Writing forces us to be concrete, to elaborate, to organize. And, when responding to well-constructed questions, writing helps us develop our critical thinking skills. Yet, in our classes, we often call on our students to make verbal arguments without the help of notes. We ask them to make complex connections without the benefit of having written anything. And we ask them to do this quickly, in front of their peers, often having called on them when they were not expecting it. No wonder they can sound unsophisticated! We have not given them time to consider carefully what they will say and we expect strong performance under difficult circumstances. Writing helps us not only remember, but also to reflect, deliberate, decide, and construct what we think. We can't make out our own grocery lists or remember what is on them, but we expect students to remember unfamiliar, complex material and answer thorny questions without writing. As a student quoted in Pelton (2013a:115) says, "Writing is also a great way to bring out knowledge and understanding—what [I] mean is, sometimes we don't think, or are unsure if we 'get it,' until we write it out and read our thoughts back."

When Maxine first heard the term "writing across the curriculum" and realized that a lot of people she admired expected her to have her students write, she was intimidated. She finds writing to be quite a challenge. The words do not flow. She often stares too long at a blank screen and she works hard on her grammar. Discovering that she was expected to use writing as a tool and even to help her students write was discouraging. While she had published journal articles, the actual writing of the articles had always been the most difficult part of the research enterprise for her. Trying to figure out how she would use writing in her classroom was one of the obstacles that almost made her give up her quest to be a stronger instructor. After all, Maxine teases, "What were all those statistics courses for if they did not get you out of having to write?"

Kath's experiences are different. She loves to write and holding back the flow of words is a bigger challenge for her than getting words on paper. Her struggle is finding the time in busy days to write, not the actual writing. However, at this point in Maxine's teaching, she considers student writing to be her single most important teaching tool and the one she uses most often. Kath agrees.

It is a truism to say that writing and thinking are inextricably linked (Hudd and Bronson 2007). Further, writing is connected to critical thinking (Armstrong 2010; Bean 2011; Massengill 2011) and we will discuss developing mechanisms to encourage critical thinking in this chapter. However, we would also argue that writing is even more fundamental and can be used in an almost endless number of important ways. We believe that low-stakes and exploratory writing—that is, the "thinking on paper" writing—is essential to good teaching and learning. Students must write to create and clarify what they think. We must require them to do so in all of our classes, large and small. Let's start with some of the basic ways Maxine and Kath use low-stakes writing in their courses.

Low-Stakes Writing

We often start a class by providing a prompt to which students respond as the class begins. That is, the prompt is presented on the board—or these days, the computer screen—and students are asked to begin to write as soon as they enter class. (This is especially useful if class members are habitually late. Papers are retrieved after the first five to seven minutes of class.) For example, a prompt might be: "In your own words, explain what Mills meant by a sociological imagination." Obviously, students who have read the sociological imagination reading assignment are likely to do better on this assignment than those who have not read it. Beginning the class with this writing prompt focuses student attention on the topic of the day, the sociological imagination. Or, if you have already discussed the sociological imagination, you might begin with, "Your parents and you obviously became adults in different historical periods of time. Many parents tell their children how their lives were lived under different social or political conditions. Provide an example of how your parents' lives were different from yours because they lived in a different historical period of time." The second prompt gives students an opportunity to think about the importance of historical context and individual lives and therefore to practice using their own sociological imaginations.

They are also practicing their critical thinking skills by applying what they know rather than simply remembering it. If you have discussed the intersection of history and biography, the prompt provides a review. Sometimes these exercises are handed in for a small amount of credit. Sometimes students are asked to share them with other students; sometimes we take them up and ask a student for permission to read their paper to the class.

We also use other writing assignments that provide more alternatives such as, "Choose one of the three articles we read on class and inequality and explain how this article contributes to your understanding of the consequences of social class." Any number of useful strategies can be used to follow up. Students might then be asked to form groups comparing the major points of the three articles. Or, a full-class discussion could follow, or you could follow up with yet another question like, "Are the consequences of social class similar to or different from the consequences of gender?"

Note that in both these instances, the questions are important. Students are not asked for simple definitions of basic concepts; rather they are being asked to think more deeply. If students are not well prepared for college or are unaccustomed to being asked to do more than recall, you might have to spend more class time helping them acquire skills or better habits. This is a perfect time to bring out Bloom's Taxonomy (1956) and have students practice moving from basic thinking skills to more complex skills (see chapter 10).

We often use low-stakes, informal writing when a discussion gets too far afield from the main topic. We might simply restate a question about the focal topic and ask students to write for three minutes, directly addressing the question. We also use writing to introduce a topic. For example, if we are teaching about gender, we might ask students to compare the concept of gender to that of "sex." (Students always seem to wake up whenever the word "sex" is mentioned.) Or, we might ask students to identify an assumption others make about men and women. We are likely to state the question something like this: "What are some stereotypical ways people think about women as compared to the way they stereotype men?" Asking for an assumption presumes sophistication that students often do not have. And we need to remember that students often get very invested in anything they state about themselves, so sometimes it is convenient for the sake of discussion to talk about "other people." Admitting that we have assumptions that are incorrect is difficult for a lot of us. This is another example of thinking carefully about the questions we ask our students. A slightly different way of phrasing a question can make a difference. Frequently, we use informal writing to bring a discussion to closure. We might simply say, "Summarize the major points we focused on in this discussion." Or, "How does this class help us reach our learning outcome for the day?"

One of the most common informal writing techniques is the "minute paper" (Angelo and Cross 1993). The minute paper is perhaps most often used for an instructor to check to see if students comprehended the day's lecture or activity. Faculty ask questions like, "What was the most important thing you learned today?" and "What do you still have questions about?" One of Kath's favorite low-stakes writing assignments is this classic minute paper. At end of theory class, she asks students to either write (1) a question they have that they don't have an answer for yet or (2) something that today's class clarified for them. These examples illustrate one of the advantages of minute papers and other types of informal writing; they allow you to see the outcome of students' learning and where they might need help. We are almost always surprised by some students' insights, question, or sometimes, obvious need for clarification.

One of Maxine's favorite low-stakes writing assignments is an example of ungraded, expressive writing. She asks students to write what they are feeling about an especially sensitive topic. Maxine acknowledges to her students that our feelings and our prior experiences affect our learning about such issues as racism, sexism, and homophobia. Before beginning an especially sensitive activity or discussing readings, Maxine asks students simply to write about how they feel about the topic, or their fears about discussing the topic, or any other related message they want to express. Students hand in their papers but are given the choice of whether to put their names on their papers. Surprisingly, most students do sign their names. She finds that honoring the affective helps students prepare for cognitive tasks. It also provides her with understanding some of the challenges students face when studying a sensitive issue and helps her get to know her students better. Frequently this exercise increases her empathy for her students.

Kaufman (2013) and Macomber and Rusche (2011) provide us with powerful examples of ungraded, low-stakes free-writes that promote reflexivity. Macomber and Rusche (2011) use an ungraded free-write to start a classroom conversation about racial inequality. They ask students to respond anonymously to the prompt: "For the next three to four minutes, free write about an early racial memory." Volunteers share their responses. Macomber and Rusche (2011) use this beginning conversation to help students learn about each other's experiences, connect to larger issues of inequality, and to begin to put a name to sociological issues. They provide the example of a student initially describing his neighborhood as only having one family who was not from the same racial background, and move to being able to identify this as an example of residential racial segregation. Kaufman (2013) presents another excellent, ungraded exercise designed to help students write to think, be contemplative, and foster reflexivity. The exercise can be done in one or two class periods and can be adapted to any class. Students anonymously respond to a question for ten minutes and pass their papers to other students. Kaufman (2013) provides examples of questions such as, "Has your education been affected by gender and/or sexuality in any way?" (p. 72) and "Do you think the use of Native American mascots in sports should be abolished?" (p. 73). Two or three more students respond to the initial student response and the original author gets the paper back and writes a concluding response. This creates a conversation. While Kaufman (2013) states that students find their original papers because they recognize their handwriting, you could easily have students mark their papers with a symbol or a number to make sure they recognize their own papers. The important point is that students must be able to write anonymously without fear of negative evaluation from peers. Although it sounds to us as though Kaufman (2013) uses this exercise in a small class, it could be adapted to large classes simply by dividing the class into sections and passing the responses among the students in the same section. Exercises such as these are much more likely to help students think deeply about sociological issues than simply stating the question in class and waiting for the most extroverted students to respond.

Pelton (2013a, 2013b) regularly uses low-stakes writing assignments to help students learn theory and write theoretically. After showing a film, Pelton (2013a) asks students to "Write for five minutes, without stopping, about anything that comes to your mind regarding Marx and the events that unfolded in the first 10 minutes of the film" (p. 112). Students are surprised at how much they have to say about Marx! Another of Pelton's (2013b) exercises requires students to fill out what we might think of as a work sheet. Such seemingly simple techniques provide scaffolding for students' writing and thinking. In one exercise, Pelton (2013a) provides four prompts on one sheet of paper and students fill in the sheet with paraphrases or direct quotes. Pelton's (2013a) goal is for students to learn theory but she is also asking them to reflect on their own learning. For example, one of the prompts is, "Assess your understanding. How certain are you that you have identified central skills of thinking sociologically? Were your typical reading and comprehension strategies effective? What adjustments did you make if those strategies did not work?" Simply asking students to focus on a specific question, even if they quote directly from the text, is helpful in increasing the probability of deep learning.

Asking students to think about their own learning and to write about it is a unique and powerful way of focusing and encouraging deep learning.

While many low-stakes writing assignments are free writes and are ungraded, some instructors count informal writing assignments as a small percentage of the grade. Journal writing is an example of a popular low-stakes assignment that helps students be more reflective and connect their lived experiences with course content. Using a large sample (n = 140) from a private Catholic university and a large state university, Picca, Starks, and Gunderson (2013) provide an excellent example of the effectiveness of a graded journaling assignment they used to help students become more aware of the effects of race, class, and gender on students' lives, and to help students learn to take field notes. They used a pretest/post-test design to measure student perceptions of the impact of race, class, and gender on their daily lives. They asked students to take field notes and write ten entries on what they observed and how they felt and then to write a summary. Picca et al. (2013) also provide an excellent discussion of the challenges of assigning journaling and suggestions for guiding questions and rules about the number and timing of journal entries. Their grading rubric is also very useful. Picca et al. (2013) used this journaling assignment as a formal writing assignment in that they asked for a summary essay that was a more finished product than many journaling exercises are. (Also see Wagenaar [1984] for an alternative journaling exercise.)

Low-stakes writing has its place in helping our students learn to think critically. In chapter 10 we discuss critical thinking, focusing on two common critical thinking typologies, Bloom's Taxonomy (1956) and Paul and Elder's (2008) "universal intellectual standards." Bloom's Taxonomy (1956) encourages us to move from the least complex thinking skills to the more complex; that is, from remembering, to understanding, to applying, to analyzing, to evaluating, and finally to creating. Paul and Elder's (2008) universal intellectual standards are clarity, accuracy, precision, relevance, depth, breadth, logic, and fairness. Low-stakes writing is most helpful at the lowest levels of Bloom's Taxonomy (1956); that is, remembering, understanding, and perhaps even applying. Paul and Elder's typology (2008) might be more helpful in helping our students create formal writing projects.

We focused on low-stakes, informal writing for a good reason. Low-stakes writing helps us with the basics of critical thinking; that is, first of all, recalling information. While simple remembering is very low-level thinking, one must think about something. The one-minute paper is a good example of recall and summary. Students must merely remember and state what they remember. Why is writing what we recall more important than simply thinking about it?

It is very easy to let our minds wander. Distractions are innumerable. When we have to write down what we remember, we have to focus. We cannot write words without thinking about them. We create what we think when we write, we clarify what we think when we write. We believe that it is essential that we include informal writing in our classes.

FORMAL WRITING

Still, we argue that it is necessary for our students to do some formal writing in all of our classes, even quantitative courses. (Remember that formal writing results in a finished product.) Writing is a life skill. All of us simply must be able to write comprehensible sentences and paragraphs. We need to communicate with others in our social world in writing. We need to communicate with others in our world of work through our writing. We fail our students if we do not help them develop their ability to communicate through the written word. While few of our students will write creatively in their occupation, the great majority of them will write professionally and will write often (Nilson 2010). Regardless of the style required in a given profession, writing clearly with a goal and an audience in mind will greatly benefit your students.

Writing to think is crucial but at some point in our curriculum, if not in every class, our students need to be able to make an argument, even if it is not a complex argument, and create a finished product. We need to be able to take a position and support it or to present alternative perspectives. We have to be able to provide information in a clear, methodical fashion. Formal writing is required to make evidence-based arguments. Are sociologists equipped to teach writing in this fashion? Of course we are! We know when someone has convinced us. We know when writing is clear. We know when someone uses evidence or writes solely on the basis of opinion! Even at the sentence level, we can critique. We know subject–verb agreement when we see it and we know when a sentence is clearly written. "Even Maxine," as she would say, can see writing errors at this level.

High-stakes, formal assignments require a supportive, developmental process. The too-common "Choose a topic and hand in a ten-page paper at the end of the class" will not cut it. Massengill (2011:3) argues, and we agree: "Meaningful writing assignments can be particularly effective in developing higher level thinking skills, but they require carefully constructed prompts, internal modeling in the classroom and deliberate feedback from the professor." Massengill (2013) deftly leads us through the steps she used in a writing–intensive course to help student develop their own arguments. The steps include class discussion of readings, sharing examples from past student work to illustrate what a successful outcome should be, practice with comparing and contrasting sources of evidence, and writing and reviewing drafts of each other's papers. Massengill's (2011) assignment asks students to read, compare, and contrast three different theoretical perspectives; apply these perspectives to a source of evidence; and develop their own original arguments. Formal, high-stakes assignments such as the one Massengill (2011) outlines are probably most appropriate for small, higher-level classes.

Alternative Formal Writing Assignments

We do not equate formal writing with traditional term papers and we do not seem to be in the minority in this view. Grauerholz, Eisele, and Stark (2013) find that very few sociologists require traditional term papers. There are many alternative formal assignments that will advance student skills. They need to know who their audience is and the purpose of the writing assignment. For example, one of Maxine's favorite formal assignments is a two- to three-page letter (adapted from Daughaday [1997]). Students are asked to write a letter explaining what their sociology class is about and why they find it useful and/or intriguing. Their audience is a family member. The instructions are simple: "Write a two- to three-page letter to a family member. In this letter you must clearly explain what sociology is in language that is easily understood by your recipient. You must provide examples of ideas, concepts, or research that you believe illustrate what the discipline is about. You must convince your family member that sociology is a discipline that contributes to our understanding of our social world and how it works."

Maxine also uses essay exams, if the class is small enough, and includes some formal writing even if it is a large class. Maxine helps students prepare for any formal writing assignments with more preparation for higher-stakes assignments. Perhaps because when Maxine teaches at the undergraduate level, she primarily teaches introductory-level courses, she spends a great deal of time on basic critical thinking skills. Before students are asked to write a high-stakes essay, her students practice in class and must hand in an organizational scheme. Her publication on the evidence matrix (Atkinson, Wills, and McClure 2008) describes this process in more depth. Maxine asks students to construct a matrix with questions on the column and sources of evidence on the rows. Students must fill in each cell, illustrating how the evidence source addresses the question. This assignment is practiced in class. Maxine also asks students to hand in short essays throughout the semester in which students are asked first to compare and contrast two authors, then three or more, so that they develop their analysis and synthesis skills. These assignments are usually very low-stakes assignments used for practice.

One of Maxine's favorite short writing projects is a sociological autobiography (see also Kebede [2009]). She asks students to begin with a description of the historical period in which they were born, including the social issues of the day and a brief and rudimentary description of the availability of major technologies such as automobiles, electricity, and computers. She asks that they follow up with a description of the current important social issues and technologies. Students focus on acknowledging how their race, class, and gender have interacted with the social issues of the day to influence their life chances. They compare themselves to someone in an older generation in their family. Maxine teaches in a large state university where many students are first-generation college students. These students often talk movingly about the effect of social class. Women often mention the opportunities they have that their mothers did not. Students of color can touchingly describe the discrimination their parents and grandparents suffered. All students are required to acknowledge some form of privilege in their lives. The historical comparison to family members not only helps them understand social context; it helps them see privilege.

Kath asks students in a social problems class to write a series of short papers that account for about 30 percent of the final grade. Students select 10 concepts from a list of about 25 that the class focuses on during the term. For each of the 10 concepts, students identify a newspaper/magazine/online news article which illustrates the concept and write a short paper about that concept. They first define the concept and follow up by explaining how the concept is illustrated in the news article. They must also correctly construct a reference for the text and the sources of the news article. Two of these 10 papers are due early in the term and Kath provides feedback. Students may choose to rewrite the early papers.

Armstrong and Fast (2004) offer two formal writing assignments that could be used in more advanced-level courses. They propose assigning a sample encyclopedia entry that asks students to include a description of the topic, a discussion of the history of the topic, and more recent developments and future directions. Classic sources should be cited. This assignment allows students some choice in topics but provides structure for the assignment. The scope of the project could be limited or more expansive. Annotated bibliographies are another example of formal writing assignments that could take the place of a traditional term paper. We suggest that assignments that require students to read and comprehend original research in sociology are more likely to be successful when students have more experience with sociological concepts. Qualitative studies may also be more accessible to undergraduates.

We use a multitude of resources to help us decide on a variety of ways to use both informal and formal writing. Both of us are, perhaps obviously, dedicated readers of *Teaching Sociology*. On the other hand, articles are never going to be as comprehensive as complete books. And here is where Maxine swears by her "writing Bible": John Bean's *Engaging Ideas* (2011). If you read no other book about teaching and writing, Maxine suggests that you choose Bean (2011). He provides dozens of suggestions for how to incorporate writing successfully into any classroom, ideas about grading, and a convincing argument that writing is a central tool for encouraging critical thinking. Most important, Bean (2011) will convince you that you can use writing in your classes. You will be more confident and more creative if you follow his advice. Ask for Bean's (2011) book for your next holiday or birthday present; you will enjoy it that much.

Your Role in Your Students' Writing Processes

One of the most important decisions you have to make about writing is what your role is in your students' writing processes. Are you the judge, delivering a final evaluation of the product? If so, there is little need for writing comments on papers. You can use a rubric and perhaps a concluding comment, but if your comments will not be used, it is a waste of time to write them. The halls of many sociology departments are littered with boxes of students' final papers that faculty spent hours writing comments on and students never bothered to retrieve. Commenting on drafts is another matter. Here your job is not to be the judge, but rather to mentor, to help students develop their thinking and organizational skills. Focus on what is important in the assignment. The most time-consuming part of all grading is line editing and you do not need to line edit for students. You can put a check mark in the margins and ask students to find their own typos and grammatical mistakes.

Consider whether or not your comments follow the dictum, "First, do no harm." Because being a parent is such a major part of Maxine's identity, she is fond of saying that every student is some mother's baby. Sarcastic, mean comments about someone's writing accomplishes nothing you want to accomplish. You probably remember hurtful comments from your own student days. Maxine remembers an otherwise kind and wise mentor who once told her that her writing was an "insult to your reader." Think about that comment. What is to be learned from it? Maxine learned that her writing was not good (and that a good cry often accompanies writing projects) but she was left with no understanding about how to make it better. When evaluating a student's written work, always find something good to say about it and start your comments with that. While this can be a challenge—particularly late at night after reading a lot of writing assignments that need a lot of work—if you look hard enough, you will find something a student did well. Once in utter frustration, Maxine wrote, "Thank you for handing your paper in on time. Being prompt is an important professional characteristic." When she handed back the paper, the student thanked her for all her suggestions for improving the assignment and thanked her profusely for recognizing how hard s/he worked to meet deadlines! The next draft was not only on time, it even had some instances of noun–verb agreement and at least one sociological insight!

What should you spend your time on? You can focus on clarity and the use of evidence. You can focus on sociological understanding and organization. You can help students learn to write well by giving them the opportunity to do so, even if the assignments are short. You do not have to require long, multiple-draft papers to get students to write formally; nor does formal writing have to be very high stakes.

How do you decide what kind of writing assignments to give? You have some exciting choices to make. One way to think of the choices is whether you want your students to write to learn or to learn to write (Anson 2007). Few of us would argue that writing is not a primary skill. Both informal and formal writing assignments help students develop writing skills. However, formal writing provides practice developing polished documents while informal writing helps generate ideas and clarify thoughts.

Developing critical thinking skills is perhaps the most prevalent of all course goals in almost every discipline (see chapter 10). Grauerholz, Eisele, and Stark (2013) argue that both formal and informal writing may be important for developing critical thinking skills and we agree. We see formal writing as likely to be associated with using evidence-based arguments and problem solving, clearly basic to critical thinking. However, informal writing, when linked to student learning outcomes and goals, is also useful for developing critical thinking skills and is central to encouraging students to write to think.

Students must practice putting their ideas into words; indeed developing their ideas is likely to require informal writing whether in the classroom or outside it.

You also must consider curriculum requirements. For example, if developing polished writing products is required for your course, you need to develop some formal writing assignments. However silly this might sound, all too often we forget to investigate the curricular requirements of our own courses. (Maxine recently committed this error. In designing a study abroad course she often teaches on her own campus, she took for granted that she knew the requirements. She had forgotten that the course must meet a university U.S. diversity requirement. Fortunately the error was easy to address, but it was simply lucky that she remembered it in time.)

And then there are the practicalities. How much time can you set aside for grading? If you have a class of 300, are you going to assign a formal project requiring multiple drafts and a lot of feedback? If you have a large class, will you have teaching assistants? How well trained will they be? We discuss considerations and suggestions for writing in large classes in chapter 19. Not surprisingly, we recommend that high-stakes formal writing assignments be reserved for smaller classes. On the other hand, we do recommend that you seriously consider some low-stakes formal writing assignments that can be graded quickly.

As we mentioned earlier, informal writing is a tool that can be used for a large variety of purposes, including assessing what your students are unclear about, writing to think, focusing the group's attention, and giving students time to think before they provide a verbal answer. We argue that informal writing is such a powerful pedagogical tool that it should be used on a daily basis. Free writes, simple phrases that remind us to focus, journaling to encourage reflexivity, critical thinking questions—the list is endless. You are only limited by your imagination and both you and your students will be pleased that you made the choice to use writing as one of your primary pedagogical tools.

▶▶▶ CHAPTER 9
GUIDING DISCUSSION

Whether the class is relatively small, a class of hundreds of students, or an online class, discussions are one of the most successful techniques you can use. But using discussion can initially be intimidating. Have you ever posed a discussion question and had that question met with omnipresent silence? If you teach online, have you ever continued to check the learning management system or website and noticed that no one is posting on the discussion? Have you ever set up a discussion only to have one group productively working away while another is discussing the latest basketball game? Have you ever had a group discussion with one student literally turning his back on the others? We've all had it happen! This chapter will provide useful tips on how to create good discussions in both face-to-face and online classes. Once you have learned to structure strong discussions, you may find yourself using this strategy more than any other.

Discussions can be used for a variety of purposes, ranging from encouraging students to focus their attention to creating a setting that inspires students to think deeply. We can focus student attention with a well-crafted question; we can help students develop critical thinking skills by posing challenging questions and creating effective discussion structures. However, careful planning and management is necessary for effective discussions and the more complex our goals, the more sophisticated our planning and management needs to be.

There is an assortment of discussion techniques but regardless of the technique we choose, active student participation is the hallmark of all discussion techniques. If you are a lecturer and want to move to interactive lecturing (see chapter 5), perhaps the first strategy to consider is discussion. If we have no plan but simply to ask students to "talk about it," or "divide up into groups and discuss," little is likely to be accomplished. On the other hand, carefully planned discussions can be vital in helping students meet higher learning–thinking outcomes. During discussion students could be asked to demonstrate comprehension by explaining a concept or principle to another student. Application outcomes could be met by asking students to apply a concept in a variety of ways or to a variety of situations. Students could be asked to analyze a document or an interaction they observe. Students could be assigned to synthesize arguments by comparing and contrasting major components of those arguments.

TYPES OF CLASS DISCUSSION

There are three logical groupings for class discussion. The entire class can discuss an issue, small groups may be formed, or pairs of students may be called on to wrestle with a question, solve a problem, or generate new ideas. Interspersing a lecture with a discussion every 10 to 20 minutes has the potential to keep students engaged. It can turn a lecture into a more interactive and more effective class. For example, rather than providing information through lecture, you could create a discussion exercise.

Maxine often presents comparative data on infant mortality and asks students to posit explanations for our poor ranking compared to other countries. She usually does this with a free write followed by a discussion or a Think-Pair-Share or a combination of both. Think-Pair-Share is one of the most basic discussion techniques and, as you may recall, is discussed in several other chapters in the book. In this example the Think-Pair-Share technique proceeds by asking students to examine a table of data, then to draft a few notes with their potential explanations, then to turn to another student to discuss their ideas. To sum up, pairs are asked to volunteer their explanations to the entire class. Discussions like these can last between about 8 to 18 minutes. Students need between a minute to three minutes to think, two to five minutes to share, and five to ten minutes to share with the class. With a fairly straightforward question like the one Maxine just suggested, the shorter time frame would probably be enough. If you are short on time, you can just use the Think-Pair part and not share with the entire class. It matters more that students actively engage with the question and talk with a peer.

Maxine usually follows the Think-Pair-Share discussion above with a consideration of infant mortality rates among demographic groups within the United States. She asks students to form groups of four students. Once the groups are formed, she gives out data tables that present infant mortality by a number of demographic and class variables. She asks students to examine the tables, to identify the U.S. families that have the highest infant mortality rates and to explain why this is the case using alternative theoretical perspectives.

How do you decide when to ask individuals to respond to a question, use pairs, or entire groups? In general, the more complex the question, the more time you will need to spend and the more likely it is that you will need to use group discussions. You might want to focus student attention on a particular concept to make sure that students understand a basic idea. If this is your goal, asking individuals to respond is perhaps most appropriate. Again, remember to allow students some time to think. However, if you want students to compare and contrast two different articles on the same topic, choosing to have students work together in pairs may be the best choice. And, if you want students to work through a complex problem, a small group may be most effective.

Class size is also crucial to take into account. While you might have good results with a whole-class discussion in a class of 20, a class of 200 is another matter. Think-Pair-Shares and small group work are much more likely to be effective in large classes. In large classes, limit whole-class discussions to brief encounters to clarify a point, or to introduce another kind of interaction.

There are many different types of small group work used for effective discussions. Discussion groups can be formed without asking students to play specific roles. The simplest approach is simply to ask students to create groups of four or five students. After some initial uncomfortable moments, they will group themselves. Or, you can ask students to count off. If for example, you have 40 students in class and you want groups of five, students would count off to eight and have all those with the same number work together. Or, students can be given colored slips of paper, choose numbers out of a bowl, etc. These informal groups are generally effective but they do allow for "free riders," and they do not necessarily encourage quality teamwork.

A more structured form of group work requires students to play different roles. This is an important technique for encouraging shy students to learn leadership and to encourage talkative students to take a turn listening. For example, you might use a technique some call a listening triad (Primary

Science Teaching Trust 2013). Divide your class into groups of three and ask one student to start by being the primary speaker. They do so by making an argument, stating a point of view, or explaining a concept or idea. Another student could take the role of questioner. This student's job is to ask for clarification, push for more information, and/or ask for evidence upon which the speaker is basing an argument. A third student could play a listening and reporting role, taking notes about the conversation and reporting to the other group members about what was said, what the main points were, and where more information might be needed. Students could switch roles during one class period or play different roles during the next class period.

Another type of group work could employ the use of envoys (No author N.d.) or what Maxine calls "go-betweens." That is, groups are assigned a task, a problem to solve or an issue to discuss. You can have all groups working on the same problem, or you can have several problems, but you must have at least two groups working on the same problem so they can share solutions. One student is assigned the role of "envoy" or "go-between" and after a specified period of time, the envoy or "go-between" moves to another group to explain their home group's response or answer. After the envoy hears the response from the second group, s/he moves back to his or her home group to share this information. The groups should be instructed to take the other students' perspective into account and decide whether or not they want to change their conclusions based on this new information. Groups should be able to justify their decisions. This technique has the advantage of allowing opportunities for students to develop their leadership, encourage listening skills, hold students accountable, and practice considering alternative points of view. Maxine usually creates groups with three students each for this type of activity and finds that the "envoy" or "go-between" carefully listens to other students and often asks for clarification from the other two members of the group. It is important to make sure that students understand that they will take turns being the envoy or "go-between." After the "go-between" has visited another group and reported back to her/his home group, the entire class should be brought back together to have the groups share their results. Here it is important to ask students what they learned from the other group and whether or not the other group influenced their later discussion. Each group should be able to explain how they used information from the other groups or why they decided to stick with their own conclusions.

Collaborative learning groups (Rau and Heyl 1990) require students to prepare for class ahead of time and then work together on a task inside class linked to the outside preparation. For example, students might be asked questions that demonstrate comprehension of content outside class and with their groups inside class. They could be asked to address more analytic questions about the same material. For the work to be completed inside class, groups of about five students are created with at least three statuses. One student is the leader, or the person who makes sure that the work gets completed. Another student is the reporter or the student who actually writes a response for the group but with input from others. The control agent makes sure that everyone in the group has an opportunity to provide input. After the groups have had sufficient time to work on the assigned task, the entire class is brought back together to discuss the problem or answer the posed questions. Students must take turns playing the various statuses.

Jigsaws (Aronson 2000–2014) are a type of group work that requires students to become experts and teach each other. First, students are assigned to become an expert on some part of a task. The task could be as simple as answering a question with multiple parts. Let's assume that a question has five parts and the class has 25 students. Five students would form an expert group on part one, five students would form an expert group on part two, etc. The experts on each part meet together to solidify their expertise. The students could be required to prepare to be experts before coming to class or be asked to pay close attention to a particular part of a lecture or demonstration. Having the experts meet together helps make sure that less skilled students or less well-prepared students can get help from a classmate. Then these homogeneous groups are broken apart and heterogeneous groups are formed with an expert on each part of the question. That is, another five groups are formed each with an expert on part one, part two, part three, part four, and part five. Each of the experts must teach their expertise to the entire group. Perhaps a simple example from statistics would be useful. Suppose you are teaching statistics and the goal is for the class to master levels of measurement and measures of central tendency. One group could be experts on the general notion of levels of measurement and why knowledge of levels of measurement is important. A second group could be experts on measures of central tendency, mastering understanding of the limits and advantages of these measures. Three more groups could be formed on the three types of measures of central tendency: the mode, mean, and median. After the experts have met with each other to make sure they understand the concepts, heterogeneous groups are formed, with an expert on each topic. The heterogeneous groups could be given a problem to solve that requires knowledge of levels of measurement, measures of central tendency, and each of the types of measures of central tendency.

An example from Maxine's history professor husband, Rich Slatta, is also instructive. Slatta hands out short excerpts of documents written from different perspectives on the Falkland war. One group of experts is given a document written from the perspective of the Argentines. Another group of experts is given a document that lays out Great Britain's counterclaims. A third group examines battle reports, and a fourth group examines maps. After experts develop their expertise, heterogeneous groups are formed with each expert presenting his or her group's piece of the puzzle. The heterogeneous groups must then synthesize the information.

Whether you are teaching a large class or a small one, jigsaws help students learn from each other and require students to be accountable to each other. Calling the entire class back together to address the problem or issue is important to make sure that groups did not get too far off track and to allow groups to share their work. Students are often justifiably proud of their work and the opportunity to display their expertise can be rewarding. Elliott Aronson (2000–2014) developed jigsaw in 1971 as a way to increase cooperation between students in recently desegregated Texas schools.

It is important to vary the discussion formats you use. Think-Pair-Shares can be used almost every day but other more elaborate strategies get to be boring and formulaic. There are too many effective techniques to use only one. On the other hand, using a different discussion strategy for every class may use more time than you want to devote to logistics. Decide on what you want the discussion strategy to accomplish for your class and choose a technique that suits your goals. For example, if you want the class to analyze one assigned article from a reader, an informal group provided with a few key questions is probably all you need. If you want to emphasize collaboration and interdependence, collaborative learning groups or jigsaws might be the best choices. If you want to pose a problem that requires creative solutions, you might choose to use envoys or "go-betweens."

The format of the discussion you use is not as important as the quality of the questions that you ask. Questions are the key to good discussions. If you ask simplistic questions that require little thought, you are not likely to inspire great insight. If you ask students to define a concept, or "yes-no" questions like, "do Marx and Weber define class in the same way?" you will not get far. You also need to be sure your questions are clear and straightforward. Bloom's Taxonomy (1956) can be used to help you structure good questions. Critical and creative thought can result from discussions as long as you create good questions to frame the discussion for your students. Nilson (2010) provides examples of good questions at every level of Bloom's Taxonomy (1956).

While students are in their discussion groups, it is important for you to walk around the room to listen to students as they are talking with each other. Do not interrupt and do not solve the problem for students; rather, listen to the approaches they are taking. Their conversations may help you tailor your responses when you bring the class back together for a summary or to incorporate into your next class.

Regardless of the structure of the discussion groups you use, it is important to provide a summary of the discussion. After the discussion groups have completed their work, make sure to have students (with your help) review most important points, connections between the discussion and the reading assignments, and the course goals. This summary is vital to the success of any discussion. Left without a summary, students may feel that they "just talked" in class and will often not be able to recognize the value of the discussion. Your role as the instructor is crucial in this summary phase. Make sure students understand how the discussion relates to student learning outcomes and to the means by which they will be evaluated in your course.

While it is tempting to reward discussion work and accept conclusions uncritically, it is not effective to do so. At the same time, we need to make sure that we do not demean students. First, remember that every group does not have to have its responses reported to the entire class. We can ask for groups to volunteer to report on their work. Then, you can follow up with a question asking how many groups agree with the conclusions. Often groups will come up with similar responses. If there is little agreement, ask for several alternatives and walk the class through evaluating each. Model for the class how sociologists evaluate arguments.

ACTIVE LEARNING AND DISCUSSIONS

If you're wondering how to fit active learning, discussions, and lectures into your class period, there is no hard line that can be drawn between "activities" and discussion. Activities, simulations, games, and other active learning techniques require a discussion. One of our favorite activities to teach social structure illustrates this point. Peretz and Messner's (2013) "Stand Up/ Sit Down Structure and Agency Activity" helps students understand social structure. The activity can be used in large or small classes and can be done quickly, or you could spend more time depending upon your course and your purpose.

Peretz and Messner (2013) suggest introducing the exercise by offering a definition of social structure taken from one of the class readings. Students are then asked, "If you believe you chose to take this class, please stand up." Most students stand and they are asked to look around to see how many of them are standing. Then, Peretz and Messner (2013) say, "This class meets the university's General Education requirements for a 'social issues' class. If it did not meet that GE requirement, please remain standing if you would still have decided to take the class." In Peretz's and Messner's (2013) experience about 15 percent of the students sit down. (You would, of course, substitute one of your own general education requirements.) Peretz and Messner (2013) take students through another iteration of the same question with this prompt: "This class meets the university requirement for a diversity class; if the class did not grant diversity credit, please remain standing if you would still have decided to take this class." Most of Peretz's and Messner's (2013) students sit down at this point. Finally, they ask students to remain standing if they would choose to take the class even if no academic credit were given for the class. At this point, almost all the remaining students sit down.

Students can readily relate to exercises like these that illustrate how social structure affects their lives. Especially in our individualistic culture, it is vital that we demonstrate how social structure acts as both opportunity and opportunity constraint. Although you could obviously simply provide many examples of social structure, actively engaging students, even if it is only having them stand up is more effective than our talking. Take every opportunity to put the spotlight on students and take it off yourself.

While it appears that Peretz and Messner (2013) followed up with a whole class discussion, we would use this excellent activity as the basis of a group discussion. We suggest creating groups of four to five students and asking them to discuss the following questions: (1) Recall what happened in the activity we just finished. (2) In your own words, explain how the activity illustrates the sociological concept of social structure. (3) Identify other structural elements of our university. (4) How does social structure work as an opportunity and an opportunity constraint? Notice that these questions build on each other and proceed from the lowest levels of Bloom's Taxonomy (1956) and move toward the higher levels.

Regardless of which active learning activity you use, discussion is likely to play a key role. There are a large variety of formats specifically designed to structure class discussion. When we conducted a generic search for "discussion techniques" we found dozens of URLs. Websites for university teaching centers are a treasure trove for discussion techniques. We have especially enjoyed websites from centers at the University of Washington (1999), the University of Oregon (2013), the University of Maryland (N.d.), and Illinois State (2006).

ONLINE DISCUSSIONS

While we have emphasized discussion formats to be used in face-to-face formats, most of us now use a learning management system (LMS) and they provide a rich resource for discussions in our face-to-face classes as well as our online courses. Maxine and Kath began to use online discussions when LMSs first became available. LMSs provide us with a number of useful attributes. First, many of us like to give credit for class discussion and online formats are easier to evaluate. Second, online discussions provide students who do not feel as comfortable speaking in class another venue for making contributions. Kath and Maxine have often been pleasantly surprised to have excellent inputs from quieter students given this alternative venue. Third, students are often more thoughtful when they write than when they speak. They usually take more care with their comments when everyone will see what they have to "say" online.

How can you create an online discussion? Emily Estrada, one of Maxine's graduate student colleagues, has created a very effective structure. Emily uses this assignment in her online course but you could just as easily use it in a face-to-face class. Emily posts a prompt at the beginning of a week; students have two days to post a reply and another two days to post a reply to another student's original post. The posts must be in students' own words. Here is an example of one of Emily's prompts: "According to the readings on gender inequality, male domination is institutionalized. What does this mean? What are some examples? Reflecting on your own life, what is an example of patriarchal culture as defined by Allan Johnson?" Notice that Emily first asks a question at the comprehension level on Bloom's Taxonomy (1956). Then, she asks an application question and follows up with another application question that requires reflection. This exercise works well in a smaller online class but if you used it in a larger online course, you might consider setting up discussion groups so that every student did not have to read through a large number of posts. Kath does exactly that in her supersections of Introduction to Sociology classes. Groups of 20 to 25 students are formed; they select a sociological namesake, such as "Team Weber" or "Team Martineau," and are assigned different weeks.

You must monitor discussions online, just as you should listen to students as they have discussions in class. Moderating discussions online can be tricky. The Illinois State University's Teaching Center (2006) offers an excellent treatment of handling online discussions. This website suggests that debates and case studies work well in online classes. The author of the website offers several helpful suggestions such as handling any problems that occur during discussions via e-mail rather than within the discussions. De-Loach and Greenlaw (2007) provide examples of common roadblocks in discussions and how an instructor can help students get past these. They recommend that instructors avoid debating with an individual student, steering the entire group toward productive directions. For example, if you see that discussions have gotten off track, you might intervene with a cautionary note and a suggestion for proceeding more productively. Such an intervention might look something like this: "Bob correctly suggests that there are at least three ways to measure social class. Judy defines each of these for us. Having established this basic information, it is important to use this information to analyze your readings. Which of your authors uses which definition? How does adopting a particular definition influence the reported findings?"

EVALUATING DISCUSSIONS AND TEACHING DISCUSSIONS

The evaluation of discussions is usually informal. The point of discussion is for students to consider alternatives, to have a meaningful and productive exchange. Discussions are rarely used as a primary means of evaluation. The most common evaluation is perhaps a simple "participate" or "did not participate," but students must be given ample opportunity to meet these criteria if grades are assigned for participation. Make sure that assignments or quiz questions reflect your class discussions. Care must be taken that more outgoing, outspoken students do not dominate conversations and that space is provided for less assertive students to demonstrate their contributions. Often if discussion is evaluated, students are asked to write summaries of their discussions as individuals or as a group effort. Trying to evaluate verbal discussions is likely to frustrate both you and your students. Online discussions are easier to assess because they are written. It is easier to use a well-developed rubric for written products.

We cannot assume that students know how to participate in effective discussion. It is worth the time to teach them. We might ask students to think of a time they have witnessed an effective discussion and explain why they considered it effective. During our own discussions, we should pause and ask students to evaluate the discussions and make suggestions for improvement. You can also encourage practice with developing the habit of reflection through the use of discussion. Consider asking your students to set discussion goals for the semester and periodically ask them to think about how they are progressing toward meeting those goals (Hollander 2002). Extroverted students might set as goals learning to listen more attentively to fellow students. More introverted students might set a goal of making contributions to classroom discussions.

Discussions are some of the most commonly used teaching strategies for good reason. With a little creativity and skill you can create an effective class discussion that focuses on student learning and makes your student look forward to coming to class. Creating an effective discussion is not only good teaching, it takes far less time than writing a lecture. Discussions provide excellent opportunities for students to teach each other, to reinforce good thinking, and to demonstrate the excitement of working together on an intellectual task.

▶▶▶ **CHAPTER 10**

CRITICAL THINKING

"Nobody Doesn't Like Sara Lee!" proclaims an old television commercial. The same can be said of critical thinking. Who could *not* be in favor of critical thinking? Indeed, a large majority of faculty agree that critical thinking is the most important goal for a college education (Bok 2006). Arum and Roksa's (2011) *Academically Adrift* garnered much attention with its report that few students make significant gains in critical thinking while in college. The consensus is clear. Critical thinking is just that—critical—and there is concern that college provides too little value added for our students when it comes to critical thinking.

Yes, you hear a "but" coming. The "but" is that there is little consensus about what critical thinking actually is. We argue that critical thinking is a term that most of us understand at some basic, implicit level without being able to define it precisely. At its best, critical thinking is our most worthy goal. At its worst, it is a clichéd, hackneyed phrase that simply takes up space on a syllabus. But, it is a concept and a skill-set that no competent teacher-scholar can ignore.

As a starting point, some of our favorite definitions of critical thinking include:

▶ "the art of analyzing and evaluating thinking with a view of improving it" (Paul and Elder 2008:2)

▶ "making a reasoned judgment based on appropriate evidence" (Lee et al. 2004:11)

▶ "developing problem-solving skills" (Goldsmid and Wilson 1980:78)

There is no perfect agreement in the literature, but these inconsistencies invite us to come to our own understandings of critical thinking. The good news is that you can help students improve their critical thinking skills without a sophisticated and nuanced understanding of the literature and the current debates.

If you have a graduate degree in sociology, it is very unlikely that you have not carefully thought about your own thinking, or made judgments based on evidence, or developed your problem-solving skills. We do after all think critically ourselves, or we would not be reading this book. What we most crucially need is awareness that it is our responsibility to help our students think in more sophisticated ways. The first step for the newest of instructors is that we must move our students beyond simple memorization. Start there. If you can do that, you are on the right track.

Fortunately, a lot of scholars have addressed critical thinking skills, and it is not that difficult to move a step, or several steps, beyond memorization. There are a number of basic tools that we can use, both to help us understand critical thinking and to help our students think more deeply. The most well-known of the critical thinking typologies is Bloom's Taxonomy (Bloom 1956), which was recently revised by Anderson and Krathwohl (2001; see Figure 10.1). A simple Google search will produce multiple sites with a large variety of visual displays in the form of Google images and verbs associated with each level, to help with understanding and writing learning outcomes. A comparison of the two shows more similarities than differences, and Anderson and Krathwohl (2001) explain the reasoning for the changes. We will continue to reference the earlier version, because it may be more familiar to most readers, and the nuances of the different versions are not central to our arguments. We focus on moving beyond memorizing content to more useful and transferable skills.

BLOOM'S TAXONOMY

Bloom's Taxonomy (1956) encourages us to move from the least complex thinking skills to the more complex; that is, from remembering, to understanding, to applying, to analyzing, to evaluating, and finally to creating. If you use Bloom's Taxonomy (1956) with students in class, it is important not to get bogged down on the details of which type of exercise fits into which category.

FIGURE 10.1 BLOOM'S TAXONOMY, REVISED

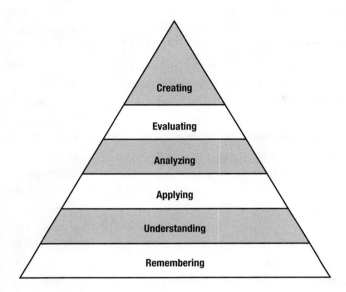

Source: Overbaugh, Richard C. and Lynn Schultz. *Bloom's Taxonomy*. Retrieved October 31, 2011 (http://www.odu.edu /educ/roverbau/Bloom/blooms_taxonomy.htm).

Emphasize that this is a sociology course and that the taxonomy is just a tool to help us think better. If it helps us think in more complex ways, it is effective.

The most basic level of thinking in Bloom's work (1956), "remembering," is being able to recall information. In the older version of Bloom's Taxonomy, this level was called "knowledge." (See Figure 10.1.) If you can remember or acquire knowledge you can list, define, identify, and/or state information. We might ask our students to recall the difference between sociology and common sense as presented in a text. If having your students be able to differentiate between primary and secondary groups is important to you, you might ask them to repeat the definitions of each. Gender scholars often want students to remember the difference between gender and sex. A simple way to start is to ask students, "What do we mean by the term *gender*?" "What is a person's *sex*?" While remembering information or demonstrating that you have knowledge is the most simplistic of all thinking skills, knowledge is very fundamental. No one can think in a vacuum. We have to have content to think about.

"Understanding," or comprehension, is the second level. Here we are asking students to describe, to put in their own words, to paraphrase, to differentiate or explain a concept or an idea. We simply want to know if they understand. We might ask students to explain the difference between sociology and common sense, gender and sex, and primary and secondary groups, for example. This is only a small step away from remembering, but it is an important one. We are asking students to do just a bit more than use the author's own words.

While the "understanding" level of critical thinking sounds simplistic, it is crucial that students understand basic concepts from the beginning of the course. One of Maxine's most important course goals is for students to see sociology as an evidence-based discipline, even though it focuses on emotionally charged topics such as religion, politics, and family values. She emphasizes the contrast between belief or opinion and fact or evidence and helps students understand what fits into the parameters of the course and what the course will not address, which helps redirect students from nonproductive, "but, that is not what I believe" conversations to examining what social forces have influenced their beliefs. For example, Maxine provides students with examples such as, "Marriage is an institution that the government should support." "There are more Republicans in North Carolina than there are Democrats." Students are asked if these are statements of opinion or statements of fact, and how one would know the difference. The class discusses what constitutes a fact and what constitutes an opinion or belief.

Sociology addresses empirical questions and interpretive questions but does not address moral or aesthetic questions (Schwalbe 2007). We do not make decisions about what is right and what is wrong and we do not decide what is beautiful or pleasing to other senses. Maxine gives students a list of statements to categorize. Examples include, "The prettiest car on the road today is a Honda." "Failure to go to church at least once a month is a character flaw." We do answer empirical questions; that is, those that can be addressed in measurable ways like counting or observing, and we do address interpretive questions, especially those that require us to give meaning to empirical evidence. A very simple example is that it is 32 degrees Fahrenheit and that is cold. What is the temperature? Is it cold? We can easily measure the temperature, but whether or not it will be perceived as cold depends on the geographical context. After providing some examples of these types of questions, Maxine starts by simply asking students to compare and contrast each type. The point is to just get students ready to think a bit more deeply about what sociology is and what sociology is not in order to define the parameters of the course. It is then easier later in the course to refer students back to what is outside the limits of the class conversations.

This exercise quickly leads to the next category on Bloom's Taxonomy (1956), "application" of knowledge. When we ask students to apply knowledge, we are asking them to use information in a new way. To show us that they can apply their knowledge, students might provide examples of some commonly held belief and how they learned to rethink that belief based on the sociological knowledge they acquired in class. When we ask students to apply we are asking them to illustrate, use, classify, or role-play, for example. When Maxine is introducing her courses and setting the stage for getting students to think sociologically, she practices with students creating sociological questions, as compared to moral or even aesthetic questions. After students have had the opportunity to compare and contrast empirical, interpretive, moral, and aesthetic questions, Maxine asks them to apply what they have just learned by providing a list of each type of question. She finds it helpful to direct their attention to a list of religious texts, including the Koran, the Old Testament, the New Testament, and the Book of Mormon. Students are asked to create questions about these texts and then to label the questions as empirical, interpretive, moral, or aesthetic. For an example of a moral question, students might ask, "Is it wrong to eat pork?" As an example of an aesthetic question, students might ask if the book of Psalms is effective poetry. While other disciplines might deal with these questions, sociologists do not. However, sociologists would address empirical questions such as, "Which religious text is used by Muslims? How do Mormons, Jews, Christians, and Muslims define the Divine?" An interpretive question might be, "Why does each faith define 'life after death' the way that it does?" Asking students to focus on religious texts helps them explore the difference between what they can measure and what they believe, though any contentious issue would work. Whatever topic you choose, we suggest keeping the focus narrow so that questions can be compared and contrasted.

Bloom's Taxonomy (1956) moves from application to "analysis." When we challenge students to analyze, we are asking them to divide a mental construct or an argument into its constituent parts. We might ask students to name three distinct points of evidence presented by the author. One of the classic approaches taken by many texts is to present material on the three theoretical approaches used in sociology. Structural functionalism, conflict perspectives, and symbolic interactionism are often presented as examples of sociological perspectives or theories. We might ask students to outline each of the other perspectives or to explain a social situation using any or all of these perspectives. This example illustrates how closely related levels in this taxonomy can be. Some might argue that using these theories is an example of application rather than analysis. We would argue that it could certainly be considered both and that the point is not so much to differentiate between Bloom's levels (1956) as it is to practice moving beyond memorization.

The fifth level of Bloom's Taxonomy (1956) in the newer version (Anderson and Krathwohl 2001) is evaluating. When we evaluate, we defend a position, we support a hypothesis, we justify a stance, we judge, we argue, we appraise. Continuing with some of the same concrete examples, we might ask students to take a common sense position that they believe is true and see if they can substantiate that position or if they have changed their minds about the legitimacy of that position. Under this circumstance we would have to make sure that changing your mind is presented as a valued trait rather than just being wrong. No one likes to be wrong! And, if students simply see the difference between what they believe to be true and what they can substantiate with evidence, we have helped them be more critical thinkers.

The sixth level of Bloom's Taxonomy (1956) in the newer version (Anderson and Krathwohl 2001) is creating. When we create, using this lexicon, we come up with a new way of thinking about perspectives, a new conclusion, or a different way of looking at information. Most of us think creatively but may not label it as such. If when synthesizing literature we come up with a new way to see a problem, we have been creative. When we derive hypotheses from theories, we are often creative. When we think of new ways to measure a construct, we are creative. Students might be asked to role-play a social scenario which encourages creativity. Debates often generate a lot of creativity because students are faced with alternative perspectives to which they respond. When asked to compare the social situations that were operative when their parents were their age to their own social environment, students often see their parents in new ways. Most anytime students recognize or use the sociological imagination, they are being creative thinkers.

A very basic way to help students begin to think critically is to simply practice using Bloom's Taxonomy (1956) with them. What would you literally do if you were using it in class? First, make sure that students have a copy of the taxonomy in front of them to use. Project it, use a document camera, or give them a handout. Let's say that you were using a reader and assigned an article based on Ehrenreich's *Nickel and Dimed* (2001). Assign the taxonomy as a part of the work done outside of class and start with a review. After a short review, your first question might be: "Ehrenreich worked at two low-wage jobs. What were they?" Allow students to use their notes, look at their books, and/or ask each other. Then, ask the students to identify the level of thinking required to answer this question. Next, ask students to identify or explain one of the points Ehrenreich (2001) was making. All they need to do is to paraphrase Ehrenreich (2001). Again, refer to the taxonomy and ask which level of thinking they are using. If they choose another level other than "understand" and they can explain their reasoning, that is great, but do not require them to go beyond simply describing or paraphrasing. Ask students the difference between the two levels on the taxonomy. Third, ask students to provide another example of a low-wage job that would have provided the same kind of experience. Fourth, ask students to analyze the article by pointing out that there are other characteristics of a low-wage job than just low pay. Ask students to explain why this is an analysis. At the beginning of the semester, stopping there is perhaps a good decision, especially if there are a lot of first-year students in the class. As you move through the semester, you can move up the taxonomy. For example, you could ask students to evaluate current social issues related to low-wage jobs, such as raising the minimum wage. Take care not to overemphasize the differences between the stages as you move up the taxonomy. The later stages often overlap.

We suggest that you ask students to practice using the taxonomy more than once and then assign an exercise that requires them to use it on their own and get some credit for thinking in a more complex way. Returning to the taxonomy several times during the semester will help students gain experience using the taxonomy and hopefully, think more critically. Emphasize the importance of strengthening critical thinking skills by including it among your student learning outcomes.

ELDER AND PAUL'S WORK

Elder and Paul (2011) created another commonly used tool that they refer to as "universal intellectual standards." While they probably would not refer to their list of intellectual standards as a "typology," these standards are helpful in many of the same ways as Bloom's Taxonomy (1956). That is, the standards are guidelines that we can use to evaluate our thinking and move us beyond memorization of content toward deeper learning and critical thinking.

Elder and Paul's (2011) universal intellectual standards are clarity, accuracy, precision, relevance, depth, breadth, logic, and fairness. While these terms are generally self-evident, perhaps not all of them are. Clarity simply refers to being clear. Clarity is foundational for Elder and Paul (2011) in much the same way that "remembering" is in Bloom's Taxonomy (1956). That is, clarity is a basic. Unless one is clear about a question or a statement, there is not much point in trying to move on to higher-level standards. In Bloom's Taxonomy (1956), we must remember or have some content to think critically about before we can move on. No one can think critically about nothing. Accuracy is next. A prejudicial statement might be clear—e.g., women are not as smart as men—without being accurate. Precision is the third standard and refers to being specific. A hypothesis would be more precise if it were directional. We might hypothesize that gender predicts height, but it would be clearer to say that men are taller than women. The fourth standard is relevance. We might ask if height is relevant to intelligence, for example. Elder and Paul (2011) use the example of students arguing that they worked hard so they should get a better grade. Relevance is at issue here. Working hard is not necessarily relevant to success in a course, or in writing this book. Just because we work hard does not necessarily mean we will write a book that is useful to the intended audience.

Depth is one of the most interesting and relevant intellectual standards for college students. Often, students have not thought about an issue in any depth. The stances they take are based on taken-for-granted assumptions and/or borrowed from their family and peers with little thought. For example, our students often say that "poor people just need to work harder." Or, immigrants should "just go back where they came from." We should all "just say no" to drugs or to unhealthy foods or going to war. Thinking more deeply is a central component of critical thinking and is the opposite of simply memorizing and being able to identify a term on a multiple-choice exam.

Breadth, logic, and fairness are the last three intellectual standards Elder and Paul (2011) assert are "universal." Breadth refers to looking at an issue from more than one perspective and is perhaps one of the biggest challenges to teaching sociology. We are asking students to use a perspective that is foreign to our culture. While our society emphasizes individualistic values and behavior, sociology focuses on context and the power of the group and the collective. Our students see trees; we see forests (Johnson 2008). It is easy to get frustrated trying to teach a sociological imagination in an individualistic culture and it is easy to think of students as just not trying when they resist sociological perspectives. On the other hand, if we think carefully, we can probably come up with examples of alternative perspectives that are tricky for us too. Homophobia, for example, is not easy for many of us to understand at any depth. While we can think of homophobia from a gendered perspective and explain it rationally, at an emotional level, many of us simply do not understand why homophobia is so pervasive. If we are politically liberal, it is very difficult to take seriously conservative positions on many issues and vice versa. Similarly, it is difficult for our students to take context seriously when individuality has been stressed for them.

Logic refers to the consistent and orderly arrangement of ideas. Our students probably know the dictionary meaning of *logical*, but they may not have had much practice recognizing inconsistencies in arguments. One of the most common fallacies we address in sociology is the difference between correlation and causation. Elder and Paul's (2011) emphasis on fairness may be one of the most sociological of their standards used to judge critical thinking. They ask that we examine our thinking to see if we are taking stances that are to our benefit. Do we benefit from a particular position? Are our own best interests our guiding principles? Can we see an issue from the perspective of others? Are we capable of taking the role of others in our thinking? Fairness and breadth are quite similar, but the fairness standard requires us to both take alternative positions and to judge whether or not our positions are to our own benefit.

Paul and Elder (2008) have published a helpful, pocket-size book aptly titled *The Miniature Guide to Critical Thinking*. The website allows you to download sample PDFs. Maxine has used this booklet when working with teachers from a variety of disciplines with good outcomes. The intellectual standards are especially good tools to use when evaluating written assignments. Clarity is the gateway standard. If something is not clearly written, you cannot use the other standards. Combining clarity with any other one or two standards is an effective critical thinking technique. For example, if an answer to an essay question is clear, presents accurate evidence, and the evidence is relevant to the argument, the student has exercised critical thinking skills.

WHAT APPROACH SHOULD YOU USE?

Our experience is that these "universal" standards are perhaps the most helpful in evaluating student essays while Bloom's Taxonomy (1956) may be the most beneficial in helping students understand how to think in a more complex manner. Bloom's Taxonomy (1956) and Elder and Paul's (2011) standards are designed to be used across the curriculum. They are generic tools that can be helpful to any student and any instructor. We might ask if these generic tools are what sociologists need. Perhaps critical thinking, and the tools we use to help our students learn to think critically, varies from discipline to discipline. It would not be the first time that sociologists argued that context is vital!

Grauerholz and Bouma-Holtrop (2003) argue that critical thinking is discipline- or context-specific and argue for a concept they term, "critical sociological thinking." Essentially, they argue that to be a critical thinker in sociology you have to be able to use evidence to support an argument and you have to have a sociological imagination. We tend to agree with this stance but argue that if you apply the generic tools of critical thinking to sociological issues and perspectives, you will help students be critical sociological thinkers. While we acknowledge that this is certainly an oversimplification, our point is that while our students' cognitive development is developmental (see Roberts 2002) so are our teaching skills. The more experienced you become, the more complex your teaching and learning about learning can be.

There are at least two ways you can learn to teach critical thinking skills, inductively and deductively. This chapter uses an inductive approach: that is, we suggest that you utilize this chapter's tips on using Bloom's Taxonomy (1956) and Paul and Elder's (2011) universal standards to move beyond memorization. Don't worry about the definitions of critical thinking and the arguments about whether one should use the older version of Bloom's Taxonomy (1956) or the newer version (Anderson and Krathwohl 2001). Rather, use this chapter, along with the chapters on constructing lectures (chapter 5), active learning (chapter 6), inquiry-guided learning (chapter 7), the importance of writing (chapter 8), and guiding discussion (chapter 9) to understand sound teaching techniques. As you become more relaxed and confident, you can go to the literature on critical thinking, especially articles in *Teaching Sociology*, for a more sophisticated understanding of what critical thinking is. Start just by moving beyond lecture and memorization. We would be very surprised if you don't find that you have been teaching at least some elements of critical thinking all along.

Or, you can teach critical thinking deductively. That is, you can start with the critical thinking literature. Digest it just as you would any other complex body of work and then create your classes based on your understanding of the literature and the issues presented. There isn't a wrong way to begin to teach well! While this is not the approach we recommend, like our students, we do not necessarily learn in the same manner. If it helps you to dive into the critical thinking literature, go for it!

We must go beyond content. If memorizing sociological facts is all we ask of our students, we do them a disservice. We teach them that life is just to be skimmed and that meaning is not to be questioned. We restrict our students and our courses to an experience that simply must be tolerated rather than considered and embraced. Teaching can be joyful and invigorating. Critical thinking with your students will help make it so. Like Sara Lee, no one doesn't like joyful and invigorating!

CHAPTER 11

FIRST-DAY ACTIVITIES

No single day in any class is more important than the first day. Students form impressions that may affect their performance and their relationship with you for the rest of the semester. One of the worst mistakes instructors make is walking in the first day, handing out the syllabus and walking out. This behavior tells the students that the course is not important to the instructor and neither are they. In contrast, one of the best ways to start off the semester is to engage the students in lively exchanges that demonstrate just how fascinating and rewarding the course is going to be. Students will be motivated to come to class again, to pay attention to the content of the course and what is expected of them. In this chapter we provide a variety of suggestions to make your first day successful and get your course off to a strong start.

On the first day of class our palms sweat, our hands shake, and we have to be careful not to stutter. Regardless of how many times we have taught a course, the first day is filled with excitement, anticipation, and yes, nervousness. "What if I blow it on the very first day? Will I ruin the entire semester by getting off on the wrong foot? What if I forget to bring something that I need? Wait—what do I need for the first day of class? There is so much to cover and I don't want to overwhelm them right off the bat." These are all questions that we have asked ourselves over the years.

Fortunately, the literature on first-day activities is rich and varied and we have tried a variety of effective ways to begin the semester. Many of the suggestions we share here can also be fruitfully used throughout the semester. The information available on first-day activities is so expansive that if you ever get stuck and can't think of an activity for any class at any time during the semester, try searching first-day activities or "icebreakers" on the web. Both topics yield a treasure trove. We just Googled "first-day activities for college" and found over a hundred links. You can easily fill your teaching toolbox with productive ideas. As we move through our suggestions for first-day activities, we will also offer suggestions for how these same activities could be used later in the semester.

Where to start planning for the first day of class? Start by thinking about what you want to accomplish. Finish this sentence: "At the end of the first day of class students will . . ." One of the most common themes in the literature on first-day activities is setting expectations. That is, "At the end of the first day of class, students will know what I expect from them in this class." That does not sound like much fun, but it can be! There are at least four goals that you might consider for the first day: clarifying expectations, setting the tone for the class, presenting icebreakers so students can get to know each other, and introducing course content.

Clarifying Expectations

What you want to accomplish on the first day of class and what your students want from the first day may not be the same. For example, if students want to know what is expected of them in the course and you want to focus on building a comfortable learning community, your first-day activity could backfire by frustrating students rather than moving them toward your goal. Ideally, you would meet more than one goal at a time. Hermann and Foster (2008) suggest an activity that helps you both communicate your expectations and serves as a means by which students get to know each other and can become more comfortable with you. This activity is a win-win. They use what is labeled a "reciprocal interview activity." Students are divided into small groups and asked to discuss a list of topics Hermann and Foster (2008) give them on a handout. These topics include their goals, how the instructor can help them achieve the goals, reservations they might have about the course, the best thing that could happen in the course, the worst thing that could happen in the course, and what resources they bring to the course (prior experience, prior knowledge). After the discussion, each group selects a reporter who conveys the group's response to the instructor and the rest of the class.

The instructor listens carefully and takes notes. The second phase of the activity requires the students to select a different representative to interview the instructor. The groups create questions for the instructor to address and are free to ask anything as long as it is related to the course. With a pretest/post-test assessment of the activity, the authors find that students felt that the activity was helpful and that they recommend the activity to other professors. They also report becoming more comfortable participating in class and with approaching the instructor.

If you do not choose to use this activity on the first day, you could easily adapt it for later use. For example, you could create questions about a set of readings or about another class activity. If you chose to use it to help students master course content the questions could include, "What do the set of readings have in common? How do they differ? Which of the readings did you find the most challenging? Which of the readings did you find most helpful to your understanding of . . . (some concept or idea)? Which of the course outcomes was most directly addressed in these readings?" After the student representatives present their findings, or after a few groups report out if you have a large class, students could reform in their groups and create remaining questions they might have about the readings that they want you and perhaps the rest of the class to address.

One of the most common set of suggestions we have heard about and used ourselves is asking students to help set the course expectations. This can be done with an entire class but we usually ask students to work together in groups or pairs. First, list the basic categories of expectations in whatever medium works for you—writing on a board, showing a PowerPoint, etc. Many of our expectations may be quite obvious to us yet unclear to our students. These categories might include expectations about handing assignments in on time, cell phone use, the use of computers and tablets in class, essay exams, etc. You may also be teaching a class that is different from most other classes in the curriculum that require special instruction. Methods and statistics classes, for example, may have very different expectations than substantive courses and upper-level courses have different expectations than introductory classes. Make sure you list the categories that are essential for your class. Experiential classes are another category of classes that require especially explicit discussion of behavioral expectations. Maxine teaches a summer study abroad class in London. She finds this to be a particularly helpful exercise because there are many expectations that students might not have encountered previously or that are more important in a study abroad class. Helping each other is more important in a study abroad class than on campus where they have many other students and faculty members to call on. When students are truly strangers in a strange land (remember Simmel?), they must rely on each other to manage their daily lives as well as classwork. One of Maxine's categories for expectations is "Being a member of a community." There are other more usual expectations that have an added significance in a study abroad class. For example, being late for class when an entire class is visiting a site that requires group tickets could ruin an outing for the entire group.

You can use students to provide input on a variety of different topics throughout the semester. For example, Maxine did not like the instructions she was using to set up the structure for student debates. As she was trying to revise them, she decided to ask her first-year students for input about successful classroom debates, expecting that she might get very little from them. Nothing could be further from the truth. She put up the categories on big sheets of paper across the room, gave out a few "stickies," and asked students to offer suggestions. They were very helpful and student debates were better that semester than at any other time!

While neither Kath nor I have ever had asking students to help set expectations for a class backfire on us, and students are usually much more strict than we are, we do strongly suggest that if there are expectations that are not negotiable, you must make that clear. For example, when Maxine teaches a small first-year seminar, any exam will be take-home essays. Multiple-choice exams are not an option. Kath expects that all electronic devices (except clickers in classes that use them) will be put away (not just put on vibrate) for every class. She asks students to let her know if they have to leave early, so that she is not distracted, wondering if she needs to send someone to see if the student is sick, etc. In larger classes, she asks students to hang a sign off desks which says the name each student would like to be called. She also explains that there is an opening activity (daily writing, a clicker question) that starts at exactly the start of class, so being on time is crucial and that students should expect to stay in class for the full time period, because there also is an ending activity every day. She then promises not to have class go beyond its required time.

Setting the Tone

Setting the tone for the class and beginning to make students comfortable with you, each other, and hopefully the structure and content of the class, is another common goal for first-day activities. Maxine has begun to place more emphasis on culture than she did in the past. Recently she discovered an exercise she is just itching to try. Stearns (1998) describes the use of a "Me-Bag," i.e., a bag of items that symbolize who we are. Stearns brings hers in the first day and models how the students will introduce themselves to each other using these physical items. Maxine's first "Me-Bag" will include a 6-ounce bottle of Coke (the kind that is an antique now), a coaster with a picture of London, two male dolls, an artificial flower, a tennis ball, and a copy of an article she published. The artifacts represent her Southern heritage, her love of London, her son and her husband, her garden, her favorite sport, and her job as a teacher-scholar. She asks that students create their own "Me-Bag" and bring it to class during the next class. The point is that everyone is a valuable member of the class, that culture includes physical artifacts, and that symbols have meaning. Maxine will follow up with asking students to draw another student's name out of a hat and ask them to write what they learned about their classmate. This is an exercise that would also fit nicely later on in the class when culture is examined more carefully. Maxine tried a version of this in her study abroad class in London asking students to bring an object that symbolized who they were at the beginning of the trip and who they were at the end of the trip. All of the 21 students indicated that they had changed because of the study abroad experience and could articulate that change.

Maxine gives out the syllabus, and asks the students to find one thing on the syllabus that interests them and one thing that they have a question about. She then asks for volunteers to share their interests and questions. Surprisingly enough, Maxine gets more "interest" statements than questions. She follows up with a "reading quiz" on the syllabus. The quiz has multiple-choice questions that include identifying readings, the major course requirements, expectations about the use of cell phones, etc. Many of the responses are serious responses but some are also silly choices like, "Dr. Atkinson expects you to swear an oath to name your firstborn child 'Maxine' and 'students who bring Dr. Atkinson Tootsie rolls every day to class get an A.'" (Invariably some student brings Tootsie rolls the next class day!) A sense of humor can go a long way toward creating a more relaxed class.

However much we want our students to feel comfortable, we also set limits. Maxine wears an "NC State Ally" t-shirt to class to be clear that she is a safe person for LGBT students to talk with and to stress that homophobic harassment is not allowed in her class. While she tries her best to set a tone of humor and comfort, she also stresses that there are lines that are not to be crossed. In large classes she has had students walk out, clearly in protest of her strong message. So be it. She does not usually wear the t-shirt the first day of class but wonders if she is doing the right thing. On the one hand, she does not want to seem overly antagonistic; on the other hand, she wants her LGBT students to feel comfortable. We would be the first to admit that we do not have all the answers.

Icebreakers

Many strong instructors use icebreakers to begin to construct a learning community. Eggleston and Smith (2005) argue that icebreakers that are relevant to a specific class are the most effective. Among the several they propose, one is similar to the "Me-Bag" discussed above. They suggest asking students to introduce themselves by sharing something that they have with them in class that says something about who they are. Students might come up with items such as t-shirts with slogans, pictures, or colors that represent something about themselves. Another example is from a developmental psychology class. There students were asked to link an object to their childhood, and a student in tennis shoes responded that when he was a child he had a hard time learning to tie his shoes.

Eggleston et al. (2005) suggest using cartoon strips with messages relevant to course content. Each student is given one panel of a cartoon when they enter the class and told to find the students with the panels that finish their cartoon. Obviously you would need cartoons that had more than one panel. Those should be pretty easy to find for sociology courses. In one day, Maxine's daily paper had several we could use. "Pickles" had one about grandparenting. "Jump Start" focused on students and teachers and "Dilbert" made fun of corporate rules about budgeting.

Introduction to the Discipline/Content

Introducing the discipline is another good goal for the first day of class. Atkinson (2010) uses an icebreaker that accomplishes this goal. She asks students to complete an identity statement 10 times. She asks students to complete this sentence: "I am _____." Once they have finished writing their 10 identity statements, they pair up and share their information. The third step is to have each student introduce their partner to the class. Maxine takes notes on each student on whatever technology is available in the classroom (e.g., the blackboard, white board, or sometimes on the class computer). She organizes these identities by gender, creating one column for women and one for men. (If the class is large, only about 15 pairs introduce themselves.) Once the introductions are made and thus the data is collected, Maxine asks students to search for patterns in the data and she proposes a hypothesis, that is, that gender predicts identity. She asks students if there is evidence to support this hypothesis. Usually there is a gendered pattern to the responses. Women students usually make identity statements that focus on relationships, such as, "I am a sister, I am a daughter, I am a good friend." Men students are more likely to say things such as, "I am a soccer player" or "I am from Raleigh, NC." Maxine makes sure that she emphasizes that sociology is an empirical discipline, noting that we did not argue whether men or women make different identity statements, rather we collected the data. She stresses that the class will be discussing data throughout the semester and that students should expect to be actively involved in every class.

Winston (2007) gives an example of another way for students to introduce themselves to the class and to learn a sociological lesson. Specifically, he says, "Please, tell us about you" (Winston 2007:161). He repeats this exact same request for each student. After each student speaks, he nods his head, smiles and says, "Thank you." What Winston (2007) observes is predictable. Quickly a pattern is established. Students give their name, class status, and major, and sometimes hometown. After the introductions, Winston follows up with a discussion of what was said and why. He leads the students to discover the definition of norm (rule about appropriate behavior), that a norm is collective, and that positive sanctions encourage the behavior and negative sanctions discourage other behaviors (Winston 2007).

Another good way to combine icebreakers with introducing the discipline is sometimes called "the circles" (Nilson 2010). Give each student a sheet of paper with a large central circle drawn in it and smaller circles around it. Students write their names in the center of the large circle. They then write the names of groups they most strongly identify with in the smaller circles, leaving space for three other students' names. The groups they might choose are home state, size of hometown, age, family size, sibling order, religion, etc. Listing possible group memberships on the board for them to choose from is a good idea. Each student then moves around the room finding students who are most like them or you might choose to ask students to find students who are least like them. Make sure you take the opportunity to talk about the centrality of groups in sociology after students have found their group members. This exercise can obviously be used at other points in the semester. For example, if you were studying religion and wanted to create heterogeneous groups, you could include religion as one of the membership choices and create groups based on this exercise.

The first day of class is unique in the semester. While making a mistake on the first day of class will not assure failure, getting off to a good start helps set the stage for success for you and your students. We suggest that you consider four goals: clarifying expectations, setting the tone for the class, introducing students to each other, and introducing the discipline.

▶▶▶ CHAPTER 12
TEACHING FAILURES

As sociologists, we understand how crucial the socialization process is for learning statuses and roles. We know that individuals learn both through doing behaviors well, but also by failing. Succeeding and failing can both be useful opportunities for growth (Rowling 2008). We thought it was important to talk about teaching failures openly in this book, for several reasons. We all have moments of success and failure. While we often share our successes via publications and presentations at professional meetings, we usually keep our failures hidden, stowed away from our colleagues, our students in other classes, and perhaps if we work hard enough to forget, from ourselves. But socialization theories show us that failures can be as important to building successful behavior as successes are. We believe that if we embrace failure as an essential part of the learning process, our social construction of what failure is, and more importantly, how we should "manage" it, when it happens to us or to our students, will shift.

Many of us try to cultivate a classroom environment which does not penalize students who make mistakes, but few of us actively cultivate failure in our classes. We believe, similar to McIntosh (2012:1) that, "If we do not encourage students to make mistakes within the controlled environment of a classroom, we might find that they will never attempt great things outside that environment." We are careful how we phrase our comments to a student whose answer is incorrect, trying to be encouraging yet also pointing out errors (Berkeley

Center for Teaching and Learning n.d.). We work hard to balance our comments on papers and always lead with a positive one (Harris 1997). Edward Burger encourages; indeed he challenges professors to urge students to fail (2012), in order that they might learn more deeply. Burger (2012) highlights a key sociological fact: how failure is processed interactionally by a faculty member and a student, and between students, can build bonds with our students or destroy them; it can deepen learning or turn students off from daring to try.

How can we help them get past this fear of failure? First, we need to listen carefully to how we talk with our students about their mistakes. Of course, we have to show them their errors, but how we do that is central to reducing their fears. Do we belittle or build them up? Second, finding ways to normalize failure in our classrooms—or even encourage it—could help to reduce their fear. For example, a friend of Kath's who teaches statistics tells her students that each student will talk every day. She simply goes around the room every day, calling on each student in turn. Some days the student will be correct and other days, incorrect. The latter, she tells them, can even be more useful than the former, because errors can diagnose a mathematical misunderstanding which is likely shared by others.

For the last decade or so, Kath has put her students' grades where her mouth is. Instead of just touting the importance of failing she now tells students that if they want to earn an A, they must fail regularly throughout the course of the semester—because 5 percent of their final grade is based on their "quality of failure." Would such a scheme provoke a change in attitude? Absolutely—with this grading practice in place, students gleefully take more risks and energetically engage in discussions.

And when a student (say, Aaron) makes a mistake in class, he exclaims, "Oh well, my quality of failure grade today is really high." The class laughs and then quickly moves to the serious next step—answering: Why was that wrong? It's not enough to console an incorrect response with a nurturing, "Oh Aaron, that's not quite right, but we still think you're the best! Now, does anyone else have another guess?" Instead, a mistake solicits either the enthusiastic yet honest response, "Congratulations, Aaron—that's wrong! Now what lesson or insight is Aaron offering us?" or the class question "What do you think? Is Aaron correct?" Either way, the students have to listen actively and then react, while Aaron sees his comment as an important element that allows the discussion to move forward.

But before we can discuss how to help students understand their own failures and guide them into turning them into learning opportunities, we need to think about the times each of us has failed in our status as professor. It is relatively easy to brainstorm a list of common failures that we might make as professors (Table 12.1) or which might happen to us.

Here's a story about one of Kath's most embarrassing moments in front of a class—a linguistic one—and how it ended up turning around the classroom dynamics. It was a once-a-week, 4-hour Sociological Theory night class, when her school was still on the quarter system. Class started at 6:00 p.m. and ended at 10:15 p.m. (fifteen minutes were scheduled as a "break"). The room was crowded and freezing cold, and everyone seemed exhausted although it was only the third week of the quarter. Kath had planned to cover the "early years" of sociology: transformative events in Western Europe from the 1300s–1700s and Comte's founding of the discipline as a response to those events, and then to cover Herbert Spencer's theories.

It was about 90 minutes into class when trouble first appeared. Kath had just started discussing Spencer, and she almost tripped over the term "organism"; but it was just an internal moment, she didn't actually misspeak it. But that sensitized her, to the point where she was on edge the rest of the night. Unfortunately, teaching about Spencer proved difficult—it seemed that in just about every sentence some version of the term "organism" popped up.

Well, it happened. She heard it the moment it came out of her mouth: she said "orgasm" instead of "organism." What should she do? Press on rapidly, hoping no one noticed? Own up to the mistake and clarify it? Bluff her way through and maybe call a break? The latter strategy immediately seemed like a good idea . . . except students were beginning to process what had happened. A few turned to each other, scribbling notes about her gaffe while a few others could be seen whispering to each other, "Did she really just say that?" A few others turned beet red; clearly they too had heard it.

So Kath decided to own up to the verbal slip. She corrected it, everyone laughed, and on went the class. Only each time the term "organism" came up in the conversation, Kath would pause and gather her thoughts, so it wouldn't happen again. Her students quickly caught on and would helpfully shout out "organism" before she could say it. With about 30 minutes to go (and after 59 more uses of "organism," according to one student who counted them), try as she might, she said "orgasm" again, and the entire class laughed hysterically. The class was tired, frazzled after a long day, and they just couldn't stop laughing. Some laughed until tears came (you had to be there!). Kath tried to pull the class back together and restore order, but the laughter just continued (hers included!). Finally, she realized that there was nothing to do—class had effectively ended! They packed up, with most of them still laughing as they walked to their cars.

TABLE 12.1 COMMON TEACHING FAILURES

Kind of Error	Possible Contexts When Error Might Occur	Examples of Errors
Content mistake	Lectures Discussions Presentation slides Notes E-mail During office hours	Mistakenly listing the types of suicide, according to Durkheim Incorrectly performing mathematical operation while teaching a statistical formula
Linguistic mistake	In class Typos in written communication	Saying "Marx" when you meant "Max" (as in Max Weber) Saying "conflict theory" when you meant to say "control theory"
Procedural mistake	In class In e-mail During office hours	Telling students that the test is over chapters 5 to 8 when it is actually over chapters 4 to 7 Telling class wrong date for next test
Technology mistake	In class In cyberspace	Sending private e-mail to entire class Responding with incorrect information to student's e-mail Forgetting electronic file needed for class Forgetting USB stick
Emotion Management	In class In office During office hours Over e-mail	Making a humorous remark to student (in person or in writing) that is interpreted by student as hurtful Displaying anger about something in one or more students' work Expressing frustration when a student asks a question that you just answered several times
Technology fails	In class In classroom management system	Computer will not turn on, so cannot show presentation slides Not having a backup plan sans technology Clicker software did not gather data from students
Classroom management	In class Online	Not enforcing classroom norms consistently Not containing an angry student's in-class tirade, and others become involved Real or apparent favoritism of some students over others

The next week, Kath was unsure how class might go—would everyone remember the verbal error? Could they rally and focus or would the twice-made error have poisoned the classroom environment? She needn't have worried. What happened was quite different. A few students teased her about blushing so much and about laughing until she cried, and then they went on to have a productive conversation about Durkheim. But throughout the rest of the quarter, students often harkened back to the "orgasm" night, even mentioning in student evaluations about how the slip of the tongue had humanized her and made it easier for them to accept her comments about misspellings and grammar errors in their written work.

The linguistic error made its way into student culture in her department. The next quarter, when she taught theory again, students, when they entered class the day of "the early years" lecture, seemed different. They seemed more alert, more attentive, even before the class started. When Kath commented on that, all the students looked down at their desks and seemed uncomfortable. Finally one brave student started to say, "Well, last quarter you said . . ." and then her voice trailed off. Before the student had said that, Kath had actually forgotten what had happened the term before. Now it all came rushing back to her. Despite the reminder, she made it through that class without the error, and at the end of the evening, the class gave her a standing ovation. Once again, even the possibility of the verbal error by the professor had brought the class together and changed its internal dynamic.

So while we as faculty often fear making mistakes in front of our students, Kath's example shows that sometimes our errors can be pedagogically useful. They can humanize the professor, especially in a highly abstract class such as Sociological Theory, and minimize social distance. Of course, that Kath's error did this was in part due to how she interactionally managed the error. Had she bluffed her way through—twice—and practiced civil inattention, pretending not to notice her verbal error, it is likely that the classroom dynamics would have been starkly different.

Owning our failures privately can keep us grounded as professors; owning them in front of/with our students keeps us human in their eyes. We don't want "hero worship" from them (and we hope that you do not, either); we aim for honest intellectual engagement with our students. And that engagement involves accepting each partner's moments of success, of confusion, and of failure. How we manage failure interactionally can be a great sociological lesson—as well as a great life lesson—for our students . . . and for ourselves as well.

PEDAGOGICAL LESSONS FROM FAILURE

Until those two weeks in her theory class, Kath had never spent much time writing about failure in her teaching journal, where she writes pedagogical notes after every class. But now she spent hours thinking about failure. Why might things have gone the way that they did? Whatever the mistake, we believe that there are at least four pedagogical lessons to be learned.

Take Responsibility

Kath owned up to the error immediately. How many times have you as faculty wanted a student to take responsibility for an error—for perhaps forgetting a due date or that there was a test? How many student excuses have you been given, that you later learned were not true? Having the professor model a better response to an error can be a great teaching moment for students. So if such an opportunity occurs, seize it. Talk it through with them.

The World Won't End If You Fail in Front of Students

Whether it is a linguistic failure such as Kath's was, or getting a date wrong in a lecture—you will likely spend more time worrying about it than they will . . . especially if you can own the error, correct it, and move on. We know of one professor who teaches statistics, who intentionally makes a mathematical mistake during the first week of class, in order to let students know that those kinds of errors are part of the learning process and that it will be okay if students make them as well. Our culture tends to construct mistakes as symbolizing failure and weakness, instead of as constructing mistakes as a routine part of learning. Burger (2013) argues, "Any great innovation or great new idea, whether it's a medical breakthrough, a sociological discovery, or a scientific realization, occurred through a sequence or succession of failed attempts." Normalizing failures just as much as we normalize being successful can go a long way to minimizing the negative pedagogical impacts of our mistakes.

Take Time to Prepare

Here's another one of Kath's failure stories. It was only the second time that she had taught Sociology of Religion (which is one of her specialties) and she was still in the "everything and the kitchen sink" mode of class coverage (see chapter 3 on coverage). Her students, by gosh, were going to learn everything that she knew! The topic of the day was Weber's concept of charisma. Students had struggled just a bit with differentiating between the more pop culture use of the term *charisma* and the Weberian meaning when she had taught it for the first time the year before. So she decided to try another technique to teach the concept. Three days before the class, she read Lewis's (1989) "Of Card Tricks and Charismatic Leaders" in *Teaching Sociology*. Done correctly, the card trick mimics a charismatic leader's ability to persuade, even manipulate, followers without being detected. What a great idea! So she decided to try the card trick in class. She practiced several times with her husband, and she felt mostly ready. An hour before class, she felt really anxious and almost bailed on using the card trick, but she calmed down and went with it.

At the start of class she asked for a volunteer to help with a card trick demonstration, who she would need later in the class period. A male student who had never seemed that interested in the class was eager to volunteer. He was nearly jumping out of his seat, waving his hand energetically. Kath was surprised that he seemed so interested, and felt that since this was the first time he'd seemed very engaged in class activities—something of course she always wants to encourage—she should select him to help her. Class proceeded, and Kath talked about how Weber analyzed different types of authority, building to Lewis's (1989) card trick to illustrate the charismatic type . . . and it didn't work. Kath was shocked, even crushed. Of all concepts to have such a momentous failure—charisma is about specialness—she had failed miserably!

All afternoon Kath fretted about what she'd done wrong with the card trick. Several hours after class, the student who had volunteered popped into her office and said, "Just so you know, I instantly knew the card trick you were going to do, so I deliberately messed it up." Well, mission accomplished! In one way, it was a relief; at least she had not made a mistake doing the exercise. But she had never considered deliberate sabotage as an explanation for what had happened.

The more she thought about this pedagogical failure, the more she realized she needed to have been much more prepared to use the card idea in class than she was. Barely giving herself two days to practice had left her more focused on doing it correctly than picking up on any interactional signals her volunteer might be giving off, because she was not yet comfortable with the card trick. Looking back, Kath realized that the volunteer had been *too* eager, given his previous level of engagement in the class. She remembered feeling that it was odd for him to volunteer, but didn't listen to that internal voice. She "shushed" it, mad at herself for not being happy that the student had finally decided to get more involved. Had Kath been more confident about her ability to do the card trick correctly, she would have had more energy for focusing on her students at that moment.

Don't Assume; Check and Check Again

Some mistakes can be prevented if we think about what issues students are likely to have and prepare for them. Here's another example of a mistake that Kath made. For probably 15 years, all her tests were worth 75 points. Then, in Fall 2012, for several reasons, she changed her tests in Introduction to Sociology to be worth 60 points. When it came time to write her first test, she just sat down and wrote it and then announced the structure of the test over the course management system's e-mail. The next time she logged on, a small e-riot had ensued! Why? Because she'd written a test worth 75 points, of course, instead of 60! Old habits die hard—and while everyone calmed down when she apologized over e-mail and in person at the start of the next class, the error didn't have to happen. If she had just looked at the syllabus before writing the announcement about the test, the situation could have been averted. With the number of classes we all teach, even if you think you know the information it is worth the time it takes to look it up. Spend a moment verifying information before announcing it to students—especially when it involves a major assignment, a test, or their final grades.

One of the most painful days of Maxine's career was also a day when she learned a lesson she has never forgotten. One of her students, who usually made strong contributions to class discussion, was initially sullen and then fell asleep. Maxine asked another student to nudge him awake and then made a remark about appropriate places to sleep. The student got up and left the class. Later in the day the student's advisor called to tell Maxine that her student's father had died the night before. Maxine has never again called a student out in front of the rest of the class for sleeping or seeming to be unengaged. She is now much more careful to talk to students individually after class.

HELPING STUDENTS WITH THEIR OWN FAILURES / COACHING THEM FOR SUCCESS

Failing, however, is not limited to those of us with faculty status. Every term we are confronted with students who fail—be it on a small assignment, a major test, or perhaps even the entire course. But we have to be honest with ourselves and with our students: we can get frustrated, even angry sometimes, when individual students or large numbers of them make mistakes. We believe we have all been there, and done that. How can we both help students learn from their failures and take steps to reduce the likelihood of these errors?

They Are More than Their Performance in Our Class

All of us have probably had one or more students whose entire identity appears wrapped up in their final grade. Many of these students, however, are not "failures" in the typical sense that they did not pass the course. Rather, their B grade is not good enough for them; they (or their parents, or both) require an A in order to feel successful. According to Lahey (2013), overparenting is a "misguided attempt to improve their child's current and future personal and academic success." She contends that when children make mistakes, it's vital that parents remember that the educational benefits of consequences—like failure, or loss of points for not turning an assignment in on time, etc.—are a gift, not a dereliction of duty by the teacher.

Students who have to have an A are fascinating; they usually are aware of their average in the class at all times and often fight for every point. They are often frequent visitors during office hours, pleading their case. Some of us initially might be happy to have these students drop by, but when it happens every time an assignment is returned, and the debate is over arcane reasons for wanting perhaps one more point, enthusiasm can turn quickly to frustration. We might even want to start labeling them as "grade grubbers" on our bad days. "'Grade grubbing,' in which students seek high grades for minimum effort, is often cited as a symptom of the consumer orientation of contemporary college students" (Delucchi and Korgen 2002:104). Delucchi and Korgen's study (2002) found 73 percent of sociology undergraduates are more concerned with obtaining high grades than with learning. But these students often have identities so connected to their academic standing, that anything we can do to help them to see that what they perceive as "failing" might be constructed differently by others.

Such students can tax faculty energy; not just our time, to be sure, but working with them to reconstruct their views of any work that is not an A can be worthwhile. Many of them are under enormous pressures. They might have parents who expect nothing less than As. For others, it is not just parents who create these expectations. Where we both teach, many of the students are first-generation college students. Some carry on their shoulders the hope that life can be made better through education, for generations of their extended families. "Failing" their families means that other family members younger than they are might not be allowed the opportunity to try college (University of Illinois Counseling Center n.d.). Their burden is enormous, and they often carry it alone.

One way to work with these types of students is by showing them that others might construct "success" differently. Many of the students Kath has in her Introduction to Sociology class hope to get accepted to the campus's Bachelor of Science in Nursing program. So Kath tries to sit down with every student who feels like a failure if she or he earned a high B on a test and together they delve deep into the admission data for the College of Nursing. By looking at the data, students quickly learn that their belief that they have to have a 4.0 GPA for admission is not accurate. This kind of interaction can be useful, because it is not the "teacher's" construction of reality versus theirs, but rather both teacher and student investigating the actual data. Of course these students know that the better their grades, the better their chances of admission, but seeing that the average GPA for the new BSN admission class for the previous year was 3.4 can ease some of the pressures that they might feel.

Understand, though, that the burden these students feel won't dissipate with just one or two conversations. They need mentors who will support them and help them to process these familial expectations as they progress through college. Kath tries to keep in touch with many of these students, long after they have completed their Introduction to Sociology course with her, supporting them through the rigorous core curriculum courses they have to take, and she will often write a letter of reference for their nursing application.

Schools need to find creative ways to work with such students, such as support groups, or using role-playing as a tool to learn how to interact with family members, and so on. If Kath has students from her Introduction to Sociology supersection who declare Sociology as a major, she works with them on how to talk with their families about the value of our major and what they can do with the degree (see also Hillsman [2012], a letter to parents written by the ASA's Executive Officer).

Sometimes It Is about Them

Other students may fail in a more traditional way; they bomb a test, or forget an assignment, and so on. Our job as faculty is to help them to analyze what happened and why, and address it moving forward in the term.

Forgetfulness. For example, many of us who teach primarily first-year students know that it can take them a while to understand they have to be organized, keeping track of when assignments are due and when tests are scheduled. Many forget daily assignments and those lost points can add up quickly. We can talk with them, letting them brainstorm about what they could do differently. Only if they seem unable to think of possible solutions, we can ask them if they want some other ideas. If they say yes, consider mentioning that they might want to keep a paper calendar or a white board in their room; or even better, that they add reminders in their smartphones. If we can keep the conversation on a practical level, not scolding them but just showing them how their continued forgetfulness could impact their grade, many will be open to our advice.

They Fear Making Us Mad and Sometimes This Can Paralyze Them. At the end of the second class after Kath's linguistic error, she asked her theory class if they were mad that she made the linguistic errors. Puzzled, they said, "No, why would you think we were?" That led to a good conversation about how some students may feel a faculty member is mad at them if they make errors in a paper/test/assignment, and therefore often stop seeking help. Each student admitted to thinking that about their college professors. Interactionally, we know that fear can create social distance—something we don't want to encourage with our students.

As the conversation about students who feared making their professors mad continued that evening between Kath and her theory students, one student asked, "Well, what are things that will piss you off, Dr. Lowney? . . . because I want to avoid them." That question caught Kath a bit off guard; she hadn't thought about student behaviors in that way too often. While she said something that night, she asked for more time and promised to answer the question more thoroughly the next week.

That was an uncomfortable week of pedagogical journaling for Kath (see Purcell 2013), because owning up to getting mad at students was not easy to ponder. But she realized that there *were* some things that did bother her and she wished students would not do them. From her journaling and subsequent conversations with students, she developed a list of behaviors (which she now includes in her syllabi) that bother her (e.g., not stapling papers which are to be handed in, compounded by not putting one's name on every page). Student failure here is not because they don't understand the content, but because each professor's list of concerns is idiosyncratic. Kath's students taught her that they would rather not fail her and that they wanted to do well.

But it is not enough to simply make the list, include it in our syllabus, or perhaps post it somewhere on the learning management system. Students need reminders in the moment. Kath now includes a short checklist of "Did you remember to do the following things?" in the directions for every assignment. She mentions them in class at least one week before major assignments are due, sometimes with an accompanying presentation software slide for a visual reminder. Starting in Spring 2013, she also included that list in the online directions "box" in the learning management system, with the additional wording of "Not doing the following things will be automatic point deductions. Have you double-checked your assignment for these issues?" These frequent reminders can coach students to take the directions seriously. Moreover, if a student still makes these kinds of errors, a follow-up conversation can focus on how he or she overlooked the frequent reminders of how to do well rather than simply pointing out the errors. As Burger noted, "A bombed assignment becomes a gift from teacher to student—an opportunity to engage in some high-quality failure, by assessing one's shortcomings and making positive changes" (Davis 2012).

Class Data Collection as Evidence. We both collect a lot of data about our students and their learning throughout the course of a term. These data then become the driving force for our course activities and assessments in future terms. Here's one example of that:

Every semester, Kath keeps statistics on what concepts caused her students the most difficulty, both on tests and on her daily clicker/student response system questions. She then uses that data to prepare scenarios for in-class group activities, and so on. Over the past three years, the concepts of role strain and role concept have been difficult for her students, especially about how to keep them separate. Students in earlier years seemed to grasp them much more quickly and confidently than her recent students. Having that data has allowed Kath to redesign her course to address the difficulty which is likely to arise. She has devised several scenarios, of various levels of complexity, which focus on differentiating these concepts. Some are in-class activities, while others are assigned before class for students to consider, and with follow-up activities in class. Others are kept for testing purposes. This has meant that other concepts, with which the students struggle less, are cut back on just a bit. This is an ongoing process of analyzing data and adjusting course content.

This kind of data collection is a large part of the "Just in Time Teaching" activities promoted by Eric Mazur and Jessica Watkins (2009). That pedagogical strategy asks faculty to think through common errors students make with the discipline's concepts and to build learning activities which zero in on those difficulties, allowing students to see how what they think they know may not be correct, and coach them to mastery.

No matter how failure emerges in our classes, the best pedagogy will use it as a teaching moment—either about sociology, about life, or about their intersection. So don't be afraid of failure—your own or theirs—but be ready to utilize it when it happens. Inevitably, failure is a part of the classroom journey teachers and students take together.

SECTION 3

ASSESSMENTS, GRADING, AND EVALUATIONS

►►► CHAPTER 13
MEASURING STUDENT LEARNING

How do we know that students are learning the sociological content that we want them to learn? This question is at the core of teaching—and therefore also at the core of the assessment of student learning. So many more stakeholders are asking that question nowadays, given what is happening in higher education. Legislators, parents, higher-education administrators, accrediting bodies, the business community, state taxpayers—and hopefully our students—are asking this question. For those of us who teach in state-assisted/state-funded institutions of higher education—where both of us teach—the pressure is on to prove the answer to that question. No longer can faculty say "trust us—our students are learning" and have that be an acceptable answer (if it ever was).

Being able to measure student learning is a critical skill; it is also one with which sociologists should be comfortable, since conceptualization and operationalization are part and parcel of the research that we conduct. In this chapter we'll offer our thoughts on measuring student learning and give several examples about how we might do so with our students. We'll begin with some of the more common strategies for measuring student learning/student success.

TYPES OF MEASUREMENT

There are two main types of measurement we want to suggest to you: embedded assessments and, for lack of a better term, "special" assessments. Embedded assessments are those moments which you organically structure into your class in order to see how your students are doing. These might be Think-Pair-Share moments, which Maxine uses frequently, especially if you require each group to report back to the entire class. Having a small notebook with you will allow you to make notes about patterns you hear (before you get back to your office or car)—be they mistakes in learning or successes, both of which you will want to share with the class. For Kath, these embedded assessments are primarily the low-stakes clicker questions which allow her and the students in her supersections to see instantaneously if students are understanding basic sociological definitions and concepts, in addition to her daily "exit ticket" questions, which students answer in written form as they are leaving class. Spending time after class going over the patterns she sees in these embedded assessments gives her an excellent overview of how students are learning and allows for rapid, targeted interventions.

What we call "special" assessments could be tests, as well as out-of-class papers, group projects which span several weeks, etc. Here students are asked to show learning of class content and weave that together with other knowledge (e.g., from other classes, from research required, from each other, etc.). Many special assessments require students to produce some sort of a product to be evaluated.

Regardless of the type of assessment, it is up to the faculty to ensure that it measures course content at an appropriate level of knowledge for the students involved. We turn now to that question.

SOME STRATEGIES FOR MEASUREMENT

The Pretest/Post-test Assessment

This approach allows you, the instructor, and the student to each see where the student started, and then to see how much new knowledge the student has gained by the end of the unit or the term. Such an assessment strategy makes the amount of new learning each student accomplished during the term quantifiable (i.e., coming to class and listening, participating in online and in-class discussions, doing the assigned readings, studying for classes and for tests, writing tasks which asked students to apply their knowledge to real-world situations, etc.).

Of course, the pedagogically intriguing issue is how to ask questions in both the pretest and post-test which get at the new learning which the student has gained. Should the same test be used for both instances of measurement? There are some advantages to asking the same questions, in particular that assessment of the same cognitive level of difficulty occurs during both tests. However, if you use this strategy, we would suggest changing the order of the questions and possibly, if it is an objective test, the order of the answer choices, to be sure that students are not just memorizing the pretest's content versus actually learning it.

On the other hand, using such a pretest and post-test strategy does not make as visible the *growth* in depth of learning. A pretest given early in the term might ask if students know what Mills meant by the phrase "the sociological imagination" and give paired answers from which the student might choose. An Introduction to Sociology student would likely not get that question correct (unless she is guessing or he had a high school sociology course) and if at the end of the term, the same student gets it correct, it can mean that the student was able to learn (or worse, just memorize) the book definition. Utilizing a different post-test, which requires students to apply Mills's concept to a short scenario and write a few sentences which illustrate the concept, gives a more detailed measure of student learning. But using different pre/post measures can make measurement more difficult.

Portfolio-based Assessment

Portfolios require that students gather work done in many/all classes in the major together and create a unified document which shows their growth as a sociological practitioner. Often this means that students use major writing projects from classes to create a paper or electronic portfolio. Some programs require final exams from classes to be included or some other objective measure of their work in each class. Faculty or outside evaluators then assess portfolios (either all of them or a sample, depending on the number of majors involved), looking for how students are expressing their sociological imagination.

Programs which use portfolio assessments often require students to respond to certain writing prompts at various points in their time in the degree program (e.g., first noncore sociology course, theory, research methods, senior capstone/seminar course). Ideally, these might be the same prompt or at least prompts which get at the same agreed-upon concepts, so that each student's learning is measured using the same assessment tool. Normally, individual students maintain their own portfolio (in paper or electronic form) and also add a summative experience which looks back on their sociological development. Faculty then can examine all or a sample of these portfolios at the end of an academic year, using a rubric which measures not only the students' sociological proficiency at each point in time but also longitudinally. This examination of students' sociological progress then gives feedback to the faculty about the program and how well students are meeting its learning goals and objectives.

Case Studies as Assessments

Introducing students to real-world problem-solving experiences can help faculty to see if students are able to go beyond mere regurgitation of concepts and definitions. Case studies show the nuances, complexities, and messiness involved in applied sociological research, policy analysis, and program evaluation (Ruggiero 2002). (For some excellent resources on using case studies, see the list at the end of this chapter.)

Here again, faculty may choose to use the same case study in order to assess student learning or may use case studies which involve similar concepts and problems to keep students' interest high. One way to use the same case study over time might be to ask first- and second-year students objective questions to assess if they can "see" concepts and apply them. In more advanced courses, students might be asked to write a policy brief based on the case study or to give sociological advice to a nonprofit organization involved in the case study. These latter ways of measurement also allow faculty to see if students can translate sociological insights to a variety of audiences through their writing, which might in itself be one of the assessments.

AN EXAMPLE OF THE MEASUREMENT OF STUDENT LEARNING: THE SOCIAL CONSTRUCTION OF REALITY

We want to begin with one of the first concepts that students in Introduction to Sociology and Social Problems classes confront—the social construction of reality—and trace how, in various courses, at different programmatic levels, faculty can assess the students' grasp of the concept. Here's how one Introduction to Sociology textbook explains the concept: "... the process by which a concept or practice is created and maintained by participants who collectively agree that it exists" (Ferris and Stein 2014:109). Years of teaching have taught us both that this is a deceptively simple concept, which many students struggle with (and confuse it with the sociological imagination). So here are some methods we use to help our students to understand the concept.

Kath devotes an entire day in her Introduction to Sociology class to the concept, with a lecture called, "When Is a Fire Not a Fire? The Social Construction of Reality." She tells the true story of Detroit Mayor Coleman Young and "Hell Night." Hell Night is the period a few days before and after Halloween. In the 1980s, Hell Night in Detroit was marked by an escalation of arson in abandoned buildings (Chafets 1991; Devil's Night [n.d.]; Risen 1989). In three nights, over 800 fires were set. Both citizens and the press felt that the mayor needed to crack down on this problem, but he seemed unable to do so in his first two terms. As he neared his third reelection, the mayor quietly redefined what a fire was. If it was in an abandoned building and did not threaten human life, then it was not called a fire and thus was not included in the fire statistics. Not surprisingly, that next Hell Night the number of recorded arson fires fell precipitously—after this new social construction of reality—and just a few days before the November election. Mayor Young swept to reelection, largely on his seemingly successful control of the hooligans active during Hell Night. It was not until Mayor Young was term-limited, and a new mayor was elected, that this new construction of what a "fire" meant became public. In reality, during the years when the numbers "fell" there had been more fires than ever before—only because the arsons did not meet the new definition of what a fire was, they therefore were not reported to the public and the press. Students enjoy this example, and wonder how something as tangible/physical as a fire could be redefined. That allows Kath to talk about how the social construction of reality involves status and power—that not all individuals have the same ability to accomplish such a reconstruction.

Kath then shifts to a less policy-driven example of the social construction of reality, by sharing two personal stories. First, when she was growing up in Seattle, beverages such as Pepsi, Sprite, and Coke were all called "pop." When she moved to graduate school in New Jersey, she learned that was not the case there. On her second day in New Jersey, hungry from moving in and wanting to make friends with her new housemates, she offered to call for a pizza to be delivered. While she was on the phone, a few housemates called out to "get something to drink too." So she asked for a big bottle of pop. The pizza employee laughed and hung up on her. Puzzled, she called back and when she said it again, the employee asked her, "What planet are you from, lady?" The pizza came, but nothing to drink. In trying to explain to her housemates that she had tried to order something to drink, she used the term "pop" again—only to be embarrassed by their hysterical laughter. They promptly informed her that the term was *soda*, not *pop*. She never said "pop" again to mean something to drink when in New Jersey. But at the end of that first year in graduate school, she went home for the summer. On the first full day back, her mom was creating a grocery list and asked Kath what she wanted. Kath promptly said "soda." When her mother came back with the groceries, Kath was unloading them, waiting for the beverages. When she pulled out a box of baking soda, she must have looked quizzical, for her mom said, "Yeah, what did you want with that anyway?" Only then did she realize she wasn't in New Jersey—where pop was soda—anymore! In groups of two, her students analyze that story, making clear links with the social construction of reality. Kath then shows the students the Pop versus Soda website (2014) and they look at how the same beverages are labeled differently, often by region. Students look at patterns and create tentative hypotheses about what might be behind the differences. This helps students to deepen their understanding of the concept.

The last story of the day involves the social construction of language. Kath tells her students that her high school Spanish class was hosting exchange students from Madrid. Kath had taken Spanish from the third grade and now was a junior in high school. She felt confident that she would be able to communicate easily with these students. Well, the day came when they arrived and a U.S. student in the class was paired up with a student from Madrid, and they were told to get acquainted. The young woman Kath was paired up with spoke *so fast*! It was hard to recognize any words; in fact for a few minutes Kath even wondered if she *was* speaking Spanish—it seemed so different from what she had learned. An hour later—defeated, upset, and more than a bit frustrated—Kath wanted to say to her partner that "I am embarrassed that I can't speak your language more fluently." Only she didn't know the word "embarrassed" in Spanish. So, she guessed and added Spanish endings to the English word "embarrassed." She whispered, "*Soy embarrassado*" (Kath's guess at spelling the word) and completed the sentence in Spanish. The young woman seemed startled, and looked puzzled. Growing more confident, Kath repeated the same sentence, only a bit louder. More puzzled looks . . . which prompted Kath to repeat it one more time, louder still. That last repetition captured the attention of the teacher. She came over and asked Kath what she was trying to say, so she said it again, even more forcefully. The exchange student was growing more and more nervous as all this ensued. The teacher almost yanked Kath from her chair, pulled her into the hallway and said, "What are you doing? You just said that you are pregnant because you cannot speak her language very well. Is that what you meant to say?" Uh, no! But like many Americans, Kath had fallen prey to the ethnocentric view that other languages must use English as their root, so she took *embarrassed* and added some "Spanish" endings. By this time in her recollection, many of Kath's students are laughing outright at the story and they say how embarrassing that must have been. And it was! But again, we can talk about how every language group creates its own grammar rules and learning them can be difficult for someone who has not grown up in the culture which created the rules, because we lack the cultural expertise which grounds the rules in real-life experiences. That ties directly back to the textbook definition.

So in 75 minutes, Kath's Intro Soc students have had the concept explained, had three disparate examples presented, and done group activities about each of them. They also have an opportunity to share an experience that they have had with the concept, first with a small group and then with the entire class if they wish. They have also had about 10 clicker questions about the concept and these examples are spaced throughout the class. In addition, Kath also uses "exit tickets"—a short writing assignment that each student does at the end of class where each can ask questions, verify if personal examples correctly illustrate the concepts we have been studying, or just admit to being lost and ask for further help. She will use the clicker question results and the exit tickets for that day's class to assess students' immediate grasp of the concept, the social construction of reality. She reads all exit tickets and writes individual responses. These allow her to offer immediate and targeted help to students. Then Kath posts common questions students asked that day to a discussion board in the course management system. She will answer them; students are welcome to reply to these posts until they feel they have grasped the concept.

Then on the first test, she asks several questions which assess students' comprehension of the concept. First she asks a rather straightforward vocabulary question which gets at the remembering level of learning in Bloom's Taxonomy (1956). This is just one way such a question could be phrased:

True or False   The social construction of reality refers to the connections between history and biography that Mills discussed.   (Answer: False)

Then she poses a question which asks students to think about the social construction of reality and link it to power (Bloom's [1956] "understanding" level), based on one of the examples used in the class:

True or False   All members of the Detroit fire department had the same power to change the definition of fire that Mayor Young did. (Answer: False)

Later on in the same test (which covers material about the sociological imagination, the social construction of reality, and a variety of concepts related to culture), there are several essay questions for students to answer. One of them is as follows:

A Martian UFO lands outside where you are living tonight and, exercising your sociological curiosity, you go out to meet the visitors. You are taken away to Mars. Congratulations! You are the first human to establish contact between our planet and Mars, so the entire planet is counting on your sociological insights to help us to understand our new "neighbors." While the Martians speak their own language, you "hear" their words in English inside your head and they hear yours in their language, so at least the very basic level of linguistic understanding is occurring. You will remain with them for one year and then you will come back to Earth and share what you have learned with the world's leaders and press. How will you go about explaining the Martian social construction of reality to us Earthlings? How will you decide what to tell us immediately? Why? Remember, the "why's" are the main sociological questions to answer. You must use "the social construction of reality" in your answer and at least two other concepts. For each sociological concept you use, you must correctly define it (2 points), use a correct example of the term as related to this question about social life on Mars (2 points), and explain why it is an example of the concept (1 point each). Total of 15 points possible (out of 75 points on this test).

This question probes more deeply into students' understanding of what the social construction of reality is, because they have to invent answers about what Mars culture might be like and the reasons why the Martians constructed their norms, values, language, knowledge, and belief systems the way that they did.

As students move through the Sociology degree program, faculty build on their knowledge of key sociological concepts and expect them to be able to handle more complex learning tasks. When Kath teaches the Sociology of Religion course (a 3000-level Institution course at Valdosta State), one of her first assignments deals squarely with the social construction of reality. In this class, all students must have had either Introductory Sociology or Social Problems, so they should have a basic working sense of the concept. And most do; what she struggles with as a teacher in this class—at least during class time—is challenging students' view of their own faith (if they have one) as the sole (right) way to be religious, so that they can better approach the faiths we will be studying with a cultural relativistic attitude. This is her way of getting students to notice how some might be ethnocentric about their own faith and too quickly criticize the faiths of others. So she asks students to construct a religion. This assignment occurs during the first three weeks of the semester. She introduces it on the very first day, so that if a student is extremely uncomfortable with the assignment they can talk about it together and the student has time to switch to another Institutions course if he or she wishes. Only two students have ever withdrawn from the class and stated that this exercise was the reason why. She usually gives students three ideas: a sport, usually American football (at any level from middle school to the NFL), some gendered item (e.g., some years it has been Barbie or a pink EasyBake Oven), and an electronic item (now she would probably say an iPhone or a generic smartphone). Individual students can also propose a different topic to center the faith around and seek her approval. Students have to create an origin story for the faith (how it was created and why it would be important to believers); list five beliefs central to the faith and their explanations; invent two prayers taught to children growing up in the faith; create a ritual wherein parishioners worship the sacred object; and explain how children, versus adults, would be socialized into the faith. In addition, they write a short paper about how they felt doing the assignment. Kath offers several questions to get them started thinking about their feelings, but most students go way beyond what she asks them to consider:

▶ Did you feel any sense of personal difficulty when you constructed a religion for this assignment? Why or why not? What was the basis for those feelings, if they arose? If these types of feelings didn't arise, why do you think that was? What might it say about your own socialization when it comes to religion and faith?

▶ How did you process any such feelings, if you had them? What did you say to yourself (or to others if you shared them) to manage the feelings about constructing a faith? Can you analyze how you processed these feelings sociologically? Think, for example, about how individuals handle occupying several statuses at a time, etc.

▶ Why do you believe Dr. Lowney created this assignment? What purpose does it have in a Sociology of Religion course? What are the one or two key concepts you think she wanted you to focus on as you were doing this assignment? Why, sociologically, did she want that?

▶ Please note: for this part of the assignment, I am only going to look at how you wrestled with the sociological concepts embedded in this assignment and how/if they became difficult for you. Feel free to be honest and I pledge to keep confidential anything you say to me, within the rules set up by VSU. I want you to engage sociologically with the assignment and the concepts. We will refer back to this assignment many times during the semester.

Kath uses a fairly simple rubric for this part of the assignment, based on her learning goals, which assess students' ability to apply knowledge (Bloom 1956): Did students understand that this was an assignment which focused primarily on the social construction of reality, ethnocentrism, and cultural relativism? If so, how deeply did they wrestle with these concepts applied to their own personal faith walk? This kind of metacognition assignment (Lang 2012; Tanner 2012) asks students to go deeper into understanding their process of learning and has been found to aid in retention of course content.

It is not unusual for her to receive a paper that goes something like this (a distillation of many papers):

I know what you were trying to have us do by constructing our own faith—you wanted us to see how all faiths are social constructions, made up over time by believers to answer the difficult questions about life. I get it. I know that is how sociology thinks. And I will strive to do that in class, I promise. However, I don't believe that when it comes to religion. It's fine to say that happens with the economy or politics, but my God [or Gods—some polytheists have also written an essay like this] gave my faith to humans and we must follow it or else. But while in class, I know that I need to be as culturally relativistic as I can be . . . and I will try.

Some students go on to talk about how it is not just religion that is not a social construction—so are the institutions of family and sexual norms. For Kath, receiving an essay that says something akin to the above is a huge pedagogical success. The student has recognized that s/he operates in several social groups at once (e.g., professionally as a sociologist and personally as a believer) and sees where they do not fit together easily. Kath created this assignment after a particularly tense time teaching the course, where several students seemed to seize every class discussion (online or in the classroom) as an opportunity to witness to the correctness of their faith. They always disparaged other faiths and could never step outside the norms and values of what they held to be sacred. Her goal in this exercise is NOT to change personal beliefs or to cast doubt on them, but to have students take this extremely important sociological concept, intellectually wrestle with it, and apply it to a thought system near and dear to many of her Southern students. Doing this early in the semester has changed the tone of many discussions later on; students are better able to catch themselves, each other, or Kath, being ethnocentric and are better able to process it when such a remark is made.

This is a time when Kath agrees with Maxine: not all students' writing has to be graded with a fine-toothed comb! Students earn most of the points for engaging with the question listed above. The remaining points are about identifying to what concepts the students believed the assignment was related. None of the personal statements are "graded" per se, although Kath will write comments on these sections, but they always are linked back to the concepts being analyzed. She also supports those students who have either chosen now as adults or who were born into households which did not have any religious socialization. Often their essays are poignant, with lots of self-disclosure about feeling lost in the religiosity of South Georgian culture.

In a third class, "Issues in Sociological Practice—Domestic Violence," Kath actually requires the class to practice the social construction of reality. The course is designed as if the members would be practitioners at a new domestic violence shelter. The class is split into working groups, who are tasked with different responsibilities: creating a name for the shelter and its mission statement/philosophy, creating and evaluating a list of possible programs to be offered, creating shelter rules for clients who stay at the shelter, and creating rules for employees. From the seemingly simple choice of a name for our fictitious shelter to whether the shelter will have batterers' programs or not, students are immediately immersed in the social construction of reality. Should the shelter be faith based? Should it be for only female adult victims (but not male victims) and their underage children? Should it serve victims of same-sex relationship violence? How dependent on the shelter should long-term clients be? Should the shelter accept state and federal monies? What are the policy implications of those decisions? This time, Kath wants to expand her students' understanding of the social construction of reality in several ways:

▶ Group decision making is required for all major decisions; ideally all decisions in the class about the shelter will be by consensus. Students quickly learn that people in different positions in the social structure have more or less ability to influence the group's social processes. So power, social location, and the interconnectivity of race, class, sex/

gender, and sexuality should be becoming more visible to students as they make these decisions.

▶ The role that other (usually outside) stakeholders/social actors play in the social construction of reality. So, for instance, if they decide to become a faith-based shelter, what sources of funds might be enhanced and/or narrowed, based on that decision?

▶ There are real-world social consequences to social construction processes. One term, the class decided to have a batterers' program held on site, in the basement of the shelter. There was quite vehement debate in the lead-up to this decision, but the idea won by two votes. Kath let it go, knowing full well that the group tasked with applying for grants would soon find out that many funding agencies do not allow a shelter program to mix victims and perpetrators. When the fund-raising group asked for a class meeting, explaining the problem and asking for a revote on this policy—many of the students felt betrayed. They talked about how the collective values of the shelter were being sacrificed to money and how that felt like a breach of ethics. It took nearly two weeks for the students to talk through this decision in class, during breaks, and in the online discussion boards.

Kath designed online weekly discussions around these class decisions and asked students to "unpack" them using their sociological imaginations. The prompts pushed students to see the complexities in the social construction of reality that they were involved in that semester as the class "built" a domestic violence shelter from scratch. These weekly discussions were graded using a 25-point rubric that asked students to:

1. Use a minimum of two sociological concepts in their several-paragraph post. (2 points each)

2. Define each concept correctly. (3 points each)

3. Explain how the concept connected to the shelter project in general and specifically about any decisions the class as a whole and/or their small group had made that week. (5 points for each concept)

4. Write: up to five points will be awarded for correct grammar, spelling, and paragraph flow, as well as ASA style in any citations used in the posting.

These examples show how the concept of the social construction of reality—central to the discipline of sociology—is introduced to students. Then, as they take more classes, their knowledge of the concept is made more complex and more sociological application and analysis of the concept is asked of them. We believe that such a progressive method of introducing the complexities of sociology—certainly for the key concepts and theories which your sociology program wants students to learn—is best for student learning. Certainly there may be other concepts or theories that will be emphasized in only one or two courses, and that too is appropriate. But students are growing personally and intellectually during their college experience and as faculty, we need to challenge them differently as they move from introductory-level courses to the more theoretical courses. In addition, and at least at Valdosta State, we believe that students also need to know how to transition "book knowledge" into sociological practice, so we push students to use their knowledge, through familiarity with case studies, service learning with community partners, or our required internship.

BUT . . . HOW DO I DO IT IN MY CLASSES?

While sociology programs are asked to show how their majors are learning, the bulk of that evidence will come from assessments embedded in courses. For many of us, a primary way that we assess student learning is via tests, so we want to concentrate our advice in this chapter on writing test questions. Other chapters will give advice about how to construct good writing assignments, etc.

Kath needs to share a true story (unfortunately!). The first test she ever created was a disaster. Students walked out in protest. She had created multiple-choice questions, often with 10 or more answer choices (many were combinations of answers). One question had 18 possible answers. What was she thinking?

So let's talk about some practical tips for creating ways to assess your students' learning through tests.

What Do You Want Them to Know (and Not Know)?

This sounds obvious, but often we skip past this step too quickly. Pull up your program's learning goals, the assessment plan, the course's learning goals and objectives, and Bloom's Taxonomy (1956) and use them to shape the content of your assessments. Then also think about your own personal values as a teacher. What do we mean? For Kath, memorizing the dates that Weber was alive and writing sociology is just not something she wants her students (at any course level) to spend their brain cells learning/memorizing.

Should they have a sense of the time period he was in? Absolutely, but she would never write a true or false question that involves the dates of a book he wrote, his birth/death, etc. She knows faculty who do that—but that is not what she wants her students to know about Weber. Therefore, she will tell students in the syllabus that specific dates are not something they need to spend time learning. So too, exact statistics are not going to be tested. Kath knows a sociology faculty member who will ask test questions just like this fill-in-the-blank question: "On the pie chart on p. 127 of our textbook, what was the percentage of the racial group whose 'slice' was colored pink? _____" The faculty member requires students to have the absolute number or else it is counted as incorrect. For many reasons, those types of questions are not getting at the knowledge Kath wants her students to have. She does share with her students, however, that names are important to know—names of theorists and the theories they created, as well as the last names of all authors whom the students read—and that she will test them on names. In first- and second-year classes that may mean she will ask some matching questions that require students to pair a famous sociological concept with its sociological "inventor," or fill-in-the-blank questions such as "Whose theory about socialization is often called the 'looking glass theory'?" She will, in first-year classes, write true or false questions, such as "Marx's analysis in the book *The Protestant Ethic and the Spirit of Capitalism* showed that religion could cause social change" to assess if students have learned course content about Marx versus Weber. In upper-division courses, Kath is far less likely to focus on this "remembering" level of knowledge (Bloom 1956) and will ask much more about how to apply the book's sociological content, etc.

Again, what you want from your students will vary by course content, level of the course, your own coverage decisions, the type of class environment (online versus face to face), and the abilities of your students. For a statistics course, do you want them to be able to calculate statistics by hand, without a calculator? Which statistics? Will you allow for calculator use during quizzes and tests? Will you specify which type of calculator they can use and which they cannot? Do students need to know how to interpret a statistical result or simply to calculate it? If you want them to show you their interpretive skills, how will you ask them to do that?

Here is an example of a question which takes students beyond rote learning and challenges them to think deeply about what they have learned, yet in a very creative way. It is one of the most intriguing exam questions that Kath has ever seen and it was written by a now-retired Anthropology faculty member at Valdosta State, Dr. Stephen Childs. This was the sole question on the senior-level Anthropology Theory course's take-home final exam. Students had one week to complete the final and had to write five to ten double-spaced pages, plus one additional page which showed the seating arrangement. The question said something like this:

> Imagine that you are having a party and inviting a minimum of 15 of these 20 anthropologists (then he would list all their names) over for a sit-down dinner. Please create the seating order around a large rectangular table, which follows these rules:
>
> 1. Anthropologists of the same "school of thought"/theoretical perspective cannot be seated all together.
>
> 2. Known "theoretical enemies" cannot be seated immediately next to each other, for social courtesy's sake.
>
> 3. As host, your goal is to have fascinating anthropological discussions between guests who are near each other, at a minimum.
>
> 4. Be sure to include yourself in the seating chart and explain why you placed yourself where you did.
>
> 5. Describe your seating chart and thoroughly explain why you put each theorist next to the people you did. As you do this, you must discuss the major theoretical elements of each guest's thoughts and how they would fit with the other guests around him or her. While some theoretical disagreements are likely to occur, do not break rule #2.

Dr. Childs said that when he first handed out this question, some students panicked, because it was not a "traditional" essay-type final exam question. But once they got into it, they loved it. The question allowed students to show their theoretical knowledge when they had to explain each guest's theoretical contributions and how they would fit with the guests around him or her, yet also tapped into their creative side. Many times he said students had insights about anthropological schools of thought that they felt would create good dinner conversation, which he had never thought of, and their insights benefitted his future teaching. But he would never have given this question to a first-year Introduction to Anthropology course's students, because it required too much in-depth learning that they had not yet had.

So matching your assessments with course content and your students' abilities is crucial. You want to push them just enough but not too much. Where is that line? While we'd love to share that "recipe" with you, we think that it is a constantly moving target. Don't assume that all sections of the same class—in one semester or years apart—will necessarily be exactly the same. Your assessments should always be fluid enough to adapt once you meet the students, etc.

How Many Students Do You Have?

We have said this before, but the size of the class you are teaching does impact the types of assessments you use. Few people will be like Kath and use partial essay tests in a class of 350 students, and we recognize that! (Maxine is one of those who will not do this.) So think about the number of students in each of your separate classes. Then consider if you are teaching more than one section of the same class, where you probably need assessments to occur at the same time. Now how many students are you talking about? Then look at the other classes you are teaching—are there tests or assignments coming due at the same time in them as well? You will have to balance your own time and energy here, as well as consider that students also have "busy times" when they will feel stressed by the number of tests and papers due near midterm and the last two weeks of the term, etc. (For more hints on grading, please see chapter 14.)

How Much Information Should Be Assessed at One Time?

Faculty often struggle with "how much information" should be on a single test. Again, there are many variables involved in answering this question: How long is the class, if you are creating an in-class test? What works for a 75-minute class might be too much for a 50-minute class. So take that into consideration. Will the test take the entire class period or not? What level of detail will you be asking students to grasp? Questions which ask for a lot of detail require more thinking, and so fewer questions might give students the time they need to pull together their thoughts and do well on your assessment.

If you feel the material is complicated and your assessment will require students to integrate a significant amount of disparate sources and theories, then perhaps an in-class assessment is not the best strategy to measure students' learning. Consider a take-home assessment instead, such as a paper or a take-home exam. Of course, once you make this decision, you need to work to create a very different exam than you would give during a class. In part, if you want students to spend time analyzing, evaluating, and synthesizing (Bloom 1956), you have to be sure that the assessment is written in a way that shows them those are the intellectual skills which are needed. Put differently, don't give a take-home true or false test! And you might want to think about the possibility of cheating. Perhaps you need to specify in your take-home directions if you will allow students to share ideas about the answers or if you consider that a breach of your class's ethical code of conduct. If your institution has an honor code, consider inserting a hyperlink to it. If you don't want students to talk at all about the assessment, be very clear about that fact. It probably won't stop that from happening but will likely diminish the number of students who do talk.

Announce clearly and often how you will assess the take-home exam or paper. Create a detailed rubric; include it with the assessment. Post it to the learning management system. Go over it with students several times. Ask some students to explain it to the class—listen carefully for any interpretations of your scoring categories that are different from what you mean. Clarify them immediately. Your goal is to blanket them with the information on how you will grade the assessment. If it is an in-class test, announce the structure of the test about 10 to 14 days before it will occur. Notice we didn't say the test had to be *written* by then (we know how busy we all are) but decide on the structure. Students often tell us that they will study differently based on the types of questions (e.g., short-answer essays, matching, multiple choice, etc.), so give them this information as soon as you can.

Types of Objective Questions to Consider Using on Exams

True or false. This type of question can work if you have large classes and want to assess basic information, especially at the "remembering" level (Bloom 1956). However, these are not necessarily easy questions to write. If you want to assess learning, we suggest you consider which concepts are the most difficult for students and then make some questions which mix up those concepts and others which do not. Kath finds that her students struggle with keeping straight all the theories of deviance which start with the letter *c* (e.g., control theory, conflict theory, etc.). So she writes questions which focus on that knowledge. But students will sometimes say these are "tricky" questions because with the exception of the one word, they sound true, yet are actually false (or vice versa). Again, if that is the type of question you are going to ask students, be sure to give them examples in the lead-up to the exam. For Kath, this is easy because these are exactly how she phrases her clicker questions, so every day, students see 10 questions that are similar to what will be on the test.

Some faculty "up" the level of knowledge in their true or false questions by requiring students to rewrite all "false" questions to make them true. This can be an effective way of assessing higher-level learning—but think about how you set up the exam. Give space for students to "fix" every question (whether it would need to be or not); otherwise if you only leave space on the "false" questions, you have signaled to students what the correct answer is! Also be sure in advance how you will score this part of the test and be certain students understand it. If a student marks a "true" question "false" and then goes on to "fix" it incorrectly, does the student lose some points for the "true" and more points for the incorrect "fix"?

Matching. These kinds of questions can assess students' knowledge of sociological vocabulary and familiarity with which theorist uses which vocabulary term. Students have a few concerns with matching questions. The first is whether you include a "none of these answers" answer in the list of terms from which students can select. We find they prefer to not have that option, because then they know that the correct answer *is* in the list of matches and can focus on them. It is for that exact reason that Kath does use the "none of these answers" on her matching tests. The second concern students have is if a term can be used once, more than once, or not at all. They prefer that a term can only be used once. This allows them to narrow their selection/guess with each question that they answer. If you do this, we would urge you to include several more choices than are necessary to answer the questions.

Fill in the blank. Again, these types of questions primarily assess students' learning using the lower end of Bloom's Taxonomy (1956). If you use this question type, be sure to mix up what part of the sentence the students have to complete. Have some questions where the noun/theorist's name is the missing information; have other questions where a student has to answer a stage in a theorist's theory, and have some other questions where a student might have to give an example of a concept or do a calculation (e.g., "Please give an original example of role conflict in your life" or "Calculate the mean of this set of numbers to one decimal place: {1, 3, 5, 7, 9, and 11}"). Think about what you want from your students. Must they name the stage of the theory exactly to earn the points? If students calculate the mean overall correctly but make a rounding error, will they lose all the points? However you choose to award points, be sure that they are explained clearly in the directions for the test. These kinds of grading concerns may mean that you want to have these questions be worth several points. That way the student might earn one point for having correctly done the addition and division required to calculate a mean and lose one point for the rounding error.

Multiple-choice questions. These types of questions require students to sort through several answers and select the correct one. There are several types of these questions. Some will ask students which is the correct answer; others may ask students to find the one concept which does not fit with the rest and select it as the answer; others may require students to link a theorist with terms which fit with the person (or don't), etc. Often there are four choices given, though that number is not sacrosanct. Some faculty use "all of the answers" or "none of the answers" as possible solution choices.

Case study or scenario-based questions. These questions begin with a case study and then ask questions based on that case study. If you are using this type of question on exams, there are several things to consider because you are asking students to move up Bloom's Taxonomy (1956). First, think carefully about the length of the scenario being used, *especially* if students have not seen it before. You want to be careful to assess your students' sociological skills, not how fast they can read. We recommend that the scenarios be relatively short (five to seven lines) and to the point. Kath uses this type of question a lot, but promises students that "every word matters" in the scenario. She coaches them that each sentence will contain sociological clues and no sentence is "filler"—so they need to read with that in mind. If the case study is longer, consider letting students have it in advance. That way they can read it at their own pace. They still will not know what the actual questions are, but will have had the chance to think about the facts, the social actors, etc. If you do give the scenario out in class in advance of the test, we recommend you also put it up on the learning management system for those students who were not present the day you gave it out. Second, scenarios allow the faculty to follow up with questions that span several levels of Bloom's Taxonomy (1956). There could be some true or false questions, some matching, and then a short-answer question that requires students to apply their sociological knowledge to the scenario. Thus case study or scenario-based questions allow faculty the opportunity to ask questions which span several levels of Bloom's Taxonomy (1956), something other types of questions do not.

SOME FINAL TIPS ON MEASURING STUDENT SUCCESS

If you are writing objective questions for quizzes or exams, we suggest that questions be not very linguistically complicated; too many clauses can make it difficult for some students to follow the point of the question. Try to avoid words like *always* and *never* in your questions. Use vocabulary that you feel most students in your classes will be familiar with and understand. Try to have a mix of answers, although we would recommend you stay away from patterns (e.g., 50 percent will be true, 50 percent false) because students may guess the pattern rather than actually learning the material.

We believe in creating multiple versions of tests, especially for classes that are large. Creating these versions could be as simple as reordering sections and the questions within each section, or you could go further and reword questions. So a "true" question on one version might become a "false" question on the second version. When grading, sort the tests by version; we find it easier to grade all of one version at a time.

Once you have graded all the questions, we encourage you to do an item analysis. For Kath, her item analysis actually starts during the test. She keeps track of which questions students found confusing during the test (because they asked her questions). Those problematic questions often give her feedback about where she needs to work on expressing herself more clearly. Then, after grading all the tests, figure out what questions were the most missed. Make a list of the concepts involved in the questions. Share that list with students, because knowing what concepts were troublesome for the class can be useful information as they review for the final exam. Save the list; you might want to reconsider how you teach these concepts or spend more time on them the next time that you teach the class.

CONCLUSION

Creating interesting and useful assessments that accurately measure what our students have learned is one of the most important tasks that we do as faculty. If you think about what you want your students to learn in the course and work backward to how you will teach those concepts and how you will involve students in actively learning them, then the assessment process can be less burdensome. One more thing: don't forget to celebrate your students' successes with them and encourage them when they show progress. No matter how large the class, reach out to students and show them that you have noticed the quality of their work.

SOME CASE STUDY RESOURCES

The Electronic Hallway. Evans School of Public Affairs, the University of Washington. Retrieved November 3, 2014 (http://hallway.evans.washington.edu/)

European Entrepreneurship Case Study Resource Centre. Retrieved November 3, 2014 (http://eecsrc.eu/case-studies/)

Free Case Study: Case Study Examples and Sample Case Studies. Retrieved November 3, 2014 (https://freecasestudy.wordpress.com/tag/sociology-case-study/)

Human Resource Council Canada. Workplaces that Work: Case Study Series. Retrieved November 3, 2014 (http://hrcouncil.ca/hr-toolkit/case-studies-workplaces-that-work.cfm)

Human Resource Management Asia. Retrieved November 3, 2014 (http://www.hrmasia.com/article-subcategory/case-studies)

Jain, Manish. Management Case Studies and Articles. Retrieved November 3, 2014 (http://www.casestudyinc.com/)

National Center for Case Study Teaching in Science. Retrieved November 3, 2014 (http://sciencecases.lib.buffalo.edu/cs/teaching/)

Resources for Research Ethics Education. Retrieved November 3, 2014 (http://www.research-ethics.net/topics/overview/)

USC Levan Institute: Online Ethics Resource Center. Retrieved November 3, 2014 (http://dornsife.usc.edu/dilemmas-and-case-studies/)

World Health Organization. World Conference on Social Determinants of Health. Case Studies on Social Determinants of Health. Retrieved November 3, 2014 (http://www.who.int/sdhconference/resources/case_studies/en/)

Yang, Kaifeng, compiler. US Case Study Online Resources. Retrieved November 3, 2014 (http://unpan1.un.org/intradoc/groups/public/documents/aspa/unpan000086.pdf).

►►► CHAPTER 14
GRADING

We have a question for you. What is the story that you tell yourself, or tell others, about grading? If you don't think you have a story to tell, imagine you are on a train/subway/airplane and someone asks you what you do (Shadiow 2013). You say "college professor" and immediately the person asks about what it is like to grade at that level. Take a moment to jot down your thoughts. Just get the narrative on paper, and don't think a lot about what you are writing yet. Done? Put it away for a few hours and come back to it. What does it say about how you feel about assessing your students? What does it say about how you feel about your job? About your students?

Kath's goes like this: Sometime during the two weeks before a new term begins, she sits down at her desk, pulls up all her syllabi on the computer screen, and begins to count: the number of tests × number of students × number of classes. For the last four years her classes have ranged in size from 150 to 350 students. Then she turns to the online discussions, then the writing assignments, and so on. About thirty minutes later, she arrives at a number. And she'll sit and stare at the screen for quite a while, pondering it. Are there too many things to grade? Or is it just the right amount? Are assignments and assessments too bunched up around midterm and at the end of the semester? No matter what the number is, she worries about it, sometimes making adjustments to her syllabi. Her worries are many: Are her assessments aligned closely enough with her goals and objectives? Has she done enough to make that alignment clear to students? There are also a few questions which she's less proud to own: Is this too much stuff to grade, in the time frame she sets for herself? (She thinks that student work should be graded within 72 hours—preferably within 24 hours—of it being turned in.) Will she still have any remnant of a life left over after grading, teaching, and other academic commitments? The number is written on a white board in her home office, and after every assessment, she adjusts the number. The visual countdown helps her, in some way. Her husband, though—also a professor, at the same school—thinks the countdown is odd and masochistic. So she's started keeping it only on her computer, where it is less visible to anyone but her.

We were surprised and amused to find that Maxine does something similar to Kath, to keep herself going on a stack of papers. Every time she grades another three papers, she gets to put up a Post-it note on her board in her home office. She loves seeing all those little Post-it notes growing. Maxine believes that this has something to do with the fact that both she and Kath are very goal oriented and find ways to congratulate themselves on meeting their goals to stay motivated.

When Kath first read Shadiow's book (2013) about the stories we tell ourselves as teachers, she grew very uneasy. Students were tangential to her story about grading—yet shouldn't it be about them and their learning?

In some ways, Kath is not that unique. We've all been there: a stack of tests or papers on our desk, staring up at us, demanding our attention. In those moments, it can sometimes be hard to remember the rationale for why we require students to produce work that requires grading. So let's step back from the pile of material to be graded for a moment, and think about how feedback is a key part of the process of learning.

In a blog post on InsideHigherEd.com about how being a Food Network fan has helped her become a better professor, Janine Utell (2013) makes an intriguing point:

> My conclusion after much Food Network watching is this: There are two types of feedback available to chefs, and possibly ordinary people like students and faculty: failure based, with an eye toward exposing weakness and asserting authority; and facilitative, with an eye towards building skills and creating opportunities for growth.

While not exactly parallel to substantive and formative evaluation processes (see for example, Juwah [2004]; Taras [2008]), Utell's comment (2013) can be helpful in developing a personal philosophy of grading. How much of the work you are requiring students to do in class is facilitative, helping them to develop a sociological vocabulary—which really means that they have internalized the sociological imagination? How much of the work is substantive—and here is where we quibble just a bit with Utell's focus on failure (2013)—requiring students to use the sociological perspective correctly, as they apply it to real-world scenarios? Is the latter kind of work always "failure based," as she said? We don't think so, though certainly a part of these kinds of learning activities will focus on correct sociological application.

Is there a correct blend of facilitative and substantive learning opportunities in any particular class? We all could likely discuss that issue forever. We believe instead, that as you are creating a class, you need to understand its place in the curriculum (be it a general education class, an introduction to the major course, a content course for primarily majors only, or a senior capstone course which sums up the student's learning). By understanding the course's social location and its learning goals and objectives, you will have a better sense of what might be the right mix of assignments and how best to grade them. So let's consider some key faculty concerns about grading.

WHAT NEEDS TO BE GRADED?

Especially in the beginning of a teaching career, many faculty may believe that every single thing that they require students to do for a class must receive the same amount of faculty time and effort spent on grading. This can be especially true for those faculty who weight all assignments equally. But research shows (Goodin 2014; Kohn 2011) that this belief is not necessarily the most effective way to understand student success and its relationship to grading.

Not Everything Has to Be Graded, or Graded the Same Way

The Writing Across the Curriculum movement has long stressed (Strong 2003; Zawacki n.d.) that writing does not always have to be graded in order to be useful to students. Practice writing, also called "writing to learn," is worthwhile and can build skills even if it is not graded. We know that students need time to digest sociological concepts, time to think about them, and to think *with* them, and designing assessments which require students to take that time expanding their sociological imagination is worthwhile in itself.

Of course, students do not always concur. They often want a good grade just for spending time with our course content and the discipline of sociology.

But that does not always mean that the work you require them to do necessarily will demand significant amounts of your time. Consider, for example, this requirement that both Maxine and Kath have used successfully in class:

> Make the last five minutes of class time for students to write a summary of that day's key concepts. Ask for the concept, its definition, and an original example. If they feel they are lost, they must instead identify which concept is confusing and where they got lost in understanding that concept. This review must be done on no more than one page of notebook paper.

Collect this writing every day (you can even ask students to keep recycling the paper until both sides are used up, then staple the new sheet to the old one, and so on for the duration of the semester) and grade it. But frequently tell students that this assessment will be graded with the following rating scale: 3 = excellent; 2 = average answer; 1 = barely acceptable answer; and 0 = not acceptable work. Tell them that you will only make a comment other than the grade on the paper if: (1) the student is lost and you will answer his or her question; (2) the work earned a 0 grade, and you will point to where the student needs to go in the book and other materials. Students doing "okay" usually will not receive comments. If it is not turned in for any reason, leave a blank in the gradebook for that day. Calculate how many days you will do this during the term, and then say how students will earn the total number of points. Even in a large class, these can be rather quickly graded, if you commit to writing few comments which are not routinized ones (e.g., "Look on p. 13 for help with this" or "let's talk after class about this"). Kath can usually grade a class of 150 in under 90 minutes, including entering grades in the learning management system. Maxine does similar writing assignments, but they focus on the assigned readings. She will use a "+" to symbolize an excellent student response, a check mark for "I can see that you read and understood," a "-" to symbolize "I can't tell if you read this or not," and a "0" to let students know that there was "no convincing evidence that they read the assigned material."

What is important, we believe, is what faculty do with the information these end-of-class writing assignments provide. You will learn where they are struggling, what concepts are still confusing to them, etc.—but how will you incorporate that knowledge into the class structure? Some may post in the course management system a summary/clarification of common conceptual errors after every set is graded. Others may take the first few minutes of class to go over this material. What is crucial for student learning is that—at least as a class—they get clarifications about any errors in learning.

If you choose this kind of low-stakes grading option, there is one thing that can slow a faculty member down considerably: if he or she decides to comment on or edit students' grammar and spelling. Here again, talk with students about your goals for this kind of quick assessment, so that they will understand your reasons for grading them the way that you are. Kath says something like this to students, both before the daily writing assignments for the first few weeks and in the syllabus:

> These end-of-class writing assignments are meant to help me spot problems in your learning sociology in-the-moment, so I am only going to focus on the sociological content in your writing. In other assignments, where you have time outside of class to think, write, edit, and revise, I will evaluate not just your sociological understanding, but also your ability to express that sociological understanding in well-written and readable language.

While Kath supports the Writing Across the Curriculum movement in general, and in sociology in particular, she is a very late endorser (as in, just this past year) of the "not all writing has to receive comments about grammar/spelling/logical argument flow." As one example, the Central Washington University's WAC website (n.d.) offers the following advice about grading grammar:

> What can I do about my students' appalling grammar? Do I have to teach grammar myself?

> These may be the questions faculty ask most frequently. First, WAC is not Grammar Across the Curriculum. Successful WAC programs focus more on writing to learn than on learning to write. No, you don't have to teach grammar, and in fact emphasizing grammar too much can make them focus on correctness instead of content.

> However, you can help students express themselves more clearly. Giving students more opportunities to write will help them write more fluently, and assigning multiple drafts will encourage them to polish their writing. Keep in mind the reasons why students make grammatical errors:

> ▶ They probably wrote the paper the night before it was due.
> ▶ Research has shown that grammatical errors increase when students confront challenging material or begin a new discipline. This is true even for graduate students.
> ▶ They may not realize that you expect them to proofread.
> ▶ They haven't fully mastered the rules.

What you can do:

▶ Require more than one draft. One way to do this is to use an in-class peer review.

▶ Make your expectations clear—but don't overemphasize grammar. Encourage them to proofread as the last step in the process. Research suggests that most students can recognize and correct about 50 percent of their errors if they proofread carefully.

▶ Avoid editing their papers. Students learn more when they have to recognize and correct errors themselves. You can note representative errors in the margin, or simply let them know that the errors are distracting and make their meaning unclear. Marking all of their errors may send the message that correctness matters more than content.

▶ Distinguish between mechanical errors and stylistic flaws. Problems like wordiness and overuse of the passive voice represent stylistic choices rather than mechanical errors.

▶ Give students a list of the most common errors you see. (Central Washington University n.d.)

Kath struggles mightily to get through the daily writing assignments and *not* write comments about grammar and structure. Don't laugh—sometimes she actually has to sit on her right hand and use her left hand to grade these assignments, so that she stops herself from correcting grammar. Since she is not ambidextrous, that is the only way she has found to get through the stack of papers—letting her nondominant hand make the 3-2-1-0s on the page! Maxine has no problem at all not grading grammar. On a daily writing assignment, she reads right past all the grammatical errors.

These daily writing assignments—especially if you want students to continue to use the paper until it is used up—create a potential problem for the next day's class: how to return them in an efficient manner so that students have them at the start of class to use at the end. In smaller classes, this can actually be a useful way to learn names—having every student come up and ask for hers. But in much larger classes, you will have to create a process whereby students can easily access their paper without creating too much of a bottleneck at the front of class and making it difficult to start on time. Kath makes bright color folders and distributes them around the edge of her super-section classroom. So, for example, students with last names beginning with A–C look for the bright purple folder in the far left corner of the room; those with last names beginning with D–G look for the bright pink folder, and so on.

Be sure to keep the folder in the same place each day, and students quickly get into the habit of going to the folder first, before sitting down.

Who Can Do Grading?

The Writing Across the Curriculum movement strongly encourages faculty to use peer reviewers/peer grading when appropriate. Students tend to pay attention to comments made by other students in the class, and so faculty want to leverage that social fact. The tricky pedagogical task is to decide which assignments are best to use peer reviewers for and then if the assignment will earn a grade or simply credit for accomplishing the task.

Students are not necessarily prepared for peer reviewing, so we urge you to plan these activities carefully. Kath uses peer reviews the week before her research proposal is due in her theory course (e.g., thesis statement, research question, statement of personal interest, review of literature over eight scholarly articles, theoretical statement, three testable hypotheses, a methodological plan for gathering data, and conclusion). Students must come to class with a polished final draft, but without their names on the papers. She collects them all and then she and her students talk about what would be helpful comments (e.g., "this paragraph flowed together well," or "I got lost a bit here—could you clarify this point more?") and unhelpful comments (e.g., "This topic isn't working for you; you need to change it"). The class goes over the grading rubric and Kath leaves it on screen so the class can see it while they are peer reviewing. In a 75-minute class, most students are able to comment on two papers. With about 15 minutes remaining in the class, Kath collects the papers and gets them back to their authors. The room goes quiet as students now look at the comments. Then Kath and her students have a conversation about "after doing two peer reviews, what do you now want to double-check in your own paper?" They explode with ideas—and the list is nearly exactly what Kath would have asked them to do. But now it means more, for it comes from their shared experiences.

Kath allows students to sign their names as peer reviewers if they want to, but she definitely signs all papers that day that she reads. And to make the numbers "work," she will bring in a paper she is writing and ask for feedback. Students salivate to get hers, and grab a pen and have at it!

Chunk Their Learning, and Thus Your Grading

Students do better when assignments are scaffolded. Assignments need to build on each other and be spaced out, in order to give students enough time to do the work you want them to do and to process their learning. If you want students to write an analytical paper, for example, think about the intellectual steps needed to complete the assignment successfully. Those steps become the "chunks" around which assignments should be built. Thus for a typical research-based paper, the assignments might be:

▶ Define topic and explain why it was chosen
▶ Create a readable number of key refereed sources on the topic and closely related topics and create a bibliography
▶ Create an outline of the paper. Faculty can specify how detailed they want the outline to be
▶ Write a rough draft of the paper (or a portion of the paper)
▶ Edit the paper individually or via peer review
▶ Turn in the final, edited paper

Each of these steps would be an assignment and you need to decide if each has to be graded, and at what level of grading. But these shorter assignments have several pedagogical advantages: (1) they stave off extreme procrastination by students; (2) they allow for earlier intervention by the faculty member if a student seems to be misinterpreting the directions; and (3) students can see how the research-writing process is not linear, but rather often takes twists and turns which can strengthen the paper.

In one sense, such a grading scheme *does* involve more grading than just saying "turn in a research paper at the end of the term." But often grading scaffolded assignments can take less time than one long paper, which the faculty member has not seen before. With these types of assignments, we can see the paper develop, see the argument being developed much earlier, learn the student's writing style (helpful in spotting plagiarism), and thus the final paper often takes less time to grade.

TOOLS TO HELP WITH GRADING

You!: How You Construct Assignment Directions

We both have learned the hard way that the better an assignment's directions are, the better the students can perform on that assignment. Kath used to think that meant "give them lots of detailed directions (sometimes more than a page or two!)." But she has come to learn that—even more than detailed directions—her students need to see why she is asking them to produce this work and how it relates to the overall class goals and objectives. This kind of information frames the work they need to do and helps them to make connections between concepts, which can lead to deep learning.

We sometimes forget that students' lives are not focused on seeing the big picture—of a discipline, of an entire term's worth of learning. Rather their days are often lived minute to minute, hour by hour, class by class. So we have to provide the overview of how any one assignment fits into the overall course plan.

If you frequently teach the same course, keep track of the questions you receive about your assignments as well as frequent errors you see. Use that data to reconstruct the directions, clarifying for future students what confused past students. While we both include in our syllabi practical rules about written assignments, we have learned that students rarely consult the syllabus as they start writing, so we suggest that you restate those norms in every assignment.

So what kinds of information do we include?

▶ How to name the file if it is being submitted electronically (Kath uses 'LastNameFirstNameNameOfAssignment' because she doesn't want to receive 300 "Assignment1" papers!). She provides a model of the format, using her name.
▶ Font and font size
▶ Staple assignment if a hard copy is being turned in during class
▶ Double space the entire assignment
▶ Acceptable margins
▶ For upper-division courses, a reminder to use the ASA's *Style Guide*, 4th edition (2010)
▶ Minimum and maximum page limits

What do you want on your "to be included in every set of directions" list? If there are specific things you want students to do in any one specific assignment, tell them, and give them examples. When Kath teaches sociological theory, part of the written requirements are that each student writes a review of literature over ten sociological published articles. Some students—even with in-class modeling, examples of former students' work, etc.—cannot "get" that such reviews need to be a dialogue between authors, not just separate paragraphs on each of the sources. So Kath now includes in her assignment directions a statement that says that every paragraph of the review of literature, save for the introduction and conclusion, must have at least two sources discussed or else points will be lost. That statement is replicated in her grading rubric for the assignment. She also includes a "skeleton model" of how the review should look, to reinforce the requirement.

By giving clear directions for each assignment—with everything students need to know about the assignment and what you are looking for right there in the directions—you are providing students all the tools they need to rise to your expectations. Provide a copy of the rubric you will use to grade their work or at least a hyperlink to it.

Grading Rubrics

Rubrics can aid the grading process. They provide a standardized format for the faculty member to give feedback and can speed the grading process. Some faculty, however, find their standardization to be constricting. But if rubrics make sense to you as a way of providing feedback about student learning, we encourage you to use them.

Creating useful rubrics will require you to match closely the goals for the assignment, your directions for how to do the assignment, and the rubric's evaluative criteria (Brookhart 2013). As you consider how many points to assign to each criterion, be sure that you "do the math." What grade would a student earn if she earned only the second-highest evaluative level on each criterion? The third? And so on. Probably you want to assign points such that all the second-highest levels would earn a B grade, and so on. Are the point totals in alignment with your learning goals and objectives? You will want to reconfigure the rubric until you are satisfied—before showing it to students.

Whether the rubric is on paper or online, be sure to leave room for your comments above and beyond the points you will assign. This is especially important if this is the only means of feedback for the assignment—common to online graded assignments. A comment section will allow for your thoughts about what the student did well (we believe in starting all comments with a positive comment), about the argument structure, frequent grammar errors, and so on. If you are creating an online rubric in the course management system, learn whether such a comment box has a word limit and/or whether you can also attach a document with more detailed comments, if need be.

Maxine never gives any formal writing assignment without providing a rubric. She finds that the rubrics help her clarify her expectations, grade fairly, and provide productive feedback. Her rubrics start with a section on "Strengths" and end with "Other comments" so that she can individualize feedback as well as preserve the common criteria for the assignment.

Students should have easy access to the graded rubric, whether it is a paper or electronic version. If you use rubrics within the course management system, show students how to see the graded rubric—don't assume that they necessarily know how to access it. This is especially true for first-year students.

GRADING BY HAND OR ELECTRONICALLY?

One of the first questions we want to ask you is this: How do you grade? Are you a "grab your favorite pen, a cup of coffee or tea, head to your favorite chair, and start" kind of grader? Up until about four years ago, that described Kath perfectly. She would grab a calligraphy fountain pen, decide on the ink color, turn on the TV, and settle in until the grading was done. That did mean, however, that she only graded at home. While she still believes that her home office provides the best environment for her to grade, as her class size grew, that wasn't always an option, especially when grading longer writing assignments. So she migrated to e-grading, using the Word documents her students uploaded. It took a while to settle on a way to add comments. Initially she would add them at the end of the sentence which provoked the comment; she had to remember to change the font color to make the comment more visible. But that was often awkward for students to understand, since her comments interrupted the flow of their writing. Then she tried only using the "Insert Comment" function in Word. While that works, it is not a perfect system either. A few students have trouble tracing the line from their text to the comment in the margin; this is especially problematic when the faculty member uses a lot of comments in one line of text. Kath has now settled on a combination of these techniques. She now writes content comments at the end of a paragraph in another color font, and comments about grammar, flow, and ASA style using the "insert comment" option. Maxine's grading system has evolved in a similar manner.

In the last five years, Kath has started using grading codes to ease the amount of writing/typing she does while grading. The list of codes is posted in the course management system for all students to review and they go over it in class after each assignment is graded. Codes are abbreviations. Table 14.1 is a copy of the list of codes Kath uses the most. If you choose to use grading codes, take a term or two to notice the most common comments you make on student work and from them, build your code sheet.

When and How to Grade

Again, there are probably as many grading strategies as there are faculty who grade, but one way to think about when to grade is to ask this question: Do you believe in the "little bit at a time" approach or are you a "just get it done" kind? The latter devotes as long as it takes to complete grading all the assignments, rarely stopping save for sleep, showering, teaching, and food. Many others use the "whenever I can" way of grading, as they try to balance

TABLE 14.1 GRADING CODES — FOR E-GRADING AND FOR WHEN YOUR
ASSIGNMENT IS GRADED BY HAND

Name of Error	E-grading Code in Comment in Margin (text will be highlighted)	Handwritten Code in Your Text
Incomplete sentence	inc sen	usually in square brackets [. . .]
Spelling error	s	usually the word is circled
Grammar error	g	usually the word is circled
Spelling/grammar in one	s/g	usually the word is circled
ASA form mistake in citation or in references	f	usually the word is circled
Capitalization error	c C	the letter is circled — should not have been capitalized the letter is circled — should have been capitalized
Punctuation error	p	the error is circled
Punctuation/ASA error	p/f	Two errors in one: usually error is circled
Indention error	pi	---> added in left margin
Add a space	a	"\" is written at location where space is needed
Delete a space	d	"x" is written at location where excess space is located

teaching at multiple institutions, childcare, and so on. Again, there is no "right way" to grade. There are, though, some things to consider.

Your physical state and grading. If you are an "in it for the duration" grader, who goes on and on until the task is done, consider how tired you may get in those last hours. Are you giving students your best effort? Would you want to have your work reviewed by someone as tired as you are? Would daily grading of a smaller amount of assignments be a better way for you?

Your emotional state and grading. Let's be honest—the process of grading can elicit a lot of emotions. There can be happy ones (e.g., elation when a student finally "gets" a concept or when a test goes well for a class) and there can be not-so-happy ones (finding an incident of plagiarism or other kinds of cheating, etc.). Your relationship with any particular class can impact how you might feel during grading of their assignments. We are human, after all. Our emotions may bleed into the grading process. The question is not *if* this happens, but how much we let it happen and what we do when we realize that it is happening.

For Kath, if she notices that she is feeling frustrated or upset during grading, that means she needs a break. She'll jump on her stationary bike and do a few miles (it also helps rehab both her artificial knees). But her responsibility to her students—to meet the 72-hour deadline—means that Kath has learned to work through negative emotions pretty quickly and let them go. She usually doesn't talk to classes about being upset.

Another emotion that can be more complicated to process is disappointment. How many of us are sure that our students "get it" only to find that they didn't on the assignment or that they did not put in the requisite time to do the assignment well? That disappointment might be something you want to share—carefully—with your students. But how to tell them that you were disappointed—that is an issue. We suggest that you first must distance yourself from the intense feelings of disappointment, so that you can talk about it with the class and remain calm. If many did not properly follow directions, talk about that and how it hurt their grades. We suggest that you don't just "pontificate"—but ask them what they feel happened. Ask if they felt any part of the directions were unclear—and be ready to listen to what they have to say. Kath likes to take notes right there, in front of her students, on a copy of the assignment, about what they have to say. But many times, students will admit that they procrastinated or didn't go back and look at the rubric or the directions and they will take responsibility. Great—that can be an important sociological and life lesson too.

INTERACTIONS WITH STUDENTS ABOUT GRADES
Pleading for Grades

It's most faculty's worst nightmare: a student yelling about the grade the student received. The situation continues to escalate; the student's emotions spiral out of control. Soon the conversation is not just about the one grade, but the entire course, your talents (or rather, lack of them) as a teacher, and so on. These are the moments that we replay over and over again, wondering where we could have de-escalated the interaction.

These faculty–student interactions often are some of the most anxiety-producing moments of the term, for both parties. We'd like to suggest a few ground rules to structure the interactions, before we talk about grade appeals, and so on.

1. These conversations should be held, ideally, in your office or at least outside of the classroom and away from other students in the class who might be around.

2. They should be conducted in relative privacy.

3. We suggest imposing a 24-hour rule: students cannot talk about their grade with you (unless it is an obvious grading/mathematical error) for 24 hours after receiving their graded assignment/test back from you. Emotions can flare when students want to talk while simultaneously beginning to process a grade worse than they anticipated, so give them some time. However, realize that for a few students, time will escalate their distress instead of reducing it.

4. Some faculty want grade appeals only in writing, for the same reason. If this is what you decide to do, provide a format for the appeal and make it easily available to students. Remind them where they can find the process the day that the assignment is returned. Be sure to put a page limit on the appeal and a due date by when it must be returned (e.g., "The grade appeal must be turned in at the start of the next class period from when the graded assignment was returned").

5. Allow the student to talk first, but do your best to keep the conversation focused. Try not to let the student start bringing up other grades (a good reason for a time limit for appeals) or other students' grades.

6. Stay calm and in control. This may not always be easy; students often try to push our emotional buttons. But know when to end the conversation. One way to end the conversation is to explain to the student your institution's formal grade appeals process, or to encourage them to see the department head/chair. If you feel physically threatened, call campus police or ask a colleague to do so.

Grade Challenges and Appeals

"Grade appeal"—the phrase can strike fear into many faculty. We each have been there, but we want to give you some advice that has helped us. First, recognize that it is the student's right to appeal a grade. Try not to take it personally, difficult as that might be. And it could be really hard at times. You might feel that your department head or chair, your dean, and the vice president for academic affairs are all scrutinizing your syllabus, your assignments, your grading policies, etc. And in a way, they will be.

Most higher education institutions have policies which set out a process for grade challenges or appeals. Know what your institution's policies are and how to find them. Kath, for instance, has the policy bookmarked so that it is easy to find or to send the link to students. Valdosta State's policies about appeals of final (letter) grades set a time frame that begins the day grades are posted in the official software we use, called "Banner." The student has to begin the appeal by talking with the faculty member and if the issue cannot be resolved, the next step is the department head, who normally meets with both the student and the faculty member (though not necessarily together). The last step is an appeal to the dean. While a student can appeal to the vice president for academic affairs, that review will only be a procedural one, not a substantive review of the grade itself.

Grade appeals will require you to produce course documents, usually the syllabus, directions for the assignment (if the appeal is over just one assignment) or all of them, a printout of the student's grades in the course, and possibly, a printout of the final grades of all students. If you awarded any student a grade that did not conform to your grading scale, expect to be asked to explain why. Then you will be asked usually for a written explanation for the specific grade(s) given to this student. If, for example, you gave the student a zero for a paper turned in late, expect to be asked to show your policy on late papers from your syllabus, perhaps a screenshot from the learning management system that shows when the student's paper came in, and that you followed your policy. If you gave a zero grade due to plagiarism, be prepared to show the source from which you believed the student plagiarized. If your institution uses software such as Turnitin, print out the report about the assignment as part of your response.

Once you explain the grade and send the paperwork on its way to the administrator who is next in the process, you really have no say in what happens. So we advise you to let it go. If the grade you gave is upheld, congratulations. If it is not, we suggest that you let it sit for a time, let your emotions settle down, and then—if you want to—ask to talk with someone about it. Who that someone will be depends on your institution. Choose the person who is most likely to help you with the decision and come to closure.

We realize that if you are a graduate assistant, an adjunct, or a nontenured faculty member, grade appeals can be even scarier, because the outcomes might impact your funding and your teaching opportunities. Many nontenured faculty feel that they must have no grade appeals and high student evaluation scores in order to be rehired. We don't necessarily dispute those claims. But as scary as that can be, we urge all faculty to maintain high standards. Ask your students to accomplish reasonable learning goals, support them as they strive to achieve them, but don't sell students short in order to get glowing student evaluations. We need to raise the bar for our students and help them to help themselves go over that bar. While sometimes stressful, giving honest, respectful feedback to students via our grades is our responsibility.

►►► CHAPTER 15
CLASS EVALUATIONS

If receiving your student evaluations creates some anxiety, welcome to the club! It happens to many of us . . . all the time! So what we want to share in this chapter are some strategies to push past the anxiety and to get to a place where you can envision student evaluations as one source of useful feedback about your teaching. And notice, we said "one source." Student evaluations ought not to be the sole measure of how any of us "are" as a teacher. We'll come back to this thought later in the chapter.

Let's start by saying that few of us necessarily enjoy hearing others' opinions about ourselves . . . so processing student evaluations can take emotional energy. Choose a good time to read them. Just because they arrived in campus mail or are released electronically does not mean that you must look at them *right this very moment*. Schedule a time when you don't have a lot of class preparation and/or grading to do, when family responsibilities are a bit less, and when you are feeling healthy physically and emotionally. But don't put it off too long into the future either—that can allow the anxiety to build into paralysis.

So, are you ready? Then start reading them. We suggest looking at one entire class's set of comments, without responding, if you can. Then take your emotional temperature. Can you continue? Great. If so, grab some paper and a pen and begin to write your initial responses to them. Don't self-edit. This writing is about feeling what you feel, be it frustration, happiness, anger, or hurt. And often you might feel all of the above emotions, and then some. If you feel you need some more time to process what you read, by all means, take it. But then come back and be the sociologist that we know you are.

IGNORE THE OUTLIERS

Haters or fan boy/girl-type comments are best to ignore. Kath once got "She's so great, buy the woman a Lamborghini." Um—okay? (And no, her department head didn't follow up on that suggestion!) But what should she have made of that comment? How did it relate to her teaching an Introduction to Social Problems class? She's also received comments like, "She is so hard, she should be fired. She expected me to learn the material—doesn't she know this is just an intro class?" Maxine had a student post to RateMyProfessor.com, "Just slit your wrists and get it over with. It would be less painful than taking this woman's class." Realize that each of us will have students who do not like us and will make their sentiments known on the student evaluations of instruction. They have that right, of course. But can those types of comments sting? Of course they can . . . *and do*. In fact, Kath realized while writing this chapter that she had only committed to memory comments that were hurtful. She had to go look for positive comments. Most people tend to magnify negative comments and memories and forget positive ones (Tugend 2012). While only remembering negative comments doesn't always seem healthy, nor would *only* remembering the positive ones.

These outliers rarely give a great deal of insight into your teaching, although they might say more about the student who authored them. Try not to go Sherlock Holmes and see if you can suss out which student wrote them, etc. While sometimes that can feel good in the moment, it really isn't useful.

LOOK FOR PATTERNS IN THE DATA

At Valdosta State, one of the questions on the required university-wide student evaluation asks students what grade in the class they are expecting to receive. Many schools include a similar question. That is the first question Kath looks at; she tries to group comments initially: What kinds of things did students who believed they would earn good grades (As or Bs) say? Those expecting lower grades? Often she learns things just from this rudimentary grouping of comments. For instance, after several times teaching theory during the day, she noticed that students expecting to receive a C or D or F grade stated that they wished she had office hours immediately *after* the class instead of before it. They wanted office hours to "keep at" their learning while the content was still fresh. Since seeing that pattern, she schedules office hours primarily after theory classes. It has been a real success. Attendance at them is about 40 percent higher and almost always from just those students who are struggling. Many students call these postclass office hours "theory class 2.0." And her student evaluation comments for the class now often include positive comments about these after-class hours.

Of course, remember that for any change in your teaching or instruction, there may be unintended consequences. So keep an eye out for reverberations based on the changes you choose to implement based on your student evaluations. Did the change impact them? If so, in what sorts of ways? Interrogating the data this way requires each of us to track comments across academic terms, not just one term at a time. After you have looked at each class individually, don't forget to examine all of them from one term together to get a picture of that particular term from the students' perspective. After Kath made this change to her theory course's office hours, she began to notice that the students in other classes began to talk more about office hours, and not in a positive way. Students began to complain that "another class is always in there, it's hard to see you anymore" and "your office is always so full, I feel like you need a 'take a number' machine. . . ." So clearly, what worked for one class was negatively impacting other classes! She is still trying to find the perfect balance of before- and after-class office hours for every class, as well as online hours in the course management system. But these comments have sensitized her to thinking more about how office hours impact her students' ability to learn as well as her own life.

If your institution permits it, consider "priming the pump" by asking students additional questions about specific pedagogical changes which you have recently instituted. This might be a set of additional questions given to students or you might make a brief speech asking them to consider commenting on the changes to help you grow as a teacher. A caution, though: you will probably get the most feedback if your students complete the evaluations during that same class period. If your institution has shifted to online evaluations, there may be a big lagtime between when you "primed" your students and when they might actually complete the online survey.

Some institutions, like NC State where Maxine teaches, allow faculty to add a limited number of questions to the standardized form. Other institutions, like Kath's, allow groups of faculty to come together to write additional questions which are asked to all classes of that type. For instance, those of us at Valdosta State who teach large sections (N = 150+ students) got together to write four additional questions about the large-class environment and how it impacted the students' learning. While meetings to craft the language of those questions were open to all faculty who taught large sections, the reality was that about 15 came or submitted proposed wording. So if you teach classes which allow for collective construction of questions, we urge you to get involved in the process, so that you are as comfortable as possible with how the data being collected is worded.

USING PATTERNS FOUND IN YOUR EVALUATIONS

Sometimes student evaluations provide us with insights we might never have known about how we teach. Kath asks students to include comments for her future students—pieces of advice, if you will, in their comments. Early in her teaching career, she was astounded to read repeatedly from students who felt they were going to earn an A or B grade that "you better learn whatever it was she was talking about when she pounds on the podium, because guaranteed, it will be on the test." She had no recollection of *ever* pounding the podium, but clearly she did! After three terms of seeing those kinds of comments, she asked students in the next term to raise their hands every time she did it, because she was trying to learn about that teaching behavior of hers. They enjoyed helping her (especially when she passed on the advice from other students about how the material would likely be on the next test). But that assisted her to have the behavior become more conscious. It took about a year for her to realize she had pounded on the podium before a student would catch it—only then could she begin working on the behavior. It was an interactional quirk she had developed and didn't know she did; the student comments alerted her to it.

Another pattern that she has learned she has, because of student comments, is that she can talk faster than they can take notes. Many students equate this with Kath being "from the North. We Southerners talk slower." A few students have referred to this as her "auctioneer mode." Phrased that way, it hurt a bit. But she now deliberately tries to slow down her talking speed, especially in the last ten minutes of the class.

Students in her theory course talk about how she writes all over their papers and that sometimes that can be demoralizing, as well as difficult to read. That prompted Kath to create a grading coding system that she now uses in all her classes (see Table 14.1). This reduces the amount of words on the page. In addition, she tries hard to summarize positive thoughts about the student's work first, before any specific criticisms. Once she began doing that, these kinds of student comments all but disappeared.

Maxine gives out her grading rubrics with essay questions so that students can clearly see how they will be evaluated. She passes those rubrics back to students with their graded essays. The first part of every rubric includes: "The greatest strength of this essay is . . ." This reminds Maxine to start with the positive.

THE PROCESS OF STUDENT EVALUATIONS

When to Administer Them

In class. Have you ever backed yourself into a corner, forgetting to do the student evaluations until the last day of class, after you have just handed out students' final grades? Or the day you handed back a test or their major writing project? Yup, we probably all have been there at least once. So we would urge you to think about the timing of when you administer evaluations in class. Here are some things to consider:

1. When will you actually receive the forms from your department or whatever part of the institution it is that sends them out? Is it a time of the term that can be predicted? If so, think about that as you are creating the syllabus and try not to do them when you are returning graded work. Kath suggests not doing them on the very last day of the term. Like the first day, many students now expect to get out early and might resent that you are "holding them" up by asking them to do the evaluation. That might not put them in the best frame of mind. However, Maxine does not necessarily agree. The last day of class could be the best opportunity you have. If you have scheduled group projects or other end-of-the-term assignments, there is no reason to fret over having the evaluations on the last day. Many of us have moved to using online evaluation forms and students have a longer window of opportunity.

2. Should you list the student evaluation as an activity on the syllabus for the day you have selected? Kath does. She believes firmly that student evaluations need to be routinized as part of the student status and so she lists it as an in-class activity. She encourages students to think about what they want to tell her and to come to class that day with comments

prepared. But other faculty might disagree. Maxine thinks that periodically asking for feedback throughout the semester is a better idea. For example, about three to four times during the semester, she asks students to write a paragraph answering these generic questions: "What is going well for you in this class? What could be better? Is this something we need to discuss outside class?" Think about it and decide what works best for you, your teaching style, and how you interact with your students.

3. What supplies will be needed to administer in-class student evaluations? Does your department have them—in enough quantity for the number of classes which might be doing them on the same day? In Kath's department, before the school transitioned to online evaluations about four years ago, we had a departmental box of about 100 pencils. But there were seven classrooms, which held up to 500 students, all of whom might be trying to do the evaluations on the same day! Obviously that did not work well, so Kath just bought her own pencils and avoided the multiple problems this created.

4. How much time should students be given for in-class evaluations? There is no easy answer to this question. We think that the faculty member should not rush the students (that might send a negative message to them about how you discount their thoughts), but there also needs to be a time limit. Kath tended to give about 15 minutes at the end of the class. She passed them out, left the class, and a student was in charge of returning them to the departmental office. That way, if students needed more time, they could take it, but they might have to sit outside of the classroom to finish and individually take their form to the department office for inclusion. Students seemed to like this option.

Online student evaluations. In the last decade, many schools have now come to use online student evaluations. Students are sent a link in their e-mails which invites them to participate. Usually the institution has a set window of time for students to do the evaluations, often a two-week period near the end of the term, which ends the day before finals begin. Some institutions, which have online evaluations, allow faculty to see which students have completed the survey—but not what any particular student has said. At Valdosta State, there are three times during the open dates when faculty can log in and see which students have completed the online evaluation, but not their actual comments. Faculty can then encourage those students who have not completed the evaluation to do it. However, students can sometimes feel this level of "checking up on them" is creepy, so Kath doesn't use this information in her classes. Instead she just sends out a few reminder e-mails.

Again, be sure to find out your institution's norms about the administration of online student evaluations. If your class is small enough to take to a computer lab on campus, can you move the class to the lab, help students to log in, and then leave them to complete the survey? Or is taking class time for the online evaluation "against the rules"?

While there is not yet as strong a body of literature about online student evaluations as there is about in-class evaluations, many institutions, which have switched to online administration of the evaluations, have seen a drop in the participation rate (Avery et al. 2006; Crews and Curtis 2011; Dommeyer et al. 2010; Stowell, Addison, and Smith 2012). This brings up some complex pedagogical and ethical issues, especially if you are feeling pressure to have "good" student evaluation statistics, which includes a high participation rate. How much "talking up"/begging students to complete the student evaluations is best? is professionally appropriate? Kath announces that the online system is open twice, and that they should check their institutional e-mail for the link to it, and it is also on her syllabus. She also says that she would appreciate learning from students how she can improve as a teacher and their help in identifying things that went well in class and any which they feel did not. One of Maxine's ideas that Kath is excited to try is having her students bring their laptops to class in order to complete the online survey.

We recognize that we are also both tenured professors, who at most have to go through post-tenure review. Student evaluations have less power over our careers now than they might for many of you who are reading this chapter, and we recognize that fact. Faculty who are adjuncts, or visiting assistant professors, or new to tenure track might feel, quite legitimately, that you have to "play the game" and figure out ways to increase your students' participation rate in the evaluation process.

That almost inevitably leads to the question of "should faculty award points—either 'regular' points or extra credit—in order to entice students to complete the student evaluations?" This became a "hot topic" at Valdosta State last year. While the situation was complex, some of the upper academic administrators publicly supported faculty offering students extra credit to complete the evaluations. This caused a lot of conversation on campus. The administration was reacting to a drop of nearly 50 percent in the number of students completing the evaluations online compared to when they were administered during class. At NC State, the Faculty Senate was opposed to offering extra credit, and the university accepted its recommendations that faculty should not do so.

Both of us argue against offering extra credit for completing the student evaluation. Kath notes that her syllabus is clear—part of the role set of being a student is to complete the online survey, to help her grow and to benefit future "generations" of students in the course. Put that way, most students in her smaller classes (65 percent) usually complete the survey. In supersections, however, it is much harder to get first-year students to participate, and she has had as low as 13-percent and as high as 70-percent participation rates. Part of Kath and Maxine's reluctance to offer points (regular or extra credit) for completing the student evaluation is that many students are skeptical of the fact that the faculty member could know by name which students completed the survey, but can't tell what they individually said. It is difficult to combat these fears. We know some faculty who take class time to log in and show students what they can and cannot see while the survey is ongoing. At Kath's institution, each student in the class who begins the student evaluation is assigned a number (first to complete it is #1, and so on). That number is also attached to comments, so if student #2 made a comment but student #1 did not, the first comment would say "Student #2" and then list what the student said. This allows faculty to run statistical analyses on the data, because elsewhere student #1 and student #2 answered a question about what grade they expected to receive in the class, etc.

If you choose to offer points or extra credit, we believe that, pedagogically, it should be for a very low percentage of the total points for the course. Too much incentivizing of this activity might make it harder for faculty who do not offer points to students (like both of us!).

USES AND ABUSES OF STUDENT EVALUATIONS

There are many faculty who report that their institutions rely heavily on student evaluations of instruction for decisions about hiring, continuation of employment, promotion, and tenure. While we both believe this is a less-than-informed use of the student evaluation data, we know it happens. Worse, it is often linked to the students-as-consumers idea now common in higher education. Student perceptions are important—we are not denying that—but they should not be the sole arbiters of good pedagogy. We prefer that this data be used by the instructor as data for reflection, self-assessment, and the springboard for pedagogical change. Only in the rarest of cases should it be used to help determine employment status.

We do offer a caveat. While we do not see students as customers, they do have rights, and student evaluations can be one way to help protect those basic rights. Maxine served as department head and in that role read all of the student evaluations for her department. She looked for patterns in the data. For example, if there was an instructor who received great reviews with students making informative remarks, she tried to find ways to reward that faculty member, including nominating him or her for teaching awards. But, she also had to look for disturbing patterns. For example, if students repeatedly reported that faculty were not coming to class, that situation simply had to be addressed.

We become concerned, however, when data from student evaluations are used in ways that harm instructors' reputations and careers, especially when administrators are not aware of the many studies that have found inequities in student evaluations (Zabaleta 2007) and fuzziness on what student evaluations are actually measuring (Clayson 2009). The literature is clear that course topic (Baker and Copp 1997; Moore 1997), appearance of the instructor, including pregnancy (Baker and Copp 1997; Campbell, Gerdes, and Steiner 2005; Felton, Mitchell, and Stinson 2004), the sex of the instructor (Anderson and Smith 2005; Baker and Copp 1997; Basow, Codos, and Martin 2013; Chamberlin and Hickey 2001; Dukes and Gay 1989; Felton et al. 2004; Foote, Harmon, and Mayo 2003; Moore 1997; Schuman 2014; Smith and Anderson 2005), the race and ethnicity of the instructor (Anderson and Smith 2005; Basow et al. 2013; Smith and Hawkins 2011; Smith and Anderson 2005; Steward and Phelps 2000; Williams 2007), and sexual orientation (Anderson and Kanner 2011; Ewing, Sturkas, and Sheehan 2003), and even the social context of the course (i.e., face to face, hybrid, or online) all can influence how students evaluate the faculty member.

The above articles and many more show that the burden of student evaluation misuse often falls on faculty who occupy one or more minority statuses, and who often are early in their teaching career. We want to offer some advice if you fall into one of these categories and want to mount a defense of your teaching.

First, try to obtain aggregate data about the course in question, the other faculty who teach the course and their student evaluation data, your departmental teaching evaluation aggregate score(s), etc. Your department chair/head likely has this data or your Office of Institutional Research might have it. Recognize that they might be reluctant to share the data, especially about other faculty. If there is only one other faculty member who teaches a specific course other than you, to share the data in effect identifies that faculty member. They might claim that they are protecting the privacy of the other faculty member. While that might well be true, this data will eventually come out during the promotion and tenure review process, but perhaps only tenured faculty will be able to see the data. If you are blocked from obtaining data from these institutional sources, try asking your colleagues directly. Many might be happy to share at least common trends they see in their student evaluation data, if not the actual numbers. Again, look for patterns. Are all the women faculty members receiving lower scores than the men, irrespective of teaching style, level of rigor, etc.? If so, then likely there are some gendered effects at work. Ask similar questions about race, class, sexual orientation, etc. Maxine suggests asking your chair/head to look for these patterns. She regularly checks for gender, race, and rank patterns.

Second, see if you can tease out the course topic from the data about you and other faculty members as individual teachers. At Valdosta State, we have longitudinal data to show that—no matter who teaches statistics, theory, and research methods—the faculty member's scores are usually lower than when the same faculty member teaches other courses. This is because the content of those courses is considered the hardest by our students and that is reflected in their evaluations, irrespective of who teaches the courses. Those of us who are tenured make sure that when a sociology faculty member comes up for promotion and tenure review who has taught any of those three courses, a paragraph is included in the applicant's letter, which explains these patterns to those who will review the application at higher levels.

Third, we suggest that you gather more information from your students than absolutely required at the end of term. As Maxine has said, evaluations do not just have to be done at the end of the term. Many of us use an evaluation instrument about one month into the class, when there is time to make corrections to the course's direction, based on student feedback. Kath often has students do a short writing assignment at the end of class every month where she asks the students to state one thing that they would like her to do differently and one thing the individual student needs to do differently as the class continues.

Fourth, use feedback from other faculty as part of your argument, if you have it. This might be a review of your teaching conducted by your mentor in the department or it might be from a faculty member associated with your institution's Teaching and Learning Center, if there is one, or even another colleague in the department. Ideally, this person will use some sort of instrument that is either sanctioned by the department or the institution, or is based on the body of literature on peer review. Consider having these kinds of peer reviews frequently in your first years at the school, so you have a pattern of data collection from colleagues/mentors about your teaching, in a variety of classes. Ideally you will have established this pattern of wanting to learn about your teaching practice *before* "a problem develops." This might help administrators to listen to your defense of your teaching—that you seek on-going feedback, not just when you feel under attack. If they go well, consider including them to your pretenure/promotion/tenure documentation to show your commitment to pedagogical critique. And don't forget to mention what you have learned from them in any required narratives.

Fifth, really sit with your student evaluations. Are there useful ideas that you can glean? It helps if you can say to your department head, "My students feel X way about this aspect of my teaching and so I plan to make the following adjustments the next time I teach that class, but I do not feel that Y comments (i.e., racist, sexist, ageist, ableist, etc.) are something that I feel I need to address at this time because . . . " (and cite some literature here). Try to have the pedagogical changes you plan on taking be measureable, so that you and your department head can track progress over the next few academic terms.

And last, recognize that not all faculty or department leaders will understand that student evaluations can be biased. Kath was just at a meeting of department heads (in 2014!) when the subject of student evaluations came up, and a male department head talked about how he was uneasy making personnel decisions based on the comments of so few students, who often seemed hostile to the faculty member. Another male department head jumped in and blusteringly rejected that idea. A female department head joined the conversation and said, "Well, I gave up on believing what they said years ago after I kept getting comments on my makeup, haircuts, and attire, and not my teaching." The second male department head said, "What?" The female department head then asked every woman in the room (about 10 of us) if that happened to them, and we said, "yes, routinely" (see for example Campbell et al. [2005]). The conversation fizzled after that, when not a single male in the room (about 25) said he had ever had a comment about appearance on his evaluations.

CONCLUSION

Learning about how our students perceive our teaching style can provide faculty members with useful data. We encourage you to carefully consider your evaluations. Let any stinging comments fade a bit before you begin processing them. As patterns emerge, begin to think about if you want to continue the behaviors or change them. Come up with a plan and then implement it. We encourage you to accept that these evaluations are but one source of pedagogical feedback that you can receive. Seek out peers who can visit a class, talk with a mentor if you have one, participate in a teaching circle—all of these individuals can help you evaluate your teaching.

►►► **CHAPTER 16**
ASSESSING YOUR PROGRAM

Ah, program assessment. That's a phrase that often generates anxiety in faculty. Few of us rush off overjoyed to meetings about program assessment. We are often nervous about how data are gathered and who is in control of the results. We are especially worried that, in ever-increasing bureaucratized institutions of higher education, if honest results could be—would be—held against us. In this chapter we want to offer strategies for how to create a plan to assess your sociology program. But let's begin with the often unspoken question, "Why *do* program assessment?"

WHY IS PROGRAM ASSESSMENT NEEDED?

As faculty, we are comfortable with course-based assessment. Our students provide their thoughts about how a specific course went in their evaluations. We might keep a teaching diary (Purcell 2013) where we contemplate how any particular class went from day to day or at particular moments (e.g., first day, midterm, end-of-term). We then synthesize our thoughts on our annual faculty evaluation to our department head/chair and in our applications for promotion and tenure. But program assessment asks a different question: What do our students know now that they didn't know before majoring in sociology (Berheide 2007; Weiss 2002)? What have the readings, the written assignments, the class discussions added to each student's ability to think critically about the social and physical worlds they inhabit? What tools (e.g., statistical analyses, table reading, theoretical frameworks, etc.) have our classes either introduced our students to or deepened their learning?

Why are the answers to those questions important to know? In a time of limited resources flowing to higher education, institutions, departments, and programs are asked to demonstrate that students are learning. The era of professors being believed just because they are professors is over—if it ever really existed. Legislatures, governors, businesspersons, and citizens alike want to know that the monies spent on higher education are well spent. Done well, program assessment can go a long way to satisfy the curiosity of such outside stakeholders. But there are also audiences that are internal to the university who request program assessment data: provosts, deans, chairs and department heads, Offices of Institutional Effectiveness—all will want and need evidence that degree programs are well designed and then that they are delivering what is promised (see Table 16.1 for common models of program assessment).

We believe that there are two more stakeholders—the two most important ones—for whom a well-designed program assessment can be helpful. First and foremost are our students. We owe them the best, most cohesive process of introducing them to the discipline we love and then gradually but consistently deepening their analytical, theoretical, and problem-solving skills, as they advance through the degree requirements. We owe them the chance to develop their own sociological imaginations and help them to understand how what they have been learning can be useful in their personal lives and in a variety of careers.

And the last stakeholders—but who are often forgotten—are ourselves. As colleagues in a program, we owe each other the knowledge that each of us is doing our part in helping students to achieve what we—hopefully collectively—have constructed. The many conversations that go into a well-designed program assessment can help to create a sense of faculty buy-in to the entire program and not just the particular classes that each faculty member teaches. Ideally, program assessment creates an environment where faculty can work together to create a learning environment across the degree program that helps students succeed.

Few of us have the luxury of designing a sociology program "from scratch." Most of us join a group of people teaching sociology classes in an institution of higher education which happens to offer a degree in sociology. The degree already exists, *sui generis*. It is a social fact. Sometimes no one on the current teaching staff had any input into the structure of the degree, while for others, a few of the faculty may have taken part in creating the current structure, but

TABLE 16.1 COMMON MODELS OF PROGRAM ASSESSEMENT

Name of Model	Description of Model	Strengths	Concerns
Portfolio-based	Faculty select particular assignments from key/all classes and students build portfolio. Each is assessed for how much student met each learning goal. Either all students' work chosen or random sample of graduates.	Can assess learning longitudinally for students. Excellent to examine critical thinking, writing, and development of sociological imagination.	Will students save work? Most now moving to e-portfolios saved on institution's servers. Still have to develop robust assessment tools. Time commitment to read/reread all this work.
Major Writing Assignment	Can be in senior capstone/thesis course or in research methods course. Student has to create a researchable question, conduct review of literature, do IRB if necessary, and collect data. Then analyze data and draw conclusions.	Provides insight into whether student is able to see world from a sociological perspective, ask researchable questions, use appropriate research methods, act professionally and ethically, and use critical thinking skills to analyze data. Gives evidence of students' writing	Lacks longitudinal data on student to show amount of learning unless also paired with another kind of assessment.
Pre-/post Learning	Done in every class or certain foundational classes. Students take a pretest about course content and then either the same test at end of term or equivalent. Looks for gains in sociological learning.	Looks for the sociological value-addedness of being in class, doing readings and other assignments. A lot of data to collect every term.	Do all faculty who teach same class cover same material, in same depth every term? Without that similarity, difficult to assess across sections of the same class. Managing and saving data can be difficult. Not always able to look at specific students' change in sociological knowledge.

most have not. Program assessment, however, asks each faculty member to live in that established degree structure, while simultaneously reconsidering it. That "both in it and outside of it" space is not always easy to occupy, as we shall see when we discuss problems that can occur during the assessment process.

What follows is our recipe (Figure 16.1) for the steps a sociology faculty would need to accomplish in order to create a *useful* assessment plan for them and their students (and hopefully, for those external stakeholders as well).

FIGURE 16.1 SIX STEPS TO SUCCESSFUL PROGRAM ASSESSMENT

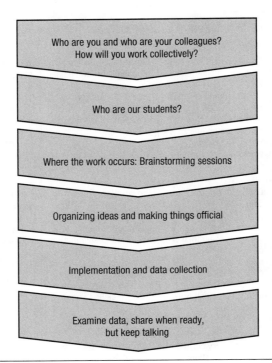

How swiftly a group of faculty could move through these steps—even the order in which you should accomplish them (or if some will need to be done simultaneously)—will be specifics which you and your colleagues will need to negotiate amongst yourselves.

STEP 1: WHO ARE YOU AND WHO ARE YOUR COLLEAGUES? HOW WILL YOU WORK COLLECTIVELY?

These early conversations about program assessment need to be not just about sociology, but about process. Under what processes will the group work? What constitutes group consensus? Does each faculty have the ability to block every decision crafted by the others? Or does each person have two "I strongly disagree" moments which can temporarily table a decision and force more conversation? These procedural conversations are important to have at this stage of the process. And be sure that they are included in meeting notes, so that all members of the faculty have them, in case they are needed later on in the process.

It is often easier to say that faculty should reach consensus than actually doing so. What will happen if one or a few faculty vehemently disagree with one of the program goals? With all of them? Should the conversation continue endlessly until consensus comes? What if it never does? How many people can disagree and still have enough buy-in from faculty for the plan to be labeled the "program's" assessment plan? These are decisions that need to be thought through in the first step, if possible, because it's likely that disagreements will occur many times throughout the process (Chin et al. 2014).

Potential Problems

We cannot forget the sociology we have learned when we enter into these brainstorming sessions. These conversations are made up of individuals with different ranks, different tenure statuses, and different personalities. Not everyone does well just thinking out loud. Some colleagues will want to consider their words and perfect them before a meeting. Others might worry about repercussions if they dare to criticize the status quo. Just saying "it will be okay to be honest" doesn't mean that those with less power in the program feel it is safe to talk. Nor will they likely feel safe saying they don't feel safe! So those with tenure need to think carefully about the mechanisms for these brainstorming sessions. We cannot assume that all will feel comfortable or even safe sharing their thoughts about the program in open conversations, even in the most collegial of programs. How might individuals be able to participate in a more anonymous way? One way would be to announce the topic a week in advance, ask each person to type up her/his thoughts anonymously. Perhaps go so far as to specify the font, etc., so that all are the same. As each person enters the room, the typed comments are put on the table. The facilitator then shuffles them up and passes them around the room and each person reads whatever comment he or she has received. This way it is not "your" comment. Or consider using software to allow for anonymous discussion. Perhaps have a discussion in the course management system and set the postings to "anonymous." What is important is that all voices who want to be heard feel as comfortable as possible in sharing their thoughts about your program.

Remember, though, that these brainstorming sessions have a social context to them—they are faculty thoughts and concerns. They need to be tempered with some data about the people in your program—your students.

STEP 2: WHO ARE OUR STUDENTS?

Early on in the program assessment process, faculty need to create an evidence-based profile of their current students. Most likely you will need to reach out to other parts of your institution for help in building this profile. The registrar, admissions, and your office of Institutional Effectiveness/ Assessment will likely be useful resources during this step. Here are some of the questions you will need to answer about your students.

When Do Our Students Enter Our Program?

Some first-year students come to college with a declared major. Many of these students choose STEM-related majors (e.g., biology, physics, chemistry, mathematics, engineering). Few first-year students declare sociology (Senter et al. 2012; Spalter-Roth and Van Vooren 2009). Many become our majors either after enjoying their Introduction to Sociology or Social Problems class or they try out other majors first. At Valdosta State, many sociology and anthropology majors were pre-nursing majors first, ran headlong into chemistry and anatomy and physiology classes, and realized that nursing was not the right career for them. Since Introduction to Sociology is required for VSU's pre-nursing program, they think back to that class and often see that sociological careers can mesh with their altruism/wanting to help people. At NC State students must choose a major upon admission and relatively few choose sociology because it is rarely taught in NC high schools. Similar to Valdosta State, they come to us when other majors do not work out or after they have had a good experience in one of our introductory classes.

It is important to know at what point students enter your program because if they enter with most of their undergraduate core courses done, they will either need to slow down until they are prepared for your upper-division classes or they might be taking some upper-division classes while also taking your lower-level or second-tier classes. This might create some academic problems for them in those more demanding classes. If your program is under pressure to "graduate students in four or five years," this kind of data will be important to learn as you consider changes to your curriculum.

What Type of Students Are Choosing Sociology?

Is your program attracting nontraditional students (e.g., military veterans, returning students) or are you attracting primarily traditional-aged students, who came directly from high school? How many of your new majors are considered at-risk academically when they enter your program (i.e., for mathematics, reading, or for writing)? What is the sex ratio of students in your program? The racial and ethnic distribution of your majors? Do you have many student-athletes? Knowing these kinds of data about your current students can give faculty a sense of who their majors are and—if the group later determines to try to change the student profile—how to market the degree differently. Is the profile of your graduates different than those who major in sociology? If so, then the faculty will have to investigate why certain types of students might have trouble in sociology classes and/or choose a different major than sociology.

Why Are Students Choosing Sociology?

Are students being asked this question during their first meeting with a sociology advisor? Are the data being collected, so that the faculty can gain a sense of students' reasons for selecting your degree? If students are being given closed-ended questions about why they chose sociology, we suggest including a wide range of options, including questions about the degree's flexibility on the labor market, their perception of the degree's intellectual heft/easiness, the amount of mathematics/statistics required for the degree, the quality and quantity of faculty–student interactions, and time to degree.

Data about why students are choosing their sociology major can help faculty customize some or all coursework. For example, if most students are interested in postgraduate studies in sociology, a more traditional "academic" curriculum might be appropriate, whereas if students talk more about using their sociological degree, with little consideration of graduate school in sociology (say, versus the MSW, counseling, or law degrees), then a more applied focus might better serve students' needs.

Potential Problems

If your admissions office and department keep good data on students, it will be easier to get answers to "when" and "who" over "why." Advisors should note that surveys conducted at the entrance to a major may reflect a rather superficial understanding of what sociology is and what one can do with an undergraduate degree in sociology, so the data may capture students' misperceptions as much as anything else. And if the program does not ask the hard questions about students' perceptions of the academic rigor of the program, then they might be getting the socially acceptable reasons for selecting sociology—which may or may not be accurate. If students have to fill the survey out in front of their advisor and turn it in to her or him, then these problems could only multiply. On the other hand, if the survey is done online, new majors may fail to take it, and then the data suffers in a different way.

STEP 3: WHERE THE WORK OCCURS: BRAINSTORMING SESSIONS

Looking at the Big Picture

Once you have established procedures and gathered data on your students, we suggest that the sociology faculty schedule some "brainstorming sessions," perhaps over a shared meal. Think broadly about who are the sociology faculty. Adjuncts who teach regularly for the program, full-time temporary faculty, and permanent teaching faculty not on tenure track should ideally be included in these conversations, not just those who are tenured or tenure track.

One topic for discussion might be "successes": What are the program and its students doing well? Don't narrow down what "success" means prematurely; let the conversation go where it goes. Some faculty will likely jump directly to academic strengths while others may see extracurricular activities such as Alpha Kappa Delta or a sociology club's involvement in the community as a success. Just let the brainstorming happen. A few people need to act as recorders, capturing the thoughts as they pour out.

Another session would need to be about "challenges to the degree program." These might be internal to the program (e.g., not enough faculty to staff the program completely, limited lab or classroom space which prohibits program growth, etc.) or external (rival programs that might be "capturing" students away from sociology [for example a Bachelor of Social Work], the level of academic preparation students bring to your program, etc.).

Another topic for brainstorming might be, "I wish we as a program could . . ." Here you all are turning the conversation from thinking about the present (your successes and challenges) to a different—hopefully better—future for the sociology program. Try not to let people throw up objections about others' wishes, but just listen to these wishes and ponder them.

Begin at the End

Good program assessment—be it of a program or of a course—begins with what you want students to know when they are "done" (see, for example, CCRP n.d.; Sample 2013; Wiggins and McTighe 2011). For a program, there are a number of questions which need to be considered:

- What should *all* students know when they graduate in sociology?
- What should most students know when they graduate?
- How well should they have learned the sociological content in order to graduate from our program? (e.g., is a GPA of 2.0 in the major enough evidence of their learning sociology? Or 2.5? Or . . . ?)
- Why is it that we feel they should know these sociological theories/ concepts and not others?
- How will we know that they have learned that sociological content? What is our evidence of their learning?
- For those students who don't learn sociology at the level we want, what resources do we offer to help them improve?
- Do we have in place a mechanism by which we collect data from (or at least try to)
  - Graduates/alumni?
  - Those who left our program and transferred to a sociology program at another school?
  - Those who transferred out of sociology and matriculated into another major on our campus about what motivated their decision to leave sociology?
  - Those who hire our students immediately after graduation? What are their impressions of our students?
  - Those who go on to graduate school? How well do they do in graduate programs? Are there elements of the undergraduate degree which they believe, in retrospect, are out of balance (i.e., not enough emphasis or too much)?

It can be tempting at this stage of the program assessment process to move too quickly from "what we want students to know" to talk of specific classes. Take the time at this stage to have the intellectual, practical, or even personality debates which may be lurking out there. It's important to do so here because having those debates at this stage (or earlier) will make future steps in the program assessment process easier.

For instance, the conversation might drift into, "Where does the theory course belong in our curriculum?" And our discipline has thoughts about that. Nearly every Intro Soc textbook and Social Problems textbook offers students an overview of "What is theory" and "Theoretical perspectives [albeit not always three]" in the early pages of the book. That is one kind of message about where theory ought to be located in the curriculum. The *Liberal Learning and the Sociology Major Updated* document (McKinney et al. 2004), while not mandating it, recommends that theory be taught as a second-level course. "The Task Force recommends that departments offer or require the theory and methods courses earlier rather than later in the major (i.e., late sophomore or early junior year rather than late junior or senior year)" (McKinney et al. 2011[2004]:12). However, many of our programs number theory courses as either a 3000- or 4000-level course, implying that the course is for upper-division students—again, another message about where theory should reside and the level of difficulty which should be anticipated.

But notice, "Where should the theory class be in our curriculum?" is a very different question than "Our students need to be able to think with and use sociological theories and how do we help them to do that?" Going too quickly to the "Where should it be" question can obscure a key fact about student learning: theoretical thinking (like every other theme you and your colleagues develop) needs to be infused throughout the curriculum, not just siloed into one or maybe two courses (e.g., Classical and Contemporary Sociological Theories). So a better question at this point is to ask, "Where are the moments in the program where theoretical skills need to be taught, refreshed, deepened, and used by students so that, upon graduation, they have a firm grasp of the theoretical tasks faculty want them to know?"

Discussing this question with other faculty members might result in a very different answer—not that theory "goes" in one class but, perhaps, that each class needs to devote time to addressing theoretical questions, at increasingly complex levels, so that students see theory in action applied to multiple sociological topics, from multiple theoretical perspectives, used differently by various faculty members. This does not preclude having one or two specific theory courses, but it also means that all faculty are more likely to "own" the theory goals and objectives. They no longer are just for the "theory faculty" to accomplish with students. Infusing theory in every course could have several useful consequences for students' learning:

▶ Students begin to get more comfortable with theoretical thinking as they see it in action more (minimizing "theory anxiety" [Lowney 1998]).

▶ Students move out of the mindset of "one theoretical perspective is 'right' and others 'wrong,'" because they will see, over time, when different research questions require different perspectives in order to find useful answers.

▶ They are given more theoretical information at different levels of curriculum and face more nuanced educational objectives about theory as they mature in the major.

▶ They see faculty make different theoretical choices about the same research topic and come to understand theory as a tool to think with rather than an absolute principle.

Another possible debate might be between how much "academic" sociology students should learn and how much applied knowledge they should get. While this debate has lessened, with calls for "public sociology" (see, for example, *The American Sociologist* 2005; Burawoy 2005; Clawson 2007), there are still those who believe that applied skills are less necessary for students to have. Others would argue the opposite; stating that fewer and fewer sociology undergraduates go on to seek a PhD in sociology (Spalter-Roth and Van Vooren 2009), and so faculty need to give students skills which can be easily transferred to work environments.

Clearly one programmatic spot which might integrate both of these differing perspectives on what students need to learn might be an internship course. But should it be required of all majors? Some majors? If not all, what criteria will be used to determine which students should take it and which would not need to enroll? And before deciding on paid or unpaid internships, be sure to read this literature about unpaid internships (Mangan 2014; McDermott 2013). This is an idea much debated in the press and in higher education legal circles right now, and sociology faculty need to be aware of the larger issues being considered about unpaid student labor.

Potential Problems

Continue to remember that even in the midst of hopefully productive and friendly conversation, there can be differences which people might not always be comfortable addressing. Is your faculty split along intellectual generations? That might create tension about newer sociological content and what its place should be in the curriculum. Are there splits between more "academic" and "applied" researchers? If these kinds of divisions, or others, exist, then the group might need a facilitator and will need to create mechanisms for allowing anonymous commenting, which could help to minimize status differences during these vitally necessary conversations. The goal is to create an inclusive curriculum which combines the faculty's intellectual goals for students with the students' interests in the best possible ways. While this process may seem easy, participants need time to build trust together, to reflect, and to share honest feelings about the current state of the curriculum and majors, without damaging relationships. We believe that the process needs thoughtful consideration over a period of time by all faculty.

STEP 4: ORGANIZING IDEAS AND MAKING THINGS OFFICIAL

After several brainstorming sessions, your faculty should have a list of so-ciological concepts/theories/theorists/skills which students need to have ac-quired by graduation. Don't edit the list—at this point in the assessment pro-cess, be a vacuum. Gather up all the ideas, mix them up, and let them churn. There will come a time for discussion, discernment, and even debate, but just generate a long list for now. This isn't as easy as it sounds; people may want to give qualifying statements, or say "I do that in X class," or even disagree. Try to keep the process focused on brainstorming skills for now.

It would be good to let everyone sit with the list for a week or so; let every-one contemplate it for a while. Then have another meeting and see if there are more items people want to add. Only when that has been tapped out, close the list-making process for now.

Then let your qualitative skills bloom! What common themes or catego-ries are there in the list? Some comments might easily fit under typical titles of classes, such as "Theory" or "Research Skills," while others might not fit so neatly into those kinds of categorizations. For example, one faculty mem-ber might have said that "students should write sociologically" while another said, "students should be able to follow the discipline's style manual." So the theme might become "writing concerns."

As you reorganize the brainstorming list into themes or categories, don't forget the "stray" comments mentioned only once or twice. At this point in the process those need to be lifted up for evaluation just as much as those mentioned by many faculty.

Often the next step in program assessment is to take the thematic list and begin to have conversations about each in turn. Let's take "theory" as a theme, with several comments from faculty such as: "Students need to know X's the-ory," and "They need to be able to understand the three theoretical perspec-tives" or "Students should be able to think about a researchable problem, and see the different kinds of questions each theoretical perspective would ask." Assume for the moment that faculty want students to be able to think with and use sociological theories to solve real-world problems. If that is a theme faculty arrive at, then how can they teach and use theory and craft theoretical assignments so that students can accomplish that skill by graduation?

Program goals and objectives should be emerging from these conversa-tions. They are the broad "promises" made by the sociology faculty about what students will be exposed to, will learn, and will be able to take with them upon graduation. Out of these conversations, faculty should be able to come to a more nuanced, shared view of what students can and will be expected to do sociologically in the program. These will be your program's outcomes. Once they are developed, then it will make it much easier to begin to talk about "classes" and where they fit in the curriculum. Out of these conversations and curricular decisions, a matrix will be developed (Table 16.2: What a Program Assessment Table Might Look Like), with sociological outcomes (skills) graduates should have acquired by graduation on one side of the table; on the other side will be presented the classes students take (required and elective, currently on the books and which might need to be proposed). Ideally, every outcome/skill should be taught/used in more than just one class (preferably several), but with higher learning expectations of students at each level. Outcomes which are just taught in only one class need the group's attention: Is that skill *so* necessary for your graduates? And if it is, why is it not repeated in multiple classes in order for students to deepen their understanding of it? Some of these "solitary skills" might be dropped as discussion continues or the group might find other points in the curriculum where that outcome could be reinforced.

It might be good to let the matrix of knowledge/skills/courses sit for a while and let the group contemplate it. Indeed, this is a good time to refer to the American Sociological Association's *Liberal Learning and the Sociology Major Updated* (McKinney et al. 2011[2004]) and *Creating an Effective Assessment Plan for the Sociology Major* (Lowry et al. 2005) and reports about majors which are collected and analyzed by the ASA's Research Department. Come back together in a week or so and see if people's views have shifted at all. Does everyone still agree that these skills get at the goals which were created? Answering that question likely will prompt more conversation. And that is the point—well-designed curricula need to have buy-in from (ideally) all the faculty so that they can "sell it" to students in ways that help students to see the connections and the unifying principles which undergird it. So take the time that you need in order to achieve that consensus.

Potential Problems

Sociology faculty are human beings, first and foremost. That means that when we are with students or with colleagues, we bring our humanness, our brokenness, our frustrations with us. Conversations about curriculum design, pedagogical strategies, grading, and faculty expectations will likely involve individuals' deeply held identities of themselves as teacher, about their experiences of being a student when they were in college and graduate school, about what is "proper" for students to be expected to do for a particular class,

TABLE 16.2 WHAT A PROGRAM ASSESSMENT TABLE MIGHT LOOK LIKE

ESSENTIAL SOCIOLOGICAL CONTENT

In this sample assessment table we chose to build on the Commission on the Accreditation of Programs in Applied and Clinical Sociology's (CAPACS) proposed assessment outcomes. A program could also use the ASA's *Liberal Learning and the Sociology Major Updated* (McKinney et al. 2011 [2004]). In line with the criteria provided by the CAPACS, every program must provide students with the essential sociological content listed here (Standards 2.0). The following is a detailed matrix that illustrates student grounding in essential sociological content. The matrix emphasizes how the required courses in Valdosta State's program provide an overview of the common core of theory, method, skills, and research ethics that constitute a desired sociological foundation for all sociological practitioners (Standards 2.2.1 a–h).

2.2.1 At minimum a Program shall:	Required Courses That Provide Grounding In Essential Sociological Content				
	Introductory Sociology	Social Problems	Statistics	Sociological Theory	Research Methods
a. *Examine in-depth a range of major sociological paradigms, theories, and perspectives.*					
b. *Cover the micro, meso, and macro levels of analysis.*					
c. *Examine a variety of methods used in both qualitative and quantitative sociological research including concept and problem formation, research design, data collection, data analysis, and interpretation.*					

d. Provide knowledge about diverse populations in diverse settings.

e. Cover a range of communication skills and appropriate use of computer technology.

f. Cover the social and political issues involved in sociological practice.

g. Infuse professional ethics throughout the curriculum and learning experiences.

h. Foster professional identity, including the responsibility to continue professional growth and development.

Adapted from the Commission on the Accreditation of Programs in Applied and Clinical Sociology's program assessment document (http://www.sociologycommission.org/).

and so on. These conversations will need skillful leadership to navigate the intellectual debates, the emotions, and the power dynamics involved. Can an insider do this or would it be best to bring in an outsider to take the facilitator status and guide the conversations? If resources are available, that might be an option to consider.

STEP 5: IMPLEMENTATION AND DATA COLLECTION

While the matrix is an important step, it is only a bridge to the next step. How will faculty in each class assess student learning of the knowledge and skills? This question most likely has been lurking over your conversations and now it is time to address it in a straightforward manner. For example, if one skill the group has endorsed is that students should be able to express themselves sociologically in clear and convincing prose, following the style of our discipline—how will any faculty member teaching a course show that her or his students have met that goal? Measurement is critical to a successful program assessment, but it is not always a straightforward process.

Consider that writing goal. What would "clear and convincing prose" look like for an Intro Soc student? A junior in a research methods course? A senior writing a capstone paper? Presumably, most of us would not expect the Intro Soc student and the capstone student to be writing at the same level. So what would sociologically convincing prose look like in different classes? How do you collectively want to measure your students' sociological writing skills? You will need to talk this through, until you come up with appropriate writing outcomes for your students. These might be, for instance:

▶ Introductory-level students:
  - have a limited number of sociological errors in writing (e.g., confusing role strain and role conflict, mixing up Weber's ideal typical characteristics of a bureaucracy with how bureaucracies "really" work, etc.);
  - have a limited number of spelling errors and grammar errors;
  - consistently use a standard reference style.

Should there be a requirement for Intro Soc students to learn the ASA style and use it in their writing? That would be up to you and your colleagues to decide. Maxine and I would probably recommend "no"—for first-year students, that they use a style consistently (any style!) might be a better outcome to assess. We wonder, in fact, if most of our sociology programs even teach the ASA style to our Intro Soc students, or only to majors (if it is taught at all).

But what does "limited number of spelling errors" mean? In this age of spellcheck and grammar check, is even one acceptable? You all will have to operationalize your goals and objectives as you write outcomes.

▶ Senior Capstone level students' papers should contain:
- a very limited number of sociological errors;
- the ability to explain sociological concepts correctly in the student's own words (i.e., not overwhelmingly dependent on quoting from references to explain concepts);
- the development of a clear and coherent sociological argument about topic;
- the ability to proof paper in advance and catch nearly all spelling/ grammar errors (i.e., independent learner of proofing and grammar skills);
- assuming your program has decided to teach the ASA style and grade on students' learning/use of the style, then an extremely small number of ASA style errors.

Of course, these are steps in the creation of the general writing goals, objectives, and outcomes for the program. There will be additional writing outcomes developed as the group arrives at what the specific writing assignments in each course will be.

There will need to be ongoing conversations as the group collectively refines these lists and operationalizes them into measurable terms. Eventually though, the faculty will have a set of:

▶ Program goals and objectives
▶ A set of agreements that detail
- Content coverage
  - What content is repeated but at more in-depth level?
  - What content is new in each course and why?
  - How will repetitive content be assessed at new levels of learning?
  - How will new content be assessed?
- What students should already know before each class (i.e., prerequisites) and will there be any sort of assessment of said knowledge at start of class?
- What should happen if students do not have the prerequisite skills even if they have passed the courses upon which those skills are based?

- What knowledge should students exit course with that will be needed in additional classes? In which specific classes? How will accumulated knowledge be assessed?
▶ Matrix of goals/objectives and outcomes where each class fits into the overall curricular plan

Once the plan is agreed to and all the measurements have been decided, it might be helpful to create a master calendar which clearly states what data need to be gathered, as well as when and by whom. Don't forget that there might be adjuncts also who will need to know these deadlines, so be sure that they are included in all communication about the program assessment plan. This way all members of the sociology faculty are aware of and can hold each other accountable for accomplishing data collection.

Potential Problems: When Agreements Are Not Honored

This feels like a good time to talk about "the elephant in the room." What happens if a faculty member either tacitly or explicitly fails to live up to these curricular agreements? For some, their refusal might be based on the fact that they didn't like the way the entire process unfolded; for others, they are fine with most of the classes they are teaching, but there are one or two classes for which they object to the consensus decisions, for whatever reason.

Some faculty may balk at the list of skills now required to be addressed in courses that they teach. Words like "I have academic freedom to teach my course" might even be tossed around! Hopefully, though, if the process has been built on listening to each other and keeping the needs of the students as the primary goal, there will be less of this. But should it happen, our advice would be that someone using "academic freedom" in the sense of, "you all are making me teach this concept/skill/theory, etc. in a class I teach and I don't want to do that" is confused about what academic freedom is. Academic freedom primarily is meant to protect faculty who—as a part of the agreed-upon content of a course—must cover controversial topics from a variety of perspectives (AAUP 2014). The freedom is that they will not be fired for their academically grounded statements about the "hot topic"; it is not the freedom to refuse to cover agreed-upon topics, which the faculty has decided that students need in order to graduate.

Instead of continuing to talk it through, this faculty member might drop out of the process, even if she or he is at the meetings, and instead might simmer, with a "they can't make me" kind of attitude, and knowingly violate the consensus by covering topics not agreed to or not covering topics which are to be covered in the course. And then again, in the rush of the start of a term, the faculty member might simply have forgotten about the curricular plan and how it should shape any particular class.

Another problem which could occur is that someone—accidentally or on purpose—forgets to gather the required data in a course which the person taught. Can students be tracked down and given some incentive to do the assessment? Or is it better to let it go, this once? What will this do to the overall assessment plan?

This raises the question of accountability. If all faculty sign on to the assessment plan, what can the negative sanctions be for not following through on one's part? Should this be reported to the department chair/head for inclusion on one's annual evaluation? Should the person be "outed" in assessment reports for failing to gather necessary data? If there is not some sort of mechanism for nonconformity, then a faculty member might choose to opt out of all the conversations involved in the assessment process, knowing full well that s/he never intends to follow through with required data collection. So conversations and consensus then become meaningless. Nothing will get the ire up of the other faculty more than someone they feel is deliberately sabotaging the process.

What can be done with such folks? At least the first time it happens, try to avoid assigning negative labels or reading too much into the faculty member's behavior. Assume the best—that he or she forgot or somehow really didn't understand how to implement these curricular decisions. Instead, this might be the time for one or two faculty to talk with the faculty member about the matter in private. If it truly was a misunderstanding or simple oversight, then fewer people know about the error and it can be corrected with less public loss of face.

But if this meeting shows that there are concerns which cannot be easily solved—that it wasn't simply forgetting, but disagreements about course content, program goals, or how, when, or why students should learn sociological skills during their time in the program—then this is a deeper issue, which will need to be talked about with the entire faculty. The leader will face a test of her or his power: how to call a meeting, ensure that as much as possible all faculty, but especially this faculty member, are given opportunities to share their thoughts and are heard, but to still arrive at consensus at the end of the meeting. The worst possible outcome is if the faculty member in question attends the meeting but refuses to say anything. Recognize that other faculty members—who thought the curriculum was a settled topic, at least for a while—might feel that the process has been derailed by one person's tantrum. They might need to express their frustration.

Curriculum creation and assessment often feels like one step forward and three backward. It happens at what can seem like a glacial pace, but more often, the time it takes to have these further conversations builds solidarity in the faculty and can create more ownership of the process and the curricular design which is the planned outcome.

As sociologists, though, we ought to recognize that it is rare that each member will agree on every part of the assessment process. Group dynamics can be messy and challenging. So keep in mind that the goal is consensus, not unanimity! Central to the assessment process will be creating an environment where all can express themselves and be heard. This is not just the task of the group leader; all who come to the table have to agree that this is the goal, work toward it, and keep their inner critic in check. As adults, we have to realize that we will be required to implement some curricular elements in the classes we teach with which we may personally disagree; that is the nature of consensus. It is for our students that we step up and live out our curricular commitments.

This might be a time, however, to think of Durkheim and how he stressed the power of rituals for group bonding (Durkheim 1995). Perhaps at the start of every academic year, faculty could have a short event/ceremony where they sign the agreements as an official step in their program assessment plan. But be sure that there is wording in the agreement about how failure to honor these agreements will be noted in annual evaluations done by department heads/chairs and in promotion/tenure/post-tenure reviews. That allows the departmental leader to begin to use the document in evaluations, even if not required at the institutional level.

STEP 6: EXAMINE DATA, SHARE WHEN READY, BUT KEEP TALKING

Assessment Audiences

Once enough data is collected then faculty will need to study the data, analyze it for patterns, and think about the meaning of those patterns. Here is another moment in a program assessment where consensus might shred. So it is helpful for all to remember that the goal of this process is a more coherent educational experience for students as they learn sociology. It is not about us (faculty), but our students. But interactionally, we know that when results might show that students are struggling with concepts from one class and we are the sole faculty member teaching that class, that it is hard not to get defensive, blame the students for not "getting" the "hard material," etc. That might all be true, but it might also be time to explore new strategies for teaching that content.

Ideally these conversations about patterns in the data will show faculty where students are succeeding in mastering sociological concepts and where they are still struggling. We can focus on analyzing precisely which outcomes/skills/theories/concepts they are struggling with and strategize how best to teach them and also, how to be sure that students get practice with those problematic elements of their sociological learning in multiple places in the curriculum.

But remember there is another stakeholder involved in the assessment process: your students. How much assessment data do you want to share with students? And when? We urge you to let students know about the general patterns. After all, their educational lives form the basis of your data. Faculty, for example, might share with students why certain assignments are required for a particular class. The more we share that the curriculum is (hopefully) a seamless whole which they will experience, and share in every class how the assignments build on earlier ones in other classes and set them up for success in future classes, the more our students will start to make the sociological connections that we want them to make. One simple way to do this is to include a "Connections" section on every set of assignment directions. Help students to see what skills which they already should know will be used in the assignment and what new skills will be involved. Show them in a few sentences how these will help them in specific assignments in future classes. Most will appreciate that knowledge.

Potential Problems

One of the reasons that some faculty complain about assessment is not that they don't want to learn how they and their students are doing, but that they worry about turning the data over to others who know less about the program, its students, and their struggles. Even worse, they fear that resources (e.g., faculty lines, departmental budgets) will be shaped around assessment data without faculty input. We are not here to say that won't happen. Of course there will be instances when assessment data can be used against a sociology program. Administrators may use results to reduce faculty lines, budgets, or other resources. But ironically, the best way to prevent this from happening is to have a program assessment plan that is designed largely, if not entirely, by you. Most administrators want to see that students are mastering the content of their major, that they are graduating in a reasonable amount of time, with a reasonable expenditure of resources on the program. A well-written assessment plan—which honestly addresses strengths and weaknesses (or "growth areas"!)—can give administrators that confidence.

We urge programs to contextualize the results and do an excellent job of writing up the results. For instance, if the numbers of majors has been declining, expect the administrator to ask "why?" But if a large number of seniors graduated on time (four to five years), then be sure to highlight that fact and celebrate the program's graduation rate success and how that plays a large role in the decline in the number of majors. Construct the data the way that best frames the program as meeting the mission of the university. Then shift the report's analysis to how the program is planning to recruit new majors (e.g., via social media, better advertising of what one can do with the degree, etc.). As sociologists we are trained in constructionism and framing; we have to use those skills in our assessment reporting.

Still, we know enough about presentation of self to realize that some of the assessment analysis might best be for an internal audience only. What you need to share with outside administrators—and how to frame those results which both honestly discuss where your program is at this moment in time and yet is not too overly self-critical in a way that will create institutional blowback—will require all the sociology faculty to work together to understand assessment politics, your campus bureaucracy, and the nuances of local budgeting and accreditation processes.

CONCLUSION

If faculty are able to come together to develop a comprehensive plan for studying how their students are learning and what sociological content they are learning, then program assessment can be a useful strategic activity. But attention must be paid to processes that help to create inclusion for this to work. Faculty need to be aware that silence—especially by nontenured or nontenure track faculty—should not be assumed to be acceptance and build in ways for anonymous participation. But done well, faculty and students alike can benefit from ongoing program assessment.

SECTION 4

TWENTY-FIRST-CENTURY
PEDAGOGY

►►► CHAPTER 17
TEACHING AND TECHNOLOGY

Times are changing. Our students are members of the first generation that has grown up almost from birth with computers and electronic toys/gadgets/communication devices. They are (or seem to be) comfortable with (some) technology, often claiming to be more comfortable than we might be.

There is a lot of debate about the implications for this technologically saturated generation, and in particular, what it might mean for the process of teaching them. We think it is important to read up on these debates and to come to your own conclusions. Howe and Strauss (2003) describe seven "core traits" shared by the millennial generation: they perceive themselves to be special; they are sheltered; they are confident; they are team oriented; they embody conventionality; they feel pressured; and they have a great propensity to achieve. Much of the generational literature talks about the fact that they are the most connected generation. We used to love going to the library to do research, flipping through those green *Reader's Guide to Periodicals*. Inevitably, we would find more treasures than we had planned, just by the process of flipping through the pages. But that is not part of how our students typically approach research and studying. They can "Google" something and find it in a few seconds. Immediacy seems to be a norm not only in their study techniques, but in their communication patterns as well. Many expect to reach faculty and staff quickly when they have problems, assuming that because they are "on" and up at all hours, that others are as well. Anything less can frustrate them.

They take pride in their technological abilities, but can become frustrated when they struggle with learning new technologies, such as a learning management system (LMS). They are so connected that some struggle to turn off their smartphone, laptop, or tablet; to stop texting; and focus on class (Hoop 2012; Khanna 2010; Moeller 2010). They are so used to media content coming at them at breathtaking speed, that even a fifty-minute "technology-free" class can seem like an eternity. When we say "please turn your electronics off," some of our students do not hear that as an invitation to learn, but as a statement of oppression. What might that kind of attitude mean for how we handle using technology in the classroom?

Let's not forget the meaning of technology—"in its narrow sense, tools; its broader sense includes the skills or procedures necessary to make and use those tools" (Henslin 2011:G7). Chalk, the ditto machine, the overhead projector, and even books have been considered cutting-edge technology in the classroom at varying points. So while there are myriads of possible technology available to use in the classroom today, it has probably always been that way—and always will be. Perhaps only the pace of the change has increased of late.

WHAT KIND OF TECHNOLOGY IS BEST FOR YOUR CLASS?

We deliberately labeled this chapter "Teaching and Technology" rather than other possible titles. We believe that sometimes having the newest technological gadget has taken center stage, instead of the teaching and learning that should be occurring between and with the students and the professor. The newest, shiniest gadget may be fun to play with, but the questions to keep in mind as one considers what technology to use are these: Is the technology being used in and out of class advancing student learning? How do you know that it is? If the technology does not increase student learning, why are you using it?

So as you sit down to create or to revise a course, we feel that one of your first questions, after creating your learning goals and outcomes, is to ask what kinds of technology might help students to learn what you want them to learn. That way, technology will always be in the service of student learning. Be forewarned—this is a more complicated question to answer than it might appear. Take, for example, the technological ability to post content slides

(PowerPoint, Prezi, Keynote, etc.) which you may create for classroom use. Many faculty have the ability to post them to a website or to an LMS. But the technological ability to post raises significant pedagogical issues. Does it foster student learning more—by requiring students to become stronger note takers—if the faculty member posts them only after class? Or would it foster better learning if the faculty member posted them before class? Giving students time to review and digest them might enhance discussions and generate more questions. Then again, might that, in some way, foster in some students a sense that they "have what they need already," and so they might choose to skip class? Other faculty might choose to not post the slides ever, notwithstanding the technological ability to do so, thinking that students need to become more self-reliant in their learning.

Which one is the best strategy? We believe the answer is, "It depends." Posting after class might be a useful strategy, especially if you also work with students to build their note-taking skills. But not to post them in advance because you assume that will lead to better note taking and learning, without testing that assumption, may be a risky pedagogical strategy. In fact, each strategy—posting before class, posting after class, or never posting—needs to be understood within an organic overview of your pedagogy. What level course is it? How complex are the concepts being covered? What is your classroom space like, especially in terms of visual access to the slides? What hour is the course being taught? How many students are in the class? Do the readings you are using cover similar content as what will happen during class time or do they provide mostly illustrations of class content and so what happens in class is the primary conduit of the basic sociological concepts you want students to learn? And so on. The answers to these questions will lead you to finding the best uses for technology for your students. What makes sense for our classes, however, does not necessarily make sense for every person's class—even if they are teaching the same course content.

Once you have begun to think through how technology might aid in your students' learning, there are more questions to consider. Many of these will be very campus specific. Unfortunately for faculty teaching at several different campuses in the same term, this can really complicate your teaching preparation.

▶ What technology is available to you for inside-the-classroom use? (e.g., audiovisual, podcasting, clickers, etc.)
▶ What technology is available to you for outside-the-classroom use? (e.g., LMS, audiovisual streaming, access to podcasts, etc.)

- ▶ How much support is available:
  - · for training in the software/hardware you may wish to use?
  - · for in-class support if the technology goes down? and what are the hours of support (especially crucial if you teach early in the morning or late at night)?
  - · Is there a FAQ for the technology for faculty which is available 24/7? One for students?
  - · How much training and support is there for students about the technology which you may choose to use? What hours?
  - · How much tech support is there for off-campus users (i.e., students and yourself)?
- ▶ What, if anything, is the cost of the technology to students?
- ▶ How much do you think students should pay for books and technological tools to succeed in your class? What is your personal "maximum" cost for students?
- ▶ Is the technology accessible to all students? (More on this in chapter 18.)
- ▶ What kinds of technology do you have access to at home? Most of us, I believe, find that class preparation happens more at home than at school, because it is hard to prepare around office hours, classes, meetings, advising, and so on. If you can only use the technology at your on-campus office, that might change your decision about using that software or piece of equipment.
- ▶ Apple or Windows? Most universities have branded their school as using one or the other software and hardware. But complications can arise with this decision:
  - · Is your home technology compatible with the school's?
  - · Faculty need to recognize that students often arrive at college as branded technology users, and are unlikely to switch just because of the college's technology decision. This means that faculty often need to become aware of common issues that might arise with other brands of technology, which students might try to use to meet your pedagogical requirements. Exceptional IT departments also will train their staff members on these issues.
- ▶ Does your school have proprietary software (e.g., SPSS/PAWS) that can only be run on school computers, thereby limiting your ability to prepare at home?
  - · If that is the case, does your school permit remote desktop access, so that you could have access to proprietary software? This kind of access allows a faculty member to download software on her home

computer and use it to connect through the Internet to her school computer. The latter, however, must be left on in order for the remote desktop software to work. Once connected from home, a new screen pops up which *is* the office computer's desktop.

· NOTE: Kath's school sells some proprietary software (MS Office, in her school's case) to faculty at an extremely low price. But there is a limited supply at any time and there is often a waiting list. This option helps out faculty who want to have the same software available on their school computers and yet not have to spend hundreds of dollars to do so. Check with your school's IT department about this.

DO YOU KNOW WHAT YOU NEED TO KNOW TO USE THE TECHNOLOGY WELL?

Congratulations—you've begun to think through your course and determined the ways that technology can assist students' success! But there is another important variable to consider, and that is you. How much technological knowledge do you have? Perhaps even more important, are you willing to admit what you don't know about technology? Do you have a personality which readily seeks assistance from those who know more or are you allergic to asking for technological help? Or are you somewhere in between? Knowing your "tech style" can be useful as you build your course. Kath has a lot of tech gadgets (iPod Touch, several laptops, two tablet computers, and a desktop computer). She usually has two of them (Touch and iPad or tablet) with her at all times at school, in addition to an "ideas notebook" that she also carries. Maxine does not have as many gadgets as Kath but she has an iPad, a laptop with a docking station, and a desktop computer. She uses two screens in her home office and her university office. Maxine is not nearly as technologically savvy as Kath but neither is she a Luddite.

We know there is a lot about technology we don't know. (If you want that last statement verified, just ask Kath's live-in tech guru/physics professor, her husband Frank.) Kath can get frustrated, especially when she tries to problem solve an issue multiple times, gets stuck, and then Frank comes in and does the exact same thing and . . . it works! Yet she is known around campus as an early adopter of much pedagogical technology. She is willing to try things if she can see how they might help students to learn. Unlike her husband though—who just opens up software and starts to play with it—she knows that she needs training before she begins to use the software. "Playing" with it—and having it not work correctly—is frustrating and she readily admits that she loses interest. Maxine is exactly the same but has less interest in technology. She usually waits until one of her graduate students or colleagues is excited about a new technology to investigate it. Kath is a frequent participant in her campus's IT training sessions. When she attends, she goes assuming the best of all possibilities—that the software will be useful to her and that she will be able to figure out how to use it. She also is eager to learn from the IT staff. We think the latter attitude is important. Kath has a story she wants to share—though the name of the person involved is changed, for reasons which will become obvious.

About ten years ago Kath attended training on how to use the gradebook in—at that time—our new LMS. She sat next to an older male colleague from the College of Arts and Sciences—let's call him Horatio—and they talked until the class began. Kath's computer was turned on when she sat down; his was not. When the class began, the trainer said to all of us, "Please turn your computer on so that we can begin." Out of the corner of her eye, Kath noticed that Horatio seemed to be having a bit of trouble, but let it go. Five minutes later, and he had still not figured out how to turn on the computer (the power button was on the back of the tower, where he never thought to look). When Kath offered to show him how to do it, he rebuffed her. After about fifteen minutes, he began to press each key, first alone, and then in combinations. He was getting a bit frantic and he attracted the attention of the trainer. The trainer offered to help, but Horatio rejected her assistance, too. And so the training went—he madly pressed combinations of keys trying to turn the machine on (and increasingly, swearing under his breath while pounding the keyboard loudly), while the rest of the group followed along with the trainer. At the end of the ninety minutes, he had still not managed to turn on the computer, and he had alienated all of the people who had offered to help him. Kath wondered what his perception of that event was. Did he go home that night, commenting on the "damned difficult software"? Her guess is he did.

So if you go for training, go with an open mind and accept help! Even if you come away knowing that a particular software is not useful for your pedagogical goals, it was not a waste of time. And don't forget to keep track of the training sessions you attend for your annual report and/or promotion and tenure packet! While there, practice what we want from our students: active learning. Don't just sit there—try out the software, ask questions, bring home the handouts, and keep using it. It might be a while before you teach a course where you need it, so you don't want to lose the skills learned.

We have one other major suggestion to make: get to know the IT staff and offer to help them. Sometimes they need a faculty member or a class to test some software. Go for it once in a while, if you feel it will not negatively impact student learning. You will help them and they will, in return, be more likely to help you in a pinch. Remember Homans's exchange theory! When they have helped Kath out beyond the call of duty, she has sent pizza to their offices or a big box of candy the next day. We think faculty and students often unload on their IT staff—more than a few of us in colorful language and with a not-so-nice attitude—so make a deliberate choice to be different. Treat them with respect and professionalism and they will notice!

WHAT TO DO WHEN TECHNOLOGY FAILS

But sometimes, even with the best preparation and training, technology fails—sometimes spectacularly. What should a faculty member do then? Our first piece of advice may seem odd, but about some things we are pessimists. We assume that it will fail and are prepared for that contingency. If it works, then it's a good day! Here are some ideas for the days when technology fails:

▶ Have all IT emergency numbers in your phone. If you have others with you in the class (e.g., a GA or TA), require them to have the information as well. Sometimes we can get lulled into thinking we don't need these numbers, because there is an "IT help" button on the computer desktop. True enough; at Kath's institution there is. And it summons help wonderfully. But what happens when we cannot even get the computer to turn on? That's when the phone numbers really come in handy.

▶ Always carry backup tools with you at all times (e.g., whiteboard pens, chalk, etc.).

▶ Carry a hard copy of your lecture/slides with you unless you feel comfortable enough not to need this in order to be able to cover the material for the day.

▶ If the use of technology (e.g., clickers) is a part of the points/grade awarded for that day, have a plan for tech failures. Students will be anxious and worried when the technology goes haywire, so know what your plan is. Ideally, tell them in the syllabus what will happen, so that you have had time to think about what to do and are not making the decision on the fly. We'll say more about this on the next few pages.

▶ If you are using an LMS, what happens if it crashes right before an assignment is due? Without a policy in advance, you could easily be deluged—especially in big classes—with hundreds of "When is the assignment going to be due now?" e-mails. And expect failures to happen at busy weeks for the institution's electronic infrastructure (e.g., at the start of the term, near midterm, during registration if it is an online process, and near the end of the term).

Through trial and error, Kath has developed the following syllabus policy for out-of-class work to be submitted using the LMS : "If the LMS goes down within 12 hours of the time an assignment is due (as verified by the IT staff), I will grant an automatic extension of 6 hours from the time the LMS goes back up. Assume this will occur; please do not write me at my school e-mail asking about an extension. If it goes down overnight, while I am sleeping, I will confirm that it went down with campus IT staff before turning on the extension" and she encourages her students to use the additional time to make their assignment even stronger!

Kath doesn't reply to students who write her outside of the LMS about what to do in case of such a technology failure, and if it is a very large class, she has sometimes added that failure to follow this policy will subtract five points from a student's final grade.

DEALING WITH STUDENTS' QUESTIONS AND ISSUES

Before discussing specific types of technology and how they might be used in sociology classes, Kath first wants to discuss one more issue. The more she uses technology in her classes and in her private life, the more "pet peeves" she has developed. They frustrate her to no end, so she lets students know what her "pet peeves" are and why they bother her. She used to be embarrassed to own that she had any such issues, but now she lets students know them so that they know she is human, that certain behaviors they might do could cause her stress and strain (e.g., trying to grade 350 assignments when each one requires nine clicks of the mouse just to get the file to open—it's not that fun!—so anything they do to add to that doesn't make her very happy). Here's some of her list—what is yours? And do you tell them to your students?

▶ Not having an assignment turned in via the LMS the way each student is asked to save it (LastNameAssignment1, etc.). She explains that in a large class, without a standardized naming system, she could easily get 100 assignments labeled "my assignment." Since she keeps all graded assignments (both the original and her graded version), adjusting files to the requested norm would involve her renaming the assignment twice for each student. That is a lot of typing for her and she refuses to do it.

▶ Not following her directions about formatting, which are included at the bottom of every assignment. She includes the following:

- Don't widen margins to make a short paper look longer. Own it if your paper is short; don't try to hide it.
- Use the spell-checker and grammar check tools. While they can miss certain spelling errors (e.g., homonyms), they catch a lot of mistakes, which if left uncorrected can detract from the sociology you are trying to show her. To support this norm, all of her assignments involve some points for spelling/writing/sentence construction as well as development of an argument.

▶ Using software she doesn't own and then expecting her to be able to grade the assignment. She specifies that documents should be uploaded in Word (.doc or .docx—her university's standard software) format or .rtf or PDF only, but many students have Microsoft Works and use that for their work. She cannot open those files. There are sometimes similar issues with students using Apple products to construct their assignments.

▶ In recent years, as the use of flash drives has become more common, she has experienced the ".lnk" error. This is when a student goes into "Recent Documents" and chooses the icon of the file to upload, but not the file itself. The LMS uploads the icon, but the file is not there.

Kath has found that if she is proactive about common issues students might have with technology, it helps with the emotional temperature of the class. She now sets up a "FA(T)Q" section in the LMS. That stands for "Frequently Asked (Technology) Questions" and their answers. As part of her requirements for uploading an assignment, she has students affirm that they have reread the assignment directions and the FA(T)Q section. Therefore, if they make mistakes discussed in either place, they are responsible for the point loss. Each of us will have different common questions, but here are the ones Kath includes:

▶ "What happens to my daily clicker grade if I forget my clicker? Can I submit my answers to the questions on paper?"

▶ "My clicker battery died and I haven't had time to replace it. Can I submit my answers to the questions on paper?" (Kath recopies the clicker policy statement from her syllabus, which answers both of these questions.)

▶ "Can I submit my assignment via LMS e-mail? Via Windows Live e-mail?"

▶ "The LMS went down. Now what?" (Here she will repeat the syllabus policy.)

▶ "I forgot how to attach an assignment using the LMS assignment function. What should I do now?" (Kath links to a Word document with screen captures of each step.)

▶ "I cannot get into the LMS chatroom for online reviews and office hours. What should I do?"

Kath's university's E-learning and IT departments have excellent help resources available by phone and a live online help desk and FAQ websites that answer the above LMS questions. In addition, her syllabus and a folder in the LMS called "Class Policies" contain the answers to the other questions. But when students have a tech issue, they often become stressed and do not problem solve by thinking of those resources; rather they will turn to the faculty member in a panic. Kath tries to change their definition of the situation and encourages them to use these other resources. But often, unless there is a deterrent (i.e., loss of points for asking a tech question answered in the FA(T)Q), you should expect to be their default choice for technology help. Do you want to become their tech guru? If so, this isn't really problematic. But if you don't want that status, provide multiple ways for them to get help and teach them where they are and how to use them. If more than five students, for example, make the same new tech error on any one assignment, consider adding it to the FA(T)Q section of the LMS.

WHAT TECHNOLOGIES ARE AVAILABLE FOR USE IN CLASSES?

Nearly every month we read about new possible technologies, so we worry that this chapter will be outdated long before publication. But we do want to talk about some of the main technologies being used in higher education classrooms right now.

Learning Management Systems *(also called class management systems)*

The number of LMSs seems to be growing nearly every month. There are open-source ones, such as Sakai and Moodle, and there are corporate ones, such as Blackboard and Brightspace. And some schools build their own LMS, so that their campus-specific needs can be addressed promptly. Regardless of how the LMS was created, they all function in similar ways. They allow all communication and documentation about a class to be stored in one place. Usually they have a variety of tools which instructors can choose to use, including:

▶ announcements/news (which quickly push out a message when students log on to the LMS);
▶ an assignment tool or dropbox tool which allows students to submit either text or attachments for faculty to grade;
▶ a calendar tool which allows faculty to post important dates (good LMSs allow for the creation of a calendar entry when assignments are created);
▶ a chat/whiteboard tool for private or multiple-person online conversations;
▶ discussion boards (which usually have the option of public or private discussions and/or blogs);
▶ e-mail;
▶ a gradebook (which usually allows the instructor to export to or import from a spreadsheet);
▶ a way to create groups of assignments/readings/tasks—usually these are called learning modules;
▶ a syllabus tool (though we find that posting Word and PDF files works better—for more on why, see chapter 18 on accessibility);
▶ a web links tool which allows for posting and organizing readings from the web.

Many LMSs also have a tool which allows an individual logged into a class to see who else in the class is currently online in the LMS. A caution though: the person might not be working on your class, but might be logged in and working on another class.

Benefits of LMS. One of the benefits of using an LMS is that faculty do not have to learn how to create, program, edit, and maintain a website for each class. Much of that is "done" for the instructor already, although there are some options (e.g., one can usually choose a font, colors of text and backgrounds, and a few other small design elements). The assignment dropbox keeps track of all student work, so issues of faculty losing papers, etc., disappear. The ability to capture all work is useful—especially in the case of a grade appeal—but that presumes that students will use the LMS to communicate with the faculty member. Often students who are less engaged with the class, perhaps having attendance issues, rarely log in to the LMS or they forget to write faculty using it, which defeats that benefit.

The way that most LMSs are created allows for multiple ways to find things. For example, all the discussions are under the "discussion" tool, but if the faculty member chooses to put them in a learning module, they can be found there as well. Each of us—faculty and students—will find the way to search for links that makes the most sense to us.

Another benefit of an LMS is that faculty can track student usage. So if a student e-mails you, worried about her grade, we suggest that before you reply to the e-mail, you track her involvement in the class. How frequently does she log on? What parts of the LMS does she use most? Has she opened files with assignment directions? And so on. While we don't suggest tracking students to the point of stalking them, especially in first-year courses, this ability can be useful to let them know you know their level of involvement and have some concerns.

Limitations of LMS. Learning management systems do have some limitations. While those of us who spend a lot of time on LMSs, smartphones, and WiFi tend to overlook this issue, the use of an LMS in a course requires that students have Internet access. Especially in rural and poor areas, that assumption may not be true for all students who live off campus. To require students to spend a lot of time on an LMS might be forcing them to come to campus or a local library with Internet access more than they had planned or that their work schedule might permit. So faculty members might want to check with students about their online capabilities during the first weeks of class.

A second limitation is that any of the LMS products has a learning curve—for you and for your students. This is particularly important to realize if you are teaching a class for first-year students in their first term at college. Some might have used an LMS in high school but many may not have done so, and they can find it overwhelming to find where you place readings, assignments, and so on. Kath resisted using the learning module tool in her campus's LMS for nearly nine years. But when the sole negative feedback she received from students in her Fall 2010 Introduction to Sociology class, on the last day of class, was about how "busy" the class's homepage was in the LMS, she realized that what she felt wasn't what was important; it was what they felt. Ever since, she has used the learning module function. Each week has its own module, and any assignment, discussion, required chat, web reading, etc., which is open or due that week, is linked in that module.

Probably the two biggest problems with LMSs, however, are beyond faculty members' control. First is the fact that, almost inevitably, they will go down during the term. This kind of failure is frustrating for both students and faculty. All any of us can do is wait for the outage to end and then communicate with students about what, if anything, has to be changed due to the failure.

The second issue with an LMS is its accessibility. Not all LMSs allow icons, such as a file folder icon, for example, to be tagged for screen readers needed by students with low vision. While many companies are getting better with accessibility issues, one still needs to be prepared to work with students who have trouble with the LMS your school has selected. We will talk about how to work around these issues of accessibility in chapter 18.

Student Response Systems or Clickers

While certainly not a "new" technology, the use of clickers in college classrooms has grown in the past decade. Clicker devices are relatively small in size (similar to a handheld calculator or even smaller), use radio frequencies, and allow faculty to post a question and then give students a range of answers from which to choose during a set period of time. After time has run out, it is possible to see the class's aggregated results. Results can provide feedback to faculty and to students about the students' comprehension of complex concepts, difficult definitions or formulas, etc. Depending on how the faculty member set up the software while writing the questions, each individual student's results can be captured and posted to the LMS gradebook or imported into a spreadsheet for points.

Benefits of Clickers. If faculty follow best pedagogical practices for using clickers, then they will space the questions throughout the class period, incorporate some questions for points and others which gather class opinions, and make the questions be low stakes (i.e., not for a lot of points [see Bruff (2009) for more on these]). Questions can be "stacked" so that a student must commit to one answer and then build on that decision in another question. Complexity therefore can be built into clicker questions.

Clickers can create student engagement, because students want to know what their peers think. In Kath's large Introduction to Sociology sections, students keep track of the class's percentage of correct answers from day to day, often trying to get to 100 percent correct on a question. They will often share how they reasoned to find the correct answer, without anyone who got the answer wrong having to admit to the error. Her students enjoy the opinion questions, such as the following example, which sets up the concept of "role conflict." Kath uses this question before introducing the concept. The question elicits lots of conversation among students once the results are shown, and keeps them interested as she transitions from the clicker question example to the definition of the concept:

> Imagine that you are a police officer, working the overnight shift on a Saturday evening. You spot a car ahead of you on a busy street, weaving in and out of the lane. You pull the car over and walk up to the window. Shocked, you see your 16-year-old child behind the wheel, buzzed on alcohol. What would you do?

> 1. Call your romantic partner to pick up the child and deal with the incident at home the next day but do not get other law enforcement officers involved. This is a family matter only.
> 2. Test your child, and if he or she is legally drunk, arrest the child and take him or her to jail.
> 3. While you are furious at your child and want to arrest him or her, you don't because you know that if you did, it would cost your family several thousand dollars and higher insurance rates.
> 4. I don't know what I would do; I feel torn between choices 1, 2, and 3.

Once students have selected their answer with their clicker, we can immediately see the class distribution and can launch into a discussion of the example. Then Kath can transition from it to the definition of the concept, and provide a few more examples.

While most faculty insert questions into their presentation software (i.e., PowerPoint, Keynote, or Prezi), companies have created the possibility of asking "on the fly" questions—unplanned in advance—which can build on conversations in the classroom.

Limitations of Clickers. While the technology still is evolving, right now most clickers are stand-alone devices, which means that students have to purchase them. While different companies have different price points for different capabilities, often a clicker could cost about fifty dollars, and that can be before a bookstore markup. That is in addition to books and any other required supplies for the course. The good news is that one clicker can be used for multiple classes, so the cost is a one-time factor in students' budgets. Enterprising students can create a "used clicker" market and lower the cost. The bad news is if your class is the one which requires the purchase of a clicker—even if students also use it in other classes—expect to hear about the price.

The clicker technology is rapidly changing; companies seem to be heading toward the use of smartphones. Students will download the clicker app, register for your course, and use it to answer questions (of course, this means that their phone will have to be out and "on" during class, if you want to use the software). This would eliminate the need for a separate device and the cost of the device, but it also assumes that all students have smartphones. Likely there still will be a cost for "enrolling" in your class, as a way for the company to make money. For the next several years, there will probably be a combination of devices being used by students and faculty.

There is no getting around the fact that there is a bit of a learning curve with clickers for both students and faculty. We would suggest that faculty who are interested in using clickers first go look at how a few other professors are using them on your campus and really think about whether clickers will add to your students' learning. If you feel they can enhance learning, then go get trained by IT or E-learning/distance learning staff. You want to learn best pedagogical practices and how to use the software (i.e., how to create questions, assign points to questions, insert them into the presentation software, download participant lists, and import grades to either a spreadsheet or your LMS).

As you would with other technologies, you have to be prepared for the software not to work correctly. Kath admits, however, that that usually means she did something incorrectly in class with the clickers, which means that the capturing of student choices and linking those to individual names did not work correctly. In her experience, when something did not work, it was usually "user error" rather than the students' or the software actually failing. Most often Kath's user errors involved setting up the clicker software, then choosing to change something in one of the slides. In order to do so, she had to rush through the steps once again, and often she forgot one (usually the step where names are linked to the students' user numbers). She had all the data, just not linked to any particular student!

Audio Capturing to Web/LMS

Here we mean several different types of technologies, such as inserting audio over PowerPoint slides or taping class and posting to the web or to the LMS. There are several types of software which allow faculty members to accomplish this (e.g., Acrobat Audition, Wimba), so we want to focus on the pedagogical aspects of the software.

Strengths of Audio Capturing. Whether the faculty member captures a lecture in advance of class and posts it for students to hear and watch (a technique often used in "flipping the classroom"; see more in chapter 19) or tapes a lecture during class and posts it afterward, having the faculty member's words available 24/7 can be an asset to students' learning. Of course, having the audio file available and having students actually use the file to learn course content are not the same thing! But certainly the possibility of listening to sociological content (for the first time or multiple times) can assist students who might not be the strongest note takers, or who feel they are more aural learners.

Limitations of Audio Capturing. Perhaps the biggest faculty worry is how this technological tool will impact attendance. The answer lies in part with the timing of posting the audio file to the LMS. If the file is posted before the class, then attendance might dip if all that will happen in class is exactly the same as what is said on the file. But those who advocate "flipping the classroom" would say that is not the correct way to implement the technique. The lecture content should be posted ahead of class, and then in class, students and faculty should apply the new content to real-world examples based on the lecture content. Faculty have to craft engaging, active learning activities which can assess learning goals, and work well with the classroom environment and class size.

A second possible limitation is whether all students will have access to the required software and Internet speed required to download and listen to the audio file.

Back Channels in the Classroom

Be it Twitter, WordPress or some other blogging software, or the LMS's ability to create a blog or discussion thread, some faculty are experimenting with back channel communication in the classroom. Imagine a large lecture hall brimming with students, engaged in an active learning activity, and students are able to tweet questions and comments to the class's Twitter site and get prompt responses from each other and the professor. The back channel can keep students engaged and thinking, asking questions as they arise. A graduate assistant can be assigned control over the back channel, deleting anything inappropriate, tagging comments with similar themes for the faculty member to come back to in discussion, and so on. The discussion can continue online after class, in Twitter's short bursts of conversation.

Since this is one of the newest ideas for using technology in the classroom, there is little data yet about how successful this can be. Certainly some faculty (Ferenstein 2010; The Modern Educator n.d.) have had success with it. But this technique requires allowing the use of computers/smartphones in the classroom instead of banning them. For many of us, this kind of teaching with technology would be an act of faith: Can students stay on task and refrain from updating Facebook, etc.? Kath had this debate with herself in the summer of 2012. Did she want to open a back channel in her 350-person class, or would that be fostering an environment where some students who could not stay on task could fall through the cracks? Her thinking then was that she was going to take it slow, and she met several times this summer with her campus's social media staff member to craft a compromise that feels comfortable to her both pedagogically and technologically. She created a class Twitter account, but students who chose to post would have 24 hours *after class* to tweet about the class topic and make connections to the "real world" (this will be one of three social media options students can choose from as a required assignment). A graduate assistant will do a thematic analysis, and we'll start off the next class with a brief review of the Twitter comments and one will earn the "Tweet of the Week."

Whether you want students to use available technology during your classroom is up to you. There are no right or wrong answers—but students are increasingly expecting us to have a rationale if the answer to "can we use our computers in class?" is "No, you cannot." What are your pedagogical goals and learning outcomes? Where can technology assist you in communicating sociological concepts to your students, be it in the classroom or outside of class? Are you building ways of assessing if and how technology is assisting your students to learn? These are the questions which need to guide your teaching with technology.

Video Inside and Outside of the Classroom

Many faculty choose to show short videos, such as commonly found on YouTube, either in the classroom or outside of it, in a "flipped" manner. Usually the videos are used to illustrate a concept. We believe that using video in this manner can be a wonderful way to reach students and engage their critical thinking.

Strengths of video. If the video is chosen well, students will find it intriguing, interesting, and will be able to see the connections you want them to see. However, this doesn't happen without effort—yours and theirs. We suggest that you teach students how to watch videos for educational purposes. Require them to take notes and to learn all key names of individuals/characters in the video. Test on this information!

If you create your own videos, consider creating a YouTube channel (Google 2014). Post your videos there and insert a hyperlink for each one in your syllabus and/or on your LMS.

Not brave enough to film your own videos? We suggest you use curators of film clips. Kath likes The Sociological Cinema (2014) best right now. This site has links to hundreds of video and film clips as well as pedagogical suggestions. For more information on how to use this web resource to its utmost (and copyright concerns), read Andrist et al. (2014).

Limitations of using video in the classroom. There are three concerns we want to raise about the use of video/film in the classroom. First, how sure are you that the clip you want to play really illustrates what you need it to do? If you find yourself having to explain it for quite a while in class, that might be a sign that you need to rethink that video selection. Second, how long is the clip versus its usefulness? Often faculty show more than they wanted to or needed to because they do not know how to clip and edit. If you have the ability to cut or edit, then you can take out extraneous moments and just show the relevant passages. If your clip has too many characters, with complicated backstories that students don't understand, the usefulness often declines precipitously.

The third limitation is about accessibility. All videos you show need to be accessible. That means that they should have screen captioning available and you should make a transcript available. We turn to the topic of accessibility in the next chapter.

►►► CHAPTER 18

MAKING YOUR COURSE
ACCESSIBLE TO ALL STUDENTS

Time to be honest: neither of us are lawyers and we don't pretend to understand the complexities of the Americans with Disabilities Act, its latest revisions, nor the numerous other laws which impact higher education's views on and requirements about students, faculty, and staff who have impairments and/or disabilities. So we won't even try to write that kind of a chapter. Instead, we want to begin where we all are—as sociologists who study and teach about how power, social structure, and identity are socially constructed. Higher education is a stratified complex of statuses, roles, social structures, and identities. While any one faculty member has little institutional power to create change, we sometimes forget that each of us as faculty do have a fair amount of power over the educational lives of the students in our class. The key sociological question is, then, how do we exercise that power? If you knew one or more of your teaching techniques unintentionally made learning harder for some of your students, would you be open to change your behavior(s)?

Kath wants to share a true story, one that changed her teaching in a profound way, but not in a way that many students are likely to even notice. About three years ago, she was invited for coffee by Dr. Kimberly Tanner, the Director of the Access Office for Students with Disabilities at Valdosta State University (VSU). In the days before the meeting, something kept floating around in Kath's brain. A few months before, there had been something posted to the campus website about a federal Department of Education grant that Dr. Tanner and VSU had received, called Project ShIFT. VSU was one of about 25 schools chosen to take part in this three-year grant. The goal was to "provide resources and professional development activities for two groups of higher education professionals: DS (Disability Services) staff and faculty.... Project participants will be supported in their activities through curriculum materials and guides, monthly technical assistance conference calls, and a Project Web site" (http://www.lanecc.edu/disability/shiftgrant.htm). Kath wondered if perhaps this was the reason for the meeting. And it was.

Since that meeting Kimberly and Kath have become close friends, advocates for change on campus, and have cotaught a class twice. They have met frequently, talked about policy changes they want to see implemented on campus and with whom to partner to accomplish those changes. In year two, they traveled to Minnesota for Project ShIFT training, including learning how to make documents more accessible. There, they came up with their campus project: together they would work to create a completely online course which was—to the best of their capabilities—completely accessible for students. The then-Provost asked them to consider teaching "Disabilities in Film"—a two-hour course he had always wanted to teach—as an elective option for the Perspectives in Interdisciplinary Studies part of the Core Curriculum. Kath had never taught completely online before and Kimberly had only done so once. So they jumped in, eager to learn and then to share what they learned with our campus community.

They started meeting weekly to develop the course's learning goals and objectives, the readings they would select, and what films the class would be expected to view and analyze. Students would have to rent the films (they were told this in advance), and of course, all had to be captioned. They contacted the major video rental places (local and national companies) to verify that fully captioned versions would be available for up to 25 students at a time (the maximum enrollment). Then they started developing the content which students would access. They knew they wanted students to be exposed to various models of disability, ending with the social model (see Table 18.1).

They worked their way through all of the things any of us do to create a course for the first time, using what they had learned about accessibility. One thing was different, though: they had an embedded technologist "in" the class as staff, available to help any student or either of them, if they ran into an IT problem. The technologist was a graduate student in the Instructional Technology graduate program, who worked at the Access Office.

TABLE 18.1 MODELS OF DISABILITIES

Key Dimension of Model	Religious Model	Charity Model	Medical Model	Social Model
Construction of Disability	As punishment for sin, either of "afflicted" person, family member, or of community where person resides	"Pitiful" conditions which afflict persons, many of whom "deserve" the afflictions	As "deficiency" or "problem" in person which needs "fixing" by medical specialists	As difference (neutral judgment)
Where Does Disability Reside?	In person or social group who sinned	Often located disabilities in the bad choices of individuals (e.g., drugs or poverty)	In the individual	In the interaction between the individual and the society; those in power select certain differences and stigmatize them
Remedy for Disability	Confession of sin, though that usually did not change the disability per se	Charitable organizations step forward to "help" the disabled. Often that help infantilizes them and diminishes their personhood and takes away rights and dignity. Example: telethons which use children with disabilities as "freaks" needing help	Medical professionals whose expertise must be followed or else person is further stigmatized	Social change, brought about by either a person with a disability, an advocate, or anyone who wishes to challenge the prevailing power arrangements which create barriers for some individuals

On the Monday of the second week of the class the technologist e-mailed Kath. It was a bit of a cryptic message: "Would you be interested in hearing your PowerPoints with the assistive technology used by a student who was blind? If so, give me a call." Um . . . sure. It seemed there was more to the story, so she called him right away. They met later that morning at the Access Office. She pulled a chair up to his computer, they logged into the school's learning management system (LMS), and opened one of the PowerPoint slide shows.

About two minutes later, she understood why he had asked her to come over. Kath was deeply embarrassed and furious with herself. Why, you might ask?

Like most of us, she had been trained to create PowerPoint slides without much if any punctuation, and never using full sentences. All the slides used phrases, but no complete sentences—hence no punctuation was needed! Well, JAWS, one of two main screen-reader software programs used for persons who have low or no vision, "read" the 45-slide presentation as ONE very long sentence. Try to imagine listening to that—45 slides' worth of information, with no stopping. It went on for about eight minutes. . . . Pure pedagogical torture.

How could any student make sense of that jumble of words? Kath couldn't, and she had written them! She thought back to the few students over the years who she knew had used JAWS, and cried. She wrote them all an apology that evening, even though in her classes at that time, she had not used Power-Point slides. But the thought that she hadn't even tried to understand what studying for her class was like for them using JAWS, made her so angry with herself. Ignorance isn't bliss—sometimes it's just ignorance. So she vowed to do better, to be better about ensuring accessibility—for her students, for social justice, for her own conscience. To teach in an accessible manner is to follow the social justice model of disability, which says that while individuals might have impairments or illnesses, it is when social structures discriminate against those persons that the impairments become disabilities. So change needs to occur in social structures and not in or by the persons with disabilities. We want you to become part of the change. Are you ready? To get started, we want to ask you some questions. Don't worry about your answers—we're here to learn together.

GENERAL QUESTIONS TO PONDER ABOUT ACCESSIBILITY

1. Have you listened to how you talk or write? Do you use what is called "person-first" language? That is to say, does your syllabus talk about "Disabled students . . ."? Or do you say "Students with disabilities who . . ."? See the difference? Students are students; some of them might have impairments which might make some ways of learning more of a challenge. Most of us have become comfortable talking about "persons with AIDS" for instance, or a "person who was a victim of a crime," instead of a "crime victim." This is the same principle, that the personhood should come first,

linguistically. So peruse your class documents (e.g., syllabus, class notes, supplemental materials, even the readings which you choose) and look for instances of non–person-first language. They are easy to change, but the change can be quite meaningful to students with disabilities, because they feel more welcomed.

2. If you use a lot of photos, for example, in slideshow presentations, how do you choose them? Are some of the people chosen differently abled? If you need a slide of a group of people, why not choose a photo where one person might be using a wheelchair as an assistive device? Think about whether you try to balance your photos in terms of race, age, and sex. Many of us do, but we can sometimes overlook including persons with (visible) disabilities when we create class presentations.

3. Do you use videos in class or as out-of-class assignments? Are they captioned for those who might have hearing loss? This is especially critical for those of us who "flip the classroom" (see chapter 19), since short videos are often a part of the flipping process. Captioning technology is not that difficult to use; moreover, if we all started requiring our libraries to only buy captioned video, it would become more and more common. Again, don't think that captioning only helps students with disabilities. Since Kath has begun using captioning in all videos she shows in her supersection, many students without disabilities have thanked her. If they missed a word (due to a speaker's accent, etc.) they are able to see immediately what was said and not miss any points.

4. Do you understand the norms for interacting with a student who is deaf and his/her interpreter? Often there is a tendency for the faculty member to engage with the person who speaks (i.e., the interpreter). Don't do that! You are, after all, interacting with your student. Think of the interpreter as simply a (human) assistive communication device. You should be looking at your student and engaging with her or him as you would with any other student with whom you speak. Perhaps especially because we are sociologists, following this norm can seem really awkward. Kath always hears this sociological voice in her head saying, "Pay attention to the interpreter too—there are three of you present in this conversation!" But that is not how members of the deaf community nor the interpreters feel. One reason for this norm is that your student may be reading your lips in addition to the signing of your words, so he or she needs to see you and especially your face. If you have a habit of putting your head in your

hands, with partial blockage of your mouth, again, try to refrain from that behavior as well.

Do you know any American Sign Language? Kath relearned some basic signs and words in order to be able to greet students who have hearing impairments the same way she'd welcome any other student to class. Sure she has messed up the signs a few times, but the student helped her out and the errors have built bonds between them.

COMMUNICATING IN WORDS

One of the main ways that faculty communicate outside of the classroom is via the written word. Examples of this might be our syllabi, assignment directions, comments on graded papers, and so on. So it is incumbent upon us to be sure that these written documents are accessible. Let's talk about one of the easiest ways to make your class more accessible: to offer students different ways to obtain written documents. Different types of visual and cognitive impairments impact how a student might be able to open, manipulate, and perceive a document. So disability service providers now urge faculty to post written documents in three distinct ways:

▶ as a word processing software (e.g., Word 2003 [.doc] or 2007/2010 [.docx]) file
▶ as a single page Web page (.html) file
▶ as a PDF file

Offering these options allows the student to select which format best suits his or her needs. A caution, however: the word processing and PDF files usually will stay how you want them to, but the HTML file sometimes can "modify itself" to fit the size of the monitor the student uses. Thus spaces may suddenly appear which are not in the other two versions of the file. If you have an assignment where spacing is crucial (for instance, if you are teaching the ASA reference style, where spacing matters), then we suggest that you not post the HTML file and instead ask any student who prefers to use it to come see you so you both can talk about possible spacing/formatting problems. But again, if that is not a concern in the document, having an HTML file as an option helps students who are using, for example, a tablet computer which might not have word processing software on it (or software that's not compatible with what you used to create the document).

Kath suggests that you make the original document as you normally would in the word processing software. Get it the way you want it to look, check that all dates and times are accurate, etc. She'll do that for a few months before a semester starts. The week or two before classes begin, she'll double-check those Word files, make any last-minute tweaks, and only then will she make the PDF and HTML files, as she is loading the files into the LMS. That saves you having to make the changes separately in all three versions. Most LMSs allow, for example, several files to be attached to an assignment being created, so just upload all three files. We suggest keeping the endings on the files so that students can quickly tell which one they want to access (see Figure 18.1).

Saving the word processing file as ".html" and as a PDF file is not complicated. During the "save as" process, there will be options for each of these file formats. Just choose one and save, then repeat—using the word processing file (not the format you just saved) over in the third format.

FIGURE 18.1 EXAMPLE OF LEARNING MANAGEMENT SYSTEM ASSIGNMENT WITH THREE VERSIONS ATTACHED

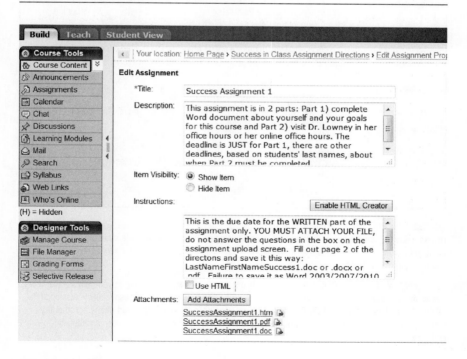

Screenshot of Accessible Assignment Files Uploaded to Learning Management System

Styles Are Your Friend in Creating an Accessible Document

Until Kath was trained in making documents accessible, she used to gripe about that "style stuff" cluttering up the top of her Word screen. Now she not only understands them, but she uses styles all the time. To help explain styles, let's picture a typical syllabus. Figure 18.2 is the first page of one of Kath's, before she learned about styles:

FIGURE 18.2 NONACCESSIBLE SYLLABUS DOCUMENT

Sociology 1101, Sections B & N
Fall Semester

Instructor: Dr. Kathleen S. Lowney, Professor of Sociology

Office: Room 1124, University Center

Office Hours: Tuesdays 11:00 – 12:00 p.m. AND 2:30 – 5:00 p.m.
Thursday 11:00 – 12:00 p.m. OR by appointment
I am in my office more than these times and would welcome you stopping by to talk about our class and how it is going.

Online Office Hours: The class and I will negotiate online office hours (at least once a week and likely more than that, particularly the weeks before exams).

Messages: Office Phone 229 333-5487 or Department Phone 229 333-5943

Website: Please use WebCT to access the website, write me emails, and post to the required discussions.

Required Text: Ferris, Kerry and Jill Stein. 2008. *The Real World: An Introduction to Sociology*. NY: W.W. Norton. AND I will place short articles from newspapers, magazines, or blogs in WebCT in the "Staying Current" class organizer. Anything placed there is required reading and is testable.

COURSE DESCRIPTION: Fundamentals of sociology, focusing on basic concepts, theories, and methods of research and inquiry. Emphasis is on applying the sociological perspective to understanding social inequalities and social stratification, culture, social institutions and groups, social change, and the relation to the individual to society. (3-0-3 credits)

WHAT WILL WE LEARN IN CLASS? Sociology will offer you a new way of looking at yourself, the world we live in, and the groups with which you associate. We will use popular culture — especially television and movies — as data with which to test our sociological imaginations. In addition, part of any introductory-level course is learning the vocabulary of the discipline, so careful distinctions between sociological concepts...

First Page of Syllabus before Making It Accessible

And Figure 18.3 is the first revised page of her upcoming class:

FIGURE 18.3 WHAT AN ACCESSIBLE SYLLABUS WOULD LOOK LIKE

SOCI 1101A
Introduction to Sociology
Dr. Kathleen S. Lowney (professor)
Fall

Contents

An Accessible Syllabus Document–Page 1

Pretty different, huh? Welcome to the role styles can play in accessibility. What is the first thing you notice about the revised version? Page 1 looks like a table of contents, doesn't it? And it is! Not only is it a table of contents, but it is now a searchable one. If a student wants to get to the "Calculation of Grades" section in all three versions of the document (.doc or HTML or PDF), he or she would just have to click on that part of the table of contents and the computer would immediately jump to that part of the file.

Why is this a good thing? Let's think back to your student who might be using a screen reader. Without using styles (which creates the "clickable" table of contents) that student would have to listen to seven pages of text read aloud just to get to the Calculation of Grades. Not so if you used styles. When that part of the table of contents is read, the student can signal the software to go there, and it will.

There are built-in styles in word processing programs, or you can override those to create your own, if you prefer. There are a few things to think about, though, as you create your own style menu or edit the built-in ones:

Fonts and font sizes. Each of us probably has one or two fonts which have become our favorites (Kath recalls that she had her "Comic Sans" period about a decade ago, but she has matured and now, her preferred font is Gill Sans MT). But personal preference notwithstanding, accessibility experts urge faculty to choose a *sans serif* font for all written documents (WebAIM 2013). Look again at Figure 18.2. Kath deliberately chose a serif font for it in order to contrast with Figure 18.3. Here are the same three words from each version of the syllabus:

Figure 18.2: Professor of Sociology

Figure 18.3: **Professor of Sociology**

The text from Figure 18.2 used Book Antiqua, size 12 font, while Figure 18.3 used Arial, size 12 font. Look at the *f*, *g*, *S*, and *y*—see the curly projections coming off the letters from Figure 18.2? Those are serifs—and they are more difficult for someone with low vision to read or for screen reading software to interpret. So choose fonts which are in the sans serif family (without serifs). Common sans serif fonts are Arial, Futura, Helvetica, Tahoma, Verdana, and Gill Sans MT. Normally experts recommend that—at a minimum—one should use font size 12. Major headings might go up one size to differentiate them from regular text.

Text color. We strongly urge you to stay with black font on a white background for all your written documents. Research (Pearson Education 2014) has shown that this combination is the easiest for those who might have low vision to see, while not causing visual strain to other readers. Again, that is pretty standard for most of us. But some built-in styles will need tweaking when it comes to their use of color. For instance, many styles will change a hyperlink to blue. This can be problematic for individuals with certain type of vision impairments, who have trouble seeing certain color combinations. Again, the standard accessibility advice is instead to underline to signal the student or the screen reader software that this text is "different." Use language which describes what the hyperlink is instead of saying "Click here" (Indiana University–Purdue University Fort Wayne 2014).

Headings and creating a table of contents. Once you have completely finished your document and have double-checked it several times, you are ready to use the styles to create a table of contents. As you move through your document, you have probably used various levels of headings (in Figure 18.3, the first-level headings appear in capital letters in the table of contents). If you did not "mark" them as first-level headings when you created the document using the styles function, it is time to do it now. Block one at a time and then hit the "Heading 1" style box, then move on to the next first-level heading in your document. Then move on to all second-level headings in your document, and so on. When that is complete, then create the table of contents. In Word 2010, that is accomplished by going to the "References" part of the ribbon, choosing "Table of Contents" at the far left and, using the pull-down menu, choosing "insert Table of Contents." Be sure your cursor is where you want to insert the table before you do it, though! If you have to make changes in your document which will change the table of contents, once you have made the changes, follow the same steps, but choose "update table" instead. Then you are ready to make the HTML and PDF versions of the document.

Creating Tables Which Are Accessible

Have you ever created a table like this: You tab over to create columns, maybe use the underline key to draw the lines between rows? Well—making documents more accessible means that constructing a table that way has to stop. Use the Table function instead—hidden codes will be embedded in the structure of the table which alert screen reader software that the following text are columns, rows, column headers, and so on. Otherwise, screen readers will read across the "columns" you created via tabbing, because they do not understand that they are meant to be columns, to be read down instead.

Don't cram contents into cells and don't cram columns and rows together to fit on one page. Keep a fair amount of white space; that makes the text easier to read. Be sure to have a textual explanation of the table in advance of where the table is located in the document, so that a student listening to a screen reader is aware that a table is coming. Don't forget to use descriptive column and row headings, to help cue the student, who is only *listening* to the table being read, about its content. And when formatting a long table which spans more than one page, choose the "repeat as header on top of each page" option, to remind the students and help them to process what they are hearing.

Images and Accessibility

If your document contains pictures or embedded charts or graphs, you will need to insert what is called "alternative text" (commonly called a "tag") for these visual objects. Since the screen reader cannot "see" these visual components of the document, what tagging the alternative text does is give students who are listening to a screen reader comparable text-based information about what they cannot see. Once a visual effect is "tagged," the alternative text will remain with it (with one exception) when the document is saved as either HTML or PDF. So like these other accessibility techniques, mastering them in one's word processing system usually continues the technique into the other two types of file formats.

Different word processing software tags visual content differently. In Word 2010, place your cursor on the effect and click "Format Picture," then "Alt Text." You will see a box that has space for both a title and then a description. A short title is fine to add, but the key text which defines what the visual effect is, should go in the "description" box. Be careful not to put *all* the text into the title box—for some reason the title is NOT included in HTML versions, but any text added to the "description" box is.

PRESENTATION SOFTWARE AND ACCESSIBILITY

If you have mastered how to make a word processing file accessible, then you have most of the skills needed to make a presentation slide show accessible. Let's review some of those techniques:

▶ Tag all visual artifacts using "Alt Text."
▶ Use sans serif fonts, and use a font size which will be easily visible from all locations in the room.
▶ Don't use a lot of font colors.

▶ Have a lot of white space (i.e., don't cram too much onto the slides).
▶ And of course, don't forget to use punctuation!

But those tips are not enough to make such a slide show accessible. You will want to create an accessible word processing file, without pictures, also, and upload that at the same time. Again, this "stripped down" file should not be thought of as just for students with disabilities. Many students have slow Internet access or might be paying for bandwidth. A file with all the images removed will load faster and save them some money.

So how does one create such a text-only file based on a slide show? This requires you to learn about the "Outline View" in your presentation software. In PowerPoint 2010, go to the "Slides/Outline" pane, then select the "Outline" tab. Your slides will appear—stripped of all visuals which you used. This can be saved as a word processing file, as well as the HTML and PDF files.

But we suggest that you tweak the file more before considering it "ready" to post. Here's why. As is, listeners won't know what text was on the first slide, the second, and so on. So the first thing we recommend that you do is to insert text that says "Slide 1 . . . , Slide 2 . . . ," and so on. Those should be Heading 1 style levels! That helps those who are only listening to the file. Second, if you wrote any further explanations in the "Notes" view, they do not appear in the "Outline" version of the text. So Kath creates two Heading 2 styles for each slide; one says "Slide contents" and the other says "Notes content." You will have to open your PowerPoint slides and cut and paste the notes content in by hand. When you are done doing that with all of your slides, then quickly create your table of contents, and save the file in all three formats. Then post the four files (PPT, word processing, HTML, and PDF) to your LMS. It sounds more complicated than it is, we promise! Kath organizes these files into subfolders. She has one called "Class PPT Presentations" and underneath that are four folders—one labeled "HTML versions," and so on. That way students don't have to sort through multiple copies of the same files to find the one they want. If they only want to look for PDF versions of the PowerPoint slides, they just open that subfolder.

AUDIOVISUALS AND ACCESSIBILITY

The central accessibility issue with video files is whether they are captioned for those with hearing impairments. If they are not, you should have them captioned before using them in class or assigning them to students. Many newer videos have captioning (although it usually needs to be turned on), but some don't. And using older videos only increases the likelihood that there is no captioning.

What then? There are a couple of options, and some involve copyright issues, so we urge you to contact your local librarian who specializes in copyright law, your university attorney, or your Disabilities Service Provider. How long a clip do you want to show with captions? What is the process to request captioning on your campus? How long a lead time do you have before it needs to be ready? (Captioning takes time—don't assume a long video can be captioned in just a few days, please.) On Kath's campus the Access Office can caption short videos, assuming that they do not violate any laws.

YouTube videos are not necessarily captioned (although this will be changing), so if you want to use one, first check to see if it is captioned. If it is not, there is software which allows anyone to overlay captions onto a video file (see the Resources section at the end of the chapter for some links). Practice captioning during a break or vacation, so that if you want to do this during a term, you are comfortable with the process.

We find it helpful to remind students, when we upload a video, that it is captioned. Unfortunately, students with hearing impairments are so used to having videos not be captioned that they might assume yours is not, and they might not always remember to toggle on the captioning. Again, don't think that only students with disabilities will use the captioning. Kath has had more than a few students thank her for the captioning, saying that it has rescued their relationship with their roommate, because they turned the volume down and just read the captions, when they were studying at 2:00 a.m.!

One more thing: don't use Flash animations either in your own documents or in videos, because screen reader software cannot interpret them.

LEARNING MANAGEMENT SYSTEMS AND ACCESSIBILITY

Unfortunately, while we as faculty can do a lot to provide an accessible environment for all our students and ourselves to learn and teach, there may be decisions made in the university which are beyond our control. One of those decisions is often what LMS is used on campus. For those of us who teach in a state system, the LMS decision may not even be made on our campus. While accessibility—we hope—is one of the criteria by which an LMS is chosen, we understand that it cannot be the sole criterion. But often that means that we are left teaching with software that is knowingly creating accessibility problems for some of our students. So let's talk about some of these possible problems.

Each course has its own set of web pages in an LMS. But often LMS pages are not necessarily as accessible as they could be. For instance, in many LMSs, there is no way to "alt tag" the folders and other visual effects on the page. So you might label folders and add descriptions to the folders using the LMS and think you are being helpful, but screen reader software will not "see" them because they are not in the preferred "alt tag" format.

One of the other issues which can arise when using an LMS is how to design the pages. Kath has been to several training sessions where other faculty have lauded the "learning module" function on VSU's LMS, but it always seemed a bit like "hand holding" to her. Couldn't students find all the required files by using the set tools such as "discussions, e-mail, web links," and so on? She had her own way of designing the "home page"—and it made sense to her.

But during the term where she and her class created a flash mob as part of a semester-long set of assignments, her opinion changed about learning modules drastically. With about 30 dance training videos, job assignment files, and data files from 135 pairs of students, plus the regular files she always posts to the website, the LMS "home page" got very "busy." It was the major complaint on her end-of-term evaluations. So she reconsidered and now uses learning modules. Most every week is its own module, and all files, readings, web links, assignments, discussions, etc., that students will need to learn successfully are located in that one place.

UNIVERSAL DESIGN

The social model of disabilities holds that it is social structure which turns differences between individuals into discrimination about "disabilities." Those of us who are faculty do have some structural power to create more accessible learning environments by the choices we make concerning the type of files we post, how we construct those documents, and how we design our learning spaces, especially in cyberspace. We also have some institutional power to raise questions about accessibility to administrators and staff members who make technology decisions.

Universal design theory flows out of the social model of disabilities (McGuire, Scott, and Shaw 2006; National Center on UD for Learning 2012). It asks that those involved in creating the built environment (e.g., buildings, etc.) and online environments practice inclusive design—that they consider all possible users, with all levels of ability. The goal of universal design is not to have to go back and retrofit accessibility on top of a software system, but to build it into the system from the beginning.

Can there be a truly "universal" design which would work for each student? Probably not, for each of us is different and may have unique challenges. But universal design as applied to higher education (Table 18.2) asks faculty to consider our students, their abilities (not just their impairments), and how to create opportunities for as many students as possible to succeed, by not denying them—even unintentionally—the access they need.

One other thing that universal design encourages is to see yourself and your own needs as part of the design process. Kath has realized that, in the past few years, she is no longer able to read essays handwritten in ink in almost the same color as the lines on the notebook paper. She now is upfront about that and tells students that if they wish her to be able to grade their test answers, they need to choose a different ink color. At first it was uncomfortable to share that information, but students were happy to learn it and easily understood and changed their behavior.

By practicing these principles of universal design for educators, we all can go a long way to ensure that our classes are equitable for all our students and therefore live up to these principles:

TABLE 18.2 PRINCIPLES OF UNIVERSAL DESIGN FOR INSTRUCTION

Name of design	Description of design	Guidelines
Equitable Use	The design doesn't disadvantage or stigmatize any group of users.	Provide the same means of use for and appeal to all users; avoid segregating; provide for the privacy, security, and safety for all.
Flexibility in Use	The design accommodates a wide range of individual preferences and abilities.	Provide choice in methods of use and facilitate the user's accuracy and precision; assure compatibility with accommodations and adaptability to the user's pace.
Simple, Intuitive Use	Use of the design is easy to understand, regardless of the user's experience, knowledge, language skills, or current concentration level.	Eliminate unnecessary complexity, be consistent with user expectations and intuition, and accommodate a wide range of language skills; arrange information in order of importance; incorporate prompts and feedback.
Perceptible Information	The design communicates necessary information effectively to the user, regardless of ambient conditions or the user's sensory abilities.	Incorporate a variety of modes for redundant presentation of essential information; provide contrast between essential information and its surroundings; assure compatibility with techniques and devices used by people with sensory limitations.

Name of design	Description of design	Guidelines
Tolerance for Error	The design minimizes hazards and the adverse consequences of accidental or unintended actions.	Minimize errors through the arrangement of elements by placing the most used elements in the most accessible location and eliminating or shielding hazardous elements; include warnings and fail-safe features; discourage unconscious actions in tasks that require vigilance.
Low Physical Effort	The design can be used efficiently and comfortably, and with a minimum of fatigue.	Allow users to maintain a neutral body position; use reasonable operating force; minimize repetitive actions and sustained physical effort.
Size and Space for Approach and Use	Appropriate size and space is provided for approach, reach, manipulation, and use, regardless of the user's body size, posture, or mobility.	Provide a clear line of sight to important elements and assure comfortable reach for any seated or standing user; accommodate variations in hand and grip size; provide adequate space for assistive devices and personal assistance.
A Community of Learners	The instructional environment promotes interaction and communication among students and between students and faculty.	
Instructional Climate	Instruction is designed to be welcoming and inclusive. High expectations are espoused for all students.	

NOTE: The information above is from the University of Washington DO-IT program. The guidelines are from The Center for Universal Design at North Carolina State University. SOURCE: Lane Community College 2014

CONCLUSION

We are humans first, before we occupy the status of student or professor. And as humans, we each have an inherent sense of dignity and personhood. As faculty, we need to ensure that our classes—the built environments, the supplemental learning materials we assign, and our own communication with students—are accessible to our students. With a bit of practice, faculty can marshall technology to assist us in accomplishing that goal.

SUGGESTED RESOURCES: GOOD PLACES TO START LEARNING ABOUT ACCESSIBILITY

Apple Products and Accessibility
- http://www.apple.com/accessibility/. This is Apple's general page about accessibility. Additional pages for each of their products (operating system, iPad, iPod, Nano, etc.) are linked off of this one.

Bobby
- (http://www.cast.org/learningtools/Bobby/index.html) is a web-based tool for checking existing web pages for accessibility. Best used if you are familiar with HTML coding.

InsideHigherEd.com articles
- "Do You YouTube? Don't Forget to Add Captions" by Steve Kolowich (http://www.insidehighered.com/blogs/student_affairs_and _technology/do_you_youtube_don_t_forget_to_add_captions)
- "Elaborating on Online Accessibility" by Steve Kolowich (http:// www.insidehighered.com/news/2011/05/27/education_department _elaborates_on_guidelines_against_discriminating_against _disabled_students_with_technology). Discussion of the U.S. government's recent focus on accessibility in higher education.
- "Online Accessibility Resources Roundup" by Eric Stoller (http://www.insidehighered.com/blogs/student_affairs_and _technology/online_accessibility_resources_roundup). Every link we have found to be useful!

Microsoft Products and Accessibility
- http://www.microsoft.com/enable/. This is Microsoft's general page. Look to the left to see many of the company's products and direct links to specific accessibility sites for those products (e.g., Windows 7, Internet Explorer 7, and Office products).
- http://www.microsoft.com/enable/news/subscribe/default.aspx. This link takes the reader to the page to sign up for free e-newsletter about MS products and accessibility.
- http://msdn.microsoft.com/en-us/windows/bb735024.aspx. Another MS resource page. Includes some links for program developers as well as users. Links include a CD for accessibility training, etc.

Open Office Products and Accessibility
- http://www.openoffice.org/ui/accessibility/. Open Office's general

page about accessibility. Some good links near the bottom of the page.

ProfHacker — a *Chronicle of Higher Education* blog (http://chronicle.com /blogs/ profhacker/) (blog entries thus far are not behind the paywall). This is a wonderful blog about the intersection of technology and peda-gogy in higher education. The blog writers frequently tackle accessibility concerns. Use the "Search ProfHacker" feature (near bottom right of screen) to find all such articles, but here are a few "gems," which we would recommend:

- "Universal Design, Usability, and Accessibility" by George H. Williams (http://chronicle.com/blogs/profhacker/universal -design-usability-and-accessibility/29501).
- "Academic Resources and Universal Design" by George Williams (http://chronicle.com/blogs/profhacker/academic-resources universal-design/26497).
- "Make YouTube Videos Accessible with CaptionTube" by George Williams (http://chronicle.com/blogs/profhacker/captiontube /29634).
- "5 Suggestions Concerning Disability, Accommodation, and the College Classroom" by George Williams (http://chronicle.com /blogs/profhacker/5-suggestions-concerning-disability -accommodationthe-college-classroom/23040).

▶▶▶ CHAPTER 19
HOW TO TEACH LARGE CLASSES

We have come full circle; in the 1970s and '80s, many colleges had large classes, especially ones in the general education core. Kath's Introduction to Sociology class at the University of Washington in 1977 was held in Kane Hall, a space that held over 500 students on the main floor, and there were also two balconies that allowed about 200 more students to enroll. But as enrollments grew and monies were flowing into higher education, many began to question the pedagogical underpinning of such large classes, and in many schools, they all but disappeared. Recently, however, in times of shrinking support for higher education, many schools are instituting or reinstituting them.

In this chapter, we want to consider pedagogical decisions which—while not necessarily specific to large classes—become even more critical with hundreds of students in one class. While there is no magic number for what makes a class "large," for the sake of this chapter, let's agree to mean anything over 100 students.

We want to begin our conversation with you—the faculty member. So whether you volunteered to teach a mass class or were assigned one, grab something to drink, a notebook and pen, and head out to your favorite contemplative spot; you have a lot of thinking to do.

YOUR TEACHING SELF AND THE LARGE CLASS

The key question to consider is this: What things about who you are as a teacher might have to change when faced with the responsibility of teaching hundreds of students at once? Let's first talk about your teaching style. How do you "own" the classroom? Sure, we don't want to do that all the time, but we know that there are times when all faculty have to be in control. How do you do that? Think about what behaviors are part of the way you control a regular-sized room. Now realize that many, if not all of those, will likely have to change.

Large classes obviously require a larger space for learning and teaching, and so your presence has to fill that space. Put differently, in a way you have to become bigger. Your voice will have to project to the far corners of the room (with or without the use of a microphone). Your gestures will need to become bigger as well, so that students can see them from a distance. What style of humor do you have in the classroom? If it is very subtle and based on facial cues, that could become problematic. Kath has found that she uses more cartoons and humor than she would in a smaller classroom.

Think about where you are while you teach in a small classroom. Do you sit on the edge of the faculty desk or stand nearby the computer, with easy access to the keyboard? Many of us do—but that is behavior that will probably be less successful in a large class. You will need to be much more mobile in a large classroom, walking around the entire space, not just at the front. This means that you will probably need to become less tied to teaching from notes. In fact, if you feel you are not able to cut that tie with notes, you will be required to be mobile, hold notes (and possibly a microphone), and move around a lot. Practice doing that, so that it is comfortable to you.

How do you interact with students before and after class? Will the environment of the large class allow you to interact in the same ways? Kath finds that she needs to greet students in a more formal way (at the door) than she would in a smaller classroom. She switches doors each day and welcomes students, answers any quick questions any student might have, etc. In smaller classrooms, she might still be putting notes up on the whiteboard, but in the large class, she's had to switch (for the first time) to using slide presentation software (e.g., PowerPoint or Prezi). She'll often get to class an hour or so early, so that once she has loaded the PowerPoint file and set up the clicker software, she will have much more time for before-class interaction than she would have in a smaller classroom. This was an unexpected gift of time with students she received when she started teaching the large class.

How are your multitasking skills? In a smaller classroom, many faculty don't use a slide changer to advance presentation software slides, but being mobile in a large classroom means that you must be talking, changing slides, and walking all at the same time. Sure, that sounds easy, but there are times when that is a lot to accomplish.

ADVANCE VISITS TO THE CLASSROOM

Visit the classroom several times, sometimes when it is empty, but ideally, try to attend several classes (no matter the discipline) in the space where you will be teaching, in advance of constructing your own syllabus. Ask the faculty member for permission (model the behaviors you would like from others, after all!) and go!

Think of these visits as ethnographic fieldwork and use all your senses. Sit in different far-flung places in the classroom in order to see how easy it is to see presentation slides. Are there places where it is very hard to see? If your class is not full to room capacity, then don't allow students to sit there! What text font and size on slides seem to work best? Look carefully at the space— are there seats which get flooded with natural light coming from the windows, which might blank out the slides? Examine student behaviors at the edges of the room, especially in the back—how engaged are they? Think about your teaching style—your "teaching front stage"—and consider how it might play in that space.

Then switch positions and listen. Can you hear the faculty member well in every location in the classroom? Is he or she using a microphone? Is it handheld or a lapel mike? Each type has its quirks, but listen for which one seems to work best in the space. Then listen for competing noises—do they come at set times or are they random? How loud can they get? Can students hear the faculty member over these noises? And if you are thinking "noises, what do they mean?" Trust us, in the brand new classroom which holds 350 students where Kath teaches, there are lots of odd noises. Sometimes it is just the AC turning on in this "whoosh" of air, but about every 50 minutes, there is this very loud stomping/trampling noise which is impossible to talk over. At first, Kath thought it was the same-sized class directly above starting to leave in a mad rush to the exits, but she has since learned that is not the case. The best we can figure out is that there is something mechanical—probably on a repeating circuit—which makes this noise in both rooms. The class just waits it out; it is so loud and has a bit of physical shaking to it, too, that there is nothing else to be done.

Are there windows in your large classroom? How much light do they let in? If there are no windows, how easily can you change the amount of lighting in the room? And how quickly do the lights react? What is the view out of the windows? Hopefully it will be less sociologically interesting than what is happening in class, but don't count on it!

After a few minutes in a class, pay attention to your body. How comfortable are the seats? Are they upright and stationary? Do they lean backward? If so, how much? How big is the pull-up desk attachment, if there is one? Is there room enough to put a full-sized notebook on the desk, or will students be fiddling all the time to make their notepaper fit on the desk? Will a computer fit on the desk? Are there both left- and right-handed desks? Or will left-handed students have to fight to take notes on a desk not compatible with their bodies? Are the desks comfortable for student bodies of all sizes? Are there some flat, long desks which could work for students with mobility impairments, who might need to pull up in their wheelchairs, or for students who need more space than the pull-up desk allows? (See, for example, Gilbert 2013.)

Speaking of different types of electronic devices, how many plugs are there in the room? Are some on the main floor, under student seats, or are they all on the edges of the room? The answers to these questions will need to play a part in your electronics-use policy.

Are there stairs in the room? If so, where are they? Will you have to traverse them to walk around while teaching? If so, that is one more task to add to your multitasking abilities. I know this seems like not a big deal, but both of us have mobility issues and need to hold on to handrails while using the stairs. So can you hold the rail, a presentation slide changer, perhaps a controller for all the electronics in the smart classroom, and perhaps your notes? And what if you need water to help you talk? See how stairs can quickly complicate things? Kath tries her best to teach big classes only in rooms with slanted floors, but not stairs, for this very reason. Her klutziness, in combination with her mobility disability, is well known, and she'd prefer not to evidence it while teaching! She suggests always wearing clothes on teaching days which have pockets deep enough to hold at least one of the electronic gadgets needed at all times.

There's one more bodily indicator to pay attention to while in the classroom space: temperature. Is it too hot? Too cold? Just right? Be sure to try to attend at least one class in the exact time slot as your class will be. Different times of the day will mean different types of natural light in the room, and will affect the temperature. The amount of light will impact students' abilities to see you and any presentation slides you are using, so this is crucial to notice.

After your ethnographic visits to other classes taught in "your room," we would encourage you to next visit the classroom when it is empty. This might need to occur after you have had training about the room's technological capabilities. Walk around, try out the software you are likely to use. Test out the mikes (are they lapel mikes or handheld or around the neck?). Remember that your voice will seem louder in an empty room than in one filled with hundreds of students. Test out your presentation slide changer—can you be in the back of the room and have it still work? Don't forget to try using it in the far corners of the room too. Do whatever you need to do to get comfortable in the room, before the students arrive and alter everything.

PEDAGOGICAL DECISIONS ABOUT LARGE CLASSES

What kinds of learning activities do you use in and outside of class when you have smaller classes? How scalable are these activities? Could they work well with large-sized classes or will you need to rethink the types of activities you select? We would urge you, first and foremost, to think about the *pedagogical advantages* of the learning activities—rather than thinking about how easy or difficult they might be for you, the instructor. Linked to this question are several more pedagogical questions: What amount of gradable work do you give? What types of feedback do you give to students on their work? How often do you give that feedback?

Large Classes and New Preps

We believe that it will be easier to "scale up" a class you have taught to a much smaller number of students than to have a new preparation be the first time you have taught a large class. Having a sense of what can work in a small class gives you a good pedagogical grounding for taking the content to the masses. But we realize others might disagree; moreover, for others, there is no say in their workload and they have to teach what is given, in whatever classroom is assigned. Still, if you are asked to teach a large class and you have the option of choosing which course to offer, we suggest first trying a class you have already taught. That way you have a sense of the content, the timing of the content, what concepts and theories are difficult for students, and you can concentrate just a bit more this first time on the mechanics of teaching that many students.

THE CHALLENGES OF A LARGE CLASS

Probably every teacher of a large class might construct a different list of challenges; we are including ones which we have experienced and which are most often mentioned in the literature.

Classroom Management

Rare and quirky student behaviors in a much smaller class can sometimes be tolerated by both the faculty member and other students. But when they are repeated by twenty or thirty students every day, they become more irksome and irritating. So how will you handle these kinds of pedagogical disruptions? Tardiness? Leaving early? Wandering in and out of the classroom, seemingly haphazardly? Talking with friends about nonsociological topics, and thus interrupting others' learning?

The good news about these bad behaviors, so to speak, is that the students have to be in class to do them. At least they are not skipping! But that doesn't mean these are acceptable behaviors (Murphy 2010; Van Brunt and Lewis 2013). Do all of these bother you to the same degree? For Kath, tardiness is not a big deal, so long as students don't interrupt the flow of the class by walking across the front of the room or coming in very loudly. But leaving early does bug her, because she is not sure why it is happening. Is the student sick and therefore she should send one of the graduate assistants to check on his or her welfare? Or did the student get a call she or he believes is necessary to take? (Kath asks students to tell her in advance if they have a call which is urgent and will require them to leave their cell phone on vibrate.) For instance, one student's wife was in the hospital with preeclampsia, and her doctors thought they might have to deliver the baby that day—his wife told him to go to class, but he was a wreck, so of course it was okay for his phone to be on vibrate.

Kath always goes to the default that "I must not be doing a good job today" when someone leaves early. Does anyone else do that? So if any of these behaviors concern you personally and pedagogically, then you need to create policy which clarifies your views, and perhaps, through points earned or points lost, encourages students to behave respectfully to you and to other students.

Cell Phone Interruptions

Most of us probably ask students to turn their cell phones off (or at least set it to vibrate) during class times. And inevitably, cells ring in the middle of class or during tests. So what are you going to do? Again, behaviors that might work in a smaller class, where you know most all of the students, might not be as functional in a larger class. We're not going to tell you that our policies are best; rather we have two pieces of advice to give about cell phones: (1) Don't let the problem fester by not addressing it the first few times it happens. That is only socializing students to the idea that your policies are meaningless—which is not a good thing! (2) Follow through on your policy, no matter who the student is or what role the student may have in class that day—students will be looking to see if you play favorites.

So has Kath asked a student—about to present and whose cell phone rang—to leave class, thereby losing presentation points? Or asked a student—whose cell phone loudly rang for several minutes until he located it, in his backpack, up on stage, where students leave their belongings—to leave in the middle of a test? Yes and yes, because leaving class for the day is her policy. It usually takes one mistimed ringing of a phone to make the point for hundreds of students that our classroom is "sacred space," not to be disturbed by outside entities during class time.

Computer Usage

Here's another classroom management issue where many of us have differing policies. There are data which say that allowing computers in class works well (Samson 2010; Wainwright 2013), and there are data which call into question the usefulness of computers in class (Fried 2008; Mueller and Oppenheimer 2014; Ravizza, Hambrick, and Fenn 2014; Rockmore 2014; Sana and Cepeda 2013). Once again, decide what works for the kinds of learning activities you want students to do in class, the level of the course, your students' note-taking abilities, the campus culture about computer usage, and then enforce your policy fairly.

Texting

If cell phones are to be put away and turned off, one would think that texting would not be a problem! But most of our students have grown up texting, often without looking at their keyboard, and so many will try to text on the sly and think that faculty can't tell when they are doing it. However, when students' intense focus is on their own crotch or underneath their desk, odds are they are texting. Again, does this bother you? Does it interfere with your ability to help them to learn? If so, then you will need a policy about it.

All these electronic interruptions occur in smaller classes too, of course, but the size of a large class exacerbates the problem. So it is up to the faculty member to construct the tone of the learning environment in part through written class policies and their explanations and in part through a culture of enforcement of the policies.

So how does one enforce a norm with 300-some pairs of eyes watching you? We suggest that policy enforcement be as low-key as possible, especially for first offenses. It begins with training any graduate assistants who are in the classroom with you, that if they see any of these behaviors, to signal you quietly what the issue is and where the student is in the classroom. (Kath and her graduate assistants have a series of hand gestures they use and they are trained to go stand right by the student until Kath can get there, but NOT to say anything.) While still mic'd, Kath quietly bends down and, whispering, asks the student to stop texting/using cell phone/computer. If this is the student's second violation of class policies, then she asks the student to pack up and exit the room, etc. The graduate assistant then follows up by asking the student to show her/his student ID card as the student is exiting OR if students have assigned seats, the graduate assistant just checks the seating chart and notes it. Kath has a notebook with her which is left on the professor's desk in the front of the classroom in every class, where conduct issues are written down. It takes usually less than a minute. But—and this is crucial—all students sign a copy of the conduct policies during the second week of class, which says that if the student is asked to leave for violating a rule, he or she will quietly leave. They promise to abide by those rules. Often a gentle reminder of that helps. Kath has never had a student escalate.

We think it is important, though, that graduate assistants or other students *not* be the ones who confront a student breaking the rules. Ultimately, that is the faculty member's job. It might not be a bad idea to write a brief note or e-mail to the student after class, perhaps with a link to the class policies. Should this be a second incident of a norm violation, a reminder of increasing penalties (if you have them) would be appropriate too. We believe it is important—especially in a large class—that the message also welcomes the student back to class the next day. Often students new to college, who have been asked to leave a class, believe that the faculty member is so angry that they never return. Kath goes out of her way to find the student the next class and informally chats. She wants the student to know that while she did not appreciate the non-normative behavior, it is not an issue anymore between them, so long as the student does not continue the behavior.

Attendance and Assigning Seats

The first thing you may want to peruse is your institution's attendance policy. Are you required to take attendance? Is it a formal norm or an informal one? What are the sanctions for you if you do not take daily attendance? We believe that having students physically in class benefits their learning, but what if they do not understand that? Talk with your students about why you are requiring attendance—and not just for bureaucratic reasons! Help them to see why you value their presence in class.

Again, think about whether you assign seats in smaller classes. If you do, why? If you don't, what is your reasoning? Now consider the exponential increase in class size you are about to encounter—would it make sense to assign seats? For many faculty, attendance is really the sole reason that they assign seats. So will assigning seats help classroom dynamics? Again, only you can see if your learning goals match your attendance policies.

We don't think there is one correct answer, but here are some issues to consider. Are there any technological tools which you could use to make taking attendance easier? For instance, some institutions install a card reader (for student ID cards) outside of each doorway into the large classrooms. Faculty will have to decide if they want students to swipe their card every day or not. Clickers in part can be used to take attendance too (though we caution you not to use them only for that purpose). There is some other software faculty can use as well (Cavender 2011; Croxall 2012). And of course, there are the tested ways of either calling roll or sending an attendance sheet around each section of the room. Both of these require some in-class time and a lot of out-of-class time by the faculty member or GA/TA noting the names in the official record.

Assigned seating takes away much of this faculty work. It is far easier and quicker to scan for empty seats and note them than work through attendance sheets. But are there any potential drawbacks to assigned seating? One thing to consider is students with disabilities. Not all students will feel free or brave enough to let you know if their assigned seat does not work well for them. This might include students with auditory or vision impairments. But don't just think that "students with disabilities" might be disconcerted with their seat assignment. If you allow students to use computers, their use often bothers those around them (and not just if students are connecting to Facebook instead of paying attention in class!) and the evidence supports this concern (Fried 2008; Ravizza et al. 2014; Rockmore 2014). So if you choose to assign seats, you might consider a "using computers" section of the class—and not put them near the front of the room.

If you decide to assign seats, be sure to announce frequently that any student who is concerned about where her or his seat is located should talk to you and that you will work it out together. Another way to address this is to let students choose their own seats, and then in the second or third week of the class, send around a seating chart and tell them that their location is now assigned only to them. This is easier to do if the seats in the room are numbered, of course.

Number of Assignments and Grading Policies

As the numbers of students rise, how to deal with all the grading—and still stay sane—becomes a central concern for faculty. And there are a number of issues to ponder as you work through this. First, what types of assignments will you require of students, given your learning goals and course objectives? If you want students to do a lot of sociological data analysis and writing, grading is, obviously, much more labor-intensive than other types of assignments which you could give. Second, how often are your assignments due? Once at the end of the term? Every day? Once a week?

We suggest that you plan all of your possible assignments and then stop and count your grading load for that class, per week. Kath likes to calculate this for every class she teaches and combine the totals, in order to see how busy her teaching life will be. She then overlays the academic calendar and looks for problems. For example, at Valdosta State, all advisees have to see their advisor in order to register, so the three weeks before registration begins means much longer days at school, meeting with her fifty-plus advisees. That means there is less time to grade, and she adjusts the schedule accordingly. So look at your entire classload's worth of grading . . . how feasible does it seem to you, along with your private life and your research commitments? Remember—sanity is still the best plan! However, if the thought of doing that calculation in advance of the term unnerves or depresses you, then please feel free to skip this step.

There Is Grading and Then There Is GRADING!

Not every assignment requires the same amount of grading time and attention. If you are asking students to do daily in-class writing to cement learning, these might be graded using a +/- system, which requires less commenting and less of your time. Or if you are using a 3-point scale (3 = excellent grasp of concept; 2 = average grasp; 1 = weak grasp; 0 = not done), then there could be less time involved. You might, for example, choose to comment only on those assignments which earned a 1. If you choose this criterion for commenting, please be sure to let students know about it. That way students understand why some students might have comments and they do not. However, if part of the daily writing involves students asking about the concept and what they don't understand and you plan on answering each student's question, then on every class day, grading will eat up a large amount of your time.

Before Kath started teaching large classes, she always had her introductory-level students write every day at the start of class. She would post a Power-Point slide with a question and they answered it, for five minutes. She used a 0–3 point grading scale. The answers would be collected and at the start of the next class, each student would pick up the graded answer and continue to use the same piece of paper until it was full. She found this not only worked well to see quickly how students were understanding the material, but as an added bonus, the eye-to-eye contact with students every day helped her to learn students' names. But when she shifted to teaching large classes, this way of daily assessment proved unworkable. It would take too much time to hand back the papers every day without eating into the class period, etc. That was the primary reason she switched to using clickers.

For the assignments which will require a more intensive commitment of time and energy from you, consider arranging them to be due before breaks/holidays/vacations, so that you have more time to work on them. Sometimes we forget that we are human too and grading is work, so by choosing to make major assignments due right before these natural breaks in the class, we give ourselves the gift of more time. And students like these deadlines too; they seem to prefer deadlines before, rather than after, breaks.

Another choice about grading you will have to make is if or how much time you will spend commenting on the mechanics of students' writing (e.g., spelling, grammar, sentence construction, and development of an argument). Scholars involved in the writing across the curriculum social movement (see, for example, Day 1989; Hobson 1998) advocate that faculty *not* comment on every single grammar mistake, but rather write a note to the student at the end of the assignment which, in part, mentions common errors and perhaps points out one or two of them in the body of the assignment. They hold that if faculty point out every error for students, we are doing students' work for them and make it easier for students perhaps to fix them for this assignment but not learn how not to make the errors in future assignments.

Another way to help with the crush of grading that comes with teaching a large class is to require all students to complete the assignment, but require different due dates. So for example, in Kath's large Introduction to Sociology class, she has students turn in their class notes from a specific class day as an assignment and she comments on how detailed the notes are and gives suggestions on how to improve their note taking. Instead of having all 350 sets of notes due on the same day, she spaces them out during the first four weeks of class. She breaks the class down by last name (A–D, E–I, and so on) and each group of students is assigned a different due date. This ensures that all students have completed the assignment in time to strengthen their note taking before the first test, but does not produce an overwhelming amount of grading on any one day. Usually there are about 30 assignments per day turned in for comment, which is much more manageable.

Similar to this is the idea of giving students a menu of assignments and allowing them choice about which they do. Each assignment might have a different due date. With a few caveats, this can spread out some of the grading (which may or may not be a plus). But there are things to consider if you use this idea. First, consider grouping assignments. Create two or three assignments about concepts of similar difficulty and make them for the same number of points. Then give students the option of choosing one or two of them. Second, be sure that your syllabus states clearly that if a student does not do any of that set of assignments, that he or she has earned a permanent zero grade. Some students—especially near the end of the term—will try to do two of a later group of assignments to "make up" for the missing one from earlier in the term. But that does not give them a learning opportunity on the missed concepts. Third, be sure that students realize that all of the concepts are testable, despite the fact that only a select few are involved in any one of the set of assignments. If you group assignments this way, try to get assignments which are, to the best of your ability, equally interesting to your students. Otherwise the goal of spacing out the grading is for naught! Fourth, be sure that no matter which assignment in each group students pick, that they are asked to do the same relative amount of work. Be sure that if you want students to write sociologically in every assignment, that every option involves a relatively equal amount of writing. Trust us—students will look at that and will complain if they feel there are inequities.

Use rubrics. Rubrics give students a sense of what is required to complete the assignment and how many points each part of the assignment is worth. They can help students who have trouble knowing how to start the assignment by giving them a suggested outline/structure. When creating a rubric for an assignment, go back to why you are having students complete this assignment: What are the key concepts you want them to use? Are you assessing just that they can recognize them? Or that they can apply them to a situation of the students' choice? If the latter is your main point in the assignment, then the section on recognizing or defining the concept should earn students far less points than the application section. If you are grading students' grammar/spelling, etc., how much of the points should that be and why? A similar question should be asked if you are requiring students to use the ASA writing style—how much of the point total should be following those style norms versus sociological content? And will you assign/subtract points for following directions, such as margins, font (type and size), line spacing, etc.? What about sexist language? Plagiarism?

We believe that while rubrics can be very useful, they need to be individualized—for you and for each of your assignments. For example, when Kath teaches Sociological Theory, the culminating assignment is a review of sociological literature of eight peer-reviewed articles on a topic of the student's choice (and faculty approved) and then testable hypotheses based on the literature review. There are assignments throughout the semester which build to this final assignment (e.g., topic/bibliography, draft review of literature, polished review of literature, theory and hypotheses, etc.), so this final assignment is more pulling the assignments together, editing them into one voice, and fixing errors rather than new writing (save for the introduction and conclusion). Initially she used a minimalist rubric, but it has morphed into a more detailed one, which gives students more hints about how to earn points. For instance, in the section of the rubric about the review of literature, there are sections and points assigned for each of these:

▶ Correct number of peer-reviewed sociologically appropriate-to-topic articles (X points will be lost for every article below the correct number)
▶ Adequate discussion of each of the articles (adequate is then defined based on how she and students have been discussing it in class all semester)
▶ No one-source paragraphs, and then states that for every one-source paragraph there will be X points taken off (she stresses that a review of literature should be a conversation between the ideas of the authors, not simply article summaries, so she requires students to have at least two sources used in every paragraph of the review of literature)

This kind of detail fleshes out the rubric and can give students more of a path to success on the assignment.

Rubrics created in a word processing software allow the faculty the ability to write comments after each section, whether by hand or on the computer. We like to use these kinds of rubrics because there is no limit on the amount of comments. However, many online rubrics, such as in learning management systems, do have a space limitation. These can be really frustrating to use and you might want to consider putting additional comments in an attachment and sending it to the student. Online rubrics are often harder to individualize;

they often require every dimension to have the same number of grading categories, etc.

We want to share a useful tip about grading online discussions in a learning management system using an online rubric: open up two browsers (not two tabs or windows, but actually two versions of the browser if the software allows—if not, open one browser (i.e., Firefox) and then open another browser (such as Chrome or Internet Explorer). Then narrow each one so that they are side by side on screen. Use one to show the student's postings to the discussion board and have the rubric open on the other. This way you do not have the posts disappear off screen while you grade them! Of course, this works much better with one of the new, wider monitors (or even two monitors!).

The time required in large classes for grading. There is no way around the fact that teaching a large class requires a significant amount of time, both to prepare and to grade. We have found that faculty members tend to have a grading style and so we encourage you to find what yours is. Are you a "little bit every day" type of grader? Or a "sit down and get it done" type of grader? Maxine is a "get it done" type of grader and so is Kath. The day of a test, Kath heads home the minute she can, immediately staples the tests if needed so that she doesn't lose any of the essays, sorts by version, makes some hot tea, and gets them done. With a class of 300, it usually takes her about 18 hours to complete the grading. Others distribute the grading over a set number of days (i.e., 50 tests per day, over 6 days). Kath normally schedules her tests for Thursdays (for a T/Th class) or Friday (for a M/W/F class), so that she has the blocks of time available on the weekend. She promises students that all assignments/tests will be graded in 72 hours, so that they can receive relatively prompt feedback. But that's just her. Give yourself an appropriate amount of time, given your campus culture, your workload, and the rest of your life. We urge you to consider letting students know when they can expect their grade, however, because that can minimize communication with you which just asks, "When will the grades be done?"

Inevitably, there are students who e-mail almost immediately after taking a test or turning in an assignment, wanting to know their grade. Kath often has several of these e-mails in the LMS inbox before she even can arrive home after a test. This used to bother her, but she has come to accept that some students are so nervous about their work—and often so driven to succeed—that sending these e-mails helps them to cope with their anxiety. Usually these are good students who are scared of "failing." So she tries not to take them personally. But if these kinds of e-mails bother you, this is another possible topic for a class norm: that no student can ask when grades will be posted for X number of days, to give you time to grade. Sometimes Kath will reply and gently let them know that the grades will be posted when she is done and other times she doesn't reply save for reminding them that she explained when grades would be posted in class (which she does) and that the information has not changed. Lately Kath has taken to tweeting (her Twitter name is @LowneySociology) when each version of a test is entered into the gradebook, so that students know those grades are available. She'll also tweet encouraging comments (if accurate) about how most of the tests are going.

Consider if there are pedagogically sound ways to make grading easier. Think about the type of tests you are giving. Could you make them shorter yet still examine students' learning? Could more frequent testing—but with fewer questions—work for students as well as for you (Wolf 2007)? Are you comfortable with peer grading? This is the practice where, after the test is completed, students pair up and go over either their own tests or others and grade them. If the pair of students do not know the right answer, they have to look up the correct answer and—hopefully—will learn it. If you do this, you might consider having students use a code (such as their seat number) instead of their names. Have them write this seat number down in their notebook before the test begins, so that in case they forget, they can easily find which is theirs. Peer grading—especially if real names are used—provides opportunities for a type of cheating (i.e., changing answers to help out friends or oneself). Another way to cut down on grading, be it of assignments or tests, might be to have some of them based on group work (Cortright et al. 2003; Slusser and Erickson 2006).

In order to reduce the amount of grading, you might want to assign group projects. If you do this, you will need to establish project ground rules (or let the class create them with you). Different members of the group might take on different statuses: proofreader, primary researcher, writer, data analyst, and so on. The best group projects include some points for the group members to evaluate themselves and award some group project points.

Maxine uses a combination of these types of grading options. She knows that she is not capable of grading a large number of exams effectively. While no grading scheme is perfect, she is better able to handle group projects than long essays from a large number of students.

Faculty can also consider using technology to assess their students' mastery of concepts. For instance, many LMS software systems allow faculty to create timed online quizzes, wherein the questions draw from a bank of questions, different for each student, in order to minimize the chance of cheating.

The problem in large classes is that one needs a fairly large number of questions, in order to ensure question randomization. Faculty therefore likely will have to spend significant amounts of time creating questions. If one is using questions from a publisher, each one will have to be evaluated to see if the faculty member finds the question stem and answers acceptable. These kinds of assessments free up class time and many of them can be auto-graded and automatically inserted into the online gradebook. Clickers also allow for some automatic grading. Testing with clickers is a bit more complicated than simply using them in class. Faculty have to set up keys and code in the correct answers, and the process by which students choose answers involves more steps than "regular" clicker use, so both the students and the faculty will need to practice beforehand. But using clickers to grade objective parts of the test can save some time and allow you to spend more energy on the analytical and writing sections of tests, which otherwise might not be included in testing in large classes.

CHEATING AND GRADING

While faculty can never completely overcome cheating, there are some pedagogical choices faculty can make which can reduce the likelihood that students will consider cheating (Lang 2013). First—and by far the most important choice—is the kind of work you are asking students to do. High-stakes tests (for example, just a midterm and final) in a big class are likely to cause so much anxiety in students that at least some will try to manage the anxiety by choosing to cheat. Kath has about 40 grades by the time a semester is done, and she has three noninclusive tests, not including the final exam. Some students see the tests as "making or breaking" their grade (which is not mathematically accurate) and so have tried to cheat. One way they try is to go to the classroom the night before (it is locked, but not until about 10:00 p.m.) and write notes on the back of the seat in front of where they plan to sit. She's learned this and so she simply arrives early to class on test day and wipes down any chair back which has writing on it. Kath has never said a word to the class, but clearly those students who did it realize that their notes have disappeared!

If you are assigning a paper for students in any size class, don't make it a "Go research X social problem and write about it." Students can easily find papers on those kinds of overly broad topics on the Internet, and pay for them. Instead, make the directions for papers be unique and specific. What do we suggest? Try using a case study as the basis for the paper and ask students in the class to analyze it from different stakeholders' perspectives. Or try asking students to find newspaper articles about the topic and use the news stories as data to analyze the social problem. Or ask students to find a song or a poem about the social problem and then analyze it using various theories. Ask students to analyze data in a particular dataset and test their own hypotheses. Or give students the option of creating a photo essay about the social problem. You'll have to explain how much of the assignment needs to be written versus visual.

GREAT—BUT WHAT SHOULD HAPPEN IN THE CLASSROOM?

Every one of us who teaches a large class will develop our own style. There is no "one way" to teach a large class. That said, it is probably easier to talk about what *shouldn't* happen first.

Do not just lecture for the entire class period. Again, that's not advice only for someone teaching a large class—it is something we'd say to anyone teaching any size class. While many of us were socialized to that model of teaching and learning, our students are not. "Chunking" material into smaller bits and then involving students in some sort of active learning technique to practice the material works better (see chapters 5, 6, and 9 for more ideas).

Kath still finds it hard, even after five years of teaching almost entirely large classes, to create space in class for active learning moments, so she has forced herself to do it using a visual cue. Most of the active learning she uses in large classes are "Think-Pair-Shares"—where students talk with each other about an application of the concept under discussion for about five minutes and then the class comes back together. (For more on them, see chapters 4, 5, and 6.) So when she is at home, creating her presentation slides, she not only inserts clicker questions, but on some slides she inserts in the bottom right-hand corner a stylized drawing of two hands clapping. That reminds her to have an active learning moment. She tells students that's what it means as well, so if she skips over it, they will stop her. To get their attention, she claps a pattern and then will say what she wants them to do in their Think-Pair-Shares. She waits for about a minute, and then starts walking around the room and popping in to listen to about 8 to 10 discussions. She asks her graduate student assistants to do the same. If we hear errors in applying the concepts, we raise them once the class comes back together and help students to see that these are common errors and can be easily overcome.

Another popular pedagogical technique right now is to "flip the classroom" (Barrett 2012; Miller 2012). Popular in the physical sciences for over a decade, more and more faculty in multiple disciplines are using this technique. Eric Mazur, a physicist at Harvard University, is one of the leading advocates of this approach (Lambert 2012; Mazur 1996). He explains that flipping the classroom shifts the location of learning the course content (via lecture, textbook and other readings, even PowerPoint/audio files) to outside of the class period. Students are required to accomplish this learning as their "ticket into" the class, where faculty and students work together to focus on applying the knowledge—often using case studies—and working on any misunderstandings. Mazur uses clickers during class as a quick way to measure student confusion and student learning.

Flipping the class requires students to step up and do their part. If students want to stay passive and have course content spoon-fed to them, they might rebel or complain. For students who have been taught in K–12 to be passive receptacles of passed-on knowledge from the teacher, flipping the classroom can be uncomfortable, even stressful. Sometimes they will say that the faculty member is not doing enough teaching for the amount of tuition monies they have paid, etc. We recommend that you explain why you chose to flip the class, show them some of the data about student success based on this pedagogical technique, but also maintain control and not get rattled by complaints. We know that is often easier said than done, though!

Kath has used a modified version of flipping the class for the past three years. She teaches on a Tuesday/Thursday schedule, and she will list a concept in the learning management system, ask students to define it, and create a short scenario which requires students to apply the concept. They have to post twice during the week. Initially, these discussions were threaded open discussions, so groups of 25 students would see each others' posts. Each week's posts were worth ten points. She graded them using a rubric.

But she began to notice several patterns which worried her. "Good" students tended to post early in the week, with fairly lengthy and detailed posts. Weaker students usually came into the discussion in the last 12 to 24 hours and often repeated what the good students said, just in their own words. On tests, however, these "late to the discussion" students did not seem to comprehend the concepts well nor could they apply them correctly. It seemed that the "free rider" problem was happening.

So last year, Kath changed things up a bit. After reading about flipping the classroom and "just in time teaching," she decided to try this: each Monday and Wednesday at 12:01 a.m., she posted a new discussion thread in the learning management system, focused only on the concept(s) for the next class (Tuesday or Thursday). The thread stayed open for only 18 hours. Instead of an open discussion, she chose the "journal" option for the learning management system's discussion, which kept each student's answers private—only the student and she saw what the student wrote. This eliminated weaker students "getting by" with the help of better students' postings. It became easy to tell which students were having trouble with every day's concepts. She would grade it that same day and use student answers (anonymously) as part of the PowerPoint slides for the next day. Thus she might start the class with a slide quoting a student's answer which exemplified a common error. Then she'd ask a not-for-points clicker question which made students decide on whether that quote was expressing the concept correctly. Then the class could work through it as they moved through the prepared presentation for the day. By including these student answers from just the day before, students could see when they were understanding the concepts well, and when they were not. Moreover, for those who had made errors, they could see they were not alone in their thinking. In the two semesters of using this private journal assignment, test grades improved by about 15 percent and discussions were more animated, because students were forced to read the material in advance. She now opens the journals up and has students comment on two of them, the week after they are due. This peer reviewing/peer encouragement has also helped with grades.

Another way to create active learning in the classroom is to use debates and other similar activities. Kath uses a modified version of Sweet's (1999) idea and combines it with an in-class debate. When she and the class cover the ethical norms in sociology, she assigns a case study which she has created. The class is divided up based on their last names and each group is assigned to one of the statuses in the case study. Individually students write a paper based on the case study which is due before the debate day. This ensures that all students are "primed" for the debate. Then on debate day, students representing the different statuses sit together and plan what they want to say. Kath acts as moderator of the debate and periodically calls time, and different students come forward to represent their "side." Students not involved in the debate can give suggestions via notes to those involved. Clicker questions appear periodically during the debate, assessing any changes in student opinions about the people's behaviors in the case study as we work our way through the ASA norms involved.

YES, VIRGINIA, YOU CAN SURVIVE—AND EVEN THRIVE— IN THE LARGE CLASS

Teaching the large class requires faculty to know themselves and their teaching style. Can you make—or are you willing to make—the pedagogical adjustments to create a "large class" persona? Are you willing to lose the notes, get up, walk around, meet with your students, and go with the flow of the class, even more than you might in smaller classes? Then leading a large class just might be something you would enjoy.

Think through the pedagogical resources available to you and how you want to use them. Plan carefully the pacing of the class, so that neither students nor you get too exhausted. Get students actively involved in class. Be sure that readings and other ancillary materials are interesting to them, so that they want to think about them. But most of all—have fun. There are great rewards as well as lots of work with classes of this size. Use your sociological knowledge and apply it to your classroom to find what works best for you and your students as you take this sociological journey together.

SECTION 5

BUILDING YOUR CAREER
AS A TEACHER-SCHOLAR

►►► CHAPTER 20

THE SCHOLARSHIP OF TEACHING AND LEARNING

As a community of scholars, we have spent a lot of time conceptualizing and defining the scholarship of teaching and learning, or SoTL. Many would argue that Boyer's (1990) work entitled *Scholarship Reconsidered: Priorities of the Professoriate*, was the impetus for a wide range of research on teaching. This single book had more influence on Maxine and Kath's careers than any other, in that it literally changed the academy. In this chapter, we offer definitions of the scholarship of teaching and learning and distinguish between SoTL and scholarly teaching. We suggest that many teachers would benefit from beginning to do research on their teaching (SoTL) and that all of us should be scholarly teachers.

● The scholarship of teaching and learning actually began as an argument that universities should value the large range of work that faculty do rather than rewarding traditional disciplinary research to the exclusion of all else (Shulman 2013). Ernest Boyer, then the president of the Carnegie Foundation for the Advancement of Teaching, became the name associated with a transformation in higher education that would help refocus efforts on undergraduate education in research institutions and stimulate inquiry on undergraduate education in all types of colleges and universities. Unfortunately for us all, Boyer passed away shortly after the publication of *Scholarship Reconsidered: Priorities of the Professoriate* (1990). In 1997, Lee Shulman followed Boyer as president of the Carnegie Foundation. Along with Carnegie colleagues Pat Hutchings and Mary Taylor Huber, Shulman led the way in helping us truly reconsider our scholarship. Shulman's conceptualizations of SoTL have been the most commonly cited (see Shulman 2000). In Shulman's definition, SoTL requires documentation of our teaching and student learning, making this documentation available for peer review, and thus providing it as a basis for use by others. This very broad definition of SoTL includes products such as teaching portfolios, blogs, entries in the American Sociological Association's Teaching Resources and Innovation Library for Sociology (TRAILS), and certainly publication in *Teaching Sociology* and other refereed journals. This inclusive definition allows recognition of a variety of types of scholarship and follows the general trends for traditional or basic scholarship. That is, while some products of basic scholarship are more highly valued than others, there is usually at least some recognition given for making contributions other than through peer-reviewed publications.

The hierarchy of SoTL scholarship undoubtedly differs by institution with some more likely to value one type of SoTL and basic research products over others. To the extent that SoTL research is valued at research institutions, SoTL peer-reviewed journal articles and research monographs are more likely to be given credence than other types of research products.

In research-intensive universities, especially in those departments that also have PhD programs, reports, presentations at conferences, book reviews, encyclopedia articles, and such are not as highly valued and rewarded as journal articles and monographs. On the other hand, in colleges where teaching is more highly valued and rewarded, such outlets are more likely to be given credence. The same is true for SoTL products.

You will not be surprised to hear that there is also no clear consensus about the appropriate venues for SoTL among sociologists. For example, Grauerholz and Zipp (2008) taught a workshop at the 2007 American Sociological Association meetings entitled "How to Do the Scholarship of Teaching." While they offered Shulman's more inclusive definition, they focused the workshop on the process of publishing about teaching and specifically about publishing in *Teaching Sociology*. Few of us would come away from reading the *Teaching Sociology* article describing the workshop without thinking of SoTL as equivalent to a peer-reviewed publication. To be fair, there is a footnote in their *Teaching Sociology* article which explicitly acknowledges SoTL work other than "formal assessment." And, if Maxine and Kath were asked to teach a workshop on doing SoTL, we might very well choose to focus on peer-reviewed publications as did Grauerholz and Zipp (2008). Why? Publication in peer-reviewed journals seems to be the most difficult challenge for SoTL scholars.

In contrast to Grauerholz and Zipp's (2008) implicit suggestion that SoTL is equivalent to refereed publication, Chin (2002) is explicit. He argues that defining scholarship as publication in peer-reviewed journals legitimizes SoTL. Chin (2002) analyzed publications in *Teaching Sociology* from 1984 to 1999 to question if a scholarship of teaching and learning is emerging. Chin (2002:55) recognizes that he is setting a higher standard than does Shulman and others but argues that this higher standard "insulates the scholarship of teaching and learning from the criticism that it is evaluated according to more lenient standards than basic research."

Maxine and Kath agree that publication in peer-reviewed journals might help elevate the status of SoTL. The more SoTL looks like basic research, the easier it is for faculty who do basic research to recognize and accept it as valid work. This may be the most efficient route to full recognition of SoTL as a research area, but we also see disadvantages to this definition. Maxine has long since argued that defining SoTL as only publishing in refereed journals limits the potential of SoTL to make a difference for our students (Atkinson 2000, 2001). Maxine asks, "How many students will benefit from having a few more academics make teaching a research area?" (Atkinson 2001:1224). A more inclusive definition encourages more types of "going public" with our teaching and making teaching community property (Hutchings and Shulman 1999:13). Limiting conceptualizations of SoTL to peer-reviewed publications devalues other forms of going public with our teaching. If other means of documenting our teaching are accepted as SoTL, more teachers are likely to make their teaching public, even those who will never publish a refereed journal article about their teaching. The more of us who accept the challenge of making teaching community property, the more likely our teaching is to be reflective and effective. Narrowly defining SoTL also lets too many of us off the hook. If SoTL is simply another research specialty, then only a few of us have to do it even though most of us teach (Atkinson 2001; Chin 2002), and we should all be carefully and systematically examining our teaching to improve it. Going public with this systematic evidence is the best way to assure that we are taking our teaching seriously and that the practice of teaching is strengthened.

Among SoTL leaders outside the discipline, there are related conversations that many call the "big tent debate." Hutchings (2013a) argues that SoTL is a big tent; that is, SoTL is not work for a group of specialists but rather work in which all teaching faculty should be engaged. We do not all have to publish, Hutchings (2013a) argues, but all of us should seriously reflect on our teaching, including posing deliberate questions, systematically gathering and examining evidence to address those questions and "engage" with others to build a knowledge base. Kath and Maxine argue that using a "big tent" vision of

SoTL is more likely to result in a larger number of faculty being willing and even excited about teaching inquiries.

Regardless of whether you equate SoTL with publication or see it as a practice that acknowledges a wider range of results, we cannot assume that we all agree. Especially if you are a junior scholar, you should carefully examine policies surrounding SoTL in your departments, colleges, and universities to be sure that you understand how SoTL is being defined. At North Carolina State University where Maxine teaches, for example, it would be rare for someone to mention SoTL and not be referring to publishing. However, at Valdosta State where Kath is on the faculty, there is probably more variation between departments. Kath also thinks that SoTL would be more likely to be rewarded at Valdosta State if an SoTL work demonstrated positive outcomes.

However, we note that even in the face of the various definitions of SoTL, there is tremendous agreement that centers on SoTL as a tool for advancing student learning through serious reflection, systematically gathering evidence to address questions about student learning, and making our teaching public. It would be difficult to emphasize this too much. It is important that we keep in mind that despite differences in perspectives on the product of SoTL, there is agreement on the process of creating SoTL.

SCHOLARLY TEACHING AND THE SCHOLARSHIP OF TEACHING AND LEARNING

If we had to choose one issue surrounding SoTL to focus on, we would first choose to expand the understanding of the strong relationship between scholarly teaching and SoTL. While SoTL scholars make important contributions to teaching, we argue that scholarly teachers play the pivotal roles in advancing higher education, especially if one assumes that SoTL is equivalent to publications. So, what is the difference between scholarly teachers and SoTL scholars? Who are scholarly teachers? Poole (2013a, 2013b) puts it most succinctly: scholarly teachers consume the scholarship of teaching and learning and apply this scholarship to their teaching. The scholarship of teaching and learning is the *production* of knowledge about teaching while scholarly teaching is the *consumption* of the scholarship of teaching and learning. In other words, scholarly teachers use the public information on teaching generated by both themselves and others. Their teaching is based on an examination and careful consideration of evidence about teaching and learning (i.e., SoTL), as compared to hunches, intuition, or other more informal ways of acquiring information about teaching. Obviously, scholarly teachers are likely to use a variety of sources of information but when we refer to someone as a scholarly teacher, we mean that he or she has read the scholarship of teaching and learning and applies what the individual has learned from the professional literature. We assert that all teachers should be scholarly teachers. No other profession that we know of would suggest that its practitioners should be allowed to practice their craft without some knowledge of it.

Pat Hutchings (2013a), one of the leaders of the SoTL movement, says that while she helped develop the distinction between scholarly teaching and SoTL, she rather wishes she had not. She emphasizes that scholarly teaching and SoTL are "related phenomena" (Hutchings 2013b). Huber (2013) agrees. She refers to SoTL as "intensification of scholarly teaching." We agree with Hutchings (2013b) and Huber (2013) that the lines between scholarly teaching and SoTL are blurred. Scholarly teaching and SoTL exist on a continuum. We begin by being scholarly teachers. You have already started this journey toward being a scholarly teacher by reading this book. We hope that you will move on to be SoTL scholars, at least in the broadest sense of the word. We all need to question our teaching and systematically address our questions.

Figure 20.1, taken from the Vanderbilt University's Center for Teaching's website (2013) illustrates the relationship between SoTL, scholarly teaching, and teaching. SoTL is at the center of teaching. Scholarly teaching is based

FIGURE 20.1 THE RELATIONSHIP BETWEEN SoTL, SCHOLARLY TEACHING, AND TEACHING

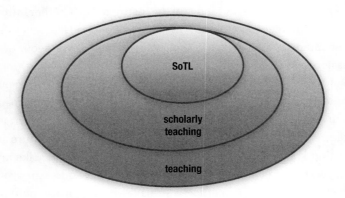

SoTL Provides the Basis of Scholarly Teaching

Vanderbilt University Center for Teaching 2013. "Why Do SoTL?" Nasheville, TN: Vanderbilt University Center for Teaching. Retrieved December 9, 2013 (https://my.vanderbilt.edu/sotl/understanding-sotl/why-sotl/

on SoTL and teaching more generically speaking can be affected by scholarly teaching and SoTL.

Lee Shulman, now President Emeritus of the Carnegie Foundation for the Advancement of Teaching, is quoted on the Vanderbilt University's Center for Teaching website (2013) as saying, "Scholarly teaching is what every one of us should be engaged in every day that we are in a classroom, in our office with students, tutoring, lecturing, conducting discussions, all the roles we play pedagogically. Our work as teachers should meet the higher scholarly standards of groundedness, of openness, of clarity and complexity." Shulman (2004:166) differentiates our scholarly teaching from SoTL when he says, "But it is only when we step back and reflect systematically on the teaching we have done, in a form that can be publicly reviewed and built upon by our peers, that we have moved from scholarly teaching to the scholarship of teaching."

DOING SoTL

What if you want to do your own SoTL? Whether you would like to publish your work or go public in other ways, the starting place is the same. Let your natural curiosity lead you. What questions do you have about your teaching and your students' learning? What is puzzling to you? The most common form of SoTL is measuring the effectiveness of a teaching technique (Grauerholz and Zipp 2008; Pike 2011) but you might be interested in a variety of other issues such as whether or not changes in the curriculum are accomplishing the goals you established, whether students evaluate online courses differently depending on the gender of the instructor, or whether introductory texts adequately treat literature on the environment, race, or any other topic of specific interest to you. Questions usually come to us from our own sense of professional curiosity. SoTL questions are no different. We are already asking ourselves SoTL questions when we create our student learning outcomes (see chapter 1) and when we evaluate the effectiveness of some aspect of our courses. If you hope to publish your SoTL research, you must situate it in the literature. Ideally, you have already examined relevant literature and have used existing knowledge to organize and frame your course. Like any other research, you have to choose appropriate methods for addressing your questions. Using more than one method will make your inquiries more powerful (Hutchings 2000) and your chance of publication will increase. For example, you might both examine student creations and survey students on their perceptions of learning.

Sociologists have two primary outlets for their SoTL. The Teaching Resources and Innovation Library for Sociology (TRAILS), the American Sociological Association's depository of teaching techniques and teaching materials, is a treasure trove for us. While TRAILS has editors, the requirements for publication are not as exacting as *Teaching Sociology*, a peer-reviewed research journal. TRAILS requires less formal assessment and a less extensive literature review. There are also many multidisciplinary journals that you might consider. For example, The University of Central Florida's Faculty Center for Teaching and Learning (2010) has an extensive list of SoTL journals.

SoTL is somewhat similar to assessment. "How is it working?" is a question to be asked for our SoTL and for assessments. However, assessments are usually not as deeply reflective nor are assessments necessarily situated in the literature. Assessments can be as simple as asking students to raise their hands to indicate if you need to repeat an explanation. Or, they can be as formal as signing off on a dissertation or giving a student a final grade. Assessments do not require making your work available for peer review; SoTL does.

There are two very important different types of assessment: formative and summative. The goal of formative assessment is to provide feedback for students or faculty to help students learn better and its focus is not evaluative. That is, the point of formative assessment is to help students improve. Summative assessment is evaluative and its goal is to provide a judgment about the quality of a learning outcome. Assessment is discussed more fully in Section 3.

formative & summative

There is a difference between the "science" most of us know—that is the "science" or tools of our particular disciplines—and SoTL. The very term SoTL has only recently been consistently used for the multidisciplinary field that focuses on teaching and learning at the classroom level in higher education. While many argue (see Felten 2013; Hutchings 2000, 2013) that SoTL is most profitably conducted with the tools of the particular discipline whose teaching/learning is being studied, SoTL is an interdisciplinary or multidisciplinary field focusing on questions related to enhancing teaching and learning. Kain (2005) offers useful parallels within other fields in sociology. For example, Kain (2005) says that sociology of the family is a broad field that often includes studies of gender, and gender is multidisciplinary. (Gender scholars might argue that gender is the broader field with family being one site of gender study; still, few gender scholars would not agree that gender is a multidisciplinary field.)

CRITIQUES OF SoTL

SoTL is a new field and there are many issues yet to be resolved. While those in the "learning sciences" have been researching how students learn for decades (Daniel and Chew 2013), SoTL research has blossomed for only about the last 20 years. Daniel and Chew (2013) provide an excellent critique of SoTL, offering several points about which we agree. They argue that SoTL is atheoretical, tied to a specific context, and that we too often fail to be comparative. That is, we test the effectiveness of a technique, but we do not compare one technique to another (Daniel and Chew 2013).

SoTL research often ignores the causes of the effects we report. We can map our research to our questions or student learning outcomes but all too often are left without an understanding of why our teaching techniques work, or why they fail to be effective. Such research lacks theoretical sophistication. While we can often use sociological concepts to help us understand our findings, we continue to work without the strong theoretical models that our disciplinary fields and subfields provide.

However, in a personal e-mail, Robert Hironimus-Wendt (2013) argues that we do indeed have "theory" but that it is implicit rather than explicit.

> The basic theory that drives SoTL is (a) teaching pedagogy are causally related to learning outcomes; (b) changing pedagogy will produce different results; (c) some pedagogy are more effective for certain forms of learning to occur; (d) changes in the way we teach can increase the amount of learning that occurs across a population of students; (e) changes in the way we teach can increase the aggregate level of learning across that population.

Hironimus-Wendt's (2013) point is well taken. We need to be more explicit about our theoretical understandings, and we need to provide more nuanced understandings of the relationships between our teaching methods and our students' learning outcomes.

SoTL typically is conducted in a very specific context, often a class taught to the members of a section of a course in a discipline at one level in the curriculum in one university. Context is controlled and as sociologists know, context is crucial. However, this very specificity of context is both our greatest strength and our greatest weakness. It is the strength and weakness of case studies. How do we know that the same technique will be as effective the next semester with a different class composition, everything else being held equal? Hironimus-Wendt (2013) argues that this weakness is typical of quasi-experimental design: "We use nonrandom, convenience samples of college students to test whether or not different pedagogy achieve the desired results."

An additional salient point Daniel and Chew (2013) make is that typical SoTL research does not compare one technique to another. We create a teaching tool or activity and ask if it "works." But, it is much less common for us to compare two teaching tools or activities. For example, we continually cite the power of active learning techniques (see chapter 6), but rarely do we test the effect of formal lectures. We often create activities that help us teach about inequalities but rarely do we compare two or more activities.

There is little doubt that creating SoTL requires us to think differently. SoTL presents both quantitative and qualitative researchers with challenges but also both will see consistencies with research designs with which they are most familiar. Quantitative researchers are not likely to be totally at ease because the sample sizes in SoTL are not always large, and SoTL is most likely to be inductive rather than deductive. We do not usually derive hypotheses from a theory and conduct research to test those theories. The extent to which SoTL research is generalizable is questionable. SoTL is grounded, local, and contextualized (Felten 2013), and any one classroom is unlikely to have a sample that is representative of some larger population. However, there are ways in which SoTL will seem more familiar to quantitative researchers than to qualitative scholars. SoTL often relies on counts, such as the number or percentage of students who are able to master a specific task, as a common and useful measurement. Quantitative data is routinely collected on our courses; we all have grade distributions and grades for individual products. Most of us have quantitative student evaluations.

Qualitative researchers will also have challenges but will see consistencies with their research designs. If you are examining social processes, as qualitative researchers do, you have to ask about the teacher's role. Can you both examine the social processes in your class and teach simultaneously? Would it be ethical to question your students like you might other respondents? Can students take the status of both respondents and learners in your classroom? Issues of power differentials make being the researcher and the teacher potentially problematic. On the other hand, there are some ways in which qualitative researchers may bridge the divides between their traditional research and SoTL more easily than quantitative scholars. Qualitative researchers do not focus on samples, populations, and generalizability. Qualitative researchers do focus on contextualized processes. Qualitative researchers are accustomed to analyzing documents, and SoTL is often based on the analysis of students' written work.

In one of the most succinct arguments about SoTL that we have seen, McKinney (2005:418) says of SoTL:

> I think there is value to readers of a strong and informative literature review; of modeling methodologies that might be replicated by others; of contributing a study that is one piece of the puzzle that forms an important picture in conjunction with other studies in the literature; of offering findings from students in one setting that provoke reflection, experimentation, and changes in practice by other instructors in their settings; of helping to support existing theory or results from other literatures; and of confirming what we believe to be obvious.
>
> Must the use of different or additional standards be interpreted as lower standards?

McKinney (2005) does not contest the fact that SoTL is different from the research that we typically do but rather she maintains that SoTL has value in and of itself.

Boyer's (1990) purpose was not to create a new field of research. Rather, his message was political. He advocated a different reward structure in our colleges and universities; a reward structure that acknowledges the wide diversity of the scholarships we create (Shulman 2013). While we cannot know if he would approve of where this movement has taken us, we would like to believe he would. For Kath and Maxine, it has taken us to work that matters, to experiencing the true joy of seeing learning happen. It has taken us to that magical place where a student sees the world in a different light, who questions, who truly wants to know and to make a difference. As Hutchings (2000:9) contends, SoTL has a "transformational agenda." That is, SoTL is produced to generate change. Usually that change is a difference in the way we teach. We continually look for the most effective techniques to teach our students in a given context. But, for many of us, SoTL goes far beyond this input/output model and represents our vision of a more just future, a future that depends on well-educated people who have a sociological imagination.

CHAPTER 21

CREATING YOUR TEACHING PHILOSOPHY AND TEACHING PORTFOLIO

Teaching philosophies serve many functions. We may construct portfolios and philosophies as a part of the materials that potential employers will evaluate, as part of our tenure and promotion packages or our post-tenure review packets, and to be considered for teaching awards. Teaching portfolios are most often thought of as the documentation of teaching credentials. They can also serve as an important means of self-reflection and teaching improvement. This chapter outlines the essential elements of portfolios and provides examples from three exemplary young teachers.

Teaching Portfolios

"Do you really have to create a teaching portfolio?" Maxine's PhD students often ask. That question comes right after, "Do I really need a teaching philosophy?" Creating our teaching philosophies and portfolios is intimidating. Teaching has been a private activity and creating a portfolio immediately conjures up images of being evaluated. Although we expect others to evaluate our research, having our teaching evaluated seems somehow more personal and more fraught with unknowns. We frequently feel that our teaching evaluations are less in our control than our research. Having a "revise and resubmit" on our research is commonplace but "R&Rs" on teaching may be harder to come by, or at least that's the way it often feels.

While we are accustomed to documenting our professional research and service obligations, we sometimes document our teaching with a list of courses we have taught and nothing more. Perhaps we differentiate between a graduate or undergraduate course, general education courses or courses for the major. Yet we may spend as much time, if not more, on our teaching than any other professional activity.

Why do we need portfolios? Why not simply ask faculty to share student evaluations with perhaps accompanying syllabi? Why portfolios? Seldin (1993) offers the analogy of flashlights as compared to searchlights. Student evaluations and other single indicators of teaching effectiveness are like flashlights; they illuminate a narrow band of teaching skills and activities. Portfolios are more akin to searchlights that show us a large range of teaching attributes, proclivities, and philosophical stances.

Does everyone really need a teaching portfolio? Most of the readers of this book will need to create at least some of the elements of a portfolio. Senior faculty are not as likely to be required to construct a collection of teaching materials unless they are nominated for teaching awards or their institution has a post-tenure review process. Maxine never constructed a teaching portfolio until she was nominated for her first teaching award. At the time, she did not know what a teaching portfolio was nor had she ever heard of a teaching philosophy. None of her friends knew either. She just started reading. It is very likely that the senior faculty who review your portfolio will not themselves have a portfolio or a written teaching philosophy.

Portfolios can be more or less expansive and can contain formative or summative materials. Let's take the most common first. Teaching portfolios, or the elements of a teaching portfolio, are most often seen as a means by which to evaluate teaching rather than as a means to improve teaching; that is, they are usually seen as a collection of documents for summative purposes. Some job ads explicitly ask for portfolios or "evidence of effective teaching." Job ads that ask for "evidence of effective teaching" are frustrating to most applicants because there is no readily agreed-upon definition of what would constitute such evidence. Unless otherwise defined for you, you should assume that "evidence of teaching effectiveness" means the three common elements of a teaching portfolio.

Three Basic Elements of a Portfolio

In general, it is useful to think of teaching portfolio materials as those created by you and those created by others or products of your teaching. Two of the most common elements of teaching portfolios are materials you create: your teaching philosophy and syllabus/syllabi. The third basic element is student evaluations of teaching, obviously material created by others. Seldin (1993) would perhaps call these three "flashlights"; that is, they only provide light on a limited part of your teaching. Still, they form the backbone of most portfolios.

Three of Maxine's friends and former PhD students agreed to allow us to quote extensively from their excellent teaching portfolios. We will use their portfolios to give you concrete examples of how recent PhDs are presenting their teaching materials. All three finished their PhDs in 2012 or 2013. All three are accomplished teachers with convincing teaching portfolios.

MATERIALS CREATED BY THE TEACHER

Teaching Philosophy

The most perplexing and difficult part of the portfolio is the teaching philosophy. Most of us have never been explicit about our philosophies. Simply put, a teaching philosophy describes how you teach and why you teach that way. One version of Maxine's philosophy begins this way: "My teaching is guided by two ideals: empowerment and partnership. I strive to assure that the people I teach are empowered by the skills they learn. My primary means of teaching is through collaboration and participation. I tell people 'why' I teach: 'empowerment.' I tell people how I teach: 'collaboration and participation.'"

Andrea Hunt (2013), a faculty member at the University of North Alabama, starts her philosophy this way:

> My role as an educator is to promote students' intellectual growth by using student-centered teaching methods that engage students in sociological inquiry. Students draw on disciplinary perspectives to reflect upon, question, and judge information about human behavior while also having an awareness of the larger social and cultural contexts that influence life decisions and outcomes. Students demonstrate how historical and cultural contexts influence individual biographies and analyze the historical, cultural, and structural factors that create, maintain, and reproduce inequality. I also strive to provide opportunities for students to learn and practice methods for creating and evaluating knowledge about the social world and critically reflect on how that knowledge applies to their own lives.

One of Andrea's "whys" is to "promote intellectual growth." She also tells us "how" she promotes intellectual growth—that is, through "student-centered teaching methods that engage students in sociological inquiry." The rest of the teaching philosophy elaborates on these themes as the remainder of this paragraph demonstrates.

Sarah Epplen (Rusche) (2013), a faculty member at the Minnesota State University–Mankato, also begins her teaching portfolio with an explanation of how and why she teaches as she does: "'If your brain hurts, you're doing it right,' I tell my students as I encourage them to engage in the process of sociological inquiry. Students in my classes *do* sociology; they don't just memorize it. My goal is that they think like sociologists as often and as deeply as possible, and I create ways to make that happen." Sarah is telling us that she uses inquiry methods of teaching and she uses these methods because she wants students to think like sociologists and to think deeply.

Kris Macomber (2013), an adjunct faculty member at Meredith College in Raleigh, North Carolina, begins her teaching philosophy by telling us the "how and why" with a student voice: "It was the last day of class, summer 2008, when a student said something to me that I will never forget. He said, 'Kris, I want to thank you for being such a good teacher. I learned so much in this class. And, the best part about it was you never told us what to think. You taught us *how* to think.' I think about this student often and hope that the sociological knowledge and insights he developed in my course have empowered him to help create a better world, even in small ways."

If you have never written a philosophy of teaching or what some simply call a "teaching statement," begin with either "why" you teach the way you do or "how" you teach. The actual document more typically begins with the "why," but as you are writing your first philosophy, it might be easier to describe your teaching and then think about why you do what you do. The "whys" are philosophical statements. What do you believe is important about teaching? What are your most important goals? What motivates you to teach well?

The "how" you teach simply reinforces the "why." It explains how it is that you accomplish your goals. The "how" you teach statements are not actually philosophical statements; rather, they are descriptive statements that help convince your reader that your philosophy is genuine. Teaching philosophies need only be about 250 words. These are not generally long statements; rather they provide an overview that you will reinforce with the other documents in your portfolio.

Sample Syllabi

In chapter 2, we discussed creating the course syllabus. We will try not to be repetitive here. Choosing which of your syllabi to present may not be a problem. If you have only taught one to three courses, present all three. If you are applying for a job and the job ad mentions one of the courses you've taught, be sure to include that one. What if you don't like the syllabus you've created? Edit it and include it. You can always list it as an update. All strong teachers update their syllabi based on their experience, new readings, and what they have learned about teaching since the last time they taught the course. Remember that a syllabus is the core of your teaching materials.

While you might get a number of requests for your teaching philosophy or teaching statement, relatively few people know how to evaluate a philosophy. As long as it is reasonably well written, most of your readers will be pleased. Most read it with an untrained eye. This is not necessarily the case with your syllabi. Many who read your syllabus/syllabi will have themselves written syllabi for a number of years. Make sure that your syllabi represent some of your best work. If, like many of us, you use a learning management system, you may not have created a traditional syllabus for a while. Still, you will have all the parts of the syllabus. If you are asked to submit a syllabus, do not make the mistake of sending in only a course calendar.

Other Materials

To continue to use Seldin's (1993) analogy, while a teaching philosophy, student evaluations, and sample syllabi are the backbone of portfolios, they are only "flashlights" rather than "searchlights." To the extent that you can go beyond these basics you will be providing a wider view of your teaching.

One of the strong points that Hunt, Macomber, and Epplen have in common is that they begin their portfolios with a table of contents. While this may seem like an organizational detail, it serves many purposes. Like all tables of content, the list allows us to quickly locate the parts of a portfolio. The table of contents tells you a lot about what is in the portfolio without having to go much further. Sarah Epplen's table of contents has a section for "Publications on Teaching." That is impressive. She also has a section titled, "What Does It Mean to Be an Excellent Teacher? A Reflection." We are intrigued and we have not even opened the portfolio yet! Epplen grabs our attention. Hunt's portfolio is equally as enticing. She lists "Sociology of the Family (Online Course)." We do not have to go any further wondering if she has taught online. She also lists "Visual Sociological Analyses" as an example of her course assignments. I am intrigued again. This is no ordinary teacher. Macomber provides us with a sample exam. This example easily convinces me that not only can she construct a good exam, she knows how to ask a good question in general, one of the most important teaching skills.

Portfolio entries that extend beyond the basics include examples of other materials you create, such as course assignments, descriptions of teaching programs you have participated in, descriptions of teaching-related activity such as advising or serving as a student club advisor, and teaching activities you are especially proud of. If you have published an article about teaching or reviewed a book about teaching, do include it. Anything in print makes a credible portfolio entry.

Course assignments and exercises are excellent additions to a teaching portfolio. Again, what Hunt, Macomber, and Epplen have in common is that they provide sample class assignments in their portfolios. These exercises or assignments do not have to be exercises you create. It is perfectly appropriate to include an exercise someone else has designed and you describe the way you use the exercise in your class. Using published exercises or exercises others have shared with you illustrates your teaching and that is the point of the portfolio. Epplen lists "Jigsaw" as one of the exercises she uses in class. Jigsaw requires that students become experts and then teach their expertise to other students. Epplen has half her class read one article and the other half reads another article. The expert group members first meet with each other to clarify the important points, any confusing ideas, etc. Then, the experts meet with nonexperts to teach them the material. The groups take turns teaching each other. As noted above, Hunt shares an original exercise detailing an assignment she gives students: take photos that represent sociological concepts, themes, or main ideas. Students take photos, explain how the photo illustrates sociological content, and cite course material to back up their arguments. This exercise quickly gives you an example of Hunt's creativity. Macomber also provides examples of class exercises. She asks her students to facilitate a class and provides us with the instructions she gives her students. She created an exercise designed to encourage students to see the connection between culture and socialization. Students choose an agent of socialization like family, education, or religion and address seven concepts that help us understand how socialization occurs through that institution. Students discuss roles, norms, sanctions, values, symbols, emotions, and material culture.

You might also include examples of teaching programs you have participated in, copies of teaching publications, and an explanation of awards you have won. Epplen includes a discussion of her work as a mentor for minority students. Macomber includes a list of teaching development activities she completed. She lists having completed a semester course on teaching sociology, for example, and several of the teaching workshops she attended. Hunt provides a discussion of her emphasis on students' reflection on their own learning.

PORTFOLIO MATERIALS CREATED BY OTHERS AND THE PRODUCTS OF EFFECTIVE TEACHING

Student Evaluations

We recommend that you present a mixture of both quantitative and qualitative student evaluations. In all three of the cases that we are using as illustrative material in this chapter, Hunt, Macomber, and Epplen present us with both quantitative and qualitative scores but they do so in different ways. They all have excellent quantitative scores so we get a quick overview of their strength. That is the primary story quantitative scores can tell us; that is, the extent to which instructors are rated highly by their students. Our experience is that as long as the scores hover around or exceed the department mean, they are unlikely to hurt your application. Nothing says that you can't pick the scores you want to present. You could show all of your recent quantitative scores if they are consistently good. Consistently high scores demonstrate that you would be a reliably good instructor. Or, if your evaluations go up over time, you can show improvement. Otherwise, you can choose examples. Or, more daringly, you could present a weak set of student evaluations and explain how you altered your class to meet the challenges the evaluations present.

There are also a variety of ways to present your qualitative student comments. Hunt presents only five comments, all chosen to represent concrete strengths. The comments focus on clarity of explanation, "Explained the material in a very easy to understand manner"; receptivity to students, "She's extremely receptive to students before, during, and after class"; emphasis on critical thinking, "taught us to think critically," "enthusiasm," ". . . loves her work"; and caring for students, "Really looked out for the students' best interest." Epplen presents a large number of comments organized around themes much like Hunt and follows up with a reflection about each. For example, after presenting a set of student comments organized around the amount of work she required and the challenges of the course, Epplen reflects: "I felt confident that my students were walking away with marked intellectual growth, not just memories of a good time in a fun class," and "I appreciate students' acknowledgement of the intellectually challenging nature of my courses." Macomber differed in her approach by presenting more comments than the other two. She also presented more quantitative scores, demonstrating the consistency of her strong teaching.

Another way to document your teaching skill is to provide examples of student work. Excellent essays, research papers, homework assignments, and data analysis modules could be used. Anything your students produce that demonstrates their learning has the potential to enrich your portfolio. Be sure to provide examples of your feedback on student work. A rubric for any student work presented is a good bit of evidence to include.

At the beginning of every course, Maxine asks her students' written permission to use their work in her teaching portfolio and in other classes to illustrate excellent work. The work is presented anonymously and only as examples of strong work. Only examples of strong achievement are presented to others. Maxine has never had a student decline permission and students are usually very pleased to have their work used in such a positive light. Some of these student materials are used in portfolios, some are used in class to illustrate a good outcome of an assignment.

If one of your students presents a paper at a conference or wins an award that speaks to your teaching, you might include that in your portfolio. Many professors provide a list of graduate students they have mentored or whose dissertation they chaired. These products of good teaching are convincing evidence of strong teaching.

You might also present letters written on your behalf by someone who has observed your class or knows your work from other experiences. Your faculty observations are obviously valuable for your file but peer evaluations can also make a contribution. If, for example, you asked a peer to observe your class and provide an evaluation, they could provide valuable insights that more experienced professors might miss. Always provide a context for these evaluations. If there is a required teaching observation rubric used by the department, be sure to tell your reader. If the person observing you is the chair of your dissertation, document that. If the person observing you teaches a class on pedagogy, let your reader know.

This chapter has focused thus far on summative teaching portfolios used for job interviews. Portfolios can also be used for tenure and promotion and for post-tenure review. The extent to which portfolios are used vary widely from college to college. It is the case that more teaching accountability has begun to be a reality at every institution, and portfolios can be an important part of that accountability. At NC State, tenure and promotion packets include teaching evaluations and a statement about our teaching, but prior to these high-stake evaluations, faculty are not asked to document their teaching activities in any detail. Annual reviews in the department Maxine is a part of, and where she served as department head, include brief statements about teaching but the requirements are minimal. University policy requires peer observations of teaching every year for assistant professors, once every three years for associate professors, and once every five years for full professors. Teaching awards are given at the departmental, college, and university level. Teaching must be documented in order to compete for awards beyond the departmental level. Those documents are forms of teaching portfolios.

THE VALUE OF PORTFOLIOS

While Seldin (1993, 2000) is the name commonly associated with asserting the value of teaching portfolios, others are more skeptical of the rewards of constructing teaching portfolios. In an especially critical essay, Burns (2000) argues that we have no evidence of the positive effect of portfolios on teaching despite the assertions of many forceful figures in the most well-known teaching organizations. Burns (2000) also suggests that teaching portfolios might actually be doing us harm by diverting our time and attention away from other work that needs to be done. This is a point well taken. In Maxine's experience, portfolios are more likely to be constructed in the process of preparing for a job interview or in a teaching seminar where they are required. Hopefully, as more and more of us are required to create portfolios, they will become an expected part of our professional lives. We would still argue that the accountability and reflection required to create a portfolio is a step forward toward better teaching.

Formative Portfolios

Portfolios can also be formative or developmental. They can help us focus and improve our teaching. We collect the teaching artifacts and use those artifacts to reflect on our teaching. The portfolio becomes an organizational scheme, a framework for developing our best practices. In the best of all possible worlds, we would create our first teaching portfolios as we create our first courses and use the portfolios as a way of documenting needed changes and effective practices that we want to include in future courses.

Maxine's teaching portfolios have been useful to her because through the process of constructing them, she has been more thoughtful than she might be otherwise. Her teaching philosophy reminds her to consider carefully why she teaches and how she teaches. While she hopes that she would always construct her syllabi mindfully, knowing that they will be public is a motivation to take care in how they are created and presented. She does not believe that she neglects her responsibilities to challenge her students in order to get good teaching evaluations but she does read evaluations carefully to try to understand how her students perceive the course as well as what she learns about their learning based on their assignments. These student evaluations help her hone her teaching practices and her portfolios.

Still, Maxine argues that we must be careful not to spend time on portfolios that might be more productively used on other teaching outcomes. A teaching philosophy is the only original product that must be created for a portfolio. The other documents are created in the process of teaching our courses. Who could possibly argue that our syllabi should not be well constructed? Student evaluations are readily available to us. We know of no colleges and universities that do not require student evaluations. Collecting a few of our class exercises should not be much of a challenge. We all should be constructing and/or using effective exercises in our class. A simple explanation of one or two exercises should not be time-consuming. Examples of student products should also be available to us. Surely our students will produce some artifacts in our classes, even if these are simply informal writing assignments. It is very likely that some students will do an excellent job. We simply have to keep some copies. Asking students to submit electronically is easy enough to do and can help us keep track of their work.

Should some of us spend more time than others creating portfolios? Probably. Those of us who want jobs in colleges that emphasize teaching may benefit from more careful and thorough documentation of our teaching, within limits. Even for those of us whose primary identities are focused on teaching, we argue that our teaching time is best spent creating significant learning experiences for our students and letting the artifacts develop as an outgrowth of that teaching. We need to take care that the tail doesn't wag the dog and the dog is certainly the teaching, not the portfolio. For those of us who keep a journal, teaching portfolios may be more reflective and more fun to put together. Even those of us who do not journal can collect our teaching documents.

Teaching portfolios are collections of teaching documents that illustrate our teaching; they do not need to take on a life of their own. Teaching philosophies are usually the only document created for the sole purpose of providing it when asked by others. The other parts of the teaching portfolio are created through the day-to-day process of teaching a course. If you do not have a teaching portfolio, draft a teaching philosophy and begin to collect your teaching documents. Focus on good teaching. A teaching portfolio should be a reflection and outcome of your good work, not another doctoral dissertation!

►►► **CHAPTER 22**
WHAT THE BEST SOCIOLOGY
PROFESSORS DO

One of Kath and Maxine's favorite books is Ken Bain's *What the Best College Teachers Do* (2004). We have both been inspired by the stories of outstanding college teachers Bain provides. We have also been heavily influenced by the very talented sociology professors that we know primarily from our work in the American Sociological Association. We wondered how "the best" sociology professors would respond to questions similar to the ones Bain (2004) posed to those he interviewed.

First, we had to decide how to measure "best," recognizing that a formal research project with a sophisticated measurement model was beyond the scope of this work. There are a variety of ways that we could have measured "the best" but we decided that we would contact winners of the American Sociological Association Distinguished Contributions to Teaching Award. While these outstanding teachers are certainly not the only skilled sociology teachers, winning the award is at least one defensible way to find excellent teachers. Note that the award is given for making an "impact" on the way sociology is taught. It is something of a measurement issue as to whether you can make an "impact" and not be a particularly good teacher yourself. We assume that is possible but unlikely.

The American Sociological Association describes the award for distinguished contributions in this way:

The ASA Distinguished Contributions to Teaching Award honors ASA members' outstanding contributions to the teaching of undergraduate and/or graduate sociology. The award recognizes contributions that have made a significant impact on the manner in which sociology is taught at a regional, state, national, or international level. These contributions may include preparation of teaching- and curriculum-related materials and publications, participation in the scholarship of teaching and learning, development and communication of innovative teaching techniques, leadership in teaching-related workshops and symposia, involvement in innovative program development, and contributions to the enhancement of teaching within state, regional, or national associations.

The award typically is given for a series of contributions spanning several years or an entire career, although it may recognize a single project of exceptional impact. The award is not designed to recognize outstanding teaching ability at one's own institution unless that is part of a career with broader impact. Individuals, departments, schools, or other collective actors are eligible. (American Sociological Association 2014)

We also realize that our choice of "best" is somewhat self-serving and we are a bit embarrassed about that. Maxine won the award in 2011 and Kath is the 2014 winner. At the time we made the decision to define "best" in this way neither of us had won the award.

Based on Bain's (2004) research, we e-mailed the winners of the American Sociological Association's Award for Outstanding Contributions to Teaching from 2004 to the present. Some were able to respond in the time period we provided. All answered our e-mail and were gracious. We asked them to respond to some or all of the following questions. (Note that this is e-mail correspondence and not an interview as sociologists would define it.) We asked them the following questions:

1. What is most important for us to remember about how students learn?

2. What are the most important lessons you have to pass on about how to prepare to teach?

3. What are (were) your primary expectations of your students?

4. What type of teaching methods do you use in your teaching?

5. What do you think is the most important thing for us to remember about how to treat students?

6. How do you check student progress in your courses (informal and formal assessments)?

7. How do you evaluate your own teaching?

We are grateful to the award winners who were able to respond to us during the time period we provided. We present excerpts from their answers verbatim as they sent them to us with only typographical errors corrected.

WHAT IS MOST IMPORTANT FOR US TO REMEMBER ABOUT HOW STUDENTS LEARN?

Caroline Hodges Persell (2005 award recipient): They learn in different ways, they have different backgrounds and prior knowledge, and they are interested in different kinds of things. Can we provide a variety of ways of learning (verbal, visual, mathematical, reading, listening, doing)?

We all learn better and remember better when we hear a story that illustrates a principle or idea.

What motivates them? Curiosity? Use value in the world? Use value in the course? What motivations do we try to encourage, and how do we do that?

Kathleen McKinney (2006 award recipient): Student learning only happens when we help/facilitate changes in the physiology of students' brains (e.g., new neuron pathways, firing of synaptic connections). When we promote student learning, we are trying to change the brains of our students. This is a tremendous responsibility. We need to be scholarly teachers who know the literature on how students learn. Many experiences can help students learn and promote these changes in their brains. We need to make use of all of our and their senses. We need to help them learn how to learn and to reflect on their learning. We need to make them active partners in their learning.

Ed Kain (2007 award recipient): At least three things are useful when thinking about how students learn:

First, everyone is a more effective learner when she/he has repeated practice at learning the same thing. You are more likely to truly learn something if you have engaged with it multiple times.

Second, students (all of us are students) are more likely to truly learn something if they *do* something, rather than just reading or hearing about

cpp! Learn by doing

something. Thus, if I am teaching about demographic differences between wealthy and poor countries, I ask students to choose a set of countries that includes both wealthy and poor countries (thus helping them review what is meant by "wealthy" and "poor," and reminding them of some countries that fall in these categories), and then collect data on a variety of demographic measures, such as infant mortality rate, expectation of life at birth, and the Total Fertility Rate (TFR). They then write about differences between the countries as well as change over time in these measures in the various countries.

Third, I would argue that learning is most effective if it is cumulative—if it begins with more simple concepts, ideas, and data, and then builds to more complex information and analyses.

Liz Grauerholz (2008 award recipient): Don't assume everyone's starting at the same level. What makes sense to some will make no or little sense to others. When it comes to important lessons, approach them in different ways.

Carol Jenkins (2008 award recipient): The latest "gimmicks" for student learning are often just that. Be cautious.

Maxine P. Atkinson (2011 award recipient): Students learn when the discipline is relevant. Nothing is more relevant than sociology but we need to make sure that students see this. We live in a culture that emphasizes, perhaps even glorifies, the individual. This makes our task a challenge.

Diane Pike (2012 award recipient): To quote Durkheim as I often do, to remember that "pedagogy depends on sociology more than any other science."

Yes, students are individuals, but it is critical to remember that we know important things about how people in general learn; those ideas need to be applied thoughtfully. The current higher education focus on a reductionist, individualized view is problematic. The obsession with technology as a solution that customizes everything—while in fact McDonaldizing and automating it—is scary.

Most people learn best in meaningful situations with other human beings.

Katherine R. Rowell (2012 award recipient): We need to remember that students learn best when they are emotionally connected to what they are learning about. I think this is something we have always known but now research on how the brain works demonstrates this as well.

Rose M. Brewer (2013 award recipient): Students learn when they are engaged with the material, the instructor, and peers, when they grow new skills and ways of thinking about the world. As professors, we have to hit all these entry points for the best student learning to happen. If students are excited about the course, that's even better. The challenge is holding and growing that excitement/engagement over time. This means understanding the fits and starts of student learning. We need to have a very good sense of who our students are, what moves them. Of course foundational to student learning is developing critical thinking, reading, and writing capacities. This really means taking seriously the dialectic of student-teacher, teacher-student learning. I tap into their knowledge; we advance our knowledge together. As they teach me, I, in turn, teach them and the dialectic continues.

WHAT ARE THE MOST IMPORTANT LESSONS YOU HAVE TO PASS ON ABOUT HOW TO PREPARE TO TEACH?

Caroline Persell: Think hard about what is important for students to know, to understand, and be able to do. Ask ourselves, what would we like them to take away from our course, or the curriculum? Then think about the best ways to help them learn, understand, and be able to do those things. How do we get them interested? How can we unpack the things they need to know and break them into smaller parts, and how can we help them connect the pieces into a more coherent understanding?

Kathleen McKinney: What we—as instructors—know, understand, can do, and can "cover" is not what matters. What matters is what our students know, understand, believe, and can do as a result of our courses, out-of-class learning experiences, and relationships. These two sets of things are not the same. Be a scholarly teacher and learn about teaching and learning. Make your teaching public (collaborative) and evidence/data-informed. Think long and hard about the student learning and developmental outcomes that you and your students hope to increase or improve. Design all aspects of your learning contexts and assessments to offer observation, practice, modeling, application transfer . . . of these learning outcomes in and outside the classroom. Remember that every decision made by any individual or group in the institution, including faculty members, involves a discussion of questions related to that decision. The primary question, for every decision in the institutions, should be, "What are the impacts on student learning?"

Ed Kain: One lesson is that we continually learn ways to improve our teaching. When something works, build upon it in future teaching. When something doesn't seem as effective, evaluate why, and either make changes that improve its effectiveness or do not use that method/assignment/technique.

Another lesson is to focus upon concepts. The specific data will change over time, but many concepts will remain useful.

Another lesson is to use the published literature on teaching—in *Teaching Sociology*, TRAILS, etc., to learn from others.

Liz Grauerholz: Be flexible and open to the unexpected. I have a tendency to overprepare—to have the class period mapped out carefully—but that can limit the spontaneous in myself and students. The best class periods have been those that took an unexpected turn; often when a student asks a "simple" question. I could give a simple answer or allow it to guide the rest of the class—the latter is the more organic and meaningful lesson.

Carol Jenkins:

▶ Transition the *"classroom as a teaching platform"* to a *"community of learners."* The classroom is a living laboratory of learners from all walks of life, all ports of call, different socioeconomic groupings, multiple languages, range in ages and (dis)abilities.

▶ Teaching well and disciplinary scholarship require the same habits of the mind. Ideally, the methods coalesce into a single teaching paradigm that views students not as "empty vessels" that exist to absorb lecture materials, but active participants who seek out answers to questions on their own.

▶ "The object of teaching is to enable the student to get along without the teacher" (Elizabeth Hubbard).

▶ Not all topics can be systematically covered. Identify the essentials and enable students to master those insights.

Keith Roberts (2010 award recipient): One of the most important elements of effective planning to teach is understanding basic principles of course design. Effective teaching requires (1) establishment of clear and measurable learning objectives, (2) determination of evaluation strategies that really do measure achievement of those objectives by the end of the course, (3) cultivation of classroom strategies or plans that are directly in line with those course goals and evaluation procedures, (4) identification of instructional resources and strategies (e.g., films, simulations) relevant to those objectives, (5) development of assignments that facilitate achievement of those objectives,

(6) selection of reading materials, and (7) determination of assessment procedures that provide feedback to the instructor on what worked and what did
not—where deep learning did and did not occur. Early in my career I thought
the first step was picking a good text or set of readings. Later I learned that
choosing the readings ought to be one of the *last* steps. The first step is establishing objectives—including objectives for deep learning rather than
surface learning. The most important part of all of this, however, is that effective courses—including *all* of these processes and steps—must be **isomorphic.** *The ends and the means must be consistent. The means, in fact, are the
end in process.* The entire course—objectives, testing methods, instructional
strategies, assignments, and assessment—must be of the same substance—
the same fabric. If the instructional strategies and the testing processes are
not totally compatible (i.e., isomorphic) with the objectives, there is very little
chance that deep learning (as opposed to short-term memorization) will occur. If the goal is critical thinking or deep learning, then using solely lecture
in the classroom and objective or multiple-choice testing for evaluation, the
course is bound to fall far short of the objectives. Learning to develop instructional strategies and evaluation methods that fit with course goals is part of
the challenge and reward of excellent teaching. The quality of the learning
was clearly better.

Maxine P. Atkinson: Most of us make the mistake of not spending enough
time preparing and thinking deeply about what we want our students to learn,
the strategies we are going to use, and how we are going to know if they have
learned. We also have to be flexible enough to abandon, or at least modify, our
plans if we see that they are not effective. That is one of my biggest challenges.

Diane Pike: Try to practice what is preached. Use our collective knowledge
in your practice and keep trying to get better (or even adequate). To prepare
to teach means taking seriously that teaching is a learned skill that requires
knowledge, practice, and feedback.

Katherine R. Rowell: Good teachers take as much time to prepare a class as
they do teaching it. Make time for preparing what you teach. In the end, the
curriculum and learning design of the course is as important (if not more
important) than the pedagogical methods used.

Rose M. Brewer:

▶ Every class is different. Every semester is new. I'm always beginning again,
assessing the terrain, keeping it fresh yet building on that storehouse of

knowledge and experience that enriches me as a teacher. This is a preeminent lesson/practice of preparing to teach.

▶ Teaching is a calling for those of us who have made it that. As with any calling you try to learn from the best teachers/modeling the best. You model but you also improvise. The improvisational aspect of teaching should not be downplayed in preparing to teach. This means making teaching our own and giving it back out as our own, having drawn on the best there is to know about this calling.

▶ Prepare. Be on the ready. Take the time to create solid lectures. Select gripping visuals/audios. Develop thoughtful small-group work. While teaching is a calling, it is also a skill requiring our time and energy to grow it, to make it powerful.

WHAT ARE (WERE) YOUR PRIMARY EXPECTATIONS OF YOUR STUDENTS?

Caroline Persell: That they were all (at least until they showed me otherwise) motivated to learn, that almost all of them were willing to work (some very hard), and that they would find the subject of sociology at least interesting if not fascinating.

Kathleen McKinney: We are all part of a community of learners (in a class or program or department or institution . . .) and should contribute to the learning in that and by that community. Students can learn from their peers and instructors; their peers and instructors can learn from them. I also expect students to take responsibility for their learning and to make choices about their learning. I am there to advise, assist, push, and support.

Ed Kain: I expect (or hope that) students will come to class prepared to engage with the material, having read all assigned materials and completed data assignments, etc. In introductory sociology I expect that students will develop the skills to read published professional research articles. Few of our students will become sociologists. They should be able to evaluate popular press reporting of research, however . . . and they can best do that if they have the skills to read original research.

Liz Grauerholz: To be open to learning something new, to at least consider alternative ways of looking at and thinking about the social world.

Carol Jenkins:

▶ Approach and complete your work with integrity on time (work ethic).

▶ Be remindful that community colleges embrace a radically inclusive student body in which all are welcome—whatever their preparation, whatever their chances of earning a certificate of completion, or an associate's degree. Learner readiness is often problematic. Underprepared students sit next to Honors-level students.

▶ Understand that there is often a gap in persistence and degree completion. Students make decisions that are beyond your control—no matter how masterful the instruction or instructor.

Maxine P. Atkinson: I expect students to show up both physically and mentally. I do my best to make sure I do the same. I close my office door and mentally prepare for every class regardless of how many times I have used a particular activity or taught specific material. I do not schedule meetings immediately before class unless I have no choice. I expect students to be respectful to each other and to me, but especially to each other.

Diane Pike: That they (to quote our college president), "Show up, pay attention, and do the work." I expect them to engage and that means I must also show up, pay attention to them, and do my work.

Katherine R. Rowell:

▶ Reading is important and so many of our students don't read. We really need to emphasize the importance of reading.

▶ Attendance and participation in class is expected.

▶ Community kinship

▶ Willingness to work outside of class

▶ Willingness to redo work when it is not acceptable

Rose M. Brewer:

▶ I expect them to show up. This is the first principle for moving the learning needle forward.

▶ I expect them to not let me off the hook in a classroom that pushes students to talk back, raise issues, advance the collective knowledge of the classroom. dope!

▶ I expect them to grow in the context of a critical classroom that takes little for granted, sharpens systems thinking/structural analysis, and generates commitments to social change.

WHAT TYPE OF TEACHING METHODS DO YOU USE IN YOUR TEACHING?

Caroline Persell: Readings, mini-lectures, videos, small- and large-group discussions, online discussions, research and writing projects (group projects in larger classes, individual projects in smaller classes).

Ed Kain: I try to have a range of methods. The mix of those methods depends upon the level of the course, the content, and the size of the class. Students typically discuss readings in small and large groups in class, lecture material is more common in introductory-level courses, students have data assignments related to the course topic (more sophisticated as the courses are more advanced), students give group and individual presentations based upon material other members of the class have not read, guest speakers are useful on many topics, videos, . . .

Liz Grauerholz: A combination of lecture (with students asking questions/commenting) and discussions (both small group and whole class). I use media clips and visual images throughout.

Carol Jenkins:

▶ Teaching at a community college is about scholarly teaching and transformational student learning. Scholarly teaching assumes a reflective practice grounded in classroom observation, relevant scholarship, and meaningful assessment of student learning.

▶ Methodologies that would enable my students to (1) capture and apply their "sociological imaginations" in the systematic study of society; (2) understand and relate their personal history and perspectives of societal life to various courses of individual and collective action; and (3) purposefully respond and make value judgments regarding matters of crucial concern to the community and society at large. It is my responsibility to provide students with an environment in which to learn.

Example: Many years ago I became intrigued with "visual sociology." I was desirous of developing a creative way to strengthen students' sociological imaginations. As an alternate to the written word, "photographic essays of social problems of interest to the student" were introduced. The photo essay is by far the most appreciated activity of the semester.

▶ I continue to mainly use the lecture method infused with biographies of theorists (context of research), storytelling (concept application), informational literacy–internet exercises (critical- and quantitative-reasoning applications), YouTube segments, and when appropriate, collaborative research with selected students (usually Honors level). I'm also a Socrates fan.

Keith Roberts: I was deeply influenced in the 1970s and 1980s when research on learning styles (later called "multiple intelligences") indicated that if I taught either the way I happened to learn or the way I was taught (mostly lecture), I was probably unwittingly engaging in a form of institutional racism and sexism. Learning styles differ somewhat between ethnic communities and gender groups, and if I was going to teach well to everyone in the room, I had to learn to utilize a wide range of instructional strategies. So I began a campaign of converting my courses—each year transforming six to eight class sessions in each course—into a more active learning environment. Within six or seven years, my courses looked very different. Some had no lecture at all; others used lecture much more carefully and judiciously. Most importantly, the students were more actively absorbed in the material and rarely missed a class session because the time in the classroom was engaging for them.

Maxine P. Atkinson: I use a variety of methods but I focus on inquiry-guided exercises, informal writing, and small-group discussion.

Diane Pike: All . . . the best method depends on what you want them to learn and must also reflect variety. Lecture is not evil, although reading a text-based PowerPoint slide is. Most all strategies work if used appropriately.

Katherine R. Rowell: I have used and continue to use multiple teaching methods. It really depends on my courses and the students I have in them. I use a wide variety. Currently, I am experimenting with flipped classroom and competency-based education.

Rose M. Brewer: I use multi-methods: discussion, lectures, and what I deem the "cold call" question, where every student is called on (at least once in the semester) to respond to a question relevant to the course material. We watch film, haunt the campus and community environments, keep journals, do research, hear guest speakers, go to campus and community events, give oral reports, write, facilitate class. The list is large.

WHAT DO YOU THINK IS THE MOST IMPORTANT THING FOR US TO REMEMBER ABOUT HOW TO TREAT STUDENTS?

Caroline Persell: To treat them the way we would like to be treated if we were students. Sometimes it is helpful and humbling to try to learn something completely new ourselves (whether another language, a musical instrument, a new computer program, new sport, or whatever) to remind us how uncertain, insecure, vulnerable, and embarrassed we feel when we're not knowledgeable or capable and how much we appreciate a teacher who encourages us and applauds the efforts and progress we make.

Kathleen McKinney: Students are simply (and not so simply) human beings. They are diverse in the broadest sense of that word . . . in gender, race, class . . . but also diverse in prior experiences, preparation, motivation, maturity, cognitive development, and in the situational contexts in which they live both day-to-day and long term. We must remember to respect them and to care for them as fellow, individual human beings.

Ed Kain: I try to treat students as I would want to be treated—as a responsible adult interested in learning.

Liz Grauerholz: If the student were your daughter or son, how would you want a professor to treat her/him? It doesn't mean being "soft"; often it's the opposite. Consider what's truly in the student's best interest—be honest and gentle. And be fair, no matter how difficult the student may be.

Carol Jenkins:

▶ With respect and dignity—always. Not all poor decisions warrant punitive responses—think about "teachable moments."
▶ Many students have no discernable moral compass—we are in a position to influence students for good.
▶ First day of class I ask students two questions: (1) Given the emergent norm of intellectual dishonesty, can I view you as men and women of integrity? What does that mean for all of us? And, (2) how do you want me to interact with you throughout the course? As high school students plus

one year, or as adult learners? What is the difference between these two types of learners?

Keith Roberts: The most important thing to remember about students is that they are *not* our "customers." *Students are far too important to treat as customers!* Customers are "always right," but to treat students this way is to do them a grave disservice. Sometimes effective teaching means being a gad-fly and irritating students rather than pleasing them at every step, for deep learning often involves some measure of "benign disruption" in their thinking. Moreover, a customer–sales person relationship is based on each party trying to get the other to do something he or she does not much want to do; it involves an effort to "pay" or "invest" the least possible for the greatest possible benefit from the other party. Both parties do this in a sales transaction, but this is a horrible model for a classroom. Instructors should not be sales reps whose first obligation is the company and making money. The long-term benefit of the student is more important than immediate "satisfaction," and the former should be my concern as an instructor. In short, students and professors should not be on opposite sides of the table in a negotiation of most benefit for least investment. Instead, instructors are mentors who should be colleagues on the same side of the table, facing a set of problems or issues together in a collegial manner. The outcome is not a zero-sum game but a positive sum game of growth for both parties. The "customer" metaphor cheapens and distorts the student–professor relationship. The outcome of the classroom is not creation of *acquisitiveness*, but *inquisitiveness*. The latter is a very different result and requires a different kind of relationship.

Maxine P. Atkinson: I am fond of saying that every student is some mother's baby. As a mother, that means a lot to me. All of our students are precious. That does not mean that our expectations should be low; far from it. It does mean that we need to remember that they are people first and our classes may not be the most important thing in their life.

Diane Pike: No one rises to a low bar and start by assuming the best of them.

Katherine R. Rowell: The best teachers practice empathy. We need to remember what it was like to be a student. We need to be empathetic each and every day. We need to listen to our students and walk a day in their shoes.

Rose M. Brewer: Always treat students with respect. They know when they've been ignored, belittled, disrespected. This doesn't mean I allow anything to go/say. I check bad behavior (as do my students) so we have a mutually respectful space. I know respect sounds like a cliché, but it works and it matters.

HOW DO YOU CHECK STUDENT PROGRESS IN YOUR COURSES (INFORMAL AND FORMAL ASSESSMENTS)?

Caroline Persell: By the looks on their faces in lectures; by their comments and questions in class; by their postings in online discussions; by the weekly mini-assignments/assessments they do, either in class or before; by their quiz, midterm, and final exams; by their oral and written project presentations.

In the beginning of the term I give them the "grading grid" that will be used to assess their final projects. They must submit a draft of their final project report which is graded and given comments about how to improve it, but this grade does not count. They have a week to work on improving the draft before they submit their final papers. My goal is to help them learn how to do a good project paper and oral presentation.

Ed Kain: Most of my assessments are formal—I have written data assignments, quizzes, and presentations. The main informal assessment is listening to discussions of readings to gauge how well students are developing their skills in reading research.

Liz Grauerholz: Multiple assignments throughout the course rather than a big one at the end or just a few throughout. So I can tell early on if a student is falling short of expectations. I also do a "check-in" around midterm to see if there are things I can be doing to help them succeed in the course.

Carol Jenkins:

▶ Checking formal student progress: all graded course activities/assignments/tests/quizzes, etc., are posted on our course management system CANVAS which computes current grade status. Students can log in at any time.
▶ Checking informal student progress: intermittent conversations before and after class, office consultations.

Maxine P. Atkinson: I emphasize informal, low-stakes activities. I use reading quizzes, free writes, and minute papers. I pose silly questions like, "If you were being named as the most outstanding sociology student ever, what would you have learned or done in this class that would make you worthy of this award?"

I do a serious evaluation three times during the semester, asking what is going well for them in the course and how the course could be strengthened.

Diane Pike: CATs, straightforward questions, and multiple data points. For example, every course I teach has at least five major assignments—a combo of essay exams, essays, small-group work/presentations, portfolios, in-class reading and writing. Learning requires attendance and engagement. Assessment of progress works best if frequent, meaningful, and used to improve the course.

I also do a significant midcourse evaluation during the term.

Rose M. Brewer: Once again, a varied set of evaluations seem to work best for my students. They have multiple strengths/weaknesses. I try to build on the strengths and minimize the weaknesses. For example, multiple drafts of a paper with feedback (peer and instructor) allows me to track writing, argument-building progress. I listen very carefully to students over the semester to detect deepening understanding of course concepts and materials. Deep listening is quite a good way to track student progress. I also give exams, assign short papers, and track small-group work. These conventional tools are useful ways to measure progress.

HOW DO YOU EVALUATE YOUR OWN TEACHING?

Caroline Persell: By looking at how well students understand the most important concepts, principles, or processes of the course. By seeing how well they do their final projects.

Ed Kain: Ultimately by how well students do in the class—on assignments, tests, presentations, etc. I also use formal evaluations at the end of the semester, and midsemester evaluations asking two open-ended questions—"In this class, what do you think is working well in helping you learn about (introductory sociology; research methods; aging and society . . . i.e., the topic of the course)?" And, "If you were teaching this class, what things would you change (and how) to increase how you are learning about (again, fill in the topic of the course)?"

Liz Grauerholz: The standard methods (midterm and end-of-term student evaluations), of course, but the best measure is the degree to which I have learned from students.

great!

Carol Jenkins:

▶ Am more concerned with the extent of student learning than evaluating best practices.

▶ Students complete evaluations for each course taken. This is the main source of information. However, on many occasions I invite colleagues to observe class and provide feedback, especially if students are not demonstrating understanding.

▶ If professional development and maintaining currency is the real question, I always attend and participate in activities that would enhance my "teaching effectiveness" and positively impact "student learning" whether provided by GCC's Center for Teaching/Learning/Engagement or discipline-based opportunities.

> KEYS TO SUCCESS:
> - Engage in reflective practice
> - Demonstrate content knowledge
> - As a scholar teacher be a good role model for other instructors
> - Inspire students and colleagues alike
> - Use feedback to improve courses
> - Be available and accessible to students

Maxine P. Atkinson: I primarily evaluate my teaching based on the quality of my students' work and the improvement in their thinking over the semester. I go to class early and leave late to keep in touch and I listen as carefully as I know how to what they tell me about their successes and their struggles.

Diane Pike: By how well I think most students are learning. Yikes . . . this is probably the most challenging thing. I try to teach my colleagues the same way I do my students, so feedback from colleagues to whom I present is useful. I team teach each year and get feedback from my coteachers. I ask students every semester, every class and do different things to learn about what they have learned. And, I read and think about the SoTL research, learn from being a TS Associate Editor and TRAILS Editor, and do my best to take it all to heart.

Katherine R. Rowell: We have department-wide assessment including pre-post assessment tools. I also use self-assessment and peer-assessment.

Rose M. Brewer: I talk to students. I listen very carefully when they tell me this works, that doesn't. I work with undergraduate teaching assistants who have very sharp radar on what works with their peers. I self-reflect on a daily basis, fine-tune, change in midcourse (if necessary), and I use student evaluations.

OUR CONCLUDING THOUGHTS

Kath and Maxine's goal for *In the Trenches* is to provide a beginning roadmap for those who are interested in improving their teaching skills. We constantly strive to improve our own teaching and are grateful for the many good resources available. Included in those resources are our teaching colleagues. We find teachers to be generous with both help and support as the quotes from the teacher-scholars above illustrate. Our hope is that this text joins the other books in your library of teaching materials. We also sincerely hope that this compendium of our own wisdom of practice and the teaching research we cite will enrich your practice and your students' learning.

REFERENCES

Adsit, Jason N. (unpublished). "Designing and Delivering Effective Lectures and Presentations." Buffalo, NY: University of Buffalo Teaching & Learning Center. Retrieved January 10, 2014 (http://ubtlc.buffalo.edu/resources/resources-files /presentation/designing-and-delivering-effective-lectures-and-presentations -2010-01-25.pdf).

American Association of University Professors. 2014. "Resources on Academic Freedom." Retrieved June 15, 2014 (http://www.aaup.org/issues/academic-freedom /resources-academic-freedom).

American Sociological Association. 2010. *Style Guide*, 4th edition. Washington, DC: American Sociological Association.

American Sociological Association. 2010. *TRAILS: Teaching Resources and Innovation Library for Sociology*. Retrieved May 31, 2011 (http://trails.asanet.org/Pages /TDLContent.aspx).

American Sociological Association. 2014. Distinguished Contributions to Teaching. Major ASA Award. Accessed May 12, 2014. (http://www.asanet.org/about/awards /teaching.cfm).

The American Sociologist. 2005. Special edition on "A Conversation about 'Public Sociology.'" *The American Sociologist* 36(3–4):3–165.

Andersen, Margaret. [2003] 2005. "The Social Construction of Gender." Pp. 197–202 in *Understanding Society: An Introductory Reader*. 2nd ed., edited by M. L. Andersen, K. A. Logio, and H. F. Taylor. Reprint, Belmont, CA: Thomson Wadsworth.

Andersen, Margaret, Kim A. Logio, and Howard F. Taylor, eds. 2005. *Understanding Society: An Introductory Reader*. 2nd ed. Belmont, CA: Thomson Wadsworth.

Anderson, Kristin J. and Gabriel Smith. 2005. "Students' Preconceptions of Professors: Benefits and Barriers according to Ethnicity and Gender." *Hispanic Journal of Behavioral Sciences* 27(2005):184–201.

Anderson, Kristin J. and Melinda Kanner. 2011. "Inventing a Gay Agenda: Students' Perceptions of Lesbian and Gay Professors." *Journal of Applied Social Psychology* 41(6):1538–64.

Anderson, Lorin W. and David R. Krathwohl, eds. 2001. *A Taxonomy for Learning, Teaching, and Assessing: A Revision of Bloom's Taxonomy of Educational Objectives.* New York: Longman.

Andrist, Lester, Valerie Chepp, Paul Dean, and Michael V. Miller. 2014. "Toward a Video Pedagogy: With a Teaching Typology with Learning Goals." *Teaching Sociology* 42(3):196–206.

Angelo, Thomas A. and K. Patricia Cross. 1993. *Classroom Assessment Techniques: A Handbook for College Teachers.* 2nd ed. San Francisco: Jossey-Bass.

Anson, Chris M. 2007. "Warp and Weft: Reflections on the Art of Communication Weaving." Pp. 2–18 in *Sustaining Excellence in Communicating across the Curriculum: Cross-Institutional Experiences and Best Practices,* edited by N. Kassabgy and A. Elshimi. Newcastle, UK: Cambridge Scholars Publishing.

Armstrong, Jeanne. 2010. "Designing a Writing Intensive Course with Information Literacy and Critical Thinking Learning Outcomes." *Reference Services Review* 38(3):445–57.

Armstrong, Jeanne and Margaret Fast. 2004. "A Credit Course Assignment: The Encyclopedia Entry." *Reference Services Review* 32(2):190–94.

Aronson, Elliot. 2014. "Jigsaw Classroom." *Social Psychology* Network. Retrieved March 7, 2012 (http://www.jigsaw.org).

Arum, Richard and Josipa Roksa. 2011. *Academically Adrift: Limited Learning on College Campuses.* Chicago: University of Chicago Press.

Association of American Colleges and Universities. 2006. "Academic Freedom and Educational Responsibility." Retrieved September 24, 2012 (http://www.aacu.org /about/statements/documents/academicFreedom.pdf).

Atkinson, Maxine P. 2000. "The Future of Sociology is Teaching? Visions of the Possible." *Contemporary Sociology* 29(2):329–32.

Atkinson, Maxine P. 2001. "The Scholarship of Teaching and Learning: Reconceptualizing Scholarship and Transforming the Academy." *Social Forces* 79(4):1217–29.

Atkinson, Maxine P. 2010. "Technique 1: Activities for the First Day, Defining the Discipline, Gender, Methods." Class Activity published in *TRAILS: Teaching Resources and Innovations Library for Sociology.* Originally published 2005 in *Innovative Techniques,* edited by S. K. Nenga and E. L. Kain. Washington, DC: American Sociological Association. Retrieved June 3, 2011 (http://trails.asanet.org).

Atkinson, Maxine P. 2014. "Possible Examples of Formative Metacognitive Activities/ Prompts." TH!NK Faculty Development Workshop. May, 2014: NC State University.

Atkinson, Maxine P. and Andrea N. Hunt. 2008. "Inquiry-Guided Learning in Sociology." *Teaching Sociology* 36(1):1–7.

Atkinson, Maxine P., Jeremiah B. Wills, and Amy I. McClure. 2008. "The Evidence Matrix: A Simple Heuristic for Analyzing and Integrating Evidence." *Teaching Sociology* 35(2):262–71.

Avery, Rosemary J., W. Keith Bryant, Alan Mathios, Hyojin Kang, and Duncan Bell. 2006. "Electronic Course Evaluations: Does An Online Delivery System Influence Student Evaluations?" *The Journal of Economic Education* 37(1):21–37.

Bain, Ken. 2004. *What the Best College Teachers Do*. Cambridge: Harvard University Press.

Baker, Phyllis and Martha Copp. 1997. "Gender Performance Matters Most: The Interaction of Gendered Expectations, Feminist Course Content and Pregnancy in Students' Course Evaluations." *Teaching Sociology* 25(1):29–43.

Barr, Robert B. and John Tagg. 2004. "From Teaching to Learning—A New Paradigm for Undergraduate Education." Retrieved January 10, 2014 (http://ilte.ius.edu/pdf /BarrTagg.pdf).

Barrett, Dan. 2012. "How 'Flipping' the Classroom Can Improve the Traditional Lecture." *The Chronicle of Higher Education* (February 19) Retrieved June 20, 2014 (http://moodle.technion.ac.il/file.php/1298/Announce/How_Flipping_the_Class room_Can_Improve_the_Traditional_Lecture.pdf).

Basow, Susan A., Stephanie Codos, and Julie L. Martin. 2013. "The Effects of Professors' Race and Gender on Student Evaluations and Performance." *College Student Journal* 47(2):352–63.

Bean, John C. 2001. *Engaging Ideas: The Professor's Guide to Integrating Writing, Critical Thinking, and Active Learning in the Classroom*. San Francisco: Jossey-Bass.

Berheide, Catherine White. 2007. "Doing Less Work, Collecting Better Data: Using Capstone Courses to Assess Learning." *Peer Review* 9(2). Retrieved May 20, 2014 (https://www.aacu.org/peerreview/pr-sp07/pr-sp07_research.cfm).

Berkeley Center for Teaching and Learning. N.d. "Responding to Students' Comments." Retrieved February 1, 2013 (http://teaching.berkeley.edu/responding-students -comments).

Bligh, Donald A. 2000. *What's the Use of Lectures?* San Francisco: Jossey-Bass.

Bloom, Benjamin. S. 1956. *Taxonomy of Educational Objectives, Handbook I: The Cognitive Domain*. New York: David McKay Co., Inc.

Bok, Derek. 2006. *Our Underachieving Colleges*. Princeton: Princeton University Press.

Boyer, Ernest L. 1990. *Scholarship Reconsidered: Priorities of the Professoriate*. Princeton: Carnegie Foundation for the Advancement of Teaching.

Brookhart, Susan M. 2013. *How to Create and Use Rubrics for Formative Assessment and Grading.* Alexandria, VA: ASCD.

Brouillette, John R. and Ronny E. Turner. 1992. "Creating the Sociological Imagination on the First Day: The Social Construction of Deviance." *Teaching Sociology* 20(4):276–79.

Brown, Peter C., Henry L. Roediger III, and Mark A. McDaniel. 2014. *Make It Stick: The Science of Successful Learning.* Cambridge: Harvard University Press.

Bruff, Derek. 2009. *Teaching with Classroom Response Systems: Creating Active Learning Environments.* San Francisco: Jossey-Bass.

Burawoy, Michael. 2005. "For Public Sociology." *American Sociological Review* 70(1):4–28.

Burger, Edward. 2012. "Essay on the Importance of Teaching Failure." Retrieved December 12, 2012 (http:insidehighered.com/views/2012/08/21/essay-importance -teaching-failure).

Burger, Edward. 2013. "Edward Burger." Retrieved February 5, 2013 (http://www .thefutureschannel.com/conversations_archive/burger_conversation.php).

Burns, Candace, W. 2000. "Teaching Portfolios: Another Perspective." *Academe* 86(1):44–47.

Campbell, Heather E., Karen Gerdes, and Sue Steiner. 2005. "What's Looks Got To Do With It? Instructor Appearance and Student Evaluations of Teaching." *Journal of Policy Analysis and Management* 24(3):611–20.

Cavender, Amy. 2011. "Android for Academics." *The Chronicle of Higher Education* (July 7). Retrieved June 15, 2014 (http://chronicle.com/blogs/profhacker/android -for-academics/344750.

The Center for Teaching. 2014. Vanderbilt University. Retrieved July 30, 2014 (http:// cft.vanderbilt.edu/).

Central Washington University. N.d. "Writing Across the Curriculum's Frequently Asked Questions about Writing Across the Curriculum." Retrieved June 20, 2014 (http://www.cwu.edu/general-education/writing-across-curriculum).

Chafets, Zev. 1991. *Devil's Night: And Other True Tales of Detroit.* New York: Vintage.

Chamberlin, Marilyn S. and JoAnn S. Hickey. 2001. "Student Evaluations of Faculty Performance: The Role of Gender Expectations in Differential Evaluations." *Educational Research Quarterly* 25(2):3–14.

Chew, Stephen L. 2010. "Improving Classroom Performance by Challenging Student Misconceptions about Learning." *Observer* 23(4). Retrieved May 25, 2014 (http://www.psychologicalscience.org/index.php/publications/observer /2010/april-10/improving-classroom-performance-by-challenging-student -misconceptions-about-learning.html).

Chin, Jeffrey. 2002. "Is There a Scholarship of Teaching and Learning in '*Teaching Sociology*?' A Look at Papers from 1984 to 1999." *Teaching Sociology* 30(1):53–62.

Chin, Jeffrey, Matthew May, Honora Sullivan-Chin, and Kaylyn Woodrick. 2014. "How Can Social Psychology and Group Dynamics Assist in Curriculum Development?" *Teaching Sociology* 42(2):86–94.

Clark, Jacqueline and Maxine P. Atkinson. 2008. "Analyzing the Social Construction of Gender in Birth Announcement Cards." Pp. 177–81 in *Sociology Through Active Learning*, edited by K. McKinney, F. Beck, and B. Heyl. Thousand Oaks, CA: Pine Forge Press.

Clawson, Daniel. 2007. *Public Sociology: Fifteen Eminent Sociologists Debate Politics and the Profession in the Twenty-First Century*. Berkeley: University of California Press.

Clayson, D. E. 2009. "Student Evaluations of Teaching: Are They Related to What Students Learn? A Meta-analysis and Review of the Literature." *Journal of Marketing Behavior* 31(1):16–30.

Coghlan, Catherine L. and Denise W. Huggins. 2004. "'That's Not Fair!': A Simulation Exercise in Social Stratification and Structural Inequality." *Teaching Sociology* 32(2):177–87.

The College Curriculum Renewal Project. N.d. "Sociology & Anthropology: Starting with the Mission." Georgetown University. Retrieved June 20, 2014 (https://cndls .georgetown.edu/ccrp/phase2/sociology.html).

Conrad, Peter and Joseph W. Schneider. [1992] 2005. "The Medicalization of Deviance." Pp. 120–26 in *Understanding Society: An Introductory Reader*. 2nd ed., edited by M. L. Andersen, K. A. Logio, and H. F. Taylor. Reprint, Belmont, CA: Thomson Wadsworth.

Cordell, Ryan. 2011. "Two More Uses for the Attendance iOS App." *The Chronicle of Higher Education. Profhacker* blog. Retrieved May 30, 2011 (http://chronicle.com /blogs/profhacker/two-more-uses-for-the-attendance-ios-app/31594).

Cortright, Ronald N., Heidi L. Collins, David W. Rodenbaugh, and Stephen E. DiCarlo. 2003. "Student Retention of Course Content Is Improved by Collaborative-Group Testing." *Advances in Physiology Education* 27(3):102–08.

Crews, Tena B. and Dylan F. Curtis. 2011. "Online Course Evaluations: Faculty Perspective and Strategies for Improved Response Rates." *Assessment & Evaluation in Higher Education* 36(7):865–78.

Croxall, Brian. 2012. "Attendance2: An Update for the Attendance App for iOS Devices." *The Chronicle of Higher Education* (August 20). Retrieved June 15, 2014 (chronicle.com/blogs/profhacker/attendance2-an-update-for-the-attendance-app -for-ios-devices/41850).

Daniel, David B. and Stephen L. Chew. 2013. "The Tribalism of Teaching and Learning." *Teaching of Psychology* 40(4):363–67.

Daughaday, Lillian. 1997. "Postcards from the Imagination: Using Letters to Teach Sociological Concepts." *Teaching Sociology* 25 (July):234–38.

Davis, Stephen Spencer. 2012. "Star Math Teacher Applies the Power of Failure, Squared." Retrieved February 3, 2013 (http://www.theglobeandmail.com/life/parenting/back-to-school/star-math-teacher-applies-the-power-of-failure-squared/article4513390/).

Day, Susan. 1989. "Producing Better Writers in Sociology Classes: A Test of the Writing-Across-The-Curriculum Approach." *Teaching Sociology* 17(4):458–64.

DeLoach, Stephen B. and Steven A. Greenlaw. 2007. "Effectively Moderating Electronic Discussions." *Journal of Economic Education* 38(4): 419–34.

Delucchi, Michael and Kathleen Korgen. 2002. "'We're the Customer—We Pay the Tuition': Student Consumerism among Undergraduate Sociology Majors." *Teaching Sociology* 30(1):100–07.

Devil's Night. N.d. Retrieved November 3, 2014. http://en.wikipedia.org/wiki/Devil%27s_Night).

Diamond, Robert M. 1998. *Designing and Assessing Courses and Curricula*. San Francisco: Jossey-Bass.

Dommeyer, Curt J., Paul Baum, Robert W. Hanna, and Kenneth S. Chapman. 2010. "Gathering Faculty Teaching Evaluations By In-class and Online Surveys: Their Effects on Response Rates and Evaluations." *Assessment & Evaluation in Higher Education* 29(5):611–23.

Dukes, Richard L. and Victoria Gay. 1989. "The Effects of Gender, Status, and Effective Teaching on the Evaluation of College Instruction." *Teaching Sociology* 14(4): 447–57.

Durkheim, Emile. 1995. Translated by Karen Fields. *The Elementary Forms of Religious Life*. New York: The Free Press.

Eberts, Paul, Carla B. Howery, Catherine White Berheide, Kathleen Crittenden, Robert Davis, Zelda Gamson, and Theodore C. Wagenaar. 1990. *Liberal Learning and the Sociology Major*. Washington, DC: American Sociological Association.

Eggleston, Tami and Gabie Smith. 2005. "Building Community in the Classroom through Ice-Breakers and Parting Ways." *Office of Teaching Resources in Psychology*. Retrieved May 8, 2014 (http://teachpsych.org/resources/Documents/otrp/resources/eggleston04.pdf).

Ehrenreich, Barbara. 2001. *Nickel and Dimed: On (Not) Getting By In America*. New York: Metropolitan Books.

Elder, Linda and Richard Paul. 2011. "Universal Intellectual Standards." *The Critical Thinking Community*. Retrieved October 31, 2011 (http://www.criticalthinking.org/pages/universal-intellectual-standards/527).

Ewing, Vanessa Lynn, Arthur A. Stukas, Jr., and Eugene P. Sheehan. 2003. "Student Prejudice Against Gay Male and Lesbian Lecturers." *The Journal of Social Psychology* 143(5):569–79.

Faculty Focus. 2014. Magna Publications. Retrieved November 11, 2014. (http://www
.facultyfocus.com/).

Felton, James, John Mitchell, and Michael Stinson. 2004. "Web-based Student Evaluations of Professors: The Relations Between Perceived Quality, Easiness, and Sexiness." *Assessment & Evaluation in Higher Education* 29(1):91–108.

Felten, Peter. 2013. "Principles of Good Practice in SoTL." *Teaching & Learning Inquiry* (1):121–25.

Ferenstein, Greg. 2010. "How Twitter in the Classroom Is Boosting Student Engagement." Retrieved June 21, 2014 (http://mashable.com/2010/03/01/twitter
-classroom/).

Ferris, Kerry and Jill Stein. 2014. *The Real World: An Introduction to Sociology*. New York: W. W. Norton.

Fisher, Edith M. 2008. "USA Stratified Monopoly: A Simulation Game about Social Class Stratification." *Teaching Sociology* 36(3):272–82.

Foote, David A., Susan K. Harmon, and Donna T. Mayo. 2003. "The Impacts of Instructional Style and Gender Role Attitude on Students' Evaluations of Faculty." *Marketing Education Review* 13(2):9–19.

Fried, Carrie B. 2008. "In-class Laptop Use and Its Effects on Student Learning." *Computers & Education* 50:906–14.

Gilbert, Marsha. 2013. "Schools Make Adjustments to Comply with Updated Standards to Make Campuses More Accessible to the Disabled." March 11. *Diverse Education* blog. Retrieved June 12, 2014 (http://diverseeducation.com/article/51840/).

Goldsmid, Charles A. and Everett K. Wilson. 1980. *Passing on Sociology: The Teaching of a Discipline*. Washington, DC: American Sociological Association's Teaching Resource Center.

Goodin, Alma Dzib. 2014. "What Is the Secret Behind Successful Students?" The EvoLLLution: Illuminating the Lifelong Learning Movement. June 2014. Retrieved June 20, 2014 (http://www.evolllution.com/program_planning/what-is-the-secret
-behind-successful-students/).

Google. 2014. "Getting Started as a YouTube Content Management Partner. Creating a New Channel." Retrieved June 21, 2014 (https://support.google.com/youtube
/answer/1646861?hl=en)/).

Grauerholz, Liz and Sharon Bouma-Holtrop. 2003. "Exploring Critical Sociological Thinking." *Teaching Sociology* 31(4): 485–96.

Grauerholz, Liz, Joanna Eisele, and Nicole Stark. 2013. "Writing in the Sociology Curriculum: What Types and How Much Writing Do We Assign?" *Teaching Sociology* 41(1):46–59.

Grauerholz, Liz and Greg Gibson. 2006. "Articulation of Goals and Means in Sociology Courses: What We Can Learn from Syllabi." *Teaching Sociology* 34(1):5–22.

Grauerholz, Liz and John F. Zipp. 2008. "How to Do the Scholarship of Teaching and Learning." *Teaching Sociology* 36(1):87–94.

Gutman, Herbert G. 1976. *The Black Family in Slavery and Freedom 1750–1925*. New York: Vintage Books.

Harris, Robert. 1997. "Recommendations for Writing Comments on Student Papers." Retrieved February 1, 2013 (http://www.virtualsalt.com/comments.htm).

Henslin, James M. 2011. *Essentials of Sociology: A Down-To-Earth Approach*. 9th ed. Boston: Allyn & Bacon.

Hermann, Anthony D. and David A. Foster. 2008. "Fostering Approachability and Classroom Participation during the First Day of Class: Evidence for a Reciprocal Interview Activity." *Active Learning in Higher Education* 9(2):139–51.

Hillsman, Sally. 2012. "A Letter to Parents of Sociology Majors." Retrieved December 23, 2012 (http://www.asanet.org/documents/research/pdfs/Hillsman_Ltr_Parents.pdf).

Hironimus-Wendt, Robert J. 2013. Personal Communique, Retrieved December 18, 2013.

Hirsch. E. D., Jr. 2001. "Seeking Breadth and Depth in the Curriculum." *Educational Leadership* October:22–25.

Hobson, Eric H. 1998. "Designing and Grading Written Assignments." *New Directions For Teaching and Learning* 74(Summer):51–57.

Hollander, Jocelyn A. 2002. "Learning to Discuss: Strategies for Improving the Quality of Class Discussion." *Teaching Sociology* 30(3): 317–27.

Hoop, Katrina C. 2012. "Comte Unplugged: Using a 'Technology Fast' to Teach Sociological Theory." *Teaching Sociology* 40(2):158–65.

Howe, Neil and William Strauss. 2003. "Millennials Go To College." Executive summary prepared by S. Eubanks. Washington, DC: American Association of Collegiate Registrars and Admissions Offices and Life Course Associates. Retrieved April 24, 2012 (http://eubie.com/millennials.pdf).

Huber, Mary Taylor. 2013. "Scholarship of Teaching and Learning vs. Scholarly Teaching." An Online Component of the International Society for the Scholarship of Teaching and Learning (ISSOTL). 2013 Conference, c/o Elon University's Center for Engaged Learning. Retrieved December 8, 2013 (http://www.youtube.com/watch?v=eedxoj1CPnk).

Hudd, Suzanne S. 2003. "Syllabus Under Construction: Involving Students in the Creation of Class Assignments." *Teaching Sociology* 31(2):195–202.

Hudd, Suzanne S. and Eric Franklyn Bronson. 2007. "Moving Forward Looking Backward: An Exercise in Recursive Thinking and Writing." *Teaching Sociology* 35(3):264–73.

Hunt, Andrea N. July 2012. Personal communication.

Hunt, Andrea N. 2013. "Teaching Portfolio." Unpublished document. Quoted with permission.

Hutchings, Pat. 2000. "Introduction." *Opening Lines: Approaches to the Scholarship of Teaching and Learning.* San Francisco: Jossey-Bass.

Hutchings, Pat. 2013a. "Big Tent Debate in SoTL." An Online Component of the International Society for the Scholarship of Teaching and Learning (ISSOTL) 2013 Conference, c/o Elon University's Center for Engaged Learning. Retrieved December 8, 2013 (http://www.youtube.com/watch?v=eM9dEwG_5eI).

Hutchings, Pat. 2013b. "Scholarship of Teaching and Learning vs Scholarly Teaching." An Online Component of the International Society for the Scholarship of Teaching and Learning (ISSOTL) 2013 Conference, c/o Elon University's Center for Engaged Learning. Retrieved December 8, 2013 (http://www.youtube.com/watch?v=eedxoj1CPnk).

Hutchings, Pat and Lee S. Shulman. 1999. "The Scholarship of Teaching: New Elaborations, New Developments." *Change: The Magazine of Higher Learning* 31(5):10–15.

Indiana University–Purdue University Fort Wayne. 2014. "ITS Training: Hyperlinks." Retrieved June 13, 2014 (http://www.ipfw.edu/training/accessibility/examples/hyperlinks.html).

Jessup, Michael M. 2001. "Sociopoly: Life on the Boardwalk." *Teaching Sociology* 29(1):102–09.

Johnson, Allan G. 2008. *The Forest and the Trees: Sociology as Life, Practices, and Promise.* 2nd edition. Philadelphia: Temple University Press.

Jones, Jason B. 2010. "The Attendance App for iOS Devices." *The Chronicle of Higher Education. Profhacker* blog. Retrieved May 30, 2011 (http://chronicle.com/blogs/profhacker/the-attendance-app-for-ios-devices/25241).

Juwah, Charles, Debra Macfarlane-Dick, Bob Matthew, David Nicol, David Ross, and Brenda Smith. 2004. *Enhancing Student Learning Through Effective Formative Feedback.* York, England: The Higher Education Academy.

Kain, Edward L. 2005. "SoTL, SHE, and the Evidence of an Incomplete Paradigm Shift. A Response to 'The Scholarship of Teaching and Learning—Done by Sociologists: Let's Make that the Sociology of Higher Education'." *Teaching Sociology* 33(4):419–21.

McKinney, Kathleen. 2005. "The Value of SoTL in Sociology. A Response to 'The Scholarship of Teaching and Learning—Done by Sociologists: Let's Make that the Sociology of Higher Education'." *Teaching Sociology* 33(4):417–19.

Kaufman, Peter. 2013. "*Scribo Ergo Cogito*: Reflexivity through Writing." *Teaching Sociology* 41(1):70–81.

Kebede, Alem. 2009. "Practicing Sociological Imagination through Writing Sociological Autobiography." *Teaching Sociology* 37(4):353–68.

Khanna, S. 2010. "Analysis of College Students' Dependence on Cell Phones." Posting on *Access to Technology in India* blog. Retrieved February 20, 2012 (http://shefali1130.blogspot.com/2010/10/analysis-of-college-students-dependence.html).

Kohn, Alfie. 2011. "The Case Against Grades." Retrieved June 20, 2014 (http://www.alfiekohn.org/teaching/tcag.htm).

Kwan, Samantha and Mary N. Trautner. 2011. "Judging Books by Their Covers: Teaching about Physical Attractiveness Biases." *Teaching Sociology* 39(1):16–26.

Lahey, Jessica. 2013. "Why Parents Need to Let Their Children Fail." Retrieved February 5, 2013 (http://www.theatlantic.com/national/archive/2013/01/why-parents-need-to-let-their-children-fail/272603/).

Lambert, Craig. 2012. "Twilight of the Lecture." *Harvard Magazine*. March–April. Retrieved June 21, 2014 (http://harvardmagazine.com/2012/03/twilight-of-the-lecture).

Lane Community College. 2014. "Universal Design of Instruction." Retrieved August 8, 2014 (https://www.lanecc.edu/disability/universal-design-instruction).

Lang, James M. 2013. *Cheating Lessons: Learning from Academic Dishonesty*. Cambridge, MA: Harvard University Press.

Lang, James M. 2012. "Metacognition and Student Learning." *The Chronicle of Higher Education*. Retrieved April 12, 2014 (http://chronicle.com/article/Metacognition Student/130327).

Lee, Virginia S., David B. Greene, Janice Odom, Ephraim Schecter, and Richard W. Slatta. 2004. 'What is Inquiry-Guided Learning?" Pp. 3–16 in *Teaching and Learning Through Inquiry: A Guidebook for Institutions and Instructors*, edited by V. V. Lee. Sterling, VA: Stylus Publishing.

Lewis, Jonathan F. 1989. "Of Card Tricks and Charismatic Leaders." *Teaching Sociology* 17(1):64–71.

Lowney, Kathleen S. 1998. "Reducing 'Theory Anxiety' Through Puzzles." *Teaching Sociology* 26(1):69–73.

Lowry, Janet Huber, Carla B. Howery, John P. Myers, Harry Perlstadt, Caroline Hodges Persell, Diane Pike, Charles H. Powers, Shirley A. Scritchfield, Cynthia M. Siemsen, Barbara Trepagnier, Judith Ann Warner, and Gregory Weiss. 2005. *Creating An Effective Assessment Plan for the Sociology Major*. Washington, DC: American Sociological Association.

Macomber, Kris. 2013. "Teaching Portfolio: Evidence of Excellence in Teaching Sociology." Unpublished document. Quoted with permission.

Macomber, Kris and Sarah Nell Rusche. 2010. "Using Students' Racial Memories to Teach about Racial Inequality." *Feminist Teacher: A Journal of the Practices, Theories, and Scholarship of Feminist Teaching* 20(3):214–25.

Macomber, Kristine, Sarah Rusche, and Maxine P. Atkinson. 2009. "Introduction: From the Outside Looking In: The Sociology of the College Classroom." *Teaching Sociology* 27(3):228–32.

Mangan, Katherine. 2014. "Colleges Ask Court for Deference on Unpaid Internships." *The Chronicle of Higher Education* (April 23). Retrieved June 22, 2014 (http://chronicle.com/article/Colleges-Ask-Court-for/146147/).

Massey, Garth, ed. 2012. *Readings for Sociology*. 7th ed. New York: W. W. Norton.

Massengill, Rebekah Peeples. 2011. "Sociological Writing as Higher-Level Thinking: Assignments that Cultivate the Sociological Imagination." *Teaching Sociology* 39(4):371–81.

Mazur, Eric. 1996. *Peer Instruction: A User's Manual*. Reading, MA: Addison-Wesley.

Mazur, Eric and Jessica Watkins. 2009. "Just-in-Time Teaching and Peer Instruction." Pp. 39–62 in *Just in Time Teaching: Across the Disciplines Across the Academy*. Sterling, VA: Stylus Publishing.

McConchie, Alan. Pop vs. Soda. Retrieved July 30, 2014 (http://www.popvssoda.com/).

McDermott, Casey. 2013. "Colleges Draw Criticism for Their Role in Fostering Unpaid Internships." *The Chronicle of Higher Education* (June 24). Retrieved June 22, 2014 (http://chronicle.com/article/Colleges-Draw-Criticism-for/139977/).

McGuire, Joan M., Sally S. Scott, and Stan F. Shaw. 2006. "Universal Design and Its Applications in Educational Environments." *Remedial and Special Education: A Journal of the Hammill Institute on Disabilities* 27(3):166–75.

McIntosh, Jamey. 2012. "Failing to Get an A." *Techniques: Connecting Education & Careers* 87(7):44–46.

McKinney, Kathleen and Barbara S. Heyl, eds. 2009. *Sociology Through Active Learning: Student Exercises*. Thousand Oaks, CA: Pine Forge Press.

McKinney, Kathleen, Carla B. Howery, Kerry Strand, Edward L. Kain, and Catherine White Berheide. 2004. *Liberal Learning and the Sociology Major Updated: Meeting the Challenge of Teaching Sociology in the Twenty-First Century. A Report of the ASA Task Force on the Undergraduate Major*. Washington, DC: American Sociological Association.

Menges, Robert J. 1988. "Research on Teaching and Learning: The Relevant and the Redundant." *Review of Higher Education* 11(3):259–68.

Meyers, Chet and Thomas B. Jones. 1993. *Promoting Active Learning: Strategies for the College Classroom*. San Francisco: Jossey-Bass.

Miller, Andrew. 2012. "Five Best Practices for the Flipped Classroom." *Edutopia* (February 24) Retrieved June 20, 2014 (http://ticharter33.org/library/TIarticle36.pdf).

The Modern Educator blog. N.d. "5 Ways to Use Twitter in the College Classroom." Retrieved June 21, 2014 (http://blog.tophat.com/5-ways-to-use-twitter-in-the-college-classroom/).

Moeller, Susan D. 2010. "24 Hours Unplugged." Retrieved February 20, 2012 (http://withoutmedia.wordpress.com/).

Mollborn, Stefanie, and Angel Hoekstra. 2010. "'A Meeting of Minds': Using Clickers for Critical Thinking and Discussion in Large Sociology Classes." *Teaching Sociology* 38(1):18–27.

Moore, Melanie. 1997. "Student Resistance to Course Content: Reactions to Gender of the Messenger." *Teaching Sociology* 25(2):128–33.

Moore, Randy. 2005. "Who Does Extra-credit Work in Introductory Science Courses?" *Journal of College Science Teaching* 34(7):12–16.

Mueller, Pam A. and Daniel M. Oppenheimer. 2014. "The Pen Is Mightier Than the Keyboard: Advantages of Longhand Over Laptop Note Taking." *Psychological Science* 25(6):1159–68.

Murphy, Kelle. 2010. "Is My Teaching Disturbing You? Strategies for Addressing Disruptive Behaviors in the College Classroom." *Journal of Physical Education, Recreation & Dance* 81(6):33–37.

National Center on Universal Design for Learning. 2012. Retrieved May 23, 2014 (http://www.udlcenter.org/advocacy).

Nilson, Linda B. 2010. *Teaching at Its Best: A Research-Based Resource for College Instructors* 3rd ed. San Francisco: Jossey-Bass.

No Author. "Debate and Discussion Formats." Retrieved March 14, 2014 (www.at-bristol.com/cz/teachers/Debate%20formats.doc).

Norcross, J. C., H. S. Dooley, and J. F. Stevenson. 1993. "Faculty Use and Justification of Extra Credit: No Middle Ground?" *Teaching of Psychology* 20(4): 240–42.

Paul, Richard and Linda Elder. 2008. *The Miniature Guide to Critical Thinking: Concepts and Tools*. Tomales, CA: The Foundation for Critical Thinking. Retrieved July 30, 2014 (http://www.criticalthinking.org/store/products/critical-thinking-concepts-amp-tools/156).

Pearson Education. 2014. Peachpit: Web Design Reference Guide. Retrieved June 14, 2014 (http://www.peachpit.com/guides/content.aspx?g=webdesign&seqNum=277).

Pelton, Julie A. 2013a. "'Seeing the Theory Is Believing': Writing about Film to Reduce Theory Anxiety." *Teaching Sociology* 41(1):106–20.

Pelton, Julie A. 2013b. Personal Communication. August 30, 2013.

Peretz, Tal H. and Michael A. Messner. 2013. "Stand Up/Sit Down Structure and Agency Activity." Class Activity published in *TRAILS: Teaching Resources and Innovations Library for Sociology*. Washington DC: American Sociological Association. (http//trails.asanet.org).

Persell, Caroline Hodges. 2010. "How Sociological Leaders Rank Learning Goals for Introductory Sociology." *Teaching Sociology* 38(4):330–39.

Persell, Caroline Hodges, Kathryn M. Pfeffier, and Ali Syed. 2007. "What Should Students Understand After Taking Introduction to Sociology"? *Teaching Sociology* 35(4):300–14.

Picca, Leslie H., Brian Starks, and Justine Gunderson. 2013. "'It Opened My Eyes': Using Student Journal Writing to Make Visible Race, Class, and Gender in Everyday Life." *Teaching Sociology* 41(1):82–93.

Pike, Diane. 2011. "2010 Hans O. Mauksch Address: *Teaching Sociology*—Leader of the Pack?—An Exploratory Study of Teaching Journals across Disciplines." *Teaching Sociology* 39(3):219–26.

Poole, Gary. 2013a. "Making a Case for SoTL." An Online Component of the International Society for the Scholarship of Teaching and Learning (ISSOTL) 2013 Conference, c/o Elon University's Center for Engaged Learning. Retrieved December 8, 2013 (http://www.youtube.com/watch?v=JlWM4K2WL3Q&feature=youtu.be).

Poole, Gary. 2013b. "Scholarship of Teaching and Learning vs. Scholarly Teaching." An Online Component of the International Society for the Scholarship of Teaching and Learning (ISSOTL) 2013 Conference, c/o Elon University's Center for Engaged Learning. Retrieved December 8, 2013 (http://www.youtube.com/watch?v=eedxoj1CPnk).

Pop vs. Soda Website. 2014. Retrieved May 18, 2014 (http://www.popvssoda.com/).

Primary Science Teaching Trust. 2013. "Teaching Argumentation in the Science Classroom." Retrieved March 14, 2014 (http://www.pstt.org.uk/ext/cpd/argumentation/unit1-listening_triads.php).

Purcell, David. 2013. "Sociology, Teaching, and Reflective Practice: Using Writing to Improve." *Teaching Sociology* 41(1):5–19.

Rau, William and Barbara Sherman Heyl. 1990. "Humanizing the College Classroom: Collaborative Learning and Social Organization among Students." *Teaching Sociology* 18(2):141–55.

Ravizza, Susan M., David Z. Hambrick, and Kimberly M. Fenn. 2014. "Non-academic Internet Use in the Classroom Is Negatively Related to Classroom Learning Regardless of Intellectual Ability." *Computers & Education* 78(September):109–14.

Ridgeway, Cecilia. L. 2013. "Why Status Matters for Inequality." *American Sociological Review* 70(1):1–16.

Risen, James. 1989. "Fire Rampant in Detroit for Devil's Night: Arson: Despite a Crackdown, Hundreds of Homes and Abandoned Buildings Are Torched." *Los Angeles Times*. November 1.

Roberson, Bill and Christine Reimers. 2008. "Rediscovering the Discipline through Research Fundamentals." Workshop presented for the First Year Inquiry Program, NC State University, April.

Roberts, Keith A. 2002. "Ironies of Effective Teaching: Deep Structure Learning and Constructions of the Classroom." *Teaching Sociology* 30(1):1–25.

Rockmore, Dan. 2014. "The Case for Banning Laptops in the Classroom." *The New Yorker* (June 6). Retrieved June 10, 2014 http://www.newyorker.com/tech/elements/the-case-for-banning-laptops-in-the-classroom.

Rowling, J. K. 2008. "The Fringe Benefits of Failure, and the Importance of Imagination." Commencement address to the 2008 graduating class of Harvard University. Retrieved July 12, 2011 (http://harvardmagazine.com/2008/06/the-fringe-benefits-failure-the-importance-imagination).

Ruggiero, Josephine A. 2002. "'Ah Ha . . .' Learning: Using Cases and Case Studies to Teach Sociological Insights and Skills." *Sociological Practice: A Journal of Clinical and Applied Sociology* 4(2):113–28.

Rusche, Sarah Nell. 2013. "Teaching Portfolio." Unpublished document. Quoted with permission.

Rusche, Sarah Nell and Kendra Jason. 2011. "'You Have to Absorb Yourself in It': Using Inquiry and Reflection to Promote Student Learning and Self-Knowledge." *Teaching Sociology* 39(4):338–53.

Sample, Mark. 2013. "Planning a Class with Backward Design." *The Chronicle of Higher Education* (May 31). Retrieved June 28, 2013 (http://chronicle.com/blogs/profhacker/planning-a-class-with-backward-design/33625).

Samson, Perry J. 2010. "Deliberate Engagement of Laptops in Large Lecture Classes to Improve Attentiveness and Engagement." *Computers in Education* 20(2):1–19.

Sana, Tina Weston and Nicolas J. Cepeda. 2013. "Laptop Multitasking Hinders Classroom Learning for Both Users and Nearby Peers." *Computers & Education* 62(March):24–31.

Scarboro, Allen. 2004. "Bringing Theory Closer to Home through Active Learning and Online Discussion." *Teaching Sociology* 32(2):222–31.

Schulz, Amy J. [1998] 2005. "Navajo Women and the Politics of Identity." Pp. 58–69 in *Understanding Society: An Introductory Reader.* 2nd ed., edited by M. L. Andersen, K. A. Logio, and H. F. Taylor. Reprint, Belmont, CA: Thomson Wadsworth.

Schuman, Rebecca. 2014. "Needs Improvement: Student Evaluations of Professors Aren't Just Biased and Absurd—They Don't Even Work." April 24. http://www.slate.com/articles/life/education/2014/04/student_evaluations_of_college_professors_are_biased_and_worthless.html.

Schwalbe, Michael. 2007. *The Sociologically Examined Life: Pieces of the Conversation.* 4th edition. New York: McGraw-Hill.

Schwalbe, Michael, Sandra Godwin, Daphne Holden, Douglas Schrock, Shealy Thompson, and Michele Wolkomir. 2000. "Generic Processes in the Reproduction of Inequality: An Interactionist Analysis." *Social Forces* 79(2):419–52.

Schweingruber, David. 2005. "Looking for the Core in the Wrong Place." *Teaching Sociology* 33(1):81–9.

Seldin, Peter. 1993. *Successful Use of Teaching Portfolios*. Boston: Anker Publishing.

Seldin, Peter. 2000. "Teaching Portfolios: A Positive Appraisal." *Academe* 86(1):36–38, 43–44.

Senter, Mary S., Nicole Van Vooren, Michael Kisielewski, and Roberta Spalter-Roth. 2012. *What Leads to Student Satisfaction with Sociology Programs?* American Sociological Association, Washington DC. Available at www.asanet.org/research /briefs_and_articles.cfm.

Shadiow, Linda K. *What Our Stories Teach Us: A Guide to Critical Reflection for College Faculty*. San Francisco: Jossey-Bass.

Sharp, Gwen. 2008. "Historical Trends in Baby Names." *Sociological Images*. W. W. Norton & Company, Inc. Retrieved July 18, 2012 (http://thesocietypages.org /socimages/2008/07/18/historical-trends-in-baby-names/).

Shared Teaching Resources for Sociology. Retrieved November 11, 2014 (https://www .facebook.com/groups/371311144336/).

Shulman, Lee S. 2000. "From Minsk To Pinsk: Why A Scholarship of Teaching and Learning?" *The Journal of Scholarship of Teaching and Learning* (1):48–53.

Shulman, Lee S. 2004. "Lamarck's Revenge: Teaching among the Scholarships." Pp. 164–72 in *Teaching as Community Property: Essays on Higher Education*, edited by L. S. Shulman. San Francisco: Jossey-Bass.

Shulman, Lee S. 2013. "Situated Studies of Teaching and Learning: The New Mainstream." Plenary address. International Society for the Scholarship of Teaching and Learning. Raleigh, NC. October.

Slay, Jack, Jr. 2005. "No Extra Credit for You." *The Chronicle of Higher Education*. May 3. Retrieved May 30, 2014 (http://chronicle.com/article/No-Extra-Credit-For -You/44956).

Slusser, Suzanne R. and Rebecca J. Erickson. 2006. "Group Quizzes: An Extension of the Collaborative Learning Process." *Teaching Sociology* 34(3):249–62.

Smith, Bettye P. and Billy Hawkins. 2011. "Examining Student Evaluations of Black College Faculty: Does Race Matter?" *The Journal of Negro Education* 80(2): 149–62.

Smith, G. and K. J. Anderson. 2005. "Students' Ratings of Professors: The Teaching Style Contingency for Latino/a Professors." *Journal of Latinos and Education* 4(2):115–36.

Social Security Administration. 2014. "Top 5 Names in Each of the Last 100 Years." Retrieved July 30, 2014 (http://www.socialsecurity.gov/OACT/babynames/top5 names.html).

The Society Pages. 2014. Retrieved July 28, 2014 (http://thesocietypages.org/).

The Sociological Cinema. 2014. Retrieved June 21, 2014 (http://www.thesociological cinema.com/).

Sociology in Focus. 2014. Retrieved July 28, 2014 (http://www.sociologyinfocus.com/).

SociologySources.org. 2014. Retrieved July 28, 2014 (http://www.sociologysource.org /nathanpalmer/).

Spalter-Roth, Roberta and Janene Scelza. 2009. *What's Happening in Your Department with Assessment.* Washington, DC: American Sociological Association. Retrieved May 31, 2011 (http://www.asanet.org/images/research/docs/pdf /ASAdeptsvybrief3.pdf).

Spalter-Roth, Roberta and Nicole Van Vooren. 2009. *Idealists vs. Careerists: Graduate School Choices of Sociology Majors.* Washington, DC: American Sociological Association's Department of Research and Development. Retrieved May 20, 2014 (http://asanet.org/images/research/docs/pdf/Idealist%20vs%20 Careerisst .pdf).

Steward, R. J. and R. E. Phelps. 2000. "Faculty of Color and University Students: Rethinking the Evaluation of Faculty Teaching." *Journal of the Research Association of Minority Professors* 4(2):49–56.

Stowell, Jeffrey R., William E. Addison, and Jennifer L. Smith. 2012. "Comparison of Online and Classroom-based Student Evaluations of Instruction." *Assessment & Evaluation in Higher Education* 37(4)2012:465–73.

Streich, Michael. 2008. "Extra Credit Can Help All Students Improve: Assessment Extras Must Be Academically Sound and Serve a Purpose." *Suite101* blog. Retrieved May 30, 2011 (http://www.suite101.com/content/extra-credit-can-help-all-students -improve-a79032#ixzz1Nr2608z0).

Sterns, Mary F. 1998. "What Works for Me: First Day Class Activities." Pp. 161–65 In *Teaching English in the Two-Year College, vol. 98, May.* edited by J. A. Pearce.

Stiggins, Richard, Judy Arter, Jan Chappuis, and Steve Chappuis. 2004. "From Classroom Assessment For Student Learning: Doing It Right-Using It Well." PBS.org. Retrieved September 24, 2012 (http://www.pbs.org/teacherline/courses/inst325 /docs/inst325_stiggins.pdf).

Strong, William. 2003. "Writing Across the Hidden Curriculum." *The Quarterly* 25(1). Retrieved June 20, 2014 (http://www.nwp.org/cs/public/print/resource/525).

Svinicki, Marilla and Wilbert J. McKeachie. 2011. *McKeachie's Teaching Tips: Strategies, Research, and Theory for College and University Teachers* 13th ed. Belmont, CA: Wadsworth Cengage.

Sweet, Stephen. 1999. "Using a Mock Institutional Review Board to Teach Ethics in Sociological Research." *Teaching Sociology* 27(1):55–59.

Tanner, Kimberly D. 2012. "Promoting Student Metacognition." *CBE—Life Sciences Education* 11(Summer):113–20.

Taras, Maddalena. 2008. "Summative and Formative Assessment: Perceptions and Realities." *Active Learning in Higher Education* 9(2):172–92.

Teaching and Learning Center at Illinois State University. 2006. "30 Ideas in 30 Minutes—A Lively Discussion about On-Line Learning." Retrieved March 14, 2014 (http://ctlt.illinoisstate.edu/downloads/symposium/2006/MemkenSympJan06.pdf).

Teaching with a Sociological Lens. Retrieved November 11, 2014 (https://www.facebook.com/groups/527741363909666/).

TeachSoc. 2005. Retrieved May 31, 2011 (http://www.mail-archive.com/teachsoc@googlegroups.com/info.html).

Tugend, Alina. 2012. "Praise Is Fleeting, But Brickbats We Recall." *The New York Times*. Retrieved June 6, 2014 (http://www.nytimes.com/2012/03/24/your-money/why-people-remember-negative-events-more-than-positive-ones.html?pagewanted=all&_r=1&).

University of Central Florida's Faculty Center for Teaching and Learning 2010. "SoTL Journals." Orlando, FL: University of Central Florida. Retrieved December 9, 2013 (http://www.fctl.ucf.edu/ResearchAndScholarship/SoTL/journals/).

University of Illinois Counseling Center. N.d. "First-Generation College Students." Retrieved February 1, 2013 (http://www.counselingcenter.illinois.edu /?page_id=142).

University of Maryland. n.d. "Large Classes: A Teaching Guide: Discussion." Retrieved March 14, 2014 (http://www.cte.umd.edu/library/teachingLargeClass/guide/ch6.html).

University of Oregon. 2013. "Teaching Effective Program: What Are Some Good Ways To Facilitate A Discussion?" Retrieved March 14, 2014 (http://tep.uoregon.edu/resources/faqs/presenting/facilitatediscussion.html).

University of Washington. 1999. "Teaching Through Discussion." *Teaching and Learning Bulletin* 2(3). Retrieved March 14, 2014 (www.washington.edu/teaching/files/2012/12/Discussion.pdf).

Utell, Janine. 2013. "What the Food Network Can Teach Us about Feedback." Inside Higher Education. *University of Venus* blog. Retrieved February 2, 2012 (http://www.insidehighered.com/blogs/university-venus/what-food-network-can-teach-us-about-feedback#ixzz2JqIRfZcn).

Van Brunt, Brian and W. Scott Lewis. 2013. *A Faculty Guide to Disruptive and Dangerous Behavior*. New York: Routledge.

Vanderbilt University Center for Teaching 2013. "Why Do SoTL?" Nashville, TN: Vanderbilt University Center for Teaching. Retrieved December 9, 2013 (https://my.vanderbilt.edu/sotl/understanding-sotl/why-sotl/).

Wagenaar, Theodore C. 2004. "Is There a Core in Sociology? Results from a Survey." *Teaching Sociology* 32(1):1–18.

Wainright, Ashley. 2013. "8 Studies Show iPads in the Classroom Improve Education." *Secure Edge Blog* Retrieved June 20, 2014 (http://www.securedgenetworks.com /secure-edge-networks-blog/bid/86775/8-Studies-Show-iPads-in-the-Classroom -Improve-Education.)

WebAIM. 2013. "Introduction to Web Accessibility." Retrieved June 15, 2014 (http:// webaim.org/techniques/fonts/).

Wechter-Hendricks, Debra and Wade Luquet. 2003. "Teaching Stratification with Crayons." *Teaching Sociology* 31(3):345–51.

Weiss, Gregory L. 2002. "The Current Status of Assessment in Sociology Departments." *Teaching Sociology* 30(4):391–402.

Wiggins, Grant and Jay McTighe.1998. *Understanding by Design.* Upper Saddle River, NJ: Prentice-Hall.

Wiggins, Grant, and Jay McTighe. 1999. "What is Backward Design?" Flec.ednet.ns.ca. Retrieved September 12, 2012 (http://www.flec.ednet.ns.ca/staff/What%20is%20 Backward%20Design%20etc.pdf).

Wiggins, Grant and Jay McTighe. 2011. *The Understanding by Design Guide to Creating High-Quality Units.* Alexandria, VA: Association for Supervision and Curriculum Development.

Williams, Dana A. 2007. "Examining the Relation between Race and Student Evaluations of Faculty Members: A Literature Review." *Profession* 2007(1):168–73.

Wills, Jeremiah B., Zachary W. Brewster, and Gregory M. Fulkerson. 2005. "The Stratification Puzzle: An Active-Learning Exercise in Hard Work and Success." *Teaching Sociology* 33(4):389–95.

Winston, Fletcher. 2007. "First Day Sociology: Using Student Introductions to Illustrate the Concept of Norms." *Teaching Sociology* 35(2): 161–65.

Wolf, Patrick J. 2007. "Academic Improvement Through Regular Assessment." *Peabody Journal of Education* 82(4):690–702.

Zabaleta, Francisco. 2007. "The Use and Misuse of Student Evaluations of Teaching." *Teaching in Higher Education* 12(1):55–76.

Zawacki, Terry. N.d. "Managing the Paper Load and Responding Effectively to Student Writing." *Writing Across the Curriculum.* George Mason University. Retrieved June 20, 2014 (http://wac.gmu.edu/supporting/writing_at_center_how_to /managing_the_load_zawacki.php).

CREDITS

Figure 5.1: Fig. 3.5, "Students' Heart Rates in Class," from *What's the Use of Lectures*, by Donald A. Bligh. Copyright © 2000 by Donald A. Bligh. Reprinted by permission of John Wiley & Sons and Intellect Books, Ltd.

Chapter 14 text excerpt, pp. 169–170: From "Frequently Asked Questions about Writing across the Curriculum," by George A. Drake, Central Washington University. Reprinted by permission of the author.

Table 18.2: "Principles of Universal Design for Instruction." Adapted from guidelines developed by the Center for Universal Design, NCSU. Reprinted with permission.

Fig. 20.1: Figure from "Why do SoTL," by Nancy Chick. https://my.vanderbilt.edu/sotl/understanding-sotl/why-sotl/. Reprinted by permission of Nancy Chick.

INDEX